Speech:
Content and Communication

SPEECH:
Content and Communication
Third Edition

CHARLES S. MUDD *and* MALCOLM O. SILLARS
California State University, Northridge   *University of Utah*

THOMAS Y. CROWELL COMPANY New York
Established 1834

LIBRARY OF CONGRESS CATALOGING IN PUBLICATION DATA

Mudd, Charles S
    Speech : content and communication.

    Includes bibliographical references and index.
    1. Public speaking. I Sillars, Malcolm Osgood,
1928-   joint author. II. Title.
PN4121.M695   1975   808.5   75-4680
ISBN 0-690-00766-3

THOMAS Y. CROWELL COMPANY

666 Fifth Avenue
New York, New York 10019

Typography by Chris Simon
Manufactured in the United States of America

Contents

Contents

Preface

We believe that thorough research of the latest studies on the nature of communication is reflected in this the third edition of *Speech: Content and Communication*. We have, however, retained the traditional and still current audience orientation of earlier editions. Communication is viewed as *transaction*, where speaker and audience join together to give meaning to messages. To establish this orientation, there is an introductory chapter on the process of communication, in which essential theory is established and key concepts of communication are related to one another.

In order to make the argumentative dimension of communication clearer to the student we have added the Toulmin system of argument and we have used Maslow's hierarchy of motivation as a basis for a practical examination of motivation in communication. A new chapter on credibility provides a greatly expanded explanation of this important dimension of communication.

In the earlier editions the chapter on group discussion was tightly linked to the Dewey reflective thinking process. We have opened this, showing the student a number of ways to pattern small-group decision making while retaining the practical advice for those called on to chair such groups.

"Interpersonal Interaction" is the title of a completely new chapter, in which the nature of roles, including the leadership role and the interpersonal problems of decision making, is discussed. This chapter is designed to complement the chapter on small-group decision making, but the principles discussed are shown to be related to all communication. All comunication *is* interpersonal interaction.

The emphasis of the book is on the practical application of the principles of effective communication in a wide variety of situations, though our concept of communication remains clearly audience-centered. We have maintained, however, a careful attention as well to the analysis of propositions. This last plus an emphasis on the careful selection of materials and on thorough preparation constitute the core of all three editions.

We have also retained the practice of providing introductory outlines of chapters, concluding summaries, and study questions to reinforce the learning process.

Most oral communication activities are dealt with, including small-group decision making; informative, persuasive, and entertainment speeches; and criticism. As before, projects are provided of small and large scope to give the student the practical experience that is of primary importance in developing the skills of communication.

We have added new examples throughout, but we have kept historically significant examples where they are appropriate. It is our belief that some of the function of the study of communication is tied to an understanding of our heritage.

We are grateful for the assistance of Professor Vernon E. Cronen of the University of Massachusetts and Professor Lloyd W. Welden of California State University at Northridge. Professor B. Aubrey Fisher made a thorough and valuable review of the second edition, which has influenced many of the changes for this edition. Charlane Sillars was our typist and proofreader and helped us innumerable times to avoid linguistic errors.

Speech:
Content and Communication

Chapter 1

The Process of Communication

During almost every day of your life, you operate as an active and functional member of a large number of groups of one kind or another. Every one of these groups—student body, class, political party, congregation—depends for its very survival on the communicative skill of its members. We can quite comfortably go even further than this to say that what are probably the most important aspects of your whole life depend upon your ability to be both source and receiver of communications in the groups through which you live your life. Developing skill in communication, therefore, is important. Everyone acknowledges the value of improved communication. But since the term *communication* is used in many senses in our society, it will be useful to take a little time to say what we mean by that term and what factors about you and those you interact with make up the process of communication.*

---

* For a brief discussion of some of the misconceptions about communication and the dangers inherent in them, see C. David Mortensen, *Communication: The Study of Human Interaction* (New York: McGraw-Hill, 1972), pp. 7–13.

I. EVERYONE IS UNIQUE

You know both from intuition and from experience that you are absolutely unique. This means that there is no other you, that there is no one in the universe past, present, or future who was, is, or will be exactly like you. The fact of your uniqueness is a source of difficulty in communicating with others who, even though they are very much like you, are not the same as you. Each of them is also unique.

You, like eveyone else, think in language. You also use language to communicate what you think. But the meanings you have for the words of the language you use are built out of your experience with what the words of the language name.* Since no one has had exactly the experiences you have had, no one has precisely the same meanings for these words and signs you have. In a sense, therefore, language can be a stumbling block to communication. It is fortunate that this stumbling block is not insurmountable, since language of one kind or another is the only means you have to transmit messages. Yet the stumbling block is there and we call attention to it because one major function of communication is to get ideas out of one head and into another —somehow.

Even though you are unique, you are like others in that you have intellect, you use symbols, you are aware of yourself and of your life style and of others and of their life styles. Certain aspects of your life style might be very much like the other members of whatever societies you belong to. For example, if you are a Democrat, you will share many beliefs, attitudes, and values with other Democrats. But you will be different from many of them too, for if you are a Baptist as well as a Democrat, you'll find a smaller number of others-than-yourself who share the whole set of your responses to both politics and religion. And again, politics and religion are only two of the limitless number of areas about which you have perceptions and judgments which, taken together, constitute your "image" of the world.†

II. EVERYONE IS SOCIAL

Skill in communication is necessary if you are to fit the unique person you are into the various societies through which you perform most

---

* It would be more accurate to say "languages," because *words* (verbal language) are not the only medium of communicative transactions. There are many sets of symbols and signs you use (consciously or not) that tell others how you think and/or feel.

† Cf. Kenneth E. Boulding, *The Image* (Ann Arbor: University of Michigan Press, 1956). See especially his "Introduction."

of your functions as a human being. How else could you answer the questions that arise as your own personality develops? Gordon Allport reminds us of some of the questions that you seek to answer: questions about your innate tendencies; the impact of the world upon you; your developing awareness of self; your conscience; your evolving manner of self-expression; your recognition of the freedom to make decisions; the way you handle problems; and the growth of your mature beliefs, attitudes, values, and goals.* All of these are rooted in your ability to engage in communication transactions with others.

Inherent in the relationships you have with others, each of whom is also unique, is the clash of the needs and goals of each one. Conflicts arise among individuals because they all have goals, because the goals of one are frequently incompatible with these of another, and because all seek their goals in active competition. Communication is necessary, then, in order for you to be able to control your environment. Gerald R. Miller stresses the point that skill in communication is one of the major ways you manipulate, control, and understand your environment so that you can reap the greatest rewards from it and minimize its punishments.†

Control of your environment, however, is only one important function of communication. In addition to this, Lee Thayer identifies another. It is that of *adaptation*. Through your ability *to be communicated to* you are able to receive information and, using it, work your way toward achieving your own personal goals.‡ The control, of course, is never perfect, either for adapting yourself or adjusting others, because the communication is never perfect. Perhaps that condition helps to account for the fact that most communicative efforts are directed toward those whom the communicator needs to adjust to and those who can help the communicator to adapt.

III. THE NATURE OF COMMUNICATION

Students of communication do not completely agree on how to define what it is they study. The situation is not uncommon. Pick up any book purporting to be, for example, an introduction to the study of philoso-

---

* Gordon Allport, *Becoming* (New Haven, Conn.: Yale University Press, 1955), p. 23.

† Gerald R. Miller, *Speech Communication: A Behavioral Approach* (Indianapolis, Ind.: Bobbs-Merrill, 1966), p. 2.

‡ Lee Thayer, *Communication and Communication Systems* (Homewood, Ill.: Richard D. Irwin, 1968), p. 33.

phy and you will see immediately that the writer is at some pains to say what it is he means by *philosophy* and what it is that a philosopher does. The same is the case in the study of communication. There are almost as many definitions of the term as there are people who study the activity. The reason for this is that it is usually quite difficult to formulate a satisfactory definition of any term which is used to name an enormously complex set of ideas.

So, what is *communication*? The term is used in many contexts. Is it what is promulgated through the mass media? Or what is transmitted by means of electronic devices? Or what happens when people feel a sense of relationship with other human beings, or with "nature," or with God? When you give your dog a command and the dog obeys you, can you say you have communicated? If you are talking to your mother, and your father (who you didn't know was in the kitchen) overhears you, have you communicated to him? Communication can, of course, be all of these things. In the broadest sense, communication can be said to have occurred when any perceived data are given significance. Thayer speaks of this act of giving significance to perceived data as the "basic phenomenon" of communication. It occurs, he says, when an individual "takes something into account."° But not all instances of communication are of interest to us here. Specifically, the kind of communication we want to examine·has these characteristics:

It is a *human activity.*
It is *interpersonal.*
It is *purposive.*
It is a *process.*

A. Communication Is a Human Activity

We asked above whether you can be said to communicate when you speak to your dog and the dog responds by obeying whatever command you have given. The answer, of course, is Yes. You have encoded a message and transmitted it. The message was received and decoded. You were given the response you sought. We wouldn't quarrel with anyone who wants to call this an example of communication. We simply say that it is not a kind of communication that concerns us here. Instead, we want you to develop both understanding of and skill in the kind of communication that engages men and women in virtually

° Lee Thayer, *Communication and Communication Systems* (Homewood, Ill.: Richard D. Irwin, 1968), p. 26.

4

every aspect of their everyday lives. We are concerned with those kinds of communication which are an absolute necessity for human existence in society. For examples of the situations we have in mind, look at the age in which we live.

The first seven decades of this century have seen issues raised on a scale never before imagined. War has destroyed many millions of people. Great economic problems have cast shadows over large areas of the world. Minority groups have successfully pressed for more rights than they have ever before enjoyed. The powerful irrationality of fascism and the deceptively persuasive message of international communism have challenged the capitalist nations of the world. The world is menaced by the specter of mass hunger and must now make a choice between the consumption of energy and the preservation of present standards of living.

All who live in these years of the twentieth century are aware that this is an age of danger. But what is surprising in that fact? Every period in the history of civilization has been faced with problems. The significant point, then, is not whether there will be problems, nor what forms they will take. The important question is, how are they met? Inherent in the creed of western democracy is the notion that people can best solve their problems through the medium of popular rule, the rule of an enlightened and sensible majority. As historian Carl Becker has put it, "Democratic government rests upon the principle that it is better to count heads than it is to crack them."

For this reason, Western democracy has always put a high value on freedom of speech. It has assumed that all ideas must be displayed and examined so that the people can make a decision. The nation, therefore, needs wise men and great speakers in every age to educate against ignorance, to analyze problems, to provide workable solutions, and to mobilize majority opinion. These difficult tasks are not the province of statesmen, scholars, and the clergy alone. If democracy is to function well, the responsibility of it falls upon all citizens and and particularly upon those who would claim the right to lead.

Adlai E. Stevenson told a 1952 television audience:

Struggle is the primary law of life. You struggle and you survive. You fail to struggle and you perish. . . . Your salvation is in your own hands, in the stubborness of your mind, in the tenacity of your hearts, and such blessings as God, thoroughly tired by His children, shall give us. The task is yours. Yours is a democracy. Its government cannot be stronger or more tough minded than its people. It cannot be more inflexibly committed to the task than they. It cannot be wiser than the people. As citizens of this democracy you are the rulers and the ruled, the law givers and the law abiding, the beginning and the end. Democracy is a high privilege, but it is also a heavy responsibility whose shadow stalks, although you may never walk in the sun.

As well as any statement we know, this expresses a realistic basis for understanding why people must speak to the public.

Public life (and not only public life) is lived in an atmosphere of facing problems: social, economic, political, moral, and many others. The resolution of problems calls for using the ability to reason, an ability that is a priceless property of humanity. In reasoning to solve their public problems, people must communicate with one another, must speak to the public. Speech supports reasoning citizenship.

B. Communication Is Interpersonal

Every human being has incomplete perceptions of the world and the people in it. No one can know everything about what is "out there" to be perceived. When you see a leaf, regardless of the detail of your examination, you do not see its microscopic cells, its chemical compounds, or its past history. If you look at it through a microscope, you do not see its overall characteristics of size, shape, texture, and color. Your perceptions, therefore, are unique to you in that you select and, to some extent, distort sensory data to conform to your own perceptual "set," which is based upon your prior experiences. These experiences are, of course, always in some degree different from the experiences of others.

Your unique perceptions become a basis for what we call *intrapersonal communication*. It is the basis by which you talk to yourself. The poet who will not publish, the painter who declines to exhibit, and the musician who will not play in public all are relying for their communication experiences on the intrapersonal aspects of communication only. Likewise, when you think but do not speak or write, you are communicating intrapersonally.

But all communication (even communication with others) has an intrapersonal dimension. Since you are a receiver as well as a source of communications, you will decode and interpret any message you receive to conform to your unique perception of the world.

Therefore, since your experiences are unique, your perceptions are unique, and your language is unique, not only are you going to see a flower differently from anyone else, but also when you talk about it, it is going to be a different flower for everyone else. Isn't it a splendid irony that when we write sentences for you to read you must tell your-

6

self what we say because we cannot tell you ourselves? In this sense, communication must always have an *intra*personal dimension.

The kind of communication we are interested in, however, is always *inter*personal even though it contains this intrapersonal dimension. It takes place in one of three circumstances: People talk to each other one-to-one; they speak to each other on a basis of one-to-many, or they communicate with each other in groups. In each of these contexts the same set of skills is necessary and operative. That is to say, the same principles of communication apply to any of these three circumstances in which interpersonal communication takes place. There is always some subject matter; it is encoded into a language; it has some kind of organization; it has a recognizable stylistic pattern, and it is delivered. Other people must, from the vantage point of their perceptions, decode the message and think or act on the basis of the meanings they have for the message.

C. Communication Is Purposive

To speak of communication as purposive may seem redundant when we have already stipulated that the kind of communication we are talking about is *human* and *interpersonal*. There is no such thing as serious communication between human beings that is not done to achieve some purpose or goal. Don't interpret what we are saying as expressing any objection to the notion of just gabbing. That's for pleasure and pleasure is a goal, and so the talking has a purpose. Of course, if you hit your thumb with a hammer, you're likely to mutter some expletive you wouldn't normally expect to hear in church. If anyone hears you, you will certainly have communicated something even though you had no intention to do so. The same is true when you sing in the shower. But all examples of this kind aside, most of your talk will be because you have some specific goal in mind and you feel that interpersonal communication is the best way to achieve it.

It isn't true that the failure of the members of a group to achieve consensus or that the failure of a speaker to get a desired response from an audience (of one or many) is the result of a "communication breakdown." This notion presupposes that there are such things as communication gaps or breakdowns. But there aren't. Communication will always occur. When the minimal conditions for communication are present, it cannot fail to occur.* A term more accurate than "commu-

* For a worthwhile discussion of this problem of communication breakdown, see Dennis R. Smith, "The Fallacy of the Communication Breakdown," *Quarterly Journal of Speech*, **56** (Dec. 1950), pp. 343–46. See also Mortensen, *op. cit.*, pp. 7–8.

nication breakdown" would be the *failure of purpose.* The only question, then, is not *whether* you will communicate, but *what* you will communicate and whether it will be what you *want* to communicate.° It is useful, in other words, to think of communication as being goal-directed, as intended to achieve a predetermined objective,† and to measure its success by its ability to maximize the possibility of achieving that goal.

Notions about what these objectives might be have changed over time. Among the Greeks, Aristotle considered the significant elements of a speech communication situation to be the speaker, the audience, the speech itself, and the occasion. He identified three kinds of occasions for speaking, and each of these occasions produced its own kind of speaking in order to achieve its own particular goal. Legal pleading was done in the courts; it sought justice through the arguments that were used in accusation and defense. Political oratory was heard in the assembly; its goal was expediency and it sought to influence the audience in matters of policy. The third kind of speaking took place on special occasions; for example, it might be used to give honor by praising some person or place or thing. For Aristotle, all three kinds of speaking had the common purpose of persuasion. This single goal was accepted as the purpose of communication for many hundreds of years. The same was true for the Romans as well as the Greeks. The primary emphasis was on persuasion. There persisted throughout the Middle Ages and the period of the Renaissance a communication theory characterized by the unquestioned assumption that persuasion was the only concern of communication.

It was during the eighteenth century that communication was recognized to have possible ends or goals other than persuasion. George Campbell, one of a group of Scottish rhetoricians of the eighteenth century who were influenced by the associational psychology of the time, brought into communication theory the notion that speech could have as its purpose to enlighten the understanding as well as to move the passions or influence the will.

Today some theorists have gone full circle, coming back to the notion that all communication will persuade. They take the position that because all communication changes a receiver's view of the world, it is persuasive. The question of the purposes of communication will be discussed at greater length in Chapter 2. We cannot resolve the

---

° Lee Thayer, *Communication and Communication Systems* (Homewood, Ill.: Richard D. Irwin, 1968), p. 111.

† See David K. Berlo, *The Process of Communication* (New York: Holt, Rinehart and Winston, 1960), pp. 7–14.

controversy here over what purposes communication has. But we can agree that all communication has *some* purpose.

D. Communication Is a Process

For literally thousands of years, people thought about communication as a series of discrete events occurring in a precise order and occurring in accordance with a rather simplistic notion of the psychology of stimulus and response. When you flip a switch, the light goes on. If you cross your knees and tap your leg just below the kneecap, your leg will jerk. Trigger the chain and the results are almost tiresomely predictable. There has been for a very long time the mistaken notion that communication occurs in pretty much the same way as turning on a light or getting a knee-jerk reflex. Not at all so. It is impossible to get a correct image of communication by likening it in any way to a static series of discrete occurrences. Instead, communication is much more correctly viewed as a number of variables, always in some relationship with each other and constantly in a state of change of flux. Miller points out that the number of these variables is indefinitely large.* It will become increasingly clear as you study communication that when you receive whatever messages are encoded and transmitted to you, you are as actively engaged in the communication transaction as the sources of those messages.

The notion of transaction is a happy one. It helps to give a clearer and more nearly correct notion of what communication is than the usual one wherein a speaker supplies stimuli to an audience, the audience reacts to the stimuli and in its turn feeds other stimuli back to the speaker, who then knows that communication has taken place. Instead, imagine a conversation. The number of people in the conversation is not important. In a lively conversational situation everyone is actively participating, sometimes as source, sometimes as receiver—giving and getting responses; encoding, transmitting and decoding messages; and shifting and causing shifts in beliefs, attitudes, and values. Because of these conditions, conversations are good examples to show that communication is processual. It is continuous, flowing, continually changing. It does not start and stop, nor is it static. Everyone is actively engaged in it all the time.†

* Gerald R. Miller, *Speech Communication: A Behavioral Approach* (Indianapolis, Ind.: Bobbs-Merrill, 1966), p. 33.

† See David K. Berlo, *The Process of Communication* (New York: Holt, Rinehart, and Winston, 1960), pp. 23–28. His discussion of the concept of process is particularly lucid.

What is most clearly discernible in conversation is characteristic of all communication even though the fact is quite often not so obvious. Communication does not begin when you stand up before an audience to speak, or when you sit down to chat with someone, or when you walk into a room for a meeting. Communication only seems to be initiated at one of these moments. It really began years ago when you first started to develop all the meanings you have for all the words you know and use. What you are doing in any communicative situation is telling people what your meanings are for the subject in discussion. It even gives a false impression of what we are saying to speak of what happens as a "communication situation," because in this context it suggests that the communication going on has a precise time of beginning and will come to an end when the situation changes. But that is exactly the opposite of what we want you to understand. For, as we have just said, the communication does not begin at the moment you start to focus on it consciously, nor does it end when the situation changes or ceases. The communication quite literally keeps going on, because whatever is communicated to you changes you. The fact that you have been changed (and have, in the process, changed others) cannot itself be changed.

Not only does the communication not have an exact moment of inception in the sense people usually think of it, and not only does it not have a precise moment at which it ends, but all during the interim communication itself is in a constant state of change, flux, flow, and development. A very large number of variables are involved in communication, which constantly shift, actively changing relationships with one another.

IV. THE RHETORICAL TRADITION OF COMMUNICATION

The kind of communication we have been talking about, communication that is human, interpersonal, purposive, and processual, has traditionally been called *rhetoric*. It is not necessarily limited to the oral, but its study began in ancient times in the study of speech communication.

It was seen by early civilizations as a necessary and practical art. The Romans learned rhetoric from the Greeks, and the subject was carried over into the Latin language. In a typically Roman manner they systematized rhetoric just as they systematized everything they put their minds to. Thus, without making significant contributions to basic theory, they introduced the useful practice of looking at rhetoric through what have come to be called the five classical "canons." The word *canon*, derived from the Greek, is used in the sense of a body of laws. In the case of rhetoric, of course, the laws are rules or principles for the composition and transmission of successful, effective messages. These canons will be discussed briefly.

The first canon is called in English, "invention." It is concerned with the *discovery* of the subject matter of the speech. When you talk, you presumably have something to say. Any considerations that help you to determine what you will say are a part of the canon of invention.

This book is probably most concerned with the canon of invention. Finding, in Aristotle's words, "the available means of persuasion" involves the discovery and analysis of appropriate purposes and propositions for communication. Such analysis requires that you examine the beliefs, attitudes, and values of an audience to find out what arguments, what motivations, what means of enhancing your personal credibility will be most effective, and what kinds of supporting material will best clarify the proposition under discussion.

The second canon is "disposition." It is concerned with *organization,* the structure of the message. Every message must have some arrangement or another so that any decisions you make about how to put a message together, how to organize it, are guided by the principles of the canon of disposition.

The third canon is "elocution." This canon is concerned with the *style* of the message. Every message, of course, must be transmitted in some language and must have some kind of style, whether it be appropriate to the audience or not. Discussions of the nature and use of language are part of the canon of elocution.

The fourth canon is "memory." It has often been called the "lost" canon because nowadays speeches are not memorized and data can be easily recovered from libraries and the memory banks of computers. Elaborate mnemonic systems for aiding a speaker's memory are no longer needed. Therefore, memory no longer has any great significance in the theory of rhetoric.

Finally, the fifth canon of rhetoric is "delivery." A speaker's judgments about how to make the transmission of a message maximally effective are guided by the principles of this canon. Everything we say in this book is directly connected with one or another of the four most important of these five classical canons of rhetoric.

Let us sum up what we have been saying about rhetoric as a field of study by giving it a somewhat more explicit definition than we have given it to this point, since we have now mentioned the elements necessary for that definition. *Rhetoric is the rationale for the management of the content, structure, style, and delivery of a message so as to improve communication by bringing the mental and physical behaviors of a particular audience as close as possible in any particular case to what the source of the message thinks those behaviors ought to be.* As we proceed through the following chapters, our discussion will make it obvious to you that when we talk about communication, we mean *rhetorical* communications—the kind of communication that affects the mental and physical behaviors of those who receive it.

V. COMMUNICATION IMPOSES RESPONSIBILITIES

The imperative to speak, which every society, be it ancient Greece or America today, imposes upon its members, in turn imposes responsibilities on those who speak. To recognize, to accept, and to carry out these responsibilities is important enough for speakers individually and for society in general to warrant some discussion of them. What is it that you should do in order to fulfill your responsibilities to yourself and to your audiences?

The notion of obligation implies that some aspect of ethics or morality is relevant to rhetoric. And this is precisely the case. But rhetoric itself is amoral. Whatever power it has is indeterminate either toward good or toward ill. In this sense rhetoric is precisely like any of the other objects and abilities human beings use, such as materials, implements, and food. Metal may be formed into plows or swords. Swords may certainly be used for good or ill. Plows help to produce food. Food is necessary to sustain the individual; it may be subverted to the ends of gluttony. Thus it is that the *people* who use rhetoric are good or bad, and the ends to which they apply it are helpful or harmful to society.

Very little profit can be derived from a lengthy discussion of the improper uses of rhetoric. To recognize that rhetoric may be ill-used, however, is important in at least one significant respect—it points to the pragmatic value of studying the subject. There is considerable truth in the notion that the significance of rhetoric to the well-being of society, to the very existence of society, imposes the burden of speaking well. Rhetoric seems, therefore, in some sense even more crucially interwoven with the fabric of ethics and morality than are the physical, material objects of human action. To speak well must imply in this context not only to speak effectively, but also to speak with care and honesty. But again we say, rhetoric is a *human* instrument and the morality of its use is a problem that must be solved by men and women every time they raise their voices to influence the thoughts and deeds of their fellows. What we are saying amounts to this: Be honest with yourself, with your audience, and with your subject.

We conclude this chapter with a final word of advice. Your conversations, your speeches, and your criticisms of the speaking of others all have a part in determining the intellectual and political climate of the nation and, eventually, the actions of its leaders. Even the speeches you give in class have an effect. The presence of any audience, large or small, formal or informal, provides an opportunity and a responsibility for a speaker. Your class should be viewed as more than a training situation; it is also an opportunity for you to fulfill your obligations as a communicator.

Learning from classroom speaking experiences will be improved if you realize that each such speaking assignment is also a real-life one. It does not occur to many beginning speakers that the class they address is an audience, subject to the same kind of ideas and feelings as any other audience. In a speech class you speak to a group of real human beings. Don't ever forget that. Think of your class as you would any other audience you are called upon to address. You may feel that your classroom listeners are different because they will criticize you. But *all* audiences criticize speakers. Therefore, seek criticism. Make this situation work to your advantage. Keep a careful record of the criticism you get from your instructor and your classmates. Then use this information to improve your later assignments. You will never get such useful help from any other audience.

QUESTIONS

1. If everyone is unique, how is communication possible?
2. Is communication manipulative? If so, can this fact be justified?
3. Explain what you mean by "process."
4. What are the "canons" of rhetoric?
5. What responsibilities do speakers have to their audiences?

I. Audiences determine speech subjects and purposes
II. Speech purposes
    A. Speaking to entertain—to give amusement
    B. Speaking to inform—to bring about understanding
    C. Speaking to persuade—to influence belief or action
III. Speech propositions
    A. Kinds of propositions
        1. Propositions of policy
        2. Propositions of fact
        3. Propositions of value
    B. Propositions in relation to purposes
    C. Sources of propositions
        1. Problems of policy
        2. Problems of fact
        3. Propositions of value
IV. Selecting the right subject
    A. Speaker competence
    B. Significance
    C. Appropriateness
V. The beginning speeches
    A. Selecting a subject and purpose
    B. Organizing the speech
        1. Organizing the body of speech
            a. Chronological order
            b. Geographical or Spatial order
            c. Topical order
            d. Argumentative order
        2. Organizing the conclusion
        3. Organizing the introduction
    C. Supporting the ideas in the speech
    D. Delivering the speech
        1. Practice

Chapter 2

The Subject and Purpose of the Speech

In late July of 1974, the Supreme Court ruled that certain tape recordings of conversations between the president of the United States and people he had talked to in his office must be turned over to special prosecutor Leon Jaworski, who was preparing a conspiracy case against defendants in the notorious Watergate affair. Before that ruling was handed down, the president's attorney, James D. St. Clair, argued that the tapes were confidential and privileged material. Two features that characterize all substantive communication can be seen in St. Clair's statements to the Supreme Court.

First, there is a *subject* under discussion. In this instance, the topic is the question, "Must Mr. Jaworski's subpoena of the tapes be honored?" That is what St. Clair is talking about. The second feature of his communication is that he has a *purpose* in speaking. His purpose here is to persuade the Court to answer the question in the negative. Looking at the example, you can see that these two facets of the communication, subject and purpose, are no more separable than are the form and substance of a sonnet. Nonetheless, because it is useful to consider them as if they were separable, we shall define them separately.

The *subject* of a speech is the substantive theme that is dealt with in the message. It is the topic under discussion.

The *purpose* of a speech is the reason that the speech is given. That reason is found in the specific influence the speech is intended to have on the mental and/or physical behaviors of the audience.

There is significance in the fact that both these definitions and the title of this chapter as well all refer to the subject and the purpose of the *speech*, and not of the speaker. It is customary to ascribe to speakers the power to determine the subject and purpose of a speech. The truth of the matter is quite the reverse. It is a perhaps surprising but unquestionably important fact that *the audience, not the speaker, determines the subject and purpose of a speech.* Or, according to Aristotle, it is the hearer who determines the speaker's end and object. A brief examination will show that there are two reasons this is so.

I. AUDIENCES DETERMINE SPEECH SUBJECTS AND PURPOSES

You see the world in your own personal, idiosyncratic way. You have your own beliefs, attitudes, and values about politics, religion and morality, aesthetics, and every other subject. The familiar notion that beauty is in the eye of the beholder is an obvious instance of what we are saying. Because of different levels of intelligence and education, varied cultural backgrounds, dissimilar experiences, and unlike biological and physiological influences, no two persons share identical beliefs, attitudes, and values. Your uniqueness (see Chapter 1) requires you to be constantly adapting yourself to the world of others, and adjusting others to your world. Whenever you speak, then, that occasion may be thought of as your attempt to get others to think and act as you want them to. You do this by trying to influence one or another of an almost unlimited number of overt listener behaviors such as buying a product, voting a certain way, waging war, or making peace; or else you try to bring about specific, predetermined changes in one or another of an almost unlimited number of covert behaviors involving your listener's beliefs, attitudes, and values. No matter whether you exhort, advise, command, inform, persuade, amuse, speculate, or question, your choice of subject and purpose is made in light of the *audience's* view of the world as it is or ought to be and in light of the audience's position in relation to *your* view or what the world is or ought to be. You must choose a subject and define a purpose for your communication that will meet these conditions in a given audience at a given time. To do otherwise would be a foolish waste of time. This is the first reason for our saying that the audience determines the subject and the purpose of a speech.

Secondly, you cannot pour ideas out of your head into the head of any listener. The transactions of communication do not involve an exchange of anything physical or material. When you encode your meanings into a message, that message stirs up meanings inside the heads of your listeners. Those meanings are their own. Only they can interpret them. But since these stirred-up meanings are the only avenue an audience has to any notion of what your subject and purpose are, its interpretations of your message *will be* your message. For these reasons, we say that the audience determines the subject and the purpose of a speech.

II. SPEECH PURPOSES

Whenever you speak, what you say will be interpreted by your listeners *in some sense*. (Hopefully, it will be in the sense you intend.) In any case, what you say will cause the audience to shift along the continuum of its beliefs, attitudes, and values. Every such shift constitutes a change in behavior. Look at these examples.

When you tell a joke, you expect a laugh or at least some response appropriate to the humor in what you say. Even if the joke fails to amuse a hearer, the judgment that it is not funny is a response and, as such, is a change in behavior.

When you ask a question, you expect an answer. Even if you get one you don't want, any response whatever, even the decision not to give an answer, modifies the behavior of your hearer.

Instead of asking a question, suppose that you make a statement. No matter what the statement, it will elicit some response. No matter what the response (and it may or may not be the one you want), it constitutes a change in behavior. These and other instances we might adduce all lead to the conclusion that no one can avoid being affected by every message, even by those that elicit a response other than the one the sender wants. We might, then, ask whether anyone speaks for reasons other than to influence the beliefs, attitudes, values, and actions of others; that is, their general response to the world. The answer is no. What a speaker does, in effect, is to say, "I'm talking to you because I want you to do something. I want you to modify your behavior in some way." But it is the *particular* change in behavior, the *specific* response of the listener, that is of primary importance to the speaker.

Thus the specific response desired from an audience determines the specific purpose of a speaker on any particular occasion. Viewed in this light, all communication can be called persuasive because it attempts to influence behavior toward a predetermined goal.

Despite the fact that contemporary theory considers all speaking to be persuasive, the 200-year-old practice of classifying the specific purposes of speeches into broad categories is still useful. Instead of considering these categories as identifying quite different kinds of speeches or speech goals, they are better viewed as arbitrary divisions of forms of communication based on such differences as the kind of response you might seek; the amount of shift you must achieve in audience behavior to reach your goal; the level of sophistication you exhibit in using certain rhetorical techniques; the degree of audience hostility toward you, your subject, or your purpose; and other criteria.

Based on these considerations, we shall establish a group of three broad speech purposes or general ends. In each case, one will be distinguishd from the others on the grounds of the primary, or at least most obvious, response you want:

General ends $\left\{ \begin{array}{l} \text{To entertain—}\textit{Amusement} \\ \text{To inform—}\textit{Understanding} \\ \text{To persuade—}\textit{Agreement} \end{array} \right\}$ *Primary response*

A. Speaking To Entertain—To Give Amusement

On many occasions, both formal and informal, you could have the primary purpose of entertaining an audience. Ordinarily, you would use humor as the means. Suppose, for example, that you were the president of the freshman class welcoming prospective members of the student body. You might decide to entertain your audience by building an amusing speech around the freshman's first experience with the college registration procedure. A speech to entertain should not be confused with an informative or persuasive speech that uses humor as a device for arousing interest. The use of humor as a means of arousing and retaining interest in a speech will be discussed at some length in Chapter 18, "Speaking To Entertain."

B. Speaking To Inform—To Bring About Understanding

When your purpose is to make something known to an audience, to clarify ideas for them, to give them facts or information, your general end is to inform. The primary response you want from your audience is understanding: of an object, an operation, a condition, or the like. To fulfill a requirement in a course on international relations, you might give a report on the organization and function of the Presidium of the Supreme Soviet of the USSR. In a report of this kind, you have no immediate concern for the attitude the audience might take toward the Presidium or toward the Soviet Union; nor are you directly concerned with what your listeners might do with the information they get from you. Your immediate goal is that they understand and remember what you say. *Understanding* and *retention* are the criteria of a successful speech to inform. The rhetorical techniques relevant to speeches to inform are discussed in Chapter 16.

C. Speaking To Persuade—To Influence Belief or Action

In a speech to persuade, you give your audience reasons for adopting your point of view on a subject wherein you and the audience hold different opinions. But for you and your audience to be at odds, the difference between your attitudes need not be one of open hostility. Indeed, you and the audience may even agree. To make persuasion necessary, it is enough for you to feel that the attitudes of your audience need reinforcement. Look at the following instance: Irritated by the fact that you cannot find a clean table in the cafeteria because students frequently fail to remove their dishes, you decide to embark upon a clean-up campaign on the campus. You would need to persuade your friends to give active support to your campaign. Even though your friends agree that the cafeteria should be clean, the need for persuasion is apparent, for otherwise the conditions of which you disapprove would not exist.

The need for giving reasons (using arguments) to support a point of view is the primary basis for making a distinction between informative and persuasive discourse. An example will emphasize the difference between the two: Suppose that you were to propose an informative speech on the operation of the Security Council of the United Nations but were to close that speech with an appeal for support of the United Nations. Such an appeal would be an indication that your primary purpose was persuasive and not informative at all. It would further indicate that you had not clearly identified the primary purpose of your own speech: to appeal for support of the United Nations. Such an appeal would require persuasive support. But the goal of informative speaking is understanding; it does not purport to give proof. The subject of a persuasive speech, however, is a matter in debate and demands proof if the speech is to change belief. Certainly, persuasion is not likely to take place in an uninformed audience, but in almost every case, more than information is needed to persuade. Since you considered your speech informative, you would not supply the necessary proof. Your audience, interpreting your primary purpose to be to urge the support of the United Nations, but failing to get from you the proof necessary to support that appeal, might well reject it. When you have accurately defined your purpose for yourself, you considerably better your odds of achieving that purpose. When you fail to do so, you can usually hope to achieve your goal only by accident.

Accurately defining your purpose in your own mind, however, will not necessarily insure that your audience will perceive the speech purpose you intend. To make this clear, let's go back for a moment to the example just above. Suppose that in making the speech on the U.N. Security Council, you had not included the appeal for support. Any part of your audience could still have concluded that the United Nations deserves our support; or, quite to the contrary, could have decided that the United States ought to get out of the United Nations. Neither of these responses would have been a part of your informative purpose and yet your speech would have been persuasive. Let's carry the example one step further. Suppose you had intended an appeal on behalf of the United Nations and had consciously developed it through the use of what you hoped would be persuasive arguments. Again, your audience could very well have judged your intent to be to inform if it agreed with you and to persuade if it did not.

So, you see, because all messages influence, it is difficult to find a truly satisfactory basis for making a theoretical distinction between informative and persuasive discourse. Further, because audiences make their own interpretations, it is difficult to predict which of these two purposes an audience will perceive you to have. Nonetheless, we shall try to make such a distinction and shall suggest some ways to predict how audiences will respond to your purpose.

For you as a speaker, the difference between persuasive and informative communication is to be found in your attitude toward the subject. In giving information, you approach the subject as if there were only one view of it to be taken. You see the need to persuade when you recognize that others may have different views. That is to say, your purpose in speaking will be to persuade when you are aware of options among which an audience may choose and you feel the need to give the audience reason to adopt the option you prefer. Your purpose will be to inform when there is only a single, noncontroversial point of view to be taken toward the subject of the speech. You will then apply to the subject the communication techniques appropriate to informative or persuasive speaking as the case may be.

The commitments of the listeners are the most important factor in determining how an audience will perceive your purpose. The beliefs, attitudes, and values of your listeners affect their interpretations of your speech as much as yours affect the kinds of messages you encode. To help you decide how an audience will perceive your purpose, ask yourself the following questions.

Does the audience consider me a credible source? If so, it is more likely to accept what you say as informative. If not, you will more likely be perceived as trying to persuade.

Does the audience consider the subject to be controversial? If not, it is very likely to accept what you say as informative. If so, the audience may interpret what you say as persuasive in intent. An example of this may be seen in a recent news item in the *Los Angeles Times*. It has to do with the old, familiar debate over whether there is life on Mars. The writer informs us that more and more scientists are beginning to believe that indeed there is life on that planet. Once we have set foot there and found out the truth of the matter, a speech on the subject that would have to be argumentative now would clearly be perceived as informative then. Yet, even though an audience recognizes a subject to be controversial, if it has no involvement or conviction or commitment in the matter, it may still perceive you as being informative rather than persuasive.

Does the audience agree with my stand on a controversial matter? If so, they are likely to consider your message informative. If not, they will unquestionably perceive what you say to be argumentative.

Does the audience view the occasion as requiring informative or persuasive discourse? Instructors talking to students in the areas of their professional expertise are usually viewed as speaking informatively rather than persuasively. Even though he may be arguing vigorously, a minister speaking from a pulpit is likely to be judged as speaking informatively. At political rallies, on the other hand, or indeed, whenever political speaking occurs, the speakers will appear to audiences as trying to persuade.

Nonetheless, your best hope for getting from an audience the response you want begins with clear thinking on your part. Before your position on a subject is presented to the audience, you should have already formulated a precise expression of it for yourself. That position is worded as a statement of the understanding you want to share, or it identifies the belief, attitude, or value you want the audience to accept, or it specifies the action you want your listeners to perform. This statement is called the *proposition* of the speech.

III. SPEECH PROPOSITIONS

The term "proposition" is part of the technical vocabulary of both logic and rhetoric, but logicians and rhetoricians use the term in different senses. The logician says that a proposition is anything that can be true or false. This means it is neither a fact, nor a sentence, nor a judgment. A fact is not a proposition; it simply *is*. A sentence is an *expression*; it is not a proposition. A judgment is not a proposition; it is a *belief*. Most importantly, the logician insists that to be a proposition, an assertion must be either true or false.

Rhetoricians, on the other hand, recognize the sometimes painful truth that in such crucial arenas of human communication as politics, the law, religion, and economics the truth or falsity of the beliefs people express cannot be known. Therefore, questions, commands, advice, wishes, prayers, and resolutions all convey meanings of importance. Moreover, they can be quite properly used as the propositions of speeches even though they cannot be either true or false. But while believing and disbelieving ought not to be confused with truth and falsity, people do make decisions on the basis of what they believe. Therefore, even though sentences expressing judgments about values or conduct are usually considered by logicians to be outside the realm of logic—they are the heart and soul of human communication.

A. Kinds of Propositions

In every case the proposition of a speech makes one or the other of two kinds of claim. It says either that something *is* or that something *ought to be*. The kind of proposition that asserts the way something ought to be is called a *proposition of policy*. The other kind of proposition, the kind which claims that something is, appears in two forms. The first of these is called a *proposition of fact*, and the other is a *proposition of value*. Let us look briefly at these three forms.

1. Propositions of Policy

Among the senses in which people use the word "policy" is the one in which they mean "course of action" or "mode of conduct." When, for example, we speak of the "foreign policy" of the United States, we are referring to the set of judgments that guide this country's relationships with other nations. During the trying 32 days in which Secretary of State Henry Kissinger successfully accomplished the awesome task of negotiating an agreement between Israel and Syria over the Golan Heights, he was guided, and to some degree constrained, by these kinds of judgments. Decisions about courses of action, however, are not restricted to international, or even governmental, affairs. Every day of your life you have to make decisions about how to conduct your life. Moreover, you very frequently find it useful for your own ends and for the benefit of others to offer them advice, to ask them to do something, or in some way to change their lives. In all these instances, the expression you use to let them know what you want, what you have in mind, is a proposition of policy.

A proposition of policy is a statement that identifies a course of action (a policy) and calls for its adoption.

Here are two examples:

The student council should establish a system of fines for students who fail to remove their dishes in the cafeteria.
The several states should adopt uniform divorce laws.

2. Propositions of Fact

Of the three kinds of proposition people use to express their beliefs, attitudes, and values, this is the only one that would be acceptable to a logician. It makes the claim that some factual condition can, upon investigation, be observed.

A proposition of fact is a statement which asserts that specified circumstances exist.

Two examples of a proposition of fact are:

There is a wide disparity among the divorce laws of the several states.
Peace will never come to the Mid-East.

Looking at these two examples, you might notice something interesting about them. The first one much more obviously meets the definition specified above: a claim that upon investigation some factual condition can be observed. When you make such a statement, it will of course, be in the belief that the proposition is true. Presumably, you would not make such a statement until you had investigated the facts and drawn the conclusion expressed by the proposition. But look again at the second of the two examples. It is not nearly so clear that in this case investigation can prove the proposition to be true. What it amounts to is no more than an expression of an opinion. Can it, therefore, be called a proposition of fact? It can because of its *form*. It is a proposition of fact because of the kind of claim it makes: that some factual conditional can (or, at least theoretically, *could*) be observed. Being an expression of opinion does not prevent its being a proposition of fact. Indeed, every proposition of any sort is precisely an opinion. Only a relatively small number of propositions of fact are anything more than expressions of opinion. All propositions of policy, all propositions of value, and most of the propositions of fact that you might utter are simply opinions, expressions of your own beliefs, attitudes, and values.

3. Propositions of Value

From all appearances, a proposition of value could be mistaken for a proposition of fact. Yet the two are different in a very important respect and you should be able to distinguish between them with precision. A proposition of fact makes the claim that something outside your head, something in the physical world, could (given the right conditions) be observed. A proposition of fact, in other words, says something about the object referred to. What it says is either true or false, depending solely upon whether the object has the property ascribed to it. A proposition of value does not ascribe properties to objects or events in this sense. What happens is that something such as a person, place, condition, situation, or event causes in you a feeling of approval or disapproval, that is, a reaction that is positive or negative on whatever grounds—aesthetic, moral, or pragmatic. When you express this feeling, you are not ascribing any property to the object you refer to. Instead, you are merely expressing the state of your mind.

A proposition of value is a statement expressing a judgment about the goodness, rightness, quality, or merit of something.

Two examples of a proposition of value follow.

Professional boxing is a brutal sport.
The American educational system is superior to the educational systems of Europe.

To conclude our discussion about the different kinds of propositions, we give you a final word of advice about how to tell one from another. It is a grave error to classify a proposition by deciding whether you believe it or not. The following often happens:

"What kind of proposition is this? Everyone should give good value for the money he receives."

"That must be a proposition of fact because it's *true*."

"No. It's a proposition of policy because of the kind of claim it makes. It identifies a course of action, a mode of conduct, a policy, and calls for its adoption."

"What kind of proposition is this? There is no life anywhere in the universe except on Earth."

"That's a proposition of value because it's only your opinion."

"No. *All* propositions are expressions of opinion. This is a proposition of fact because of the kind of claim it makes. It identifies a condition and claims that the condition could at least theoretically be observed in the physical world."

You are not likely to be easily confused in identifying propositions of policy. They are so clearly different from propositions of fact and value that they are easy to recognize. But there are not such hard and fast lines between propositions of fact and value and in everyday life we tend to mingle them. The differences between them, however, are real, and not to identify each one correctly makes for fuzzy thinking and blurred notions of what you want to say.

B. Propositions in Relation to Purposes

Speech propositions identify the subject matter of a speech much more precisely than they do the purpose of the speech. Consider these two propositions of policy:

Congress should impose a 10 percent surtax on personal incomes.
Congress should give Manhattan Island back to the Indians.

There is little reason to wonder which of the two examples is more likely to be the proposition of a speech to persuade. The number of times that your response to serious comments has been "You're kidding!" makes it clear that either statement could conceivably be the proposition of a speech to persuade. Furthermore, probably no statement can be made that cannot be used as the proposition of a speech to entertain. But there is no reason to think that an audience would interpret either of the above subjects as the proposition of a speech to inform.

Consider next the following proposition of value:

Women are better cooks than men.

Is this statement the proposition of a speech to entertain or to persuade? Without saying anything about the merits of *any* speech on this subject, we can see clearly that a speaker could have either purpose. We can also see that it is highly unlikely that an audience will consider this statement to be the proposition of a speech to inform. What about propositions of fact?

> Golf is for little old ladies.
> An earthquake is the result of complicated causes.
> Astronauts from Earth will land on Mars within 10 years.

It is reasonable to suppose that the first of these sentences expresses the proposition of a speech to entertain, the second a speech to inform, and the third a speech to persuade. In each instance, the speaker's goal will influence the development of the topic. In each instance also, however (and the point is worth repeating), it will be the audience who determines whether it is the speaker's purpose to entertain, inform, or persuade. The point to be made here is that only the proposition of fact clearly and easily lends itself to all three kinds of speaking we have been discussing.

To summarize briefly the relationships between speech purposes and speech propositions:

1. A proposition of policy or a proposition of value will be interpreted by an audience as voicing the purpose to entertain or to persuade. In making its interpretation, the audience will be guided in part by the subject matter, in part by the subject as developed, and in part by the condition of its own attitudes, opinions, and beliefs.

2. A proposition of fact can be used to express any one of the three purposes. The audience's interpretation will be based on the same factors that determine its reaction to propositions of policy and value.

We have developed the notion that of all the propositions you might adduce to identify the subject and purpose of any particular speaking situation, the one you do select is determined by the audience. Perhaps a better way of stating what happens is to say that a speaking situation will not usually come about until you recognize that the beliefs, attitudes, values, and actions of someone else constitute an obstacle to some goal of your own. You then adduce a proposition that you present and develop with an eye to changing the thinking or actions which are inimical to your goal. Such terms as "obstacle," "goal," and "inimical" suggest too strongly that all speakers must overcome active opposition. Not so.

Suppose your goal (the response you want from the audience) to be amusement. The obstacle: "These people don't see the laughable in such-and-such a concept." That concept is then identified in a proposition of policy, value, or fact, and you try to influence the audience's meaning for that concept to include "laughable." What happens may be called a speech to entertain.

In another instance, the goal may be: "I want people to know how earthquakes happen." The obstacle: "They don't understand how complicated the process is." Thus the proposition of the speech is indicated. Your purpose would be to inform.

Again, assume the goal to be: "Elect Harrison to the state assembly." The obstacle: "This somewhat conservative audience thinks Harrison is too liberal." The proposition: "In matters most important to you, Harrison is a moderate." The purpose of this speech is clearly persuasive.

In this manner, then, speakers identify the subjects, purposes, and propositions that particular audience conditions require them to choose on particular speaking occasions.

All that has been said thus far in this chapter has been directed toward your better understanding the part played by the audience in the formulation of the proposition of a speech. Perhaps you have said to yourself, "All right, I've never thought of it that way before and it sounds a little odd to say that an audience determines what a speaker's proposition will be. Even so, the speaker has to *find* the proposition, he doesn't directly ask the audience to give it to him. You've been saying that of all the propositions in the world, the speaker chooses the one that is right for a particular audience at a particular time. But what I want to know is, where do all these propositions come from?"

You have asked a good question, one worth thinking about for a while.

C. Sources of Propositions

Suppose that you and a group of friends wanted to run a candidate for student body president. Several questions would arise: Who should your candidate be? How should you conduct the campaign? And so on. You and your friends would explore the subject to understand better the problems involved and to make decisions about them. As a result of this exploration, you achieve understandings and beliefs you did not have before your inquiry began. In talking about the campus election, you might come to conclusions like the following: "The candidate who can get the support of the Interfraternity Council will swing the election." "Fred Byron is the best man to unite the council behind him." "Fred Byron should be selected as our candidate for the office of student body president." "Fred's campaign should be built around the idea of getting for the students a more decisive voice in appropriating money from the student activities fee." This example makes evident that the general source of propositions is questions. You will recognize that each of the conclusions you draw as a result of exploring the questions arising in connection with the student body election is a proposition: The first is a proposition of fact, the second is a proposition of value, and the last two are propositions of policy.

These questions are given the general name of *problems*. The conclusions you reach in your attempts to solve whatever problems you meet become the propositions that you may, in speaking to others, choose to explain or to prove.

The need to solve problems of one kind or another is something that none of us escapes. The foregoing example of some of the problems that might need to be explored in a student body election assumes that problems might be attacked by a group. This is clearly not a necessary condition. Many problems are by their nature the sort of things which, for political, social, or other reasons, one prefers to explore alone. Nonetheless, there are problems whose scope and import make appropriate a cooperative attack. Their number is great enough so that group decision making has attracted the detailed interest of industrialists, politicians, and investigators in such fields as psychology, sociology and, of course, rhetoric.

The usefulness of exploring problems in a group situation has warranted a chapter in this book devoted to that kind of speaking occasion. Note, however, that it is not considered to be a fourth "kind" or "general end" of speeches coordinate with speaking to entertain, to inform, and to persuade. We take group decision making to be not a *purpose* but rather an *occasion*. It equates, therefore, with such other forms of communication as public speaking. The goals of the participants in group decision making, the responses they seek, you have met in our earlier consideration of speeches to inform and to persuade. The members of a group intend to give and get information for *understanding* the problem (and this is the purpose of speaking to inform). Moreover, they seek *agreement* on a solution (and this is the purpose of speaking to persuade). The rhetorical techniques appropriate in group decision making are the same as those used in speaking situations of other sorts: identification of the subject (in group discussion the subject is a *problem* rather than a *proposition*), specification of the purpose (*understanding* the problem, *agreement* on a solution), collection and organization of evidence and ideas, selection of meaningful

28

language, and effective communication through appropriate delivery.

The outcome of successful exploration of a problem is the formulation of a proposition that is presumably an acceptable solution to the problem being explored. Thus the source of any proposition is a problem to which the proposition is at least a relevant answer. This definition implies that problems are of three kinds: *policy, fact,* and *value.*

1. Problems of Policy

A problem of policy is a question that asks for a formulation of policy. It asks what procedure, what method of operation, or what mode of conduct ought to be adopted. It says in effect, "What course of action should we follow in such-and-such a situation?"

The question that phrases a problem of policy should be stated in such a way that it calls for a choice among several possible alternative courses of action. It does not ask for acceptance or rejection of any one proposal. This point can be clarified by an example. Suppose we were to ask, "Should the United States finance a search for a source of oil outside the Arab world?" The question is obviously concerned with a matter of policy. Is it not, then, a satisfactory question of policy? It is not, and for this reason: A specific course of action that the United States might follow in solving a problem of energy shortage is suggested in the very phrasing of the question. Instead of asking which one of *all* possible courses of action ought to be adopted, the question as stated demands a Yes or No answer with regard to *one* alternative proposal. As such, it is an invitation not to explore but to persuade. A properly phrased problem of policy would read, "What should the Federal government do to prevent an energy crisis in the United States?"

2. Problems of Fact

A problem of fact is a question that asks what the conditions in a given situation are. We may ask, "What procedure does the Federal Reserve Bank employ in controlling credit spending?" Other examples range from such questions as "What were the causes of the Vietnam War?" and "What principles govern the operation of the neutron bomb?" to such simple matters as "What time is it?" and "What's for supper?"

3. Problems of Value

A problem of value is a question that asks about the merit or lack of merit in a person, an item, or an idea. A value judgment must be made before an answer can be given to such questions as, "What is the greatest play in the English language?" or "When did the most significant advances in science take place?"

A problem of value is both like and unlike a problem of fact in precisely the same way in which propositions of value and fact are different and alike. That is to say, a problem of value and a problem of fact both ask that a judgment be made. There is, however, a difference between the kinds of judgments that these two problems require. As the name implies, the problem of value asks for a value judgment; the problem of fact does not. An example will make the distinction clear:

> PROBLEM OF FACT: In how many schools is art a required part of the curriculum?
> PROBLEM OF VALUE: How important is art in the college curriculum?

To insure that problems of fact and value will be explored rather than debated, avoid phrasing them as questions that can be answered Yes or No. Instead of asking "Is the defendant guilty?" ask "Who committed the crime?" Instead of asking "Is Babe Ruth the greatest baseball player in the history of the game? ask "Who is the greatest basball player in the history of the game?"

IV. SELECTING THE RIGHT SUBJECT

An audience will probably not listen to you if you fail to give it reasons for judging you to be competent. Your competence is a matter constantly at issue, and an audience judges it from moment to moment during a speech. The first opportunity you have to make a step toward earning an audience judgment that you are competent comes when you choose the right subject. We say the *right* subject, rather than a "good" subject. There is, in fact, no such thing as an inherently good subject, nor is there any such thing as a bad one. Rather than good or bad subjects, there are only good or bad speeches on any subject whatsoever. A subject is right when it is one upon which you are *competent* to express your beliefs, attitudes, and values; when the audience will judge it to be *significant*; and, most important, when it is *appropriate* to whatever changes in thinking and action you want as an audience response. A subject with these qualities is the one you want to select if you expect to achieve your goals.

30

IV Selecting the Right Subject

A. Speaker Competence

The assumption that a good speaker can talk well on any subject is an erroneous one. Winston Churchill, one of the great speakers of the modern world, spoke on propositions growing out of the political, economic, and social problems to which he devoted his public life. He would not try to tell engineers how to build a bridge or biochemists how to design a laboratory for manufacturing antibiotics. Good speakers are avid readers and investigators. They pursue all kinds of knowledge, but they cannot be expert on everything. They must, therefore, speak on subjects chosen from areas of their own greatest competence.

But a subject you choose need not be in an area of your competence *before* you choose it. If this were the case, the number of topics would be so limited that you would be reduced to virtual impotence in your own society. In fact, when you choose a subject, you may know very little about it; you may be incompetent in the sense of not having detailed knowledge. If you add to your knowledge through study, then your initial knowledge and your research can combine to make you competent. The important thing is that you be competent *before* you make a speech.

B. Significance

For a home economics major, the fact that the spool of thread which used to cost a nickel now costs 15 cents is likely to be of considerably greater interest than it is to an art major whose creativity takes forms other than sewing. An anthropology major might go out of the way to hear a lecture on the Hopi Indian. A student of political science might gladly spend time tabulating returns of a campus election in which the anthropology major had perhaps not taken time to vote. All four students would respond sharply to news that tuition at their college was to be increased 25 percent. In each of these instances, the students would be giving attention to those events which each one considered significant.

The same condition applies to your speech subject. It will be of interest to an audience if it involves matters that are of significance to the audience. The greater the significance, the greater the interest. The listeners may not be aware of the extent to which the topic does concern them. Indeed, they may not have any feeling in the matter. This indifference does not mean that the subject is necessarily a poor one. Instead, it means that you must stimulate interest in the subject. You stimulate it by helping your listeners perceive the significance the topic has for them. Unless you make clear why your listeners should be interested, unless you show how and why the subject is of significance for them, they will pay you little heed. Then it will not matter that the subject offers information the audience has not heard before or new insights into familiar ideas, or that the material of the speech is organized with great clarity, eminently well supported, and delivered with superior skill.

C. Appropriateness

The subject of a speech is appropriate only if you can hope to gain the response you seek: enjoyment, enlightenment, action, or belief. There is not much point in trying to get an audience to do something it cannot do: high-school students under 18 cannot vote for a sheriff. Nor is there much use in asking the audience to accept an attitude you know it is highly probable they will reject: Liquor dealers will scarcely endorse prohibition.

Examples of these exercises in futility can be heard in any college speech class: "Here's how I think you ought to raise your children"; or "You can have a full life after retirement." This is not to say that college students will not some day have children or retire. It is to say, however, that speeches on subjects of this sort are not directly and immediately salient to the audience.

In other kinds of speeches, speakers explicate their own personal value systems without any real hope of getting any audience other than a friendly (already convinced) one to enter into the discussion at all. "Gambling is immoral" or "He was a conscious tool of the communists." Such a speech is a cathartic experience for the speaker and is delivered because there is an audience.

Usually, it is a specific occasion that draws men and women together to form an audience. In choosing a subject you must, therefore, consider the occasion. You would not deliver a partisan political talk at a church meeting any more than you would tell jokes at a funeral. An address delivered on Lincoln's birthday should indicate at least an awareness of the great president's philosophy and deeds, and on the Fourth of July some phase of patriotism is traditionally in order.

Some speakers, on the other hand, use the limitations of the occasion as an excuse for not taking a responsible part in the affairs of the community. Franklin D. Roosevelt's speech on the threat of aggression prior to World War II was delivered at the dedication of a Chicago bridge. It might seem better to have delivered this "Quarantine of Aggressors" speech at a foreign-policy meeting, and to have made his appearance in Chicago the occasion for a speech on public works. The demands of the times, however (it might be called the "larger occasion"), *made* this a right occasion. Certainly, the people of Chicago are interested in the question of war and peace. It might have been easy for the president to delay until Hitler marched into Poland two years later, excusing himself by saying that the right occasion for stating his views had never come along.

Similarly, you will be given many opportunities to voice your opinion on questions that concern you. Do not hesitate to let others know what you think because "the occasion is not right." This is an excuse rather than a reason. If you are to take your place as a responsible citizen, you must be willing to state your views on the pressing problems of the times. The world is full of people who are happy to shirk this responsibility.

V. THE BEGINNING SPEECHES

Proficiency in the art of speech grows out of the combination of understanding and experience, of theory and practice. Which should be taught and studied first? If you wait until you have a good background of theory before you begin to make speeches, your speaking suffers from lack of practice; if you make speeches from the beginning, you lack the guidance of theoretical knowledge.

To begin speaking at the outset seems the better choice. The theoretical basis of your speaking will admittedly need development, but the value of practice is great, and your knowledge of theory will grow as you examine the principles of speaking in greater detail. It will be helpful and necessary to learn enough of the theory to do a satisfactory job early in the course.

Effective speaking may be considered to be what an audience thinks is worth listening to. Audiences tend to respond in this fashion to speakers who have something significant to say; who give their ideas order, coherence, and form; who provide adequate grounds for their credibility; and who present their materials well. This chapter examines briefly these four elements of any effective speech: subject, organization, supporting material, and delivery. Our purpose here is to give you an introduction to the basic skills of communication. You will study each of these elements in more detail during the coming weeks.

A. Selecting a Subject and Purpose

On any speaking occasion, two restrictions will limit your choice of a subject. You will be limited by the need for finding a subject that will be of interest to both you and your audience, and you will be limited in the amount of time you will have to speak.

Because of the restriction in time, the general subject you choose must be narrowed in scope so that it can be adequately discussed in the length of time allowed. The narrowed subject is then further specified by phrasing it as a *statement of specific purpose*, which indicates what you intend to convey to your listeners about the subject.

GENERAL SUBJECT: Transistors
SPECIFIC SUBJECT: How a transistor works
SPECIFIC PURPOSE: To inform the listeners about the way in which the phenomenon of electron borrowing makes transistor radios possible

GENERAL SUBJECT: Skin diving
SPECIFIC SUBJECT: Skin-diving equipment
SPECIFIC PURPOSE: To inform the audience about the minimum equipment necessary for the beginning skin diver

GENERAL SUBJECT: Capital punishment
SPECIFIC SUBJECT: The effect of capital punishment on crime
SPECIFIC PURPOSE: To persuade the audience that capital punishment is a deterrent to crime

Notice how concrete these statements of specific purpose are. Each points to one clear-cut effort and excludes any others. Compare them with the following statements of purpose, which are alleged to be specific but are multiple, diffuse, and therefore badly drawn:

SPECIFIC PURPOSE: To inform the audience of the popularity of the transistor radio and how it works, especially how it uses electron borrowing

SPECIFIC PURPOSE: To inform the audience of the equipment necessary for skin diving and how skin diving is not only safe but fun

SPECIFIC PURPOSE: To persuade the audience that capital punishment deters crime and, as a matter of fact, that severe punishment is effective, even with children in the home

All three of these statements of purpose are poor. They show that the speaker does not have a clear, single purpose in mind. Instead, the statements give only vague notions about what the subject will be. The specific purpose, once it has been carefully drawn, becomes a guide to test the organization and materials of the speech. Every statement in the speech, every piece of evidence or supporting material used, will relate directly to the accomplishment of that purpose. If it doest not help to achieve the purpose of the speech, no piece of material can be justified and should be excluded from the speech.

B. Organizing the Speech

Your speech will be organized into three parts: an *introduction*, the *body*, and a *conclusion*. The body is organized first, because it bears the primary responsibility for accomplishing the purpose of the speech. The introduction and the conclusion are developed after the body of the speech has been prepared.

1. Organizing the Body of the Speech

If human beings were able to use some method of direct psychic communication such as that commonly called telepathy, it would perhaps be possible for your listeners to receive a whole complex of ideas in a single perceptive flash. Since audiences do not have this ability, however, you must build understanding in your listeners piece by piece. Think of the subject of your speech as a jigsaw puzzle you have made. If you give it to someone else as a jumble of pieces, he will have to work it out for himself to make an intelligible picture of it if, indeed, he bothers to do so at all. Should you, instead, hand him the pieces one at a time and in such an orderly fashion that he can easily fit them together, the picture you have made grows readily before his eyes. Organizing a speech is very much like these two processes: first, putting together the parts of the puzzle so that you can see the picture yourself, and second, handing the pieces in proper order to someone else.

To make sure that all the parts of your speech fit together in their proper places in the minds of your audience, that is, to make sure that it sees the same picture you do, you will need to divide the subject of your speech into a series of main points and then to arrange these in an organizational pattern that brings order to the materials and clarity to the ideas. Together with their supporting material, these main points constitute the body of your speech. We mention four organizational patterns here. These, and others, will be discussed further in Chapter 16, "Speaking To Inform," and in Chapter 17, "Speaking To Persuade."

a. Chronological Order. The sequence of main points in the body of the speech may be arranged in the order of their occurrence in time.

> SPECIFIC PURPOSE: To inform the audience about Germany's submarine-warfare policy in World War I
>   I. February 1915, the British Isles were declared a war zone.
>   II. May 1916, Germany pledged not to sink ships without warning.
>   III. January 1917, Germany commenced unrestricted submarine warfare.

b. Geographical or Spatial Order. The sequence of main points in the body of the speech may follow the order of their arrangement in space. The points occur in the speech in the same order in which the listener might visualize himself moving physically from one to another.

> SPECIFIC PURPOSE: To inform the audience about the major dialects of English spoken in the British Isles
>   I. Ireland
>   II. Scotland
>   III. Northern England
>   IV. Southern England
>   V. Wales

c. Topical Order. The main points in the body of the speech may be a list of the important parts of the idea discussed by the speaker. Added together, these parts or "topics" make up the whole idea.

> SPECIFIC PURPOSE: To inform the audience about the operation of the speech mechanism
>   I. Respiration
>   II. Phonation
>   III. Resonation
>   IV. Articulation

d. Argumentative Order. In speeches to persuade, the body is organized in what may be thought of as a form of topical arrangement. The main points in the body of the speech to persuade are arguments, reasons for believing the truth of what the speaker is trying to prove.

> SPECIFIC PURPOSE: To persuade the audience that prices at the college book store are too high
>   I. The book store has increased its prices every year for the past three years.

II. The book store made an excessive profit last year.

III. The same books cost less at neighboring colleges.

2. Organizing the Conclusion

After you have organized the body of the speech, you will want to plan a *conclusion* to pull together the main ideas in the speech. One customary and effective way to end a speech is with a brief summary which recalls for the audience the specific purpose of the speech and the main points that develop it. A summary conclusion is particularly valuable in speaking because a listener cannot go back and rehear as a reader can go back and reread. Not all conclusions take the form of a summary, but you will find it useful in your beginning speeches. More sophisticated kinds of conclusions will be discussed later. Use these when experience has developed your skill.

3. Organizing the Introduction

The last section to be developed is the introduction, even though it is to be spoken first. In preparing a speech, the introduction is left until last because once the body of the speech and the conclusion are prepared, you know what you want to say to the audience. You will then be able to prepare an introduction that is more directly related to the ideas contained in the speech.

The introduction has two essential parts. First, there is some interest factor: a story, incident, description, startling statement, or quotation that will catch the attention of the audience. This interest factor should be immediately pertinent to the subject of the speech because its primary function is to arouse interest in what you are going to say and to direct that interest toward the purpose of the speech.

The second major part of the introduction is the subject sentence. In informative speeches, this is a statement which expresses the specific purpose of the speech in an informal oral style.

> SPECIFIC PURPOSE: To inform the audience about the way in which the phenomenon of electron borrowing makes transistor radios possible
>
> SUBJECT SENTENCE: Transistor radios are made possible by the phenomenon of electron borrowing

The subject sentence of a persuasive speech is very often much less direct than it might be in an informative speech. If the audience has no strongly negative attitudes toward the proposition you advocate, you will do the cause no harm by telling them openly what you want them to accept. On other occasions, however, a specific statement of what you advocate might solidify any negative attitudes the audience may have toward what you want to say and cut off communication before the speech gets under way. In addition, suspense and movement toward a climax have interest value. These two factors may cause you to avoid committing yourself to a specific position before you have a chance to build a case for it. In any event, however, you must give the audience a clear notion of the subject area of your speech.

C. Supporting the Ideas in the Speech

The statement of specific purpose and its development in the body of the speech constitute the definite idea you want the audience to have. But the idea you have in mind may not be the idea the audience understands from what you say. Your task in every speech is to improve the fidelity of your communication. This you may do, at least in part, by the proper use of supporting materials to maintain the *interest* of the audience and to lend *clarity* to what you say. Examples, statistics, quotations, and arguments all help to make your ideas more clear, interesting, and believable. Always use *at least* one item of such specific material in support of each important point in the body of the speech. (Usually, two or more pieces of supporting material are necessary and desirable.) This specific material will help you to make the ideas you have developed more precise and vivid, and thus serve to clarify the subject, add interest, and establish belief.

When you have determined the content and organization of the speech, you may want to prepare some notes to help you in delivery. Whatever notes you use should be in outline form. Here is an example of standard outline form suitable for organizing either an informative or a persuasive speech early in the course. As your experience grows and you develop skill, your outlines will increase in complexity to meet the demands of more sophisticated materials and ideas.

INTRODUCTION
I. Interest factor
II. Subject sentence

BODY
I. First main point of the speech
   A. Supporting material
   B. Supporting material

38

    II. Second main point of the speech
       A. Supporting material
       B. Supporting material
       [And so on]

CONCLUSION

    I. Summary statement noting the purpose
       A. First main point
       B. Second main point
       [And so on]

D. Delivering the Speech

The ideas, organization, and supporting details in any given instance of communication can be the same whether the communication is written or spoken. Except for some few differences in style (the way language is used), what most distinguishes writing from speaking is that a speech must be delivered. Indeed, it doesn't become a speech until the moment of delivery. Consequently, good delivery makes a significant contribution to effectiveness in speaking. It is the vital, physical means by which ideas are transmitted to a listener. Good delivery is direct and spontaneous, shows your involvement in the subject, and is intelligible to your audience.

1. Practice

An audience will judge your speech as it is delivered, so you need to prepare it in terms of that delivery. Practice the speech aloud and listen to it as it might be heard by the audience.

When you have what you think is the final draft of your outline, practice speaking from it several times to set the ideas in your mind. If you can find an audience to practice on, so much the better. Don't write the speech out or try to memorize it. Use the words that come to you at the time of each practice delivery. The oftener you practice during the preparation period, the better you will be able to find the words to get the reaction you want from the audience.

SUMMARY

All good speaking is aimed at influencing the beliefs, attitudes, values, and actions of an audience. The condition of an audience (the way it thinks and acts) is, therefore, the determining factor in the selection of a speech subject and purpose. Speech subjects are expressed as propositions of policy, value, or fact.

The primary responses a speaker seeks are amusement (in speeches to entertain), understanding (in speeches to inform), and agreement (in speeches to persuade).

The sources of propositions are problems. These appear as problems of policy, value, or fact and are frequently explored in group discussions.

The right subject to choose is one within the speaker's competence, one that is significant for the audience, and one that is appropriate to the audience and the occasion.

Develop your beginning speeches through attention to these four basic steps: subject, organization, supporting material, and delivery. Formulate a specific purpose. Study the possible ways to divide the speech into its main points. Search for the right supporting materials to make the ideas clear, interesting, and acceptable to your audience. Practice while you are preparing the final outline and after it has been established.

QUESTIONS

1. What responses might a speaker seek?
2. How does the audience determine the subject of a speech?
3. What are the differences among problems of fact, value, and policy?
4. Discuss the qualities of the right speech subject.
5. From the general subject "Education," select a specific subject suitable for a short informative speech. Prepare a statement of specific purpose and a subject sentence.
6. Give an example of each of three types of order for the body of a speech.
7. What is the twofold purpose of an introduction?
8. Why should a speech have a conclusion?
9. What are the supporting materials mentioned in the text that make ideas most precise and vivid for an audience?

EXERCISES

1. Select some campus problem and, using the examples in this chapter as models, state it as a problem of policy. Rephrase it into a proposition of policy indicating what you believe should be done.

2. Phrase a proposition of fact and a proposition of value from the same general subject. Explain, by using these examples, the difference between fact and value.

3. Select one of the audiences below or one assigned by your instructor and make a list of five speech subjects which you believe would interest them. Write a brief note after each one indicating why you think this audience would be interested.

    (a) A church club you belong to.

    (b) An assembly of the high school from which you graduated.

    (c) The freshman class at your college.

    (d) An organization to which your parents belong.

4. Make a list of five general subjects on which you believe you are qualified to speak and explain why you feel each would or would not be right for your classmates.

5. Examine the following list of expressions and determine whether each is (1) a problem or a proposition; (2) concerned with policy, fact, or value; (3) properly phrased—and if not properly phrased, why not.

    (a) Girls aren't very reasonable.

    (b) Should we go to the movie?

    (c) What day does school open?

    (d) Who is the most valuable member of the football team?

    (e) What nation produced the most steel last year?

    (f) The United States should give economic assistance to Poland.

    (g) War is caused by greed.

    (h) What should our city do about the increase in crime?

    (i) Hasn't Senator Morgan lost the confidence of the people?

    (j) Which automobile is best for students?

    (k) What should be the college policy toward smoking on campus, or should there be one?

    (l) Wouldn't Doris make a beautiful Homecoming Queen?

6. From an issue of *Vital Speeches* magazine or a volume of speeches such as *Representative American Speeches*, select a speech and briefly outline it showing the division of the speech into introduction, body, and conclusion, and the main points in the body. Then write a few paragraphs analyzing the speech, noting the following:

    (a) Would the beginning of the speech arouse interest?

    (b) Is the subject sentence clearly stated?

    (c) Does the speaker have enough or too many main points in the body?

    (d) How does he conclude his speech?

7. Organize and deliver a three-minute informative speech explaining to your classmates some historic or scenic location within 100 miles of the college.

8. From one of the general subjects mentioned below or from others assigned by your instructor, select three specific subjects and phrase them into statements of specific purpose.

(a) Automobiles   (b) Dating practices of college students

(c) Juvenile delinquency   (d) United States foreign policy

(e) Psychology   (f) Athletics

9. Listen carefully to the delivery of an instructor's lectures in another class. Compile a list of the characteristics of the instructor's delivery that aided your understanding and a list of those that detracted from it. How many of the detracting factors do you suppose you would have noticed if you hadn't especially looked for them? How important do you think delivery is to a speaker?

A LIST OF SUBJECT AREAS

The following list is intended to help you think of a speech subject. These subjects will need to be narrowed. Each of these could be a subject for entertaining, informing, persuading, or discussion. Taking the first subject on education, for instance, you might choose one of these specific purposes:

ENTERTAIN: To indicate what a large university looks like to a very small freshman.

INFORM: To inform the audience about the academic organization of Columbia University.

PERSUADE: To persuade the audience that students get a better education at a large university.

Education

Large universities	Progressive education
Private versus public education	College students today
Teaching a child to read	Revisions in the high schools
Federal aid to education	Foreign languages
The place of athletics in education	Student government
The teaching of reading	Changes in education
Foreign and American colleges	Honors programs
Grading systems	Junior high schools
Vocational aptitude	Counseling
Junior colleges	Drop-outs
Campus political parties	Academic cheating
Small colleges	Honor system

42

V The Beginning Speeches

World Politics

Disarmament
United Nations
Israel and the Arabs
Japan's economy
Dictators
Alaska and Russia
The Middle East
International spies
Underdeveloped countries
Russia's leaders
American tourists
Yugoslavia
Berlin

Africa
China
Cuba
Canada and the United States
India
Russia's army
Past wars
Propaganda
Ambassadors
Franco's Spain
Satellite nations
Southeast Asia
Vietnam

National Politics

Military men in public office
Revision of the Supreme Court
Constitutional amendments
Antitrust laws
The Electoral College
Straight party voting
Lobbying
Social welfare
Wiretapping
Pump-priming
Should Congress be televised?
Impeachment

Presidential elections
How different are the parties?
Labor disputes
Ex-Presidents
Filibuster
State offices
Public power
Withholding tax
Closed shop
Civil disobedience
Watergate

Science

Great scientists
Ants
Microscopes
Photosynthesis
Growth
Man in space
Psychiatry and psychology
Radiation
Atoms

Should nonscientists study science?
Solid state physics
Butterflies
Cell division
Perception
Dentistry
Fission
Disease
Computers

Humanities

The value of the study of history
Great writers

Liberal versus technical education
Recent novels

43

How to understand poetry
"Time spent in reading is time lost
   from living."
Civil war
Transcendentalism
Semantics
Representational versus abstract art
Huck Finn revisited
Should a novel have a happy ending?
The Trent affair

Modern art
Sculpture
Does history repeat?
Rationalism
Bertrand Russell
Modern music
Popular fiction
Morality in art
Sigmund Freud
Movies made from novels

Society

The Hopi Indians
The ideas of an ethnic group
"All men are created equal."
The police force
Subliminal advertising
Personal liberty
Distinctive features of American
   society
Television give-away programs
"A woman's place is in the home."
Human beings are unalike.
Social Security
Marriage laws
Population explosion
Birth control

Child-beating syndrome
Censorship
Poverty
New roles for women
A double standard?
Are Americans disliked?
High salaries for entertainers

Polish wedding
Racial barriers
Science in advertising
Traffic accidents
Capital punishment
Juvenile criminals
Divorce
Retail price control

Religion

The sermon in Protestantism
What is a saint?
Varieties in Judaism
"The Great Awakening"
Mohammedanism
Hinduism
Psychology and religion
The education of the clergy
The symbolism of the Mass

The election of the Pope
Puritanism in New England
Religious wars
Zoroastrianism
Confucianism
Science and religion
Buddhism
Evolution versus divine creation

Definitions

Capitalism
The Great Plains

New Yorker
Loyalty

V *The Beginning Speeches*

Liberal education
Morality
Ethics
Rumor
Gossip

American
Individualism
Success
Socialism
Communism

I. Issues defined
II. Analysis—the method for finding issues
    A. Analyzing propositions of policy
        1. Finding the issues in propositions of policy
        2. Phrasing the issues
        3. Reducing the number of issues
        4. Classifying the issues (stock issues)
    B. Analyzing propositions of value and fact
III. The five *loci* of potential issues
    A. Issues located in the stated advantages and disadvantages
    B. Issues located in the criteria
    C. Issues located in the relative importance of the criteria
    D. Issues located in the application of the criteria to evidence
    E. Issues located in the evidence
IV. How issues are used
    A. To indicate the lines of argument
    B. To group the arguments
    C. To determine emphasis
    D. To determine the nature of the argument

Chapter 3

Analyzing the Proposition

Ministers and salesmen, governors and student body presidents, lawyers and housewives all have ideas they want others to accept. You are barraged with efforts to persuade you—appeals and arguments of enormous variety. You try to persuade others, both individuals and groups, to accept the truth of something you believe, to value something you like, to do something you want done.

Suppose that you and your friend Bob would like to take the same elective course so you can study together. You favor cultural anthropology. You might say:

"A bunch of us are going to take DeSilva's course in anthropology next semester. Diane says DeSilva's an easy grader; he doesn't even check on whether you do the reading. Last semester, he didn't call the roll half the time."

But Bob is not looking for a snap course; he wants one that will be worthwhile and interesting. He isn't worried about whether the professor is an easy grader. He likes to do the reading for the courses he takes. Although he recognizes that anthropology could be interesting and worthwhile, he has heard reports that the instructor is dull and he is afraid that the course may be a bore. Therefore, while the arguments you have used seem plausible to you, they probably won't be convincing to Bob; they fail to deal with the specific questions that concern him.

I. ISSUES DEFINED

Before you can expect to persuade Bob, you will need to find arguments that deal with his real attitudes, motives, and values which cause him to have a negative reaction to your proposal. Before you can find these arguments, you will need to see where your attitudes and motives are likely to conflict with his. These points of disagreement are called *issues.*

In the question of whether Bob should take the course in anthropology, his position is something like the following:

"I hear that DeSilva is a very dull lecturer. He just stands up in front of the room and reads from those yellow pages he hasn't revised in 20 years; he doesn't even look at the class. I don't think it would be an interesting course."

The position you should take if you are to argue effectively must be somewhat along these lines:

"Anthropology is an interesting subject. The course has field trips to Indian burial grounds and to museums. You're already interested in sociology, and DeSilva's course covers the cultural background of this very area."

The *issue* Bob raises lies in the question: "Is anthropology an interesting course?" If you argue on any grounds other than this issue that concerns Bob, your efforts more than likely will fail. Your only alternative to identifying your proposal with his interests is to change his interests. This is generally more difficult to do, although in some cases it is the only obvious alternative. But whether you argue the issue, "Is cultural anthropology an interesting course?" or "Is the ease of a course more important than its interest value?" notice that both you and Bob express your attitudes about the anthropology course in the form of *argument.* Both of you give *reasons* for the attitude. Moreover, when you carefully express the arguments, they directly oppose one another. In this relation you find the *issue,* that is, *the question over which the opposing arguments clash.* So, in your discussion with Bob, you attempt to enlighten him on the nature of the course in cultural anthropology:

"Cultural anthropology is a study of primitive peoples, their social structures, living conditions, and mores. The course consists of lectures and discussions of reading assignments. There is a midterm and a final examination, both of which are to be answered in essay form, and each student writes a term paper on some particular phase of a primitive society."

You have probably given the necessary information for your friend Bob to understand what the course in cultural anthropology is. You have covered what are, for him, the salient points: the issues. It might be fun to go back and ask whether these are the same kinds of evidence that would interest your friend Diane, who was quoted previously.

II. ANALYSIS—THE METHOD FOR FINDING ISSUES

In any communication situation the careful analysis of issues is essential to success. Certainly, advertizers spend millions of dollars every year to discover what we expect from an automobile, a refrigerator, or a tooth paste and then build print and video media campaigns to meet those issues. Public speakers must discover the points of controversy that must be resolved if their speeches are to be effective. Even in informal discussions, although you may not be so formal about it, you are effective communicators to the extent to which you find the issues that matter to people and address yourself to those issues.

In the previous chapter we discussed the three kinds of propositions: fact, value, and policy. In this chapter we shall see how each of these is analyzed for issues and how they relate to one another.

A. Analyzing Propositions of Policy

We begin examining the process of analysis by looking at the most complicated proposition: the proposition of policy. In order to prove a proposition of policy, you must convince your listeners on one or more propositions of fact or value, which are analyzed quite differently. In all of this analysis, however, it is essential to keep in mind that no unchangeable law governs your decisions about what the issues are—all come from the attitude of the audience and, consequently, this chapter is closely allied to the next one on analyzing the audience.

1. Finding the Issues in Propositions of Policy

An example will most easily explain the method of analyzing a proposition of policy. Gun control legislation has been a source of controversy for a long time. The assassinations in the 1960s of President John F. Kennedy, his brother Robert Kennedy, Martin Luther King, Jr., and Malcolm X, and the 1972 wounding of presidential candidate George Wallace have brought the demand for stricter gun control, even the elimination of private ownership of guns.

If you were to become involved in the controversy, you would need to defend your point of view. No matter what position you take, here is how you might analyze the policy proposition, "Federal licensing of all firearms should be required."

First, draw a line down the middle of a sheet of paper. On the left side of the sheet, list all the arguments you can find that support the proposal. On the right side, list the arguments that oppose the proposition. Match the opposing arguments by pairing them against each other.

All Firearms Should Be Federally Licensed	Firearms Should Not Be Federally Licensed
The Federal licensing of all firearms will keep guns out of the hands of potential killers	It is impossible to prevent a a murderer from getting access to a gun

An identical statement sometimes supports opposing views:

All Firearms Should be Federally Licensed	Firearms Should Not Be Federally Licensed
The crime rate is a serious problem in America	The crime rate is a serious problem in America

On the surface there would appear to be no disagreement and, thus, no issue. In circumstances of this sort, wherein statements are agreed to by the opposing parties to a conflict, the propositions accepted without objection constitute what is called *waived matter*. Such claims as, "Ninety-four police officers were killed with hand guns in 1971," "Shotguns are used less often in crime than hand guns," or "Governor

Wallace was shot with a gun purchased out of state" would be accepted as waived matter by any knowledgeable person discussing this proposition.

The fact that both parties to a conflict make the same statement does not necessarily identify waived matter. In the case at hand, the statement that the crime rate is a serious problem in America only appears as waived matter when taken alone. The statements do clash when pertinent sentences are added, according to viewpoint: "Thus guns must be more closely controlled" or "Thus people need to have guns to protect themselves and gun licensing would take them away."

An argument in one column or the other may appear to admit no opposition, or at least in your study you may not find an opposing argument:

All Firearms Should Be Federally Licensed	*Firearms Should Not Be Federally Licensed*
In other countries with gun control laws there are fewer crimes committed using guns	No apparent argument

It is unwise to assume automatically that such unopposed arguments constitute waived matter. The offering of the argument suggests that an issue exists. To make the analysis complete, look carefully for a possible answer that may clarify the issue, for example:

All Firearms Should Be Federally Licensed	*Firearms Should Not Be Federally Licensed*
In other countries with gun control laws there are fewer crimes committed using guns	This is not a true statement Or This is true but it has nothing to do with gun licensing—it is caused by the socioeconomic nature of the society

Some arguments may not be answered because they are considered too trivial.

All Firearms Should Be Federally Licensed	Firearms Should Not Be Federally Licensed
This is based on an unwarranted assumption, but even if it is true it is trivial compared with the real problems of controlling crime	Sportsmen and gun collectors are afraid that their records will not be confidential and they will be more subject to the theft of their guns

When you have eliminated waived matters and found the opposing points of view on all the arguments, your analysis sheet will look like this:

All Firearms Should Be Federally Licensed	All Firearms Should *Not* Be Federally Licensed
There is a need for the licensing of firearms to cut down on the assassination of public figures and policemen, the high murder rate, robberies with guns, and gun accidents	Licensing of firearms will not control such actions because the criminal can always get a gun
Gun licensing will weed out the criminal and those of unstable character	The criminal can always get a gun and licensing will not restrict the crime of passion
The courts have often said that the Federal government can regulate deadly firearms	Federal gun licensing is unconstitutional because it violates the second amendment and because, except in interstate

Continued *next page*

52

	commerce and taxation, the police power is vested in the states
Not true *Or* Yes, that would be a good thing	Federal licensing would be a step toward the arbitrary denial of gun ownership
This is probably not true, but it is a trivial argument in any event	Although confidentiality is promised by the proponents of the measure, information would leak out and sportsmen and gun collectors would be more subject to theft
No more so than licensing an automobile or a fisherman	Licensing is burdensome and inconvenient
Only Federal licensing will assure adequate enforcement	Current legislation is adequate

2. Phrasing the Issues

After the analysis sheet is prepared, the points at which the two opposing sides clash are more easily seen. The next step is to phrase as a question the clash implied in each of the set of opposing arguments. This is done in the same manner that the clash was phrased in the example of the Anthropology class arguments given above. The questions that result are the issues; for example:

Only Federal licensing will assure adequate enforcement	Current legislation is adequate

The issue that separates the opposing positions is the question: "Is

Federal legislation essential to adequate enforcement of licensing controls?"

Examine each of the issues to see that all are *clearly stated*. The following issue is badly drawn:

> ISSUE: "How much of a gun problem do we have in this country?"

As it is phrased, the question presents no issue between clearly opposed points of view. Moreover, it assumes that there is a gun problem when there is disagreement over that question. A popular catch phrase in opposition to gun control says that there is no gun problem: "License criminals, not guns."

3. Reducing the Number of Issues

Not all of the issues that are discovered by your analysis of the proposition will need to be argued. The issues in any proposition should be reduced to the smallest number which will accurately identify the important elements of the clash.

Wherever possible, combine issues that seem to overlap. The following issues involve only one point of conflict:

> ISSUE: Will licensing of firearms cut down on assassinations, the murder rate, robberies with guns, and gun accidents?
> ISSUE: Will licensing weed out criminals and those of unstable character?

Eliminate issues that would seem to be trivial to your audience.

| The National Rifle Association is not enough | The National Rifle Association's hunter safety program is more valuable in controlling gun deaths than Federal licensing |

Eliminate issues that seem to be irrelevant.

The National Rifle Association is not acting in the best interest of the country in opposing Federal licensing	The National Rifle Association is a patriotic and law abiding group of citizens

When the job of analyzing the proposition is done, you will have a list of issues somewhat like the following:

ISSUE 1: Will the licensing of firearms cut down on assassinations, the murder rate, robberies with guns, and gun accidents?

ISSUE 2: Is Federal gun licensing unconstitutional?

ISSUE 3: Is Federal gun licensing a step toward the elimination of gun ownership by citizens? If it is admitted that such is the objective, substitute the issue: Is the eventual elimination of private ownership of guns a good idea?

ISSUE 4: Would sportsmen or gun collectors be more subject to theft?

Or

Is it important to this disagreement that they might be subject to theft?

ISSUE 5: Is licensing burdensome and inconvenient?

ISSUE 6: Is Federal licensing essential to provide adequate enforcement of gun control?

4. Classifying the Issues (Stock Issues)

There are a number of ways to approach the organization of the issues once they are found. If you are not experienced in this area, you will probably find it useful to classify the issues by three stock contentions which you assume a person must prove if his proposal is to be acceptable: that the problem is severe enough to warrant a change, that the proposed change is more desirable than the policy currently in operation, and that the proposed policy is workable. These are frequently called, in brief, the issues over need, desirability, and practicability.

Although the concept of stock-issue analysis is useful, it can be misused when real issues are forcibly grouped under these three general heads. Not all propositions respond to such classification. Issues are created, as we have seen, not from arbitrary formulas but from the clash of reasoning in the minds of people holding two opposing positions.

One can imagine situations wherein stock-issue analysis would serve well: Is local law enforcement unable to cope with crime? (need) Would a national police force responsible to the federal government do a better job of controlling crime? (desirability) Would such a federal police force be a workable solution? (practicability)

However, if you will look back over the six issues we have defined in the gun licensing proposition, you will see that in issue 1 need and desirability are combined and that the practicability of licensing is not even a question. The decision on that proposition will be based not on resolving stock issues but on the relative advantages and disadvantages of two opposing alternatives. To a large extent this is caused by the fact that we have chosen a problem in which everyone agrees that crime should be curbed.

But stock issues are useful in two ways:

1. They help you to identify and interpret the specific issues you have discovered in your analysis.
2. They sometimes offer a means of grouping the specific issues by putting each one into a recognizable, workable class.

In an argument over the abolition of capital punishment, for example, some would contend that to abolish capital punishment would be desirable because innocent men are sometimes put to death (that is, the problem is severe). On the other side, you hear it argued that to abolish capital punishment would lead to an increase in crime (that is, the proposed policy is less desirable than the present one).

These two arguments and their answers constitute issues that relate to the stock issues of need and desirability. Assuming, for the moment, that no other issues were troublesome to a listener, you need not concern yourself with, or even mention, workability. You are interested in finding *issues that divide opinion*. However, it is valuable to know when a broad question identified by a stock issue is not at issue, or is relatively less important, in the proposition. You can use this knowledge to put proper emphasis on the more important factors.

B. Analyzing Propositions of Value and Fact

If you look back at the issues we have identified on various propositions of policy in this chapter, you will recognize in them a common characteristic: In every instance, the question that states the issue must be answered with a proposition of value or fact. Then, in order to resolve any such issue, you must be able to prove the proposition that states your position on the issue. Issues, in other words, are resolved and policy decisions are made on the basis of judgments of value and fact.

Proving a proposition of fact or value requires giving arguments to support it, arguments that will eliminate ground the audience may have for rejecting it. Any issues that stand between you and the audience must be resolved. Propositions of fact and value, whether they be argued for their own sakes or in order to prove a proposition of policy, have issues of their own, and these issues must be discovered. At first glance, propositions of fact and propositions of value would appear to be very much the same. Syntactically, they are quite alike. Every proposition of value or fact has two elements: first, a *subject term* which refers to some idea, thing, or event; second, a *judgment term* which in a word, phrase, or clause says something about the subject term. But sentences of this sort can be used to express two very different kinds of judgments. The difference between these two kinds of judgments is what distinguishes propositions of fact and value from each other. Simply put, the difference lies in whether a *value* judgment is made. In 1491, Spaniards debated whether the world was flat, whether by sailing west Christopher Columbus would sail off the edge of the world. These arguments were over matters of *fact*. The judgments expressed were not the same as the value judgment no doubt widely current at the time: Christopher Columbus is a fool! But whether a proposition is one of fact or of value, the same method of analysis is applied.

The first step in finding the issues in propositions of fact and value is to formulate a successful definition of the judgment term. This definition will serve as a set of criteria for evaluating the subject term. Analyze, for example, the proposition: "Federal gun licensing is unconstitutional." Here "gun licensing" is the subject term. The judgment term is the word "unconstitutional." An unconstitutional law might be defined as one that

1. Is explicitly prohibited by the wording of the constitution.
2. Has been ruled unconstitutional by a court, particularly the Supreme Court.

If these criteria satisfy you and your audience as a definition of being unconstitutional, the next step is to prove that Federal gun licensing has one or more of these characteristics (meets the criteria). If you can convince your listeners that the proposed legislation fits the definition, they will agree with your proposition.

III. THE FIVE LOCI OF POTENTIAL ISSUES

When there is disagreement on any proposition, each issue will arise at one or another of five points. These are the *loci* of the issues, the points where they are located. In analyzing a proposition you intend to prove, you may expect to find in these five regions of potential issues the conflicting attitudes that identify a division of opinion. The first region applies only to propositions of policy. The last four are the sources of issues that arise from propositions of value and fact as well.

A. Issues Located in the Stated Advantages and Disadvantages

The broadest basis of potential issues is the relative value of comparative advantages and disadvantages. One can see how this issue arises when advantages of the existing system are judged against the advantages of the new proposal. Debaters using stock-issue analysis usually phrase this point of issue: Does the need justify the plan? One might argue that a massive Federal program of public works is an essential part of the solution to the problem of poverty in America. Another might argue in reply that such a program would be too expensive for the country. Although these seem to constitute separate issues, they may constitute a single issue: Would a program of massive public works do enough good for the society to be worth the cost?

B. Issues Located in the Criteria

There may be disagreement over the validity of the criteria. That is, an issue may arise over whether the judgment term of the proposition (of fact or value) has been acceptably defined. Many speakers whose use of logic and evidence is good base their conclusions on standards that appear to be false. There is grave danger that issues will arise over definition unless such abstract terms as "good," "truth," "peace," and "prosperity" are defined with great care.

Imagine an argument that Abraham Lincoln was a great president because he was (1) more than six feet three inches tall, (2) bearded, and (3) governed in wartime. Certainly, the evidence is available to show that Abraham Lincoln meets these criteria. The issue is with the criteria, which constitute a nonsense definition of a great president.

Even when the criteria have been acceptably defined, they may generate issues. Cost, for example, is usually a factor in any decision. But some will argue that in some situations money should be no criterion. "Nothing's too expensive for my Annie." "When it comes to national defense, cost is no object." Thus issues are defined that have their *locus* in disagreement over whether a particular criterion should be applied at all.

C. Issues Located in the Relative Importance of the Criteria

Even when there is general agreement on the criteria that should be used in making a judgment, and even when the criteria are acceptably defined, an issue may arise over the relative importance (a proposition of value) the criteria should have in influencing a judgment. Suppose you were to evaluate a college by using as criteria: (1) its endowment or level of public support, (2) the research reputation of its faculty, (3) the buildings and other facilities, (4) the concern of the faculty for students, or (5) the quality of its extracurricular program. Large numbers of people might agree that all of these are worthy of consideration. Their relative importance will differ from one person to another and issues will arise over these criteria. A potential graduate student in physics might put much higher value on the research reputation of the faculty and the laboratory facilities. To an athlete, the extracurricular athletic program has greater value than to other students.

D. Issues Located in the Application of the Criteria to Evidence

A fourth area of potential issue is in the application of the criteria to evidence. Assuming that there was complete agreement at all three of the preceding points, there might very well be an issue at the point where the actual judgment of fact or value is made. The United Nations is much concerned of late with aggression. Any delegate to the United Nations will acknowledge that the elimination of aggression is a universally accepted criterion which guides that body in many of its deliberations. No issue there. You might even get markedly similar definitions of the term "aggression" from members of widely disparate political points of view. But ask several of these same members whether Israel committed aggression against the Palestine Arabs. This is an issue.

E. Issues Located in the Evidence

At the base of all controversy is the possibility of disagreement over evidence (a proposition of fact). Such issues arise in the Mid-East conflict between Israel and its Arab neighbors. Which nation attacked first? How many refugees are there in the Sinai? Neither faction will agree that the other side's evidence is true.

Analyzing propositions in terms of the five points at which conflicts of opinion will arise helps you to formulate the issues. This formulation helps you to identify and deal with the doubts and contrary opinions of the audience that constitute the barriers to persuasion. These barriers can be eliminated—persuasion can take place—when the doubts are resolved and the opinions changed.

IV. HOW ISSUES ARE USED

A. To Indicate the Lines of Argument

Analyzing the proposition lays out the groundwork for communication. Finding the issues points the direction the line or argument must follow. If you are to resolve the doubt and opposition in an audience, the central arguments in your speech, those which are best developed and best supported, should be the arguments that deal with the issues. As a candidate for Student Council Treasurer you may be an honest, intelligent, and trusted member of the college community. But if your fellow students doubt your ability to keep a good set of records, that doubt is the issue your supporters need to attack.

This emphasis on issues raises a question: Does a speaker always talk about issues? Do you ever use generally accepted ideas? In one sense you do always talk about issues, but in so doing you will use noncontroversial ideas in a very helpful way: When you analyze a proposition, you discover points of agreement as well as areas of dispute and doubt. These points of agreement are the *waived matter* described above. There are also unstated value judgments or warrants for arguments. Together with waived matter, they serve as a common ground between you and your audience; they are the base upon which you support your position on the matters at issue.

During the campaign for Student Council Treasurer, your fellow students recognize you as a trusted person, an honest person, and a person with good ideas about student government. These acknowledgments are waived matter. Your supporters can use them as arguments to help minimize the fact that you have not had the training in accounting which many of the students believe a treasurer needs. Waived matter should not be used to hide or avoid an issue. The issue is "Does the Student Council Treasurer need to be trained in accounting?" And the issue must be resolved. But by giving a more complete picture of the contest, arguments built on waived matter help to establish the probability that as treasurer you might do a better job than your opponent *even though the opponent is an accounting major.* In this sense, even noncontroversial waived matter should be emphasized *in relation to the issues.*

B. To Group the Arguments

The practice of grouping the specific issues in a proposition of policy under stock issues is used successfully by many speakers. It is a good practice because it accomplishes several goals:

1. It avoids giving the audience the impression that you have a loose collection of scattered arguments.
2. It creates the idea that you have blocks of arguments and evidence, first in one area and then in another.
3. It makes transitions easier, because similar issues are annexed to one another.
4. It gives your speaking a sense of thoroughness and adds to your credibility as a person with knowledge about the proposition.

C. To Determine Emphasis

Since your time is limited, you must know what to emphasize for the greatest effect. The proposition that capital punishment should be abolished has been a recurring controversy in our history. We have all heard arguments for and against it, but we have probably not analyzed these arguments to identify the issues. Suppose you did so, with this result:

1. Does capital punishment deter crime?
2. Is retribution (an eye for an eye) a proper standard for our society?
3. Does capital punishment save the taxpayer money?
4. Would the abolition of capital punishment return to society men who would kill again?

61

5. Is capital punishment discriminatory against minority groups and the poor?

6. Do innocent persons die through capital punishment?

You can recognize that some of these issues are more important than others to an audience such as a group of college students. They are unlikely to be as concerned as some over cost or to think in terms of "an eye for an eye." There is one great rallying point for such a group, where defenders of capital punishment get their support. If you wished to persuade students that capital punishment should be abolished, you would need to show that it does not deter crime. All other points are less important to the average middle-class college student.

The final determination of emphasis requires audience analysis, which is discussed in Chapter 4. However, the adequate use of audience analysis is possible only if the issues have been clearly identified and related one to another.

D. To Determine the Nature of the Argument

Chapter 8 will look in more detail at the nature of arguments. As a prelude to determining what kinds of argument to use, it is essential to know what kind of issue demands your attention. An issue over the criteria is obviously an argument over definition and must be answered by the development of reasonable definitions. Issues over evidence can only be answered by a careful look at the sources of evidence. Issues of advantage or disadvantage lead deep into the value systems of the audience. Knowing the *locus* of an issue, then, is an important prelude to effective argument.

SUMMARY

In order to prove a proposition, you must analyze it to find the points at which your audience is likely to be influenced by arguments against your proposal. These points of conflict are called issues.

To find the issues in propositions of policy, the propositions are analyzed by drawing out of directly opposed arguments the essential elements of clash and phrasing them as clearly stated questions. The number of these questions is reduced by combining issues that overlap, by eliminating waived matter, and by eliminating issues that seem to be trivial or irrelevant. The issues that make up the resulting list are sometimes grouped according to the stock issues that embrace them. The stock issues are three questions that apply to all propositions of policy, and which the audience must be able to answer affirmatively before a proposition is accepted.

To find the issues in propositions of fact or value, define the judgment term in the proposition. This definition is used as a criterion for determining whether available evidence warrants the judgment one makes about the subject term.

Issues will arise at one or more of five *loci*:

1. Questions of the relative advantages and disadvantages of the proposed policy.
2. The acceptability of the criteria used to evaluate judgments of value and fact.
3. The relative importance of the criteria.
4. The judgment that is made when the criteria are applied to the available evidence.
5. The accuracy of the evidence itself.

The issues you find when you analyze a proposition help you find the lines of argument you should use in proving your proposition, as a means of grouping your arguments for greater strength in either attack or defense, as a basis for the application of audience analysis to determine emphasis, and as help to selecting proper forms of argument.

QUESTIONS

1. What is an issue?
2. When does an argument not identify an issue?
3. What are stock issues?
4. What is the use and limitation of stock issues?
5. How are propositions of fact and value analyzed?
6. What must be done first to resolve disagreements when abstract terms such as "good," "truth," or "peace" are used?
7. How are noncontroversial ideas used to argue issues?
8. For what four purposes are issues used?

EXERCISES

1. What are the issues in the following controversy? On November 7, 1972, the voters of the State of California voted on a highly contro-

versial proposal. Proposition 20 would have amended the Constitution of the State of California to place strict regulations on development of the coastal area. It was conceived as an ecological measure to protect the environment. (It failed to pass.)

The following statements are taken from the pamphlet compiled by the Legislative Counsel George H. Murphy and distributed to all California voters by the then Secretary of State, Edmund G. Brown, Jr., *Proposed Amendments to Constitution, Propositions and Proposed Laws, Together with Arguments, General Election, Tuesday, November 7, 1972, pp. 51–55.*

PROPOSITION 20

COASTAL ZONE CONSERVATION ACT. Initiative. Creates State Coastal Zone Conservation Commission and six regional commissions. Sets criteria for and requires submission of plan to Legislature for preservation, protection, restoration and enhancement of environment and ecology of coastal zone, as defined. Establishes permit area within coastal zone as the area between the seaward limits of state jurisdiction and 1000 yards landward from the mean high tide line, subject to specified exceptions. Prohibits any development within permit area without permit by state or regional commission. Prescribes standards for issuance or denial of permits. Act terminates after 1976. This measure appropriates five million dollars ($5,000,000) for the period 1973 to 1976. Financial impact: Cost to state of $1,250,000 per year plus undeterminable local government administrative costs.

Argument in Favor of Proposition 20

Save California's beaches and coastline for the people of California, vote YES on this proposition.

THE PROBLEM

Our coast has been plundered by haphazard development and land speculators. Beaches formerly open for camping, swimming, fishing and picnicking are closed to the public. Campgrounds along the coast are so overcrowded that thousands of Californians are turned away. Fish are poisoned by sewage and industrial waste dumped into the ocean. Duck and other wildlife habitats are buried under streets and vacation homes for the wealthy. Ocean vistas are walled off behind unsightly high rise apartments, office buildings, and billboards. Land speculators bank their profits, post their "no trespassing" signs and leave the small property owner with the burden of increased taxes to pay for streets, sewers, police and fire protection. The coast continues to shrink.

THE REASONS FOR THE PROBLEM

Massive construction projects are often approved solely to benefit corporate landowners. We need a coastal plan, but responsibility is fragmented among 45 cities, 15 counties and dozens of government agencies without the resources to evaluate and prevent developments whose destructive effects may overlap local boundaries.

THE SOLUTION?

Your **YES** vote!

YOUR YES VOTE WILL:

(1) Give the people direct participation in planning. No important decisions will be made until commissions hold public headings and the citizen is heard. Coastal commissions are composed in equal number of locally elected officials and citizens representing the public;

(2) Furnish immediate protection of California's beaches from exploitation by the corporate land grab;

(3) Prevent tax increases resulting from irresponsible developments;

(4) Stimulate growth of the $4.2 billion annual tourist industry and make new jobs;

(5) Stop our beaches from becoming the exclusive playground of the rich;

(6) Bring a runaway construction industry back to the cities where jobs and new homes are needed;

(7) Use the coast to enrich the life of every Californian;

(8) Prevent conflicts of interest. Tough provisions modeled after federal law will keep coastal commissioners from planning for personal profit.

(9) Develop a fair Statewide Plan for balanced development of our coast.

(10) Increase public access to the coast.

THE SAFEGUARDS:

(1) This act will *not* impose a moratorium or prohibit any particular kind of building, but ensures that authorized construction will have no substan-

tial adverse environmental effect;

(2) Homeowners *can* make minor repairs and improvements (up to $7,500) without any more permits than needed now;

(3) The '.egislature *may* amend the act if necessary.

YOUR YES VOTE ENACTS A BILL:

(1) Supported by more than 50 *Republican* and *Democratic* state legislators;

(2) Almost identical to legislation killed year after year by lobbyists in Sacramento;

(3) Modeled after the San Francisco Bay Conservation and Development Commission established by the Legislature in 1965, which has operated successfully to plan and manage the San Francisco Bay and its shoreline;

(4) Sponsored by the California Coastal Alliance, a coalition of over 100 civic, labor, professional, and conservation organizations.

VOTE *YES* TO SAVE THE COAST

Rebuttal to Argument in Favor of Proposition 20

The proponents' Argument for Proposition 20 is a textbook example of circumvention of the facts.

It is filled with such misleading statements as "protection of California's beaches from exploitation by the corporate land grab"; "stop our beaches from becoming the exclusive playground of the rich"; "this act will not impose a moratorium"; "give the people direct participation in planning."

The truth is that the only "land grab" is that planned by the proponents of Proposition 20, who have devolved a scheme for appropriating private property without paying for it.

The truth is that Proposition 20 would make beach lands a haven for the rich who have already developed "exclusive playgrounds." The foremost motivation of the Initiative's elitist proponents is to preclude the enjoyment of coastal areas by retired and working people.

The truth is that Proposition 20 would, as a practical matter, establish a two to four year moratorium on virtually all building in the coastal area, including development for recreational purposes. The result would be a sharp reduction in land values, assessments, and local tax collections which would create a severe economic depression in every one of the 15 coastal counties.

The truth is that people would have no direct participation in planning, which would be the sole prerogative of super-State and regional agencies composed of appointed commissioners.

Proposition 20 is discriminatory legislation and should be roundly defeated so that the people's elected representatives can get on with the job of completing sensible environmental and zoning controls over California's coastline.

Argument Against Proposition 20

Proposition 20 on the November 7 ballot represents bad government for all Californians. Proposition 20 is bad because it takes government from the hands of the voters.

In the name of coastal protection, Proposition 20 would impose an appointed, not elected, super-government to control the destinies of almost 3½ million people who live near and over 1 million who work close to our ocean shore.

CALIFORNIA'S 1,087 MILE COASTLINE IS NOT ENDANGERED

The State's official Comprehensive Ocean Area Plan, which has inventoried the total coastal area, shows that 74% of the land is in open space, 65.1% is undeveloped in any way, and 54% is already in public ownership.

PROPOSITION 20 IS A POWER GRAB—AND A LAND GRAB—BY THOSE WHO WOULD BY-PASS THE DEMOCRATIC PROCESS

It would substitute for that process the judgment of a vast new bureaucracy and appointive commissioners largely representative of a single purpose point of view.

It is on the ballot because its sponsors have ignored all reasonable efforts by the State, by local government, by labor, by business and civic organizations to develop an orderly land management policy for California through the legislative and regulatory process.

THESE ARE THE TRADITIONAL PROCESSES AND THEY ARE WORKING

A recent State-adopted plan for ocean waste discharges, for example, will cost $770 million—about $5.70 a year for every Californian—but the plan was approved in democratic fashion.

Yet the sponsors of Proposition 20 would lock up California's coastline for at least three years, and probably forever.

The results of Proposition 20 if it should pass include:

—Loss of $25,750,000 in tax revenues annually as values in the coastal zone are reduced and assessments dropped, thus forcng higher taxes on coastal counties, cities, and school districts.

—Loss of millions of dollars and thousands of jobs in needed development projects, jobs especially important to racial and economic minorities in the construction industry.

—Delay of needed oceanfront and beach recreational projects because of the measure's disastrous fiscal implications to the State as a whole.

—Loss of local control and local voice in local affairs.

—Threat of increased power shortages and possible brownouts because of delays in construction of new power generating plants.

—Loss of property rights through inverse condemnation without compensation as private land use is denied but properties are not purchased by government.

Even more important if Proposition 20 passes, what's next?
WILL THE ELITISTS WHO WOULD GRAB OUR COASTLINE FOR THEIR OWN
PURPOSES THEN BE AFTER OUR MOUNTAINS, OUR LAKES AND STREAMS,
OUR FARMLANDS? AND AT WHAT COST?

Nowhere in the planning principles set forth in Proposition 20 are the words "economy" or "economics" used once.

If the people of California want statewide land planning such planning must apply equally to all areas of the State, not just the coast. The federal government, the California Legislature, state and local government plus regulatory agencies are ready to complete the job.

Proposition 20 would halt that effort.

Don't lock up California's coastside.

VOTE *NO* ON PROPOSITION 20

Rebuttal to Argument Against Proposition 20

The *real* opponents of the Coastline Initiative—the oil industry, real estate speculators and developers, and the utilities—are primarily concerned with profits, not the public interest. Their arguments are simply *not* true.

—Every government study, every scientific report, every trip to the beach proves that our beaches *ARE* endangered.

—The public has been denied access to hundreds of miles of beaches and publicly owned tidelands by freeways, private clubs, residential, and industrial developments.

—Two-thirds of California's estuaries and many of our beaches have been destroyed.

—Of California's 1072 miles of coast, 659 are privately owned; of the 413 miles publicly owned, only 252 are available for public recreation.

—Proposition 20 represents an open beach and public access policy for Californians now locked out from swimming, beach recreation, surf-fishing, and skin diving.

—The initiative process, the essence of democracy, gives the people this opportunity to enact themselves what unresponsive government has for years refused to do.

—Proposition 20 contains *NO* prohibition on the construction of power plants. Rather, it offers a sensible plan to determine *where*—not if— new plants may be built.

—*One-half* the membership of the six coastal commissions will be *locally elected officials.*

—The opponents claim revenue and job losses. These scare tactics have *no* basis in fact.

—Many labor unions, including the ILWU, Northern and Southern Districts Councils, are on record in support of the Coastline Initiative.

VOTE *YES* ON PROPOSITION 20

I.   Beliefs, attitudes, and values
     A. Definitions
     B. Salience
     C. Identification and dissociation
II. The nature of audiences
III. General attitudes of audiences
     A. Attitudes toward the speaker
     B. Attitudes toward the subject
     C. Attitudes toward the occasion
     D. Attitudes toward itself
IV. Demographic factors influencing audience attitudes
     A. Attitudes associated with sex
     B. Attitudes associated with age
     C. Attitudes associated with economic position
     D. Attitudes associated with social background
     E. Attitudes associated with group membership
V.   Speech development determined by audience analysis
     A. The amount of material
     B. The kind of material
     C. The central tendency of the audience
     D. Cross pressures in the audience
     E. Premises for argument
     F. Language fitted to the audience
     G. Organization
     H. Motivation

Chapter 4

Analyzing the Audience

Audiences are made up of individuals. When you attempt to communicate with an audience, you must search for factors which make people in that audience alike. Try to categorize their beliefs, attitudes, and values in such a way that you can better design a message which will achieve your purpose. Although you know that no two individuals are exactly alike, you also know that even across quite different audiences people are similar in many ways. They generally prefer wealth to poverty, pleasure to pain, truth to falsehood, and a host of other alternatives that must immediately come to mind.

It is these general preferences and the special preferences of a particular audience which you must discover and adapt to if your communication is to be effective. In Chapter 3 we discussed the analysis of the proposition; at all times we were considering the listener. In later chapters we shall examine how arguments are made and reinforced with supporting materials, argument, motivation, and credibility. Each of these requires knowing more about people and their beliefs, attitudes, and values. Therefore, audience analysis is fundamental to all successful communication whether the audience is one person, a small group, or the U.S. Congress. This chapter is concerned with the principles, the process, and the use of audience analysis.

Let us consider a simple social situation. An elderly man and a teen-age boy are seated in a living room talking. Perhaps it is a man and his grandson, who is in high school. The boy has recently been awakened to a whole new world of football, girls, automobiles, and jobs. For him his studies have a remoteness about them though he knows they are, in some vague way, a part of his future and he has learned to enjoy some of them.

The older man wants the best for his grandson. He "knows" that, by the standards of the adult society the boy must soon join, success will be measured in terms of a good job, a home, a family, and enough money to enjoy life and provide for his family. The boy also "knows" this situation, not as he "knows" an MG or the Saturday night dance, but because he has been told about it by adults.

"What kind of work do you think you will be going into, Frank?" asks the man.

"Well," says Frank, "I thought I would study engineering. I got a B in algebra last semester and I am pretty good at mathematics and science."

"Oh, is that so?" continues the man. "Well, it is good to study hard so that you can get into a profession and it is also important to find something you enjoy doing. What college do you plan to attend?"

"I thought I would go to Harvard if I can get the money. Othewise, I will go to State U."

"Don't you need better grades to get into Harvard?"

"Yes. I plan to study harder next semester."

Even though he is asking questions, the man is trying to tell Frank that he should study harder and be a success. His statements clearly indicate that Frank needs guidance, and he sees himself as a source of that guidance. Nothing the man says is "untrue," but it is clearly not central to the boy's thoughts. Engineering is a vague but respectable profession about which he knows little and Harvard is a university he has accepted as a symbol of the best in higher education. Frank thinks that his grandfather is always concerned about vague things in the future. Frank's response is predictable. He has played the role he was cast into by the older man: a student preparing for a profession. But he fills such other roles as second-string linebacker, lunch-time comic, Volkswagen driver, and good dancer.

Chances are that both man and boy know the communication situation is not right. Each has cast the other in a role and the verbal currency transacted between them has produced little new meaning

72

beyond reinforcing the other's predetermined roles.

The factors in this speaking situation, then, are the speaker with his image of himself and his predictions about the listener, the listener with his image of himself and his predictions about the speaker, and the message that changes in meaning for each of them as image and prediction change.

Messages are used to bring these two sets of images and predictions together. Too often we think of a message, a speech, as being a thing with which a speaker does something to a listener. The action, instead, is reciprocal. Listeners with their images and predictions do something to a speaker. Problems in communication, represented by such statements as "He didn't understand what I said," or "He deliberately misinterpreted me," indicate how a listener can affect a speaker.

I. BELIEFS, ATTITUDES, AND VALUES

The communication transaction between the older man and the teenage boy is a simple example of what goes on in even the most complex situations. Verbal and nonverbal signs and symbols are used to effect behavior changes in others.

Between the stimulus of what one person says and the response of another, there are certain mental activities (conscious and unconscious) that take place to mediate the experience. Thus we postulate that there are certain beliefs, attitudes, and values which receivers have that will affect how they will behave in response to a particular message.* It is important, therefore, to consider the beliefs, attitudes, and values of an audience, be it a nationwide television audience or a single listener, if you wish to gain a desired response to what you say.

A. Definitions

A *belief* is "any simple proposition, conscious or unconscious, inferred from what a person says or does, capable of being preceded by the phrase, 'I believe. . . .' "† Beliefs are represented rather directly by

---

* There is no point here in wondering whether attitude will always be related to behavior. The research on this has been well reviewed and its inconsistencies resolved by Cronkhite. Gary Cronkhite, *Persuasion: Speech and Behavioral Change* (Indianapolis: Bobbs-Merrill, 1969), pp. 6–15.

† Milton Rokeach, *Beliefs, Attitudes, and Values* (San Francisco: Jossey Bass, 1968), p. 113.

behavior and can be virtually infinite in number. They also can be subdivided into categories of propositions: fact, value, and policy. You believe the world is round, the Rockies are high, it is a mile from home to the city hall, candy is made with sugar, etc. You may also believe that the St. Louis Cardinals are the best baseball team, America is a great country, swimming is fun, and the Toyota is the most economical car. Likewise, you might claim that we should ban arms sales to foreign countries, join a church, buy a Buick, eat an ice cream cone, and so forth. You must realize, then, that you have beliefs on all kinds of conceivable subjects.

An *attitude* is "a relatively enduring organization of beliefs around an object or situation predisposing one to respond in some preferential manner."* Thus you have attitudes toward kinds of foods, people, automobiles, ideas, policies, and the like. Although you may believe that social psychology is a good course, it takes an attitude to classify your general preference for social science courses over courses in the humanities.

Much of the research literature has concernerd itself with attitudes and their influence on communication. We shall not emphasize attitude because, while their study tells us a lot about communication, attitudes are not as functional as values for understanding the practical problems of analyzing an audience for the purpose of designing a successful message. "An adult," says Milton Rokeach, "probably has tens or hundreds of thousands of beliefs, thousands of attitudes but only dozens of values."† Thus, for a practical beginning study like this, values are far more useful.

Values are "abstract ideals, positive or negative, not tied to any specific attitude, object, or situation, representing a person's beliefs about ideal modes of conduct and ideal terminal goals."‡ Your values constitute broad bases for your behavior; you may value hard work, or truthfulness, or cleanliness, or love, or strength, or all of them. Values are general conceptions of what you regard as good or bad and, therefore, are critical in audience analysis. From knowing the values of the

---

* Milton Rokeach, *Beliefs, Attitudes, and Values* (San Francisco: Jossey Bass, 1968), p. 112.

† Milton Rokeach, *Beliefs, Attitudes, and Values* (San Francisco: Jossey Bass, 1968), p. 124.

‡ Milton Rokeach, *Beliefs, Attitudes, and Values* (San Francisco: Jossey Bass, 1968), p. 124. This definition is quite close to that of anthropologist Clyde Kluckhohn, "Values and Value-Orientations in the Theory of Action," *Toward a General Theory of Action*, Talcott Parsons and Edward A. Shils, eds. (New York: Harper & Row, 1951), p. 395.

audience, you can better anticipate what strategy to develop in order to provide a basis for affecting the behavior of your listeners.

B. Salience

Although values are more useful than beliefs and attitudes in determining strategy for communication, you can not ignore specific beliefs and attitudes of audiences. Those beliefs and attitudes which are most *salient* at a particular moment can be more important than the values the listeners hold. Regardless of the general value system, if listeners have a strong attachment to a particular belief which is important to a particular subject, it can be critical. If you wish to convince your audience that a particular candidate should be elected and they believe he is corrupt, that belief is much more important than the hard work which he displays and which the audience values.

Salience of belief or attitude is essential for a particular belief or attitude to be important in a communication situation. No matter how strongly held a belief is, if it does not seem to apply in the particular communication situation, it will have no effect. You could be a devout Roman Catholic and yet see your beliefs as having nothing to do with your political preferences, favorite hockey team, or club membership. Thus, in each new communication situation, the communicator will look for those values which are basic to the audience on the chosen topic and which beliefs and attitudes are salient.

C. Identification and Dissociation

Here the term *identification* becomes useful.* Let us think of communication as a process whereby a speaker identifies a cause with the opinions of the audience. Everyone is, as we have said, a complex of these mental postures. They are either positive or negative, and one clings to them with varying degrees of tenacity. In the same sense that a weather forecaster may say there is a 60 percent chance of rain, so a person may be 60 (or 50 or 80) percent in favor of the Democratic party, open housing, fraternities, or the Methodist Church. In similar varying degrees, such a person will be negatively inclined toward other subjects. Thus a speaker tries to make the proposal consonant with the way the audience views the world. When such a practice is successful, the audience will identify the speaker's position with their own.

When, for example, a speaker proposes adoption of the local school

* Kenneth Burke, *A Rhetoric of Motives* (New York: George Braziller, 1955), pp. 19–29.

board budget to a listener who values calm, careful consideration of all sides of a subject, the speaker will stress the hours of thoughtful study that have gone into preparing the budget.

Again, suppose that a speaker favors massive spending in poverty areas. Addressing an audience negatively disposed toward taxation, such a speaker will have to give the listeners some ground upon which to identify with the proposal: for example, that poverty spending will result in general economic benefits, or that it will aid law and order, or that it is supported by many persons who are generally known to oppose increased taxes.

The counterpart of identification is dissociation. At the same time the speaker identifies a proposal with positive values in the audience, it will be dissociated from negative ones.

Thomas Jefferson came to the presidency in 1801 after some stormy political conflicts. Many Federalists feared that he would institute repressive actions against them. After a campaign and a close election that had to be decided in the House of Representatives, Mr. Jefferson had to allay Federalist fears. In his Inaugural Address he dissociated himself from the rancor of the past by characterizing it as the natural excess of political campaigning and identified his presidency with such widely accepted values as unity, law, and reason.

During the contest of opinion through which we have passed, the animation of discussions and of exertions has sometimes worn an aspect which might impose on strangers unused to think freely, and to think and write what they think; but this being now decided by the voice of the nation, announced according to the rules of the constitution, all will of course arrange themselves under the will of the law, and unite in common efforts for the common good. All too, will bear in mind this sacred principle, that though the will of the majority is in all cases to prevail, that will, to be rightful, must be reasonable; that the minority possess their equal rights, which equal laws must protect, and to violate which would be oppression. Let us then, fellow-citizens, unite with one heart and one mind. . . . We have called by different names brethren of the same principle. We are all Republicans; we are all Federalists.

II. THE NATURE OF AUDIENCES

Look back for a moment at the conversation between Frank and his grandfather. With minor variations, could this conversation have taken place with Frank's friends Randy or Bruce? Would there be greater variation in the conversation, however, if it were held with his grand-daughter Sally? Why? Because the aspirations which a grandfather in our society has for Sally are different from those he has for Frank. Although he probably would not suggest that she become an engineer, he certainly could expect her to work and study hard, and get good grades in any subject. In this situation, however, the grandfather's aspirations for Bruce are little different from those he has for Frank.

Note the grandfather's words which tell us something about what is important to him: "Work," "study hard," "something you enjoy doing," "better grades." And Frank responds with words that will have the greatest import for the other: "Study engineering," "B in algebra," "good at math and science," "Harvard," "if I can get the money," "study harder." Taken as a whole, these words imply a value system which emphasizes hard work for tangible results in a socially approved way. A clearly secondary value is that one should enjoy what he does. The conversation reveals through its language a facet of what is known as the Puritan value system, a major one in our society, and one with which Frank's grandfather can identify.

It is of primary importance that you study audiences in order to discover which of their values are relevant in a particular communication situation. You especially want to find out which of their beliefs and attitudes are salient. When you have this information, you can select and adapt materials that will reinforce the beliefs, attitudes, and values that will help to identify your proposal with the value system of the audience.

The findings of research investigations on the nature of audiences cannot always be quickly adapted to the practical problems of audience analysis. Experimental evidence is frequently less useful than common sense. There is, for instance, quite a bit of research on which classes of persons are most persuasible.* But if, as some research shows, women are generally more persuasible than men, or if open-minded people are more persuasible than closed-minded people, or if persons with high self-esteem are more difficult to persuade than others, such information isn't particularly useful to you when you confront an audience with which you wish to communicate. It is valuable information for the researcher but for you in a practical situation, it may not be very useful. As a practical communicator, you must look to

---

* Gary Cronkhite, *Persuasion: Speech and Behavioral Change* (Indianapolis, Ind.: Bobbs-Merrill, 1969), pp. 130–39, presents a good summary of the literature on the subject of persuasibility.

the characteristics of your audience which can be translated into practical communicative acts.

First, make a list of the things you know about the *general attitudes of the audience.*

Second, gather information about the specific *demographic factors influencing audience attitudes.*

These facts will help you to find the relevant values and the salient beliefs and attitudes of the audience with which to identify your proposal. After we have discussed these two points, we shall conclude this chapter by suggesting how the information you get from analyzing an audience will answer a number of questions about other aspects of speech development.

III. GENERAL ATTITUDES OF AUDIENCES

A. Attitudes toward the speaker

Perhaps the most difficult attitude for you to attain is an objective understanding of the audience's predictions about yourself. It is natural to think that others see you as you see yourself. You may be competent, honest, and intelligent; but, as a speaker, what you think you are or what you actually are is not as important as what others consider you to be. You must examine your audience carefully to gain some understanding of what they probably think of you. In most cases the effectiveness of a speech will be increased by the realization of the audience that you are an expert. If you are a football player, a musician, or a campus leader, an audience may be likely to accept your information on sports, music, or student government. However, in some instances this expertness can stimulate audience resistance. Thus, if a football player asks for more aid for athletics, or if a musician wants a required course in music, or if a student leader calls for more participation in extracurricular activities, each of these views is expected and the speaker may be suspected of bias. In such instances you must be aware of possible negative reactions and develop your speech accordingly.

The football player might argue that if it were not for athletic scholarships, many students would not be able to attend college. An audience made up of students seeking or holding athletic scholarships would find this argument valid. But a cross section of the student body might have an entirely different reaction. Their response would be:

"Of course, he favors athletic scholarships because he gets one. But what about people like me? I'd like to have a scholarship, too." The speaker would do much better if he were to recognize the possibility of such a response. He would not then argue that without scholarships many athletes would not be able to go to school, or that scholarships are the only way to build a football team. Instead, he would choose arguments that reduce the implications of his own self-interest. He might begin by noting that he already has a scholarship, and therefore is not arguing for personal gain, and then build his arguments on the benefit to the college.

This example can serve as a useful basis for noting how audiences respond to speakers. Listeners make predictions and final judgments about speakers and their messages on the basis of three characteristics: trustworthiness, competence, and dynamism. Applying this analysis to the football player just mentioned, we might see a particular listener making a prediction about the speech. "Bob is a nice guy (trustworthy) who knows what he is talking about (competent), and he is a good talker (dynamic). He will probably give a good speech but it may be a 'snow job' because he will advocate more athletic scholarships because he is an athlete (another kind of trustworthiness)." Or imagine these predictions: "Janet? What does she know about football?" Or, "Scott? He is so stuck-up I just don't like him." Or, "Sure he knows a lot, but is he a dull speaker!"

Obviously, listeners don't always consciously frame their thoughts, but there is no doubt that they make predictions. As a speaker you must consciously plan your message to reinforce favorable predictions of the audience and diminish unfavorable ones. This problem will be discussed in greater detail in Chapter 10, "The Credibility Dimension of Communication."

B. Attitudes toward the Subject

Audiences have general reactions to the subject of a speech. After a political campaign, listeners are frequently "tired of hearing about politics." Church groups may prefer not to be exposed to additional missionary drives, and in your speech class, a fourth talk on racial prejudice may be overworking a theme that was interesting in the first three. Each set of listeners must be analyzed to determine what their reactions are likely to be.

But what do you do when what *you* want your listeners to know or believe seems to conflict with what *they* want to hear? Change your subject and tell them what they want to hear? Certainly not. Too many speakers fail to realize that listeners don't really want to hear innocuous talk without any conviction any more than they want to be told what they are ignorant or wrong.

When you feel that your listeners are not interested in your subject but you think they ought to be, you can bridge the gap by building an interest in your subject from other interests your listeners already have. Through your analysis of the audience, discover what their interests are and relate your ideas to these interests. Thus you must know not only the audience's attitude toward your subject but also its attitude toward many subjects. A group of businessmen may not be interested in religion, but they could be interested in a subject that related business law to the moral systems which religions teach. Are young people interested in the problems of the aged? Perhaps not, but they could be interested in the subject if it were related to their own problems in understanding their grandparents in the difficult adjustments of old age. A good speaker who analyzes his audience carefully can make any subject interesting.

C. Attitudes toward the Occasion

Although the occasion of a speech is a part of the role of the listener, we must isolate it here to call attention to some of the special problems that occasion creates in defining an audience.

The occasion upon which a speech is given can either help or hinder the response a speaker wants to obtain. When a geology class is assembled to learn about earthquakes and fault lines, it is not prepared to hear an appeal to support the Campus Fund. The members of a sociology class may be interested in hearing about the recently inaugurated and highly publicized charity drive, but they also may not be interested at the time; the speaker should be prepared for possible negative reactions.

If there is audience hostility, it does you as a speaker little good to ignore it. Faced with negative reactions, you should treat them honestly. You can acknowledge that your listeners are met for a purpose other than to hear you speak. To overcome your disadvantage, you need to build a speech associated with interests your audience has.

The attitude an audience has toward an occasion frequently can be used to strengthen the speech. If the occasion has some special meaning to the listeners, you can identify your subject with the occasion to build interest. Holiday speeches invariably do this. The speaker at a

Labor Day meeting may want to speak on world affairs but will link the subject to the aspirations of the working man.

One of the most significant effects of a specific occasion is to limit the scope of the audience's conception of itself. Two men sit side by side at a lodge meeting. Although one is a Democrat and the other is a Republican, they think of themselves, on this occasion, as lodge members. For a time they forget, or at least submerge, their political preferences. They see themselves, as "brothers," and in this sense they think alike. The audience's narrowed conception of itself in terms of the role it is then taking helps to polarize the group and makes it easier for the speaker. The religious convictions, political loyalties, and economic stations of the members, however, are still present, although they may be latent. What you, the speaker, say can awaken these latent associations in the audience to your own advantage or disadvantage.

D. Attitudes toward Itself

The attitudes that listeners have toward themselves are a vital determinant of how they will respond to the speaker's message. Frequently, this attitude will be directly related to their attitude toward the speaker. If a man plays golf with his boss, he may be less inclined to see himself as the good golfer he is because more central to his thinking is his relation to the other man as "Boss." When a political science professor stops to chat with a student who is lead cellist with the university orchestra, they discuss music. The student's attitude toward self is considerably different from the attitude toward self inside the classroom, where comparative government is being discussed.

If listeners are to receive a message with reasonable fidelity, the speaker must take into account what the listeners think of themselves.

Fred is excitedly telling his Aunt Alice about the play he saw. "Several of us went together to see *Hamlet*. It was the best play I have seen in a long time. After we left the theater, we all went over to the Hoosier Tavern and sat discussing it for hours. The thing that was so great about it was . . . ."

Aunt Alice is thinking to herself, "Fred always did have confidence in me. This is his way of telling me that he drinks. Of course, I wouldn't tell his mother. She would have a fit."

Aunt Alice's perception of herself as confidante to Fred clearly influenced her interpretation of his message.

Attitudes that listeners have toward themselves may also be unrelated to the speaker. The president of the Kiwanis Club has a role as leader of that group which he takes regardless of the particular speaker at any particular Thursday noon luncheon. As a speaker you must be careful that what you say will not seem to be an insult or an affront to the role such a person takes and to the members who have their roles also. The officers and members of any organization have attitudes toward themselves that the speaker must consider.

IV. DEMOGRAPHIC FACTORS INFLUENCING
AUDIENCE ATTITUDES

We have noted that listeners' attitudes toward the speaker, the subject, the occasion, and themselves will affect the kinds of predictions they make about a speaking situation and the kind of response they will give to it. Although the list is by no means exhaustive, we shall isolate five factors that will tend to influence listeners' attitudes: sex, age, economic position, social background, and group membership. Differences in these areas will reveal differences in value systems and, therefore, differences in audience attitude.

A. Attitudes Associated with Sex

Recent years have made great changes in our assumptions about the differences in values between men and women. The Women's Liberation Movement has brought to our attention the many ways in which women, particularly upper middle-class, educated women, have attitudes and values about professions, political activities, and social action which are more similar to men's than we previously thought. Any male student speaker today who characterizes his woman classmates as husband-hunters and sees their potentials essentially as housewives, is bound to get a real argument.

Yet there are still differences between men and women that contribute to an understanding of the values that might motivate an audience made up predominantly of men or of women. Even if a modern college audience would not differ much between men and women, this is surely not the view of most middle-class, middle-aged men and women. For them there are between men and women real differences of self-image and of role.

In any event, it is essential to consider the self-image of the listeners. Whether you are a man or a woman, if you are addressing a group of women who see themselves as being "liberated," the values with which they will identify and the beliefs and attitudes which will be salient will be different from those of the average male and from many other women. Women who seek to convince others of the values of liberation will need to consider the sex of the listeners and their self-image.

B. Attitudes Associated with Age

Young people, it is said, tend to be flexible in their political and religious affiliations and are, perhaps, more idealistic. As they grow older, they tend to become concerned about the practical operation of ideas and to develop somewhat fixed attitudes toward religious and political affiliations. Although these generalizations do not apply to all, they do provide a starting point for more specific analysis.

The age group of an audience may help a speaker anticipate reactions to specific subjects. A group of college freshmen and sophomores will usually be more skeptical of plans to reintroduce the draft for military service than will an older group. Why? Because such a proposal affects them directly and inconveniently. Older people may be concerned if they have sons of draft age.

C. Attitudes Associated with Economic Position

Many problems have implications for a listener's pocketbook. Proposals that involve an increase in taxes are usually less acceptable to those who must pay the taxes than they are to those who may avoid them. Also, proposals that will benefit specific groups economically, such as support for farm income, airline subsidies, and tax preference for the oil and gas companies, will find acceptance among these groups more readily than among groups that do not benefit. In your local community or college, some of the same reactions can be seen. Athletes and students interested in athletics may strongly support an increase in the student activities fees by which athletic programs are financed. Other students who have no lively interest in athletics may object to an increase in their student fees.

It is easy to put more emphasis on economic position than is justified. Many people have come to consider all reactions as economic. These "economic determinists" ignore the many other factors that determine attitudes. Because of a strong belief in education, an upper-income person without school-age children will frequently favor aid to education despite increased taxes. And so, while their economic position can tell you much about your listeners, it must be viewed only as one of the many factors that influence their reactions.

Sometimes economic position can be misleading. More important frequently than present economic position is the economic class in which people see themselves. Persons who grew up in poverty, in the ghetto or the *barrio*, or even in a white Anglo-Saxon poor neighborhood, will frequently see themselves as poor even though they are now in a higher economic class. In economic position as in all other demographic factors affecting attitudes, it is the self-image rather than the actual situation that determines the values with which a person will identify.

D. Attitudes Associated with Social Background

The past conditions of people's lives—the way they grew up, and the kinds of attitudes and values their parents had—make up the social background of audiences and have a significant effect on how they react to ideas. You can easily imagine that the views of one group might differ from the views of any other. Does an audience meet as a group of Polish-Americans? Of Nisei? Of Blacks? Of Southerners? Of Roman Catholics? Of Sons or Daughters of the American Revolution?

Most people find it impossible to escape their background completely. Even though a woman may leave behind certain ties, such as the "old-fashioned" ideas of her parents, these ties still have the power to color her thoughts and to affect her responses. Her own ideas have changed, but she still lives in the atmosphere of her background. The old values must at least be tolerated and the people who still hold them expect her to act in accordance with the value systems of the old background.

Not only does the immediate social pressures of parents and community influence people to maintain old ways and attitudes, but these values are built into the individual. Each has been conditioned to them for years and when new associations produce attitudes that are antagonistic to older attitudes, they produce cross pressures which must be resolved.

Under such cross pressures a person is more susceptible to persuasion than the person who is free of them. One who has been raised with the religious conviction that abortion is immoral, and then in college associates with people who believe otherwise, is more likely to shift position than is one who has not grown up in such a background or one who associates in college with people who also consider abortion immoral.

Many authorities believe that social background is perhaps the strongest factor in determining attitudes. Thus it may be more important that the listener you address is a Chicano, a White Anglo-Saxon Protestant, a Jew, or a Catholic, than that this one is a woman or that that one is twenty years old.

E. Attitudes Associated with Group Membership

While the analysis of sex, age, and economic–social backgrounds tells much about audiences, a knowledge of their affiliations will help to pinpoint analysis much more sharply. Knowing that an audience has a substantial percentage of American Legionnaires, National Organization of Women, or Democrats can help you judge its probable attitudes toward a subject. These specific affiliations do not tell all that one needs to know about a group, but as part of total audience analysis, they give helpful clues. Organizations such as the American Legion have specific statements of principles that will help to guide you in developing a topic. Chambers of Commerce, farm groups, and labor unions usually represent recognizable social and economic attitudes. Service clubs, such as Rotary, Kiwanis, and Lions, all have projects that are important to them. Specific religious organizations—the Knights of Columbus, B'nai Brith, the Women's Club of the First Baptist Church—have distinctive approaches to questions of faith and morals. Political clubs have their obvious partisan positions. Knowledge of the aims of these specific groups will help you do a better job of persuading their members.

Group membership is an easier factor to learn than are some others; easier, for instance, than ethnic background and it is a fairly good measure of attitudes. Studies seem to show that people join groups with ideas and goals similar to their own. The group further reinforces these ideas and goals.

In groups that are brought together because of some firmly held opinion or position—as differentiated from groups such as the Kiwanis Club or the Lions Club, whose members share general goals without an issue—important factors must be considered. Such issue-oriented groups attain greater solidarity in their opinions and attitudes the more controversial their opinions are and the more they are in the minority. The Rotary Club will be less solid in its attitudes than is a Young Republicans Club, for instance.

Individuals who claim great independence and who join together to claim it are really not independent, and they merely exchange one influence (perhaps parental) for another. Although quite different from the general society, the Flower Children or Jesus People conform quite closely to the attitudes of their own group.

If you can identify the group memberships of an audience, you can tell much about the beliefs, attitudes, and values of the listeners and, therefore, know better how to choose values with which to identify your proposal.

V. SPEECH DEVELOPMENT DETERMINED BY AUDIENCE ANALYSIS

It is impossible for you to give an audience all the evidence and reasoning that supports your position. You must find some basis on which to select the material. That basis is the audience. Audience analysis helps to determine eight elements of the content and development of a speech: (1) the amount of material to use, (2) the kind of material, (3) the central tendency of the audience, (4) cross pressures in the audience, (5) premises from which to reason, (6) language, (7) organization, and (8) motivation.

In all cases you will need first to draw together all the insights you have about your audience, particularly in relating the subject of the speech to the demographic factors. What factors does the subject of the speech particularly give salience to and what attitudes, beliefs, and values become most important to the self-image of this audience?

A. The Amount of Material

The amount of material needed to clarify or to prove a specific point within a speech is determined by the need of the audience. In a speech to inform, for example, you will need few specific details if you know that the audience can easily understand a given point. In persuasion, the keynote speaker at a political convention judges the amount of evidence needed to support arguments from knowing that the members of the convention will already agree with many of the points to be made. When student body funds are allocated to various campus activities, a lack of student interest in music may motivate the members of the student council to cut the budget for the opera program. A speaker who is aware of the student council's attitude will give a great deal of evidence to that group, when asking for more money for the opera program.

B. The Kind of Material

As you prepare a speech, you will gather more information than you can use in one speech. The process of selecting the items that are best for your purpose will be based on the nature of your audience. You will choose quotations not only because they say exactly what you want them to say, but also because the authorities you quote are respected by your audience. You will draw illustrations from experiences that are understandable to the group to which you speak. If you are speaking to students who have never had a chemistry course, you will need to adjust your talk on atomic energy to take account of this fact.

C. The Central Tendency of the Audience

From your knowledge of the composition of the audience, look for some central tendency around which your listeners' attitudes can be grouped. Will they tend to be liberal or conservative on economic and social problems? Do they have strong religious convictions? Does the age of the group affect the kinds and amount of experience they have had? What is the proportion of men and women in the audience and what effect is this likely to have on the way they view the subject of your speech?

Naturally, this central tendency provides only a general picture of what an audience is like. You cannot, in one speech, take into consideration all the possible attitudes an audience may have. Prepare your speech to appeal to the bulk of the audience. *You cannot please everyone.*

D. Cross Pressures in the Audience

Although many audiences will have strong central tendencies on which a speaker can build an appeal, others will be under cross pressures. Whenever two or more central tendencies conflict in an audience at any one time, cross pressures exist.

Investigations of the American electorate in the 1952 presidential campaign revealed this example of cross pressures: Although a majority of the American people had a strong emotional attachment to the Democratic party, there was also present strong dissatisfaction with conditions in the country. The Republican party resolved this cross pressure by nominating for the presidency a man who could convincingly argue that he could improve conditions in America but who was at the same time sufficiently nonpolitical to neutralize the strong emotional attachment of many people for the Democratic party. Many Democrats in 1952 were able to say, "Eisenhower is almost a Democrat. He really isn't a Republican at all." Twelve years later, in 1964, many Republicans were able to dissociate themselves from Barry Goldwater by convincing themselves that he wasn't really a Republican but was instead associated with some undefined "far right." Thus they could justify voting for President Johnson without betraying their Republican loyalties. And in 1972, apparently, many Democrats voted for Richard Nixon because George McGovern's policies seem to them to be too radical.

A common example of cross pressure is furnished by the teenager whose parents have always emphasized the need to do well in school. The young man agrees with his parents but he also needs the companionship of his own friends. When his friends want him to "go with the gang to the movies" on the night before a chemistry test, he is under cross pressure. If he can find a way to go to the movie and still get his studying done, the cross pressure will be resolved and he will go to the movie after all.

It is an important part of audience analysis to discover whatever cross pressures are in the audience. You must then find evidence, argument, and motivation which will resolve them. The examples given above of the elections of 1952, 1964 and 1972 show how these cross pressures are resolved. You do not simply argue the case. You provide a rationale in terms of the values, attitudes, and beliefs that already exist within the listeners. People put labels on things in order to capsulize their attitudes in language. These attitudes may differ from one person to another. Some college students may be opposed to having a fraternity man as student body president because to them a fraternity man is rich or snobbish. To argue that Gordon Silver should be student body president because he is the best qualified and most dedicated is not enough. Nor is there time enough to change listeners' assumptions about fraternity men. The speaker must show that Gordon "is not a fraternity man," that is, he does not have the characteristics of a fraternity man which the listeners predict he will have. The listeners' cross pressure is that they must choose between the most qualified candidate who is a snob and the less qualified candidate who is not. The attitudes which form the basis of cross pressures are not formed by any significantly systematic examination of evidence. Although Gordon Silver is best qualified because he was last year's vice-president, he is a fraternity man (snob). The speaker resolves the cross pressure by showing that Silver is not a snob (in effect, that he is not like their image).

While audiences under cross pressure are more complex and, therefore, require greater skill in understanding, they also provide the greatest possibility for change. In general, the greater the cross pressure the greater the challenge and the opportunity for persuasion.

E. Premises for Argument

Frequently, reasoning is based upon starting points or premises that speakers do not need to prove. Such unproved and sometimes even unmentioned premises are called assumptions. It is not necessary for a speaker to prove certain assumed premises because they are already accepted by the audience. A minister begins a sermon on the assumption that there is a God and that the congregation believes it. Frequently the minister assumes other theological principles which are accepted by the congregation. In most Christian churches, for example, it is assumed that God is triune but not in the Unitarian church.

It is virtually impossible to argue without assumptions. If speakers felt compelled to go back to first principles on every argument, they would both bore their listeners and waste valuable speaking time.

Look at such traditional documents as the Declaration of Independence and the Constitution. Observe from the Constitution the excellent examples of premises stated without proof.

We the People of the United States, in Order to form a more perfect Union, establish Justice, insure domestic Tranquility, provide for the common defence, promote the general Welfare, and secure the Blessings of Liberty to ourselves and our Posterity, do ordain and establish the Constitution for the United States of America.

The writers of this document assume without submitting any proof that union is desirable, that justice ought to be established, that domestic tranquility should be insured, that the general welfare is worth promoting, and that liberty is a blessing. What proof is necessary?

A speaker should know enough about the group addressed to be able to use arguments based on premises that the audience already believes. To know what premises will be acceptable to a given group, the speaker must determine what assumptions the audience holds and use them as premises for arguments.

F. Language Fitted to the Audience

Language is affected, even determined, by such factors as time, place, sex, and circumstances. At a Presbyterian convention, a man does not use the same language that might be heard at a convention of Lion's club members. In many significant ways, there are differences between the language of men and the language of women. Certainly, the language of the educated person is different from the language of the uneducated. Adlai Stevenson was criticized in 1952 because he "talked over the heads of the American people." But Stevenson was not being criticized for not knowing the language. Most people lauded his language. The real criticism was of his audience analysis. The Democratic party countered with the charge that Mr. Stevenson's critics were underrating the American public. In this instance, analysis of the contemporary American political audience became an actual issue in the campaign.

G. Organization

In Chapter 17, "Speaking To Persuade," we discuss the way in which the organization of a speech is determined by the nature of the audience you address. You will want to use different methods of organization depending on the extent to which the audience agrees or disagrees with what you say.

H. Motivation

As has already been pointed out, the greatest use of audience analysis is to provide the basis on which you may adapt a speech to the listeners' salient beliefs and attitudes and identify with their values. If you are talking to a friend about the punishment and rehabilitation of persons convicted of a crime, it is important to know that your friend believes that capital punishment is an unacceptable means of punishment. It is also important to know that your friend generally favors proposals in any field embodying humanitarian ideas, which assumes that people are essentially good, and which places a high value on the individual. When you pull together these salient beliefs, attitudes, and values, you will want to find an overall basis for motivating your audience to see the situation as you do. It is not enough just to know the relation of your proposal to beliefs, attitudes, and values; you must motivate the audience to an active state of awareness and action. In

Chapter 9, the hierarchy of motivation is discussed in greater detail.

Even if you do not know anything about specific beliefs and values, you can at least begin to infer them from the demographic information. What kinds of values do people in this age bracket tend to have? What values are members of this organization likely to hold? These are the kinds of questions you must ask yourself before you speak. And after you begin to talk, you can watch for reactions from your listeners that will help you test your assumptions about the audience to see if you have chosen the best possible motivation.

The experience of the supervisor of a group of electricians working on high-tension lines illustrates this point. The accident rate among the workmen was quite high, and all attempts to frighten the men by telling them of the physical dangers of not grounding the line and of not wearing safety helmets failed. Even the death of a friend who failed to heed the warnings did not succeed in changing their habits.

The supervisor was completely frustrated until he realized that self-preservation was not an acceptable motivation for the men. To them, not wearing a safety helmet and not grounding the wire were signs of manliness. They were, in their own minds, strong and able people; others had made errors because of their weakness. The emotional motivation was changed. The ego of the men was utilized as a basis of persuasion. They were told that no one cared if they wanted to kill themselves but that only fools did what they were doing. The workman who violated the safety rules was ridiculed as silly or even worse. When the men identified themselves with this concept, the number of accidents decreased. The success of this second motivation was the result of a more realistic analysis of the audience.

SUMMARY

To be effective, you must adapt your speech to your listeners. You must study their beliefs, attitudes, and values before you prepare your speech. The process of audience analysis, through which you gain your knowledge of your listeners, is one that demands continued study and observation of people. There are no infallible rules for knowing how audiences will respond. However, some clues to the nature of the audience can be found and used to help you identify your proposition with the values of the audience.

As a speaker you must determine the kinds of attitudes an audience has toward you, toward your subject, and toward the occasion of your speech. There are, moreover, specific factors that you can use to gain insight into the ideas and attitudes of your listeners. You need to know the makeup of the audience in terms of its sex, age, economic position, social background, and affiliations.

Once you have made your analysis of the audience, you can use it in a number of ways to strengthen your speech. Your analysis will help you choose the amount and kind of material you should use. You can estimate what the central tendency of audience attitude is, or, in cases where there are conflicting central tendencies, you can determine what cross pressures are operating. You use the information you gain from analyzing the audience to determine what premises you can assume without the need for proof. Your language and the organization of your speech will be influenced by what you know about the audience. Most important, you use your analysis of the audience to help you adapt to the salient beliefs of your listeners and identify your proposal with their values so that they will be motivated to an active response.

QUESTIONS

1. What general attitude of an audience is the most difficult for a speaker to assess?

2. Your class being your audience, select a specific topic and then speculate as to which of the five factors of audience analysis are most important? Least?

3. How do cross pressures affect audience response?

4. How is argument affected by the assumptions of an audience?

5. If you say that someone "talks over the heads of his listeners," do you mean his language is poor? If you do, then in what way?

6. How might the value system of teenagers about safe driving be different from those of their parents?

EXERCISES

1. Write a brief paper (no more than three double-spaced typewritten pages) in which you explain what you need to know about one of your parents or a brother or sister before you ask a favor. You will probably find it easier to write this paper if you select a specific favor to ask. Your purpose in this paper is to make an "audience" analysis of that one person, so do not write about the techniques you would use to get the favor. For instance, what do you need to know about your

father's ideas and attitudes in order to successfully ask him to let you use his car Saturday night?

2. Select any one of the five factors that determine the specific attitudes of an audience. Also select for consideration some specific question of current news interest. How do you think the attitudes of any two groups of people within the classification (for example, men and women, teenagers and middle-aged people, well-to-do people and poor people, Blacks and Caucasians) would differ *generally* on the question? What limitations do you see in this generalization? If you believe that on the question you have chosen there are no differences, explain why you believe so.

3. Make a careful and honest assessment of yourself as an "audience" for a speaker. What do people who wish to communicate with you have to know about you?

4. Think for a moment about the following subjects and audiences. Which demographic factors are most important and what beliefs, attitudes, and values will come into play in each of the nine possible combinations?

Subject	*Audience*
1. To inform the audience about the training of a fashion model.	A. Young black women from urban areas who are college students.
2. To persuade the audience to support the university football team.	B. White Protestant businessman at least 40 years of age.
3. To persuade the audience to support greater funds for urban renewal.	C. Students at a Roman Catholic college of both sexes and a variety of races.

Do certain factors seem less important than others? Do some factors immediately give you some clues as to how you ought to prepare your speech for maximum effectiveness? And don't forget, who are you? What is the audience's attitude toward you likely to be? What is the occasion?

I. The nature of attention
II. Audience conditions that influence attention
    A. Habits
    B. Set
    C. Values
    D. Suggestion
    E. Projection
III. Attention factors
    A. Intensity
    B. Change
    C. Unity
    D. Familiarity
    E. Novelty
    F. Repetition
IV. Principles in the use of attention factors
    A. Attention factors should appear throughout the speech
    B. Attention factors should be emphasized in the introduction
    C. Attention factors should be pertinent to the speech
    D. Attention factors should be appropriate to the interests of the audience

Chapter 5

Attention and Communication

From a psychological standpoint, a book about speech is a study of perception. It examines the ways in which you may encourage a listener to receive sensory impressions and then to perceive their meaning. You have an idea; you want your listeners to understand it. You want that idea to be reproduced in the listener's awareness in such a way that it will have essentially the same meaning and significance for the listener that it has for you.

The speech serves as a kind of map. It is a complex series of reference points made up of literally thousands of visual and auditory impressions that merge to form for the listener a single, overall interpretation of the idea. The listener's perception of your idea is a part of a transaction that takes place between the two of you. The many events, thoughts, attitudes, and values existing both inside and outside your nervous system and that of the receiver affect the meaning of the message as it is perceived by each. Thus, in engaging in communication, a receiver reacts to stimuli but he also creates them.*

* C. David Mortensen, *Communication: The Study of Human Interaction* (New York: McCraw-Hill, 1972), p. 71.

95

I. THE NATURE OF ATTENTION

The image most often conveyed in popular lore of the dynamic speakers who enforce, however subtly, their ideas on passive listeners is an inaccurate one. Emerging from recent developments in psychology, says psychologist Paul Bakan,

is a model of the organism as an active selector of stimuli rather than a passive recipient of stimulus impingements. In view of a limited capacity to deal with the available potential stimuli, the organism must somehow select those stimuli which will influence its behavior. It is this process of stimulus selection that constitutes *attention.**

Attention is, of course, very important to the communication process, and some communication theorists (most notably, James A. Winans) have considered it the central factor.†

Since there is, as we have noted, an almost infinite number of stimuli for a receiver to attend to at any moment, it is essential for you to concern yourself with the principles of attention. Such attention is particularly important at the beginning of a speech, where attention-getting is essential or no communication can take place, but it is also important throughout the communication transaction.

It is quite reasonable to believe that a person cannot attend to more than one event at a time and perceive each clearly. You may be able to move your attention rapidly from one to another of several events, but your understanding is likely to be more general than if you concentrate on one.‡

It becomes most important, therefore, to look seriously at the conditions that influence receivers to attend to particular stimuli. You should also be familiar with some of the attention factors that you can build into your messages so as to help receivers attend to your message and absorb the idea you want to communicate.

II. AUDIENCE CONDITIONS THAT INFLUENCE ATTENTION

Five major conditions determine the stimuli to which a member of an audience will respond: habits, set, values, suggestion, and projection.

* Paul Bakan, *Attention* (New York: Van Nostrand–Reinhold, 1966), p. iii. (Italics added.)

† J. A. Winans, *Public Speaking* (New York: Century, 1917), p. 194.

‡ Magdalen D. Vernon, "Perception, Attention and Consciousness," in Paul Bakan, ed. *Attention* (New York: Van Nostrand–Reinhold, 1966), pp. 38–39.

A. Habits

People perceive objects and ideas as they have been in the habit of perceiving them. When a sensitive critic looks at a poem, he sees form, idea, and quality of language. An untutored reader sees in poetry only words, and perhaps dull words at that. The one responds to the beauty of the poem, the other to its dullness. The poem is different only in the habitual response of its two readers. Much of education is a process of developing new habits of looking at things. Students learn new habits of perceiving a picture, a microscopic organism, an event in history, a novel, or a business organization.

You may change some of your listener's habits but you cannot, with a speech, expect to construct new systems on the instant. Since audiences have certain habits of perception, you must make some adaptation to those habits.

Politicians have learned to say "federal health insurance," instead of "socialized medicine." Psychologists, psychiatrists, and social workers use the term "mental illness" in discussing what used to be called "insanity." Words like "health" and "insurance" evoke favorable habitual responses, while "socialism" and "insanity" tend to evoke habitual negative responses.

B. Set

The habits in an audience are the personalized, internal dispositions of the individual listeners. The set of the audience is a generalized, external predisposition. Listeners tend to have certain predispositions about what should come from a speaking situation. Their interpretations of what you say are determined in part by their expectations, by their set. We know a man, a clever, witty speaker, who frequently addresses groups of high school students to explain to them, among other things, the entrance requirements of the college he represents. He knows his business and he speaks well. At the same time, he always manages to amuse the young people he addresses and, as a result, has acquired the reputation of being a very funny man. Some time ago he was invited to deliver the commencement address at the graduation of a high school he had visited on several occasions. He prepared what he intended to be a straightforward and serious set of remarks appropriate to such an occasion. His audience laughed at virtually every sentence he uttered. After some uncomfortable moments of surprise and chagrin, he realized that his audience, many of whom knew him by reputation and many of whom had heard him speak before, *expected* him to be funny and so laughed at everything he said. The lesson to be learned here is that a speaker either must meet the anticipations of his audience or must change its set. If he does not do either, he will be misinterpreted and the response he gets will not be the one he wants.

How would you like to be introduced to an audience of a thousand people in a strange town this way: "And now I give you Miss Mary Watkins, whom we all know as one of the most inspirational speakers of our times. We are all anxious to hear what Miss Watkins has to say to us, for we know that our lives will be enriched by her message." If you wanted to fall through the floor at that moment, no one could blame you. The chairman establishes a set in the audience which you know you cannot meet on those terms. Apropos, a word of warning to chairmen of meetings: give the audience a set which will help the speaker. When you introduce the speaker and the topic, create a favorable impression for them both. But do not make the audience expect too much.

C. Values

An audience's values will affect its response to your ideas. Value differences have been demonstrated by an experiment with children and coins. A group of children were shown various coins. A beam of light was then projected on a screen and the children were told to adjust the circle of light to the size of the coins. Invariably, the children from poorer families perceived the coins as larger than they actually were. The coins had a greater value for them than for the other children.

Some audiences see greater value in religious ideas than others. Some audiences will give higher values to athletics, agriculture, politics, or books than others do. To be a skillful speaker, you must understand the system of values that is operative in an audience and adapt your speaking to it. If you want to gain and hold the attention of your listeners you will need to adapt what you say to the values they hold. You need not sacrifice your own principles to do this, but you must relate your point of view to the values of the listeners. It is essential to understand what has value for a listener. For what has value will frequently determine what that listener will attend to.

D. Suggestion

Listeners are influenced by those around them. One form of political suggestion is known as the "bandwagon" technique. Candidates for office try to create the impression that there is no doubt they will be elected. If this notion can be established, other politicians and some voters may support them because everyone wants to be on the winning side. In one well-known experiment, an audience was told that a bottle containing a fluid with a strong odor had been opened in a room. Members of the audience were asked to hold up their hands when they could smell the odor. Actually, there was nothing in the bottle. The most suggestible members of the audience soon put up their hands and others followed. Some never did. One significance of the experiment is the fact that the people who raised their hands later were clustered in groups around the more suggestible whose hands had gone up first. This reaction seems to indicate not only that some people are more suggestible than others, but also that they help to influence those around them.

This fact is important to you as a speaker. When several individuals agree, they reinforce each other's convictions and modify, by suggestion, the ideas of other listeners in the group.

E. Projection

Perhaps the most frequently overlooked conditions influencing a listener's attention is the phenomenon of projection. You are aware of the projective techniques used by psychologists. The Thematic Apperception Test presents a series of pictures that are deliberately vague. When viewers are asked to tell a story based on a picture, they will project themselves into the picture and express their underlying values and attitudes. An auditory form of projection technique is the "tautaphone," an instrument that produces meaningless sounds. When listeners are asked to interpret these, they project their own ideas into the meaningless sounds.

If purposely vague pictures and sounds convey meaning because listeners or viewers project ideas into them, is it not also to be expected that listeners will do the same with a vague speech? Listeners not only *accept* or *reject* what you say because of habits, set, values, and suggestions; they actually *change* your ideas to make them mean what they want to hear. They reconstruct the speech into something they want to attend to. The more vague the speech, the more the listeners will "hear" you say what they would say or want to hear you say.

The implications of this phenomenon are clear. You must make sure that ideas and words are concrete. You must repeat your main ideas and use specific examples, for if you are vague in word and idea, the listeners will fill the gaps with what they want or expect to hear. Experiments have been conducted with classes of college students who were read a meaningless speech like the one in Chapter 12, "Cooperation—An Opportunity and a Challenge." When asked to explain it, most of the students who thought they understood the speaker's point had heard ideas that were compatible with their own. An overly technical speech will also encourage projection. If your language is so technical as to be unclear, then listeners who expect (and therefore want) to find meaning will project their own meaning, perhaps an incorrect one, into what you say.

Projection can also work to your advantage. Realizing that a listener has certain interests in an idea, you know that you need not go into great detail. In argument, for example, some of the steps in the reasoning process are omitted. The audience will fill them in. It is a necessary condition of the speaking situation that you cannot completely develop all your ideas. Listeners would become bored if they were subjected to every detail. "The Anti-Defamation League," a speaker says, "does a real service for America because it fights discrimination," and the listener projects the essential but missing part of the argument, "Discrimination is bad." But note that the possible projections here are limited. Suppose the speaker had said, "The Anti-Defamation League, which does a lot of things, is interested in discrimination, and that is a very controversial topic."

You must know your listeners and build a framework that will cause them to project those ideas which are compatible with your ideas.

III. ATTENTION FACTORS

Thus we see that certain conditions influence a receiver's tendency to attend to and respond to a message. People with certain habits, set, or values, for instance, will attend more closely to ideas that conform to their perceptions of the world. If, for instance, you are particularly interested in horses, that is, put a high value on horses, you will quickly attend to any discussion of horses. But, even subjects that do not meet the habits, set, values, and so forth, of an audience can be made interesting by a speaker who employs attention factors.

Six factors will normally command attention regardless of the selectivity of the listener. These are intensity, change, unity, familiarity, novelty, and repetition.

A. Intensity

Among a group of stimuli, listeners will tend to respond to those that are most intense. Thus a loud noise, a bright light, or a strong smell will attract attention. This means that when you speak, the stimuli you convey must be the most intense in the room. You must be louder than the general babble around you. You must be more forceful in stating your case than your competitors.

Intensity here does not mean just loudness or gross physical gesture. It includes, also, your attitude toward the situation and your subject. If your attention seems to wander, if you look out the window, if your arguments sound copied without interpretation from last month's *Reader's Digest*, if the total impression the audience gets is that you don't really care, you can be said to lack intensity. If you want an audience to pay attention to what you say, you must show that the subject you discuss is of concern to you and that you have a commitment to your own convictions.

B. Change

If intensity were the only criterion, then the loudest, most positive, and most physically active speaker would get the most attention. You know that is not what happens. You know that unrelieved intensity in speakers frequently makes listeners tired of hearing them. The intensity of loudness, for instance, can be so constant that it becomes a general characteristic of the occasion. It has nothing about it that sets it apart from the background and it is, therefore, no longer useful in differentiating the speaker from competing stimuli. The audience's attention moves as yours does when you are studying in your room and someone begins to use the typewriter. It attracts your attention because it is different from the stimuli you have become used to. As you become habituated to the sound, however, it fades into the background and as you study you do not even hear the typewriter. This fading is an example of the way we attend to *changes* in the nature and intensity of stimuli more than we do to a continuous level of stimulation.

Not all stimulation that involves change will command attention. A repeated pattern of flashing lights, like a neon sign above a grocery store, fades into the background of attention after the viewer becomes habituated to the patterned change. When you speak with a singsong pattern although you change pitch and quality, once the listener finds the pattern, your rhythmic patterned changes command as little attention as a monotone.

Speakers make use of change to build attention and thus give greater emphasis to ideas. If, at certain points in the speech, you seem more intent, argue more carefully, and heighten the motivational aspects, your audience will give more attention to those points. You can thus direct the attention of the audience to your major ideas. But don't emphasize minor points in this way, or the audience will pay more attention to them. You would be putting them in the foreground of your listeners' observation and relegating your major points to the background. Frequently, you will be confronted by the insistence that someone did not "hear" a point when you are sure that you "said" it. Both you and your listener are right. You "said" what you thought you said but not in a way that made the listener "hear" it. The listener did not perceive from your manner that the point was important, so it was either ignored or forgotten.

C. Unity

If speaking were like the visual perception of a bright light, which is a single stimulus, intensity and change could be regulated more conveniently. But speaking is not this simple. It involves subtle abstractions of language; it involves a visual image that is not a single strong light but many different stimuli which reach the eye from clothes, stance, facial expression, and movement. The vocal characteristics of pitch, force, time, and quality also provide multiple impressions. Over and above such external stimuli as the hard seats, the ventilation, the whispering in the row behind, the audience receives millions of stimuli from the speaking situation. If you are to comprehend them, they must be organized. You must, therefore, order your actions so that at any given moment the audience will receive all the discrete stimuli as if they were one.

Ideally, every movement and change in voice should support your idea. There must be a focusing of attention: The diverse stimulus components must be so related to one another that they may be taken as a whole. An analogous element in visual attention is sharpness of outline. You must assure yourself that all the stimuli at any given moment focus on a central idea.

It is with the purpose of helping speakers to achieve this focus that teachers caution against unnecessary physical movements, unusual patterns of speech, or irrelevant ideas. Unless all stimuli are linked together as a unified stimulus field, the listener will respond to distracting elements that stand out. These distracting sensations will produce injurious reactions like "He kept fumbling with his keys," "She sounded as if she were 'preaching' to us," and "What was all that talk about his uncle's farm for?" Unless there is unity, the listener may well fail to perceive the central purpose of the speech.

D. Familiarity

Things that are familiar to an audience will frequently command attention. When the ideas in a speech are unfamiliar to the listeners, their minds will tend to wander, to look for more understandable stimuli, in which they are already interested. You must, therefore, relate your subject to what is familiar to the audience. "You may not know or care what a differential is, but if your car didn't have one you wouldn't be in class today," said one student speaker. "The Chinese food you get in a restaurant is not the same food the people in China eat," said another. In each case the speaker was trying to link the subject to what was familiar to the audience.

E. Novelty

A habitual cigar smoker might give attention to the sight of a man smoking a cigar. What kind of cigar is he smoking? How many does he smoke per day? Questions like these occur to the cigar smoker; someone who does not smoke cigars is likely to say, "Who cares?" But anyone will pay attention to a woman smoking a cigar. That sight is novel.

The out-of-the-ordinary will almost always attract attention. A student speaker brings a strange machine to class. The members of the audience look up. "I wonder what that is all about," they say to themselves.

While novelty will get immediate attention, it must be linked to the familiar if interest is to be sustained. Most listeners will cease paying attention to a thing after they become aware that it has little to do with their interests.

In Chaper 18, "Speaking To Entertain," the principles of humor will be discussed in greater detail. But it can be noted here that the attention-getting quality of humor is based on its novelty.

F. Repetition

Since attention span is short and listeners are continually attracted by competing stimuli, it is quite common for main ideas to be forgotten, even those which have been forcefully stated. One method of reinforcing a listener's attention to an idea is repetition.

The judicious repetition of ideas and phrases will strengthen the speech. You can make use of repetition through parallel sentence structure and phrasing. In one section of his Annual Message of January, 1936, President Franklin D. Roosevelt used 14 consecutive rhetorical questions beginning with the word "Shall." Ten of the 14 questions begin with the words "Shall we say." (This passage is quoted at length later. "That government of the people, by the people, and for the people shall not perish from this earth," has a repetition of phrase pattern and words that holds attention. When you weave each new point into the pattern of your speech by associating it with the central thought, you are using repetition to reinforce your main idea.

If, however, repetition is used too much or wrongly, it is likely to become all the listener hears; it will draw attention away from important ideas and make the audience conscious only of the repetition. Unconscious periodic repetition of distracting mannerisms like "ah" and "uh" reinforce the unnecessary and force the main idea of the speech into the background.

IV. PRINCIPLES IN THE USE OF ATTENTION FACTORS

Attention will be attracted to a communication because that communication is congruent with the interests which are a part of the audience condition or it may be attracted by the deliberate use of attention factors. If you have natural conditions in the audience helping to gain its attention, that is a help, but even then and particularly when these are not working, attention factors must be developed with skill to gain and hold attention.

You should first assess the factors in the audience that will gain and detract from attention; then look for attention factors that may be built into your speech. Let us look now at some of the principles which should control that use.

A. Attention Factors Should Appear Throughout the Speech

You need the attention of your audience throughout your entire speech. When and if attention lags, something important may be lost.

IV Principles in the Use of Attention Factors

Because the span of attention is quite limited, it must be constantly renewed. Material should be selected, points should be organized, and delivery should be used to sustain the attention of an audience from beginning to end.

B. Attention Factors Should Be Emphasized in the Introduction

The first and perhaps the most important point at which attention must be developed is in the introduction of the speech. When you arise, you are, in a sense, a blur of movement, unfocused in the attention of your audience. As you go to the speaking stand and arrange your notes, you become a human being; you have distinctive clothing and a distinctive face. Then you begin to talk. If the audience continues to see just a human being without distinguishing characteristics of feature or of intellect, you will not hold attention. So it is that the introductory part of your speech must direct the attention of your hearers to your main idea. If you fail to seize the attention of the audience at the beginning of your speech, it will be extremely difficult to do so later on.

C. Attention Factors Should Be Pertinent to the Speech

It is easy for you to catch attention by using methods that are completely extraneous to the ideas in the speech. A young man began a speech one day by holding out his hand at arm's length and dropping a large number of glass marbles on the floor. The marbles made a marvelous flash of color as they rolled around the room. The audience was immediately and completely attentive—not to the speaker but to the marbles. To make it worse, as soon as they discovered the marbles had nothing to do with the speech, their attention was lost. Such *involuntary* attention is like the response to a sudden bright light, or the firing of a shot. It will not last long and is of little use to a speaker.

Listeners will also give a kind of *voluntary* attention that is motivated by something extraneous to the speech itself. For example, you may voluntarily set yourself to hear a dull lecture because you want to get a good grade in a class, or workers will force themselves to listen to instructions that they must have in order to hold their jobs.

Outlandish attention techniques will send listeners away remembering the technique and not the idea. "Boy, was he loud!" was a remark we once heard from a listener leaving a lecture hall. "That was really a funny joke he told. I have to remember to tell my wife when I get

105

home," said one man after a political speech. Such reactions as these indicate that what may be popularly regarded as a "good speech" may actually be a poor one because the idea of the speaker is lost in the techniques of attention. You want responses to your *ideas*. You must be sure, therefore, that your attention techniques complement rather than overshadow the ideas.

D. Attention Factors Should Be Appropriate to the Interests of the Audience

The kind of attention you get when you appeal to the habitual concerns of an audience is the most useful. You must look for the best attention factors in a speech and not just the obvious ones. You look for the factors that will be close to the experience of the audience, for the ones to which the audience can most easily respond.

SUMMARY

In addressing an audience, you initiate systems of stimuli that the listeners accept, reject, or interpret in terms of their own interest. Five conditions influence the response that an audience will make to your message and help to determine whether listeners will select the stimuli you intend them to select:

1. Habits
2. Set
3. Values
4. Suggestion
5. Projection

In order that listeners may perceive your ideas correctly, you should use certain devices to focus the attention of your audience on the central idea of your speech. These devices are called attention factors:

1. Intensity
2. Change
3. Unity
4. Familiarity
5. Novelty
6. Repetition

To make your communication effective, use these attention factors throughout the speech but apply them with particular care in the introduction. Choose attention factors that are appropriate to the ideas in your speech.

QUESTIONS

1. How do both speaker and listener affect the way an act of communication takes place?
2. How valuable to a speaker is involuntary attention in an audience?
3. How do listeners' habits affect their responses?
4. What is set?
5. What kind of a speech will invite the greatest listener projection?
6. The chapter discusses six different attention factors. What three do you consider most important? Why?
7. How is a singsong pattern of speech like a monotone?
8. What principle of attention is in danger from unnecessary physical movement, unusual patterns of speech, or irrelevant ideas?
9. Why should attention factors be emphasized in the introduction?

EXERCISES

1. Report some experiences that show how people are suggestible.
2. Develop and bring to class the outlines of two or three different introductions to the same speech, emphasizing different attention factors in each.
3. Write a paper in which you analyze a specific audience, explaining what values you believe would be most significant to them. Consult Chapter 4 in writing this paper.
4. Evaluate some speech delivered in class in terms of what the speaker did, or failed to do, to arouse your attention and sustain your interest.

I. Clarity and interest
II. Types of supporting material
   A. Definition
     1. Logical definition
     2. Operational definition
     3. Definition by description
     4. Definition by comparison and contrast
     5. Definition by example
     6. Definition by figure of speech
     7. Definition by usage, etymology, or history
   B. Statements about facts: Examples
     1. Real examples
     2. Secondary examples
     3. Hypothetical examples
     4. Extended examples
     5. Using examples for clarity and interest
     6. Using examples to prove
   C. Statements about facts: Statistics
     1. Using statistics for clarity and interest
     2. Using statistics to prove
   D. Opinions about facts: Testimony
     1. Using testimony
     2. Evaluating testimony
   E. Comparison and contrast
III. The use of visual aids
   A. Types of visual aids
     1. Diagrams and graphs
     2. Maps and globes
     3. Pictures
     4. Models and actual objects
   B. Principles for the use of visual aids

Chapter ⑥

Supporting Materials and Visual Aids

The ideas in your speech are reflections of your experiences, and they include your research and your knowledge. An audience understands those ideas in terms of its own experience, however. Hearers interpret language based on their experience with the concepts and objects to which the language refers. To be an effective speaker, you must use language that makes it easy for an audience to visualize the concepts and objects that you are discussing. Abstractions must be made concrete; generalities must be made specific; obscurities must be made clear. Concrete, specific, vivid details help your listeners visualize your ideas in terms of their own experiences. These details are called supporting materials.

In any serious effort to communicate, you must select the materials best calculated to make your meaning clear. In a very real sense, for every set of verbal symbols you use, you have a meaning and your listener has a meaning, but they will never be precisely the same. Unless you select materials carefully, you will be less likely to modify the listener's meaning so that it shifts toward your own.

In every kind of speaking—to inform, to persuade, to entertain—the kinds of materials used are of the same sort. As the purpose in speaking differs, however, and you work toward different general ends, you make different uses of the material. No matter what your goal, your materials should provide the listener with a balance of clarity and interest.

I. CLARITY AND INTEREST

In a sense, the qualities of clarity and interest are antagonistic. Clarity increases as the listener is able to predict your meaning with greater certainty. Interest increases with novelty and change, when the situation is less predictable.

Clarity without interest will produce a speech that is dull and therefore difficult to listen to. Actuarial tables, for example, can be eminently clear, but they do not make good listening. On the other hand, there is harm in using materials which may be interesting in themselves but which add nothing necessary to the clarification of the ideas. A major artistic factor in all communication is striking a careful balance between the dull and the exciting, of finding the point where your meaning is both interesting and clear.

All supporting materials are designed to provide meaning, but these materials are not things; they are statements about things. They have meaning for the listener because they refer to something in the listener's experience: things, people, thoughts, attitudes, values. We speak of giving evidence to support a point. Sergeant Joe Friday of *Dragnet* asks the witness to "Give us the facts, just the facts." But no one gives "facts"; he makes statements about facts. The law of gravity is a statement about a fact. A definition of communism is a statement about communism. A college president's opinion on the pass-fail system of grading is a statement about that system.

Your purpose in using such statements is to make the listeners believe that through these supporting materials they are learning about reality.

II. TYPES OF SUPPORTING MATERIAL

Supporting materials may be classified in four categories: *Definitions* are used to clarify your meaning for words or concepts which may be unfamiliar, obscure, or different from the listener's. *Statements about facts* are details found in the forms of examples and statistics. *Opinions about facts* occur in the form of the testimony of others. *Comparison and contrast* establish a relationship for the listener between the known and the unknown.

A. Definition

A druggist labels a bottle of medicine so that there may be no confusion about the contents or the dosage. In a similar sense, language provides labels for ideas. The labels put on ideas, like the labels of bottles of medicine, should be recognizable, clear, and precise. But language is not always easy to use in speaking about complex or abstract ideas. "Democracy," "communism," "union shop" are not "seen" in the same sense as "aspirin" or "vitamin C." When you use words like *aspirin* or *vitamin C*, listeners recognize your simple denotative meaning, even though they may not have full insight into the chemical components of the concrete things named. *Democracy, truth,* and *honesty,* however, are abstract terms. These labels are used with a greater variety of meanings than are those of more concrete objects. There is a tendency to use language as if the labels for such abstractions were understood as easily and universally as the labels put on concrete things. Too often listeners are confused because they do not understand the labels in the sense you use them. They will, therefore, project their own meanings into what you say rather than shift their meanings toward yours. Consequently, an abstract, unfamiliar, or obscure term will need to be defined.

No amount of effort at clear definition will make certain that doubtful words have precisely the same meaning for every listener. Universal understanding is impossible, but fortunately it is also unnecessary. Ideas can be communicated adequately in spite of the inherent ambiguity of language. The closer you and your audience come to a mutual understanding of language, the better the communication will be.

The basic requirements of a good definition are (1) to indicate the sense in which you use the term and (2) to bring your meaning within the scope of the listeners' experiences.

1. Logical Definition

There are many different methods of definition, but the one that traditionally has been considered to fulfill these two requirements best is definition by classification, so-called *logical* definition. Logical definition puts the thing defined into a class with which the listener is already familiar. Then, to restrict the meaning and eliminate ambiguity, the definition distinguishes the thing defined from all other members of that class. To the baseball player, a "Texas Leaguer" is a safe hit on a short fly ball that falls to the ground between the infielders and outfielders. It belongs to the class of safe hits but is differentiated from other safe hits by the facts that (1) it is a short fly ball and (2) it hits the ground between the infielders and outfielders.

2. Operational Definition

When someone tells you what you must do to discover what something is, he is giving you an operational definition. He is telling you the operation you must go through to experience the meaning of the term.

Maybe you have been somewhere for the first time, and you know that it is the first time you have ever been there, yet you have the feeling that you have been there before, even to the extent that you could predict things about the place that you couldn't possibly have known. Last summer I was driving through a town I had never been in before on a road I had never traveled before, and suddenly I felt that I had been there before. I even knew that around a corner up ahead would be a large stone church, although I couldn't see around the corner, and I knew that I had never been around that corner. I got to the corner, and there was the church, just as I knew it would be, and just where I knew it was. The feeling that I had which you may have had at some time in your life, is called *déjà vu.*

3. Definition by Description

To say that South College is the 100-year old, red-brick, four-story building built in two wings will help a person to recognize it. It will not, however, indicate anything about the function of the building (the Linguistics Department, The Office of the Dean of Arts and Sciences, and the Debate Union are located there) or the nature of its general usefulness. But it does define its general physical characteristics so that a listener can recognize it. For some items such a description goes a long way toward defining it. For most people, a description of a gambrel roof, a Georgian column, or a Cape Cod house is a definition.

4. Definition by Comparison and Contrast

In defining by comparison and contrast, you try to show your meaning for a term either by likening it to something (comparison) or by differentiating it from something (contrast) with which your listeners are already familiar:

Writing is like speaking in that its major purpose is to communicate an idea.

The union shop is not exactly like the closed shop. Workers can get jobs at a union shop before they join the union, but they must already belong to a union before they can be employed in a closed shop.

Comparison and contrast may be used together for clarification. The government of the state of Nebraska is much like that of the federal government. It has three branches—executive, legislative, and judicial —which carry on the usual functions of those branches. But Nebraska has only one house in the legislature.

5. Definition by Example

Speakers may explain their meaning for a term by citing examples. In 1974, Senator Sam J. Ervin, Jr., of North Carolina, defined intellectual freedom by turning to Thomas Jefferson and his contemporaries and using the principles of the Bill of Rights for examples that would define.

The greatest exponent of intellectual freedom among the men and women who made America a living reality was Thomas Jefferson, who said: "I have sworn upon the altar of God eternal hostility against every form of tyranny over the mind of man."

His contemporaries shared Jefferson's abhorrence of tyranny over the mind, and for this reason they adopted the First Amendment. When this amendment is read in conjunction with the Due Process Clause of the Fourteenth Amendment, it compels the governments of the states as well as the federal government to extend to every human being within our borders these intellectual, political, and religious freedoms:

1. Freedom to think whatever he pleases.
2. Freedom to speak and publish his thoughts with impunity, provided what he says or publishes is not obscene and does not falsely slander or libel another, or tend to obstruct the courts in their administration of justice, or create a clear and present danger that it will incite others to commit crimes.
3. Freedom to associate with others to accomplish any lawful objective.
4. Freedom to meet peaceably with others for consultation and protest, and to petition those invested with powers of government for redress of grievances, real or imagined.
5. Freedom to entertain such religious beliefs as appeal to his conscience, to practice his religious beliefs in any form of worship not injurious to the rights of others, to endeavor by peaceful persuasion to convert others to his religious beliefs, and to be exempt from taxation for the support of any institution which teaches religion of any character.

These freedoms are exercisable by fools as well as by wise men, by agnostics or atheists as well as by the devout, by those who defy our Constitution and laws as well as by those who conform to them, and by those who hate our country as well as by those who love it.*

6. Definition by Figure of Speech

Not all definitions express a specific denotative meaning for a word. In the above illustration of definition by example, the user clearly has a connotative meaning for the term. Even more connotative is definition by *figure of speech*. To say "The world is a stage" or "The devil is a roaring lion" helps the listener to visualize but in a connotative way. In most speaking situations you will be more interested in clarity of definition, but sometimes you will want definitions that convey attitudes. In such cases more connotative forms of definition will be useful.

7. Definition by Usage, Etymology, or History

A dictionary always reports the usage of a term:

showdown, *n.* 1: In poker, the play in which the hands are laid on the table face up. 2: Any action or disclosure that brings an issue to a head.

The dictionary may also report the *etymology* of a word or the *history* of its development. The meaning of the word "persuasion" may be clarified by showing that it comes from the Latin phrase *per suasionem*, which means "through sweetness." To the etymology of the word may be added something of its history: The tribes of Europe, who found the declensions of the Latin language difficult and awkward, dropped off endings and used words in their root forms. Thus the phrase *per suasionem* lost its *em* ending and became the single word "persuasion." The concept of sweetness is still an important connotation of the term. The dictionary's report of usage makes no precise definition of a term; neither does the etymology of a word or the history of its development. By telling these, though, you could convey enough of your meaning to make it understood.

One brief word of caution is necessary about the use of definitions. Although audience analysis may reveal that many of your listeners do not understand what you mean by a word, there may be in the audience many who already have a meaning for the term. So, avoid comments such as, "I know that you don't understand what this term

* Sam J. Ervin, Jr., "Our Basic Liberties," *Vital Speeches of the Day*, 30 (May 15, 1974), p. 455.

means, so let me define it for you." If your listeners do not understand the term, you scarcely need to tell them that they don't. It is far better to put the responsibility on yourself: "To make myself clear, let me point out that by———, I mean———."

B. Statements About Facts: Examples

Examples are the product of experience and observation, either yours or someone else's. Grand Teton National Park is in Wyoming. The United States was attacked at Pearl Harbor on December 7, 1941. The British burned Washington, D.C., during the War of 1812. John F. Kennedy was elected president of the United States in November 1960. All of these are statements about facts that may be used as examples to illustrate some point.

If you want to become a truly effective speaker, learn to use examples well. Think of the interesting speakers you have heard, whether on a public platform or in your own living room. Remember the many examples they used to illustrate the subjects they discussed.

Examples may be secondary or hypothetical, brief or extended in length.

1. Real Examples

An example is an account of an incident or occurrence that you relate to illustrate a point, or an object or condition that you cite. A real example refers to an incident that has actually occurred or an object that actually exists. "A good example of a great football team was the old Chicago Bears." "St. Stephen's Church down on Orange Avenue is a good example of what I mean by modern church architecture." Although both of these examples are real examples, there is a significant difference between them. It is quite clear that an audience may have actually experienced St. Stephen's Church. The speaker is asking it to remember the building as the listeners probably saw it on Orange Avenue. On the other hand, it is quite likely that the average listener never experienced the "old Chicago Bears." Some examples are more immediate in the listeners' experience than others and, therefore, presumably require less detail for their understanding. In this case you might have to give a lengthy explanation about the Chicago Bears of 20 years ago, while St. Stephen's Church would be instantly recognizable. In such a situation, perhaps, the Pittsburgh Steelers or Minnesota Vikings would be a better football example because they too, like St. Stephen's Church, might be instantly recognizable.

2. Secondary Examples

Because the personal knowledge that both you and your listeners bring to the communication transaction is limited, many of the examples you use are not real to you. You accept them as being real on the credibility of someone else. You cannot usually testify to starvation in an African nation, brutality in a foreign jail, or the beauty of the French countryside. On all historical subjects except the most recent, you must use examples you receive from others. These we can call secondary examples. They are not in the experience of the speaker or the listener.

In November of 1974, the United Nations World Food Conference convened in Rome. The occasion motivated one of our students to make a speech in which appeared a clear instance of secondary example. As we recall, the speaker said something like this:

For the 77 million people of Bangladesh, famine has become a dreaded nightmare. More than 100,000 human beings have starved to death in the past two weeks. And there is no hope for perhaps a million more of these Bengalis because the next rice crop won't be harvested for another month. Even more pitiful is the fact that the emergency food supplies now on their way there from other countries won't get there in time.

You and I are strangers to hunger. For us, the thought of starvation has never been a nightmare. And yet, while here in the United States calves are being shot to dramatize the soaring costs of feed, and milk is being dumped into gutters because the market price is too low, children in Asia and Africa are starving to death.

3. Hypothetical Examples

If an example describes an incident that has not actually occurred, but might, it is a hypothetical example. Harry Schwartz, Visiting Professor of Medical Economics in the Columbia University Medical School, used this hypothetical example in a speech delivered at New York University*:

As an intellectual experiment, let us begin by considering two conceivable, opposite extremes of therapeutic practice. The first will be a model based upon recommendations of believers in maximum free enterprise; the second upon recommendations of believers in maximum practicable total control.

In the first variant, we may think of a society in which anyone who wishes is freely permitted to set up shop and offer his services as a healer. Imagine a row of stores on an urban street, the first one occupied by a chiropractor,

* Harry Schwartz, "Responsibility and Accountability in American Medicine," *Vital Speeches of the Day,* 41 (Jan. 1, 1975), p. 175.

116

the second by a homeopathic physician, the third by an allopathic physician, the fourth by a naturopath, the fifth by a witch doctor, the sixth by an Iroquois medicine man, the seventh by a faith healer, the eighth by a religious science practitioner of one persuasion or another, the ninth by an expert in voodoo incantations, the tenth by an acupuncturist, and so on. In this model each of these self-licensed and self-designated therapists competes for the trade of the sick, the lame and the halt. In this situation of open competition, the consumer has maximally free choice and so has the therapist. Presumably over a long enough period of time, consumers would develop preferences based upon experience and some therapists would prosper because of their perceived performance efficacy and efficiency, while others would be compelled to shut up shop because of lack of trade. In such a model, we may suppose, there would be no need for any formal mechanisms to assure responsibility or accountability since consumers would quickly perceive differences in effectiveness among the competitive healers. The untrammeled competition would be relied upon to give results that in more constricted models might require formal governmental measures.

At the other extreme we may conceive of a medical system, perhaps attainable a few years or decades from now, under which each self-designated sick person would be required to present himself at a designated computer terminal complete with all possible computer-attached sensors and manipulative instruments. At this terminal a semi-skilled attendant would have only the task of applying various sensors and instruments to the appropriate portions of the patient's anatomy. Once applied these sensors and instruments would record and transmit to the computer's central processing unit all necessary information about the patient's conditions, including all information needed to diagnose any disease. The central processing unit would presumably have all available medical knowledge and be appropriately updated daily to assure that it was fully current with the latest scientific findings. For most patients, presumably, the computer would immediately supply a complete diagnosis plus an optimal therapeutic regimen which might include the administration of appropriate drugs, the use of indicated operations or radiation therapy, etc. We may suppose that in this futuristic medical system all drugs, surgery, radiation etc. are administered by computer-directed machines so that no problem of human negligence arises. At most mechanical or electromechanical faults in the machinery might produce errors, but for these problems the computerized medical system might have maintenance computer systems that kept eternal watch and sought to prevent any malfunction. Presumably in this future computerized Utopia there might sometimes be patients who presented themselves with symptoms and internal data readings so discordant that no satisfactory diagnosis could be made by the central processor. In such cases the recommended treatment might be provided by some appropriate random choice mechanism. But in all cases where diagnosis was possible, the patient could be confident that he had received the best care that was computerly possible. In this system, too, presumably, problems of responsibility and accountability would be minimal.

117

4. Extended Examples

On occasion, you will want to develop an example at somewhat greater length and in more detail than is possible in the brief form the example ordinarily takes. Such illustrations are called extended examples and may be either hypothetical or real.

On March 15, 1965, President Lyndon B. Johnson delivered what is probably his most well-received speech. That speech on the right to vote was delivered to a joint session of the Congress. In it he developed an extended personal example to illustrate the idea that "You never forget what poverty and hatred can do when you see its scars on the hopeful face of a young child."

My first job after college was as a teacher in Cotulla, Texas, in a small Mexican-American school. Few of them could speak English and I couldn't speak much Spanish.

My students were poor and they often came to class without breakfast and hungry. And they knew even in their youth the pain of prejudice. They never seemed to know why people disliked them, but they knew it was so because I saw it in their eyes. I often walked home late in the afternoon after the classes were finished wishing there was more that I could do. But all I knew was to teach them the little that I knew, hoping that it might help them against the hardships that lay ahead.

And somehow you never forget what poverty and hatred can do when you see its scars on the hopeful face of a young child.*

5. Using Examples for Clarity and Interest

There are some rules for using examples which you ought to remember.

1. Use extended examples only when the point to be described is an essential one. For minor points, brief examples are sufficient.

2. Use the best example you can find for the particular idea you are discussing. Unless examples are carefully chosen, there is a danger that they will not clearly exemplify the point you are making. An example that fails to illustrate your point precisely forces you to say, "This isn't exactly what I mean, but . . ." The listener is thrown off the track, and after a few such instances, may well give up listening.

3. Be sure that the necessary value characterizations are given with the example: The Pittsburgh Steelers are not just *any* football team; they are a *great* one, while the Reseda High School Regents are a "typical high-school" team.

* Lyndon B. Johnson, "The Right to Vote," *Vital Speeches of the Day,* **31** (April 1, 1965), p. 356.

4. If necessary, use more than one short example for a specific point. A single example might enlighten part of the audience and not the rest, or may only partly enlighten the audience as a whole. A greater number and variety of examples will often clarify or prove when one example might fail.

5. Use real examples whenever it is possible and give them the kind of detail that will make them seem more directly related to the listener's experience. Be specific as to time, place, and circumstance. If real examples are not available, give to secondary and hypothetical examples as much of the characteristics of real examples as possible. If only a hypothetical example is available of how to use your brakes on a slippery pavement, you can say, "Suppose you were coming down Ventura Boulevard at about 25 miles an hour in a heavy rain when a truck pulled out of Balboa Boulevard. Here's what might happen. . . ." Although your hearers never experienced this event, they can visualize it and can profit by the description. This hypothetical example has the characteristics of the real example: The experience on Ventura Boulevard is not real, but hearers recognize the event and have had similar experiences or have heard of similar experiences, which is enough to make it seem real.

6. Using Examples To Prove

When you use examples to prove a point in a speech, you must not only choose illustrations for their value in achieving clarity and interest, but you must also select instances that meet three further criteria. If the answer to all three of the following questions is Yes, the examples may be considered acceptable.

Are the examples representative? Examples must be typical, not exceptions to the rule. You may do all kinds of favors for a person but the first time you refuse you may hear, "What kind of a friend are you? You never help me out when I need help." The person singles out what is perhaps the only atypical example in an otherwise clear pattern of behavior as the basis for an unfounded generalization. A specific instance must give a true picture of the situation it illustrates if it is to be effective as a means of proof.

Are the examples sufficient in number to give clear support to the point you are making? The number of instances that will be necessary is not the same in every case. One may be enough: The first sunburn you get on a cloudy day will be quite enough to establish for you the generalization that exposure to the sun is dangerous even on a cloudy day. On the other hand, it takes quite a number of baseball games to demonstrate which is the best team in the National League.

Are negative instances accounted for? It is not reasonable to expect to establish belief in an idea if there is substantial evidence to the contrary. A wealthy man may on many occasions show civic pride and social responsibility, and a speaker might try to characterize him as a good and philanthropic citizen. The speaker would not be notably successful if his audience knew that the man's fortune was made in legal but morally doubtful operations in slum-area real estate.

C. Statements About Facts: Statistics

Statistics are figures you use to clarify an idea or prove a proposition. Ronald Reagan of California was brought into the political spotlight by speeches he delivered in support of Senator Barry Goldwater's candidacy for the presidency in 1964, and after that for conservative politics in general. Extensive use of statistics characterizes these speeches. Here is an example from a speech the future governor of California delivered in 1965.

Our Government is spending $260 million a day and that's $10 million more that we were spending a year ago. Our Government is responsible for a deliberate and planned inflation that has reduced the purchasing power of the dollar in the last three decades to 44½ cents. In the last 20 years, we have eroded the value of our savings and insurance by $190 billion. My father, when I was a boy, and I can hear him now, said the country needed a good 5-cent cigar. What this country needs is a good 5-cent nickel.*

1. Using Statistics for Clarity and Interest

When statistics employ large numbers (roughly four or more digits), it is wise to round them off. For instance, the 1970 population of Philadelphia was 1,950,098 but if you wanted to use this in a speech you would probably say, "In 1970 the population of Philadelphia was almost 2 million." Even though 49,902 is a substantial number of people, "almost 2 million" is accurate enough for most purposes and much easier for the listener to remember.

After statistics have been rounded off, they can be made still more meaningful by comparison. The round figure of 2 million is easier to comprehend if it is compared: "That's approximately four times the

* Ronald Reagan, "A Moment of Truth," *Vital Speeches of the Day*, 31 (Sept. 1, 1965), p. 684.

size of our own city of Atlanta." Percentages, fractions, and proportions all help to put the compacted examples we call statistics into a clear relationship with other facts. Statistics, then, can add clarity and interest if you round them off and, by using comparison, show their relationship to other ideas.

2. Using Statistics To Prove

When statistical data are used as illustrations to clarify an idea, it is important, of course, that they be accurate and meaningful as well as interesting and clear. When figures of this kind are used as evidence to support a proposition, however, it is even more important that they be examined carefully.

1. *Check the currency of the data.* The date of compilation is one of the first things to ask about statistical information. Recency is of little concern, of course, in matters that change slowly or slightly if at all. A statement of the number of times a human heart beats per minute need not be doubted today just because the subject was studied years ago. The infant mortality rate in American hospitals does not change rapidly enough to demand new study every day. If, however, you see a report on the number of jet fighter planes Syria is supposed to have, you would want to know when the count was made. Air power is not static.

2. *Check the reliability of the source of the statistical data.* Completely apart from any interpretation put upon figures—the validity of any comparison between, let us say, the air powers of Israel and Syria —accurate reporting depends upon the reliability of sources. You must ask: Who made the statistical study? Did the information come from sources that may be intentionally misleading?

Certain governmental agencies such as the Bureau of Labor Statistics are generally accepted as a source of honest reports. The Brookings Institution is a private economics research group that has earned general acceptance. But, as any television viewer can tell you, many so-called independent agencies are nothing more than sources of advertising copy.

3. *Be sure the statistics measure what they appear to measure.* It would be doubtful to conclude that one-fourth of the student body of an entire college is Italian because two of the eight students in an advanced class in the Language Department happen to have been born in Rome. This is an insufficient sampling.

Suppose, moreover, that the average age of the same eight students is 30 years. This measure of the sample is probably a poor measure of the age of the students in the whole college, and it can be misleading in reference to the class itself. The two Italian students may be a man and his wife who came to this country after the man had retired from business and both may be 65 years old. If four of the other students in the class are 18 and two are 19, this distribution makes the *average* age of the class 30, but no one in the class comes within 10 years of the average.

Finally, it would be wise to ask how the word *average* is used: Does it refer to the mean, the median, or the mode? The *mean* is a simple arithmetical average. To find it, add together the quanity of each item in a series and divide by the number of items. The *mode* is the figure that appears most frequently in a series. The *median* is the point above and below which half of the items fall. In the example cited above, the mean age of the students is 30, the mode is 18, and the median is between 18 and 19. In other words, statistical data are subject to scrutiny and interpretation. The old saying that "figures don't lie" is itself a generalization that bears investigation; although the remainder of the saying, "but liars figure," is above reproach.

D. Opinions About Facts: Testimony

Often the material you have gathered reflects some judgment on the part of its source and comes to you as an interpretation of the data involved. These interpretations are called *testimony* and are *opinions* about facts.

1. Using Testimony

Using testimony in a speech makes it possible for you to tap the resources of generations of thought and expression. All that human kind has written and said becomes a vast reservoir from which you can draw the authoritative testimony of expert witnesses. You add clarity and interest to your ideas and strength to your propositions when you associate your attitudes and opinions with the thoughts and feelings of people your audiences know, respect, and admire.

The privilege of using testimony in a speech is one that brings certain obligations. Honesty demands that you identify ideas and language that you have taken from someone else. This is not merely a moral injunction against plagiarism; two other considerations are involved. First, by failing to identify your source you pass up the opportunity to add the credibility of your source to your own and, second, if a listener recognizes that the statement is not your own, it will tend to diminish your credibility as an honest person.

Putting directly quoted testimony into a speech may bring some awkward moments. To avoid these, it is generally wise not to use the words "quote" and "unquote" to identify the beginning and end of a direct quotation. Instead, identify the source of your material as thoroughly as honesty demands, then let your voice (through pause, change in tempo, or other means) indicate which words are yours and which belong to your source.

Your use of testimony need not be in the form of a direct quotation, that is, word for word. It can be presented in your words with an indication that the explanation or comparison has some respected person as its source. If the explanation of an authority is particularly clear, you may want to quote it *verbatim*, but, in general, putting the idea into your own words will keep it on the level of language used in your speech.

Regardless of the form, testimony is always opinion *about* facts, not fact itself. Consequently, the best use of testimony will reveal how the authorities cited arrived at their conclusions. Testimony that merely states an opinion asks listeners to accept the conclusion simply because they trust the source. It is far stronger to support this trust with the facts and reasons behind the judgment.

2. Evaluating Testimony

Before you decide to use a piece of testimony, you should ask yourself two questions about it:

Is the authority competent? The background, training, and experience of the persons whose opinions you use as supporting material should put them in a position to know what they are talking about. To be qualified, they should be speaking in an area of competence. A theologian is not usually an authority on biology. A former heavyweight champion who happens to be Black is not necessarily any greater authority on race relations than any other Black. Look for sources whose competence will be clear to the listener. Sometimes, with less well-known authorities, it is necessary to give the audience evidence of their competence.

One would like to believe that competence can be objectively measured. Like all factors in rhetoric, however, it is a judgment in the minds of the audience. You might be tempted to think, "Well, if you don't know who Charles Percy is, you are pretty dumb." But, objectively, if the listeners don't recognize the name of the Senator from Illinois, it is your responsibility to see that they are informed.

Is the authority trustworthy? Even when an authority is accepted as competent, he may not be considered thoroughly trustworthy on a subject. Ex-Senator J. William Fulbright of Arkansas is one of the most knowledgeable men in this country in the area of American foreign policy, but many people think him to be biased on the subject. For them, his credibility is less than it is for others. A frequent mistake of beginning speakers is to assume that any senator, historian, physicist, or economist is a source of useful testimony. Their biases, whether real or only imagined by the audience, will decrease their credibility.

E. Comparison and Contrast

Although they can be treated separately, *comparison* and *contrast* are in essence the same process. Comparisons show how things are *like* other things; contrasts show how things are *unlike*.

In comparison, choose something familiar to the audience and liken it to the unknown factor you wish to explain. One student speaker, in explaining the principle of radar, compared it to bouncing a ball off a garage door, in that the farther away from the garage the player gets, the longer it takes the ball to bounce and return. If he could measure the amount of time and the speed of the ball, he could determine the distance to the door. He then went on to say that ball-bouncing is roughly comparable to the way radar works. Radio waves, whose speed is known, are thrown against an object and the length of time the reflected wave takes to return indicates the distance of the object from the sender.

Contrast is used to show differences. An audience may not be clear on the difference between radar and sonar. After explaining the basic nature of radar by comparing a radio wave with the ball bounced off the garage door, a speaker can explain sonar by noting that, while radar employs radio waves, sonar employs sound waves.

III. THE USE OF VISUAL AIDS

Frequently, ideas will be clearer if the supporting materials, particularly the examples and statistics, are put in visual form to aid the listeners' understanding.

A. Types of Visual Aids

Most visual aids can be classified into four categories: (1) diagrams and graphs, (2) maps and globes, (3) pictures, and (4) models and actual objects.

1. Diagrams and Graphs

Diagrams are useful when you want to explain some process. If you were to talk about the basic operation of a spring motor or an internal-combustion engine, a schematic diagram would help to show the relationships among the various parts and functions of the object under discussion. See Figure 6.1.

Graphs provide a means for showing relationships among statistical data, such as the yearly crime rate, the federal government's tax collections, or the increasing school population. Such graphs are generally of three types. *A line graph* will give the viewer an idea of a general trend over a period of time. A *bar graph* shows comparative quantities clearly where the comparison is among a relatively small number of

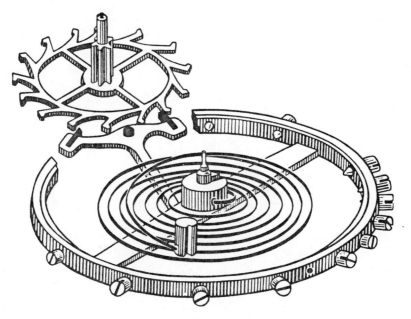

Figure 6.1. A simple diagram that can be enlarged for viewing by an audience or shown by a projector. (Courtesy of the Hamilton Watch Company.)

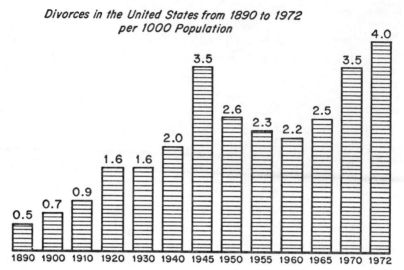

Figure 6.2. A bar graph made from data compiled by the National Center for Health Statistics. Most graphs published in books, reports, and magazines require redesign to make them satisfactory as visual aids for speakers. This one is relatively simple and clear; it could be enlarged for easel display or projected on a screen.

years, companies, nations or what have you. It is simple to make. Figure 6.2 shows a bar graph.

A *pie graph* is useful for showing how the parts of a whole are divided. See Figure 6.3.

2. Maps and Globes

Maps will frequently help to explain geographical relationships. Globes are ordinarily less useful than maps because of the distance that is likely to separate you from your audience. If listeners are gathered about you, a globe may be useful; otherwise, a globe is difficult for all to see and for you to use. When you need to give particular emphasis to the shape of the earth and to the relationships which are brought about because of that shape, a globe becomes a functional visual aid.

3. Pictures

It is not always true that "a picture is worth a thousand words" because a picture has a particular disadvantage which graphs and maps do not have. Whether it is a drawing, a painting, or a photo-

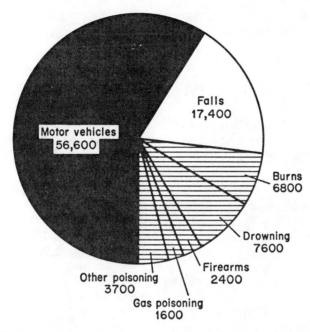

Figure 6.3. A pie graph showing principal types of accidental death in 1965–1970. When these aids are used for wall display or projection, the sections should be clearly distinguished by color or by strong contrasting shading. This graph was prepared from 1970 data of the National Center for Health Statistics.

graph, whether it is shown directly or projected as a slide, a picture necessarily encompasses a narrower scope of material than a graph or diagram. Furthermore, it does not make comparisons and contrasts immediately comprehensible as do graphs. A picture becomes most useful when it portrays an object that is unfamiliar to an audience.

4. Models and Actual Objects

When you want to explain some object, displaying the object itself or a model of it during the speech will help an audience visualize what you are saying. Like pictures, however, these visual aids often seem more useful than they actually are. The mere presence of an object does not make its explanation more clear. To explain the aerodynamic principle of lift, a diagram of an airplane wing showing lines of air flow is probably more illustrative than a small model of an airplane. If you wanted to explain the functioning of the *f* stop and the time mechanism on a camera, you could do a better job with a diagram than with the actual camera because the latter is so small that the members of the audience couldn't see it nearly as well.

B. Principles for the Use of Visual Aids

A little common sense is about all you really need to use visual aids properly. Here are some common-sense principles to keep in mind when you design and use visual aids.

1, The visual aid must be large enough to be easily seen by all the members of the audience. If it is too small, it is of no help.

2. Talk to the audience and not to the aid.

3. Your language should be as vividly descriptive as if there were no model, map, or diagram. The visual aid should support your language and not be a substitute for language.

4. Avoid blocking the audience's view of the visual aid.

5. Be sure that the visual aid has only enough detail to make your point. The visual aid should be as simple as it is practical.

6. The visual aid should be at the intellectual level of the audience. Clarifying notations that the audience would already know should be omitted.

7. The relationships among various items on the visual aid should be clearly indicated.

8. The visual aid should be an integral part of the speech. Avoid using pictures, models, and the like unless they clearly add to the clarity of your main idea. Remember, an attractive visual aid that is not related to the main purpose of the speech will do much to draw attention away from the speech.

9. In using a blackboard for diagrams to be made during the speech, you must draw well enough to get a favorable response from your diagrams and you must be sure that you don't take too much time doing it.

10. When you are finished with your visual aid, put it out of view of the audience. Otherwise, it will be a continuing distraction.

SUMMARY

Effective speaking is interesting and clear. Supporting materials supply clarity and interest by helping an audience visualize ideas concretely and specifically. In all speaking, the supporting materials are of four types: (1) definition, (2) statements about facts—examples and statistics, (3) opinion about facts—testimony, and (4) comparison and contrast.

The materials selected for a speech should be suited to the general end; they should be accurate; they should be of such quality and quantity that they satisfy the expectations of the audience.

You can also add to the effectiveness of your speech by visual aids. Most visual aids can be classified as diagrams and graphs (among which are the line, bar, and pie graphs), maps and globes, pictures, and models and actual objects. The rules for using visual aids are largely matters of common sense. Keep these points in mind:

1. Make the aid large enough.
2. Speak to the audience, not to the aid.
3. Continue to use descriptive language; the aid is not a substitute.
4. Avoid blocking the view of the members of the audience.
5. Try to keep the aid as simple as possible but be sure to use enough detail to cover all the points that must be covered.
6. Keep the aid at the intellectual level of the audience.
7. Indicate relationships clearly.
8. Make the aid an integral part of the speech.
9. Take special care with preparation and practice if you plan to use the blackboard for visual aids.
10. When you are finished with the aid, put it out of sight of the audience.

QUESTIONS

1. What are the two major requirements that speech materials must meet?
2. Why do some words require definition while others do not?
3. What are the two basic requirements of a good definition?
4. What is a logical definition?
5. Explain three other kinds of definitions.
6. Differentiate among real, secondary, and hypothetical examples.
7. What three questions are asked as tests of examples that are used to prove?
8. Explain how statistics can be made clear and interesting.
9. How should you test the statistics you use?
10. What value does testimony have in a speech?
11. What two questions should be asked in evaluating testimony?
12. Explain comparison and contrast.
13. Explain the nature of the different kinds of diagrams and graphs mentioned in the text.

14. What is the potential disadvantage to using models?

15. The text lists 10 principles for the use of visual aids. Which 5 do you consider most important?

EXERCISES

1. Develop a one-point speech in which you support that one point with at least one instance each of three of the four different types of supporting material.

2. From one of the other classes you are enrolled in, select a term you had never heard before. Define that term in a brief logical definition and by three other methods of definition. Decide which of the four methods has given the clearest explanation of the term. Decide which method was the least clear. Why do you think the one method is better than the other for defining this term?

3. Make a survey of opinion among some group of students on campus. For instance, what do the men at the Phi Kappa Tau fraternity house think about rock and roll? What generalization can you make from the statistics?

4. Develop three hypothetical examples, each of which has "the characteristics of a real example." Indicate the point the hypothetical examples would be used to support.

5. In *Vital Speeches of the Day* or in *Representative American Speeches* find speeches that illustrate the use of:

operational definition   statistics
extended example   comparison and contrast
testimony (direct and
    indirect quotations)

6. Prepare a 5-minute informative speech in which you use visual aids to clarify the main purpose of the speech. Be sure that the speech you choose needs visual aids and that the aids are essential to the whole speech, not to just a part of it.

Chapter 7

Supporting Material: Sources

One of the nearly infallible ways you can destroy your effectiveness is to be inadequately informed about the subject of a speech. No matter what your purpose is—to inform, to persuade—if you are to achieve that purpose, your audience must judge you to be competent, to be worth listening to. Ignorance of your subject is one of the really great offenses you can commit against your audience. No matter what the subject, audience, or occasion, by appearing before a group, you profess to have something to say. Unless you know what you are talking about, you can hardly expect the audience to pay much attention to you. To have your audience believe you are worth listening to, you must supply yourself with supporting materials of a kind and to a degree adequate to the demands of the audience and the subject.

Making an audience identify its thoughts, feelings, attitudes, and beliefs with the purpose of a speech is rarely a simple task. A mature, resourceful speaker and a person of good judgment will not, therefore, leave any avenue untraveled in the search for clear and interesting material. The preceding chapter considered the kinds of material that are useful to a speaker and discussed the ways in which they are used.

This chapter examines some of the more useful sources of this material and the tools for discovering it.

I. PERSONAL EXPERIENCE

No other person can look back to precisely the same set of experiences you have had. Your life, the things you have done, and the things that have happened to you are unique when they are viewed as a whole. This uniqueness in your own personal experience has important implications for your speaking. First, there are some things that you know more about than anyone else. This special knowledge alone qualifies you to speak authoritatively about some subjects. A second consideration, however, qualifies the usefulness of your unique knowledge: Not merely have no two persons had identical experiences; indeed, very few of your experiences have been shared by everyone. Consequently, that which is most valuable in your experience, its uniqueness, is also the most difficult to communicate. Successful communication demands a common ground of shared experience in order to bring about identification between you and an audience. Although you may, for example, know more about automobiles, teenage language habits, or ice hockey than any member of your audience, you can use your own personal experiences in communicating this knowledge to others only if you help your audience to interpret these experiences in the light of their own personal and unique backgrounds.

Good speakers sense readily which of their own experiences are common to other people. When they draw on these common experiences and interpret them intelligently, they achieve clarity and create interest through this common bond. If you recognize both the advantages and the limitations of personal experience as a source of supporting material, you can use this kind of material to bring clarity and interest to what you say. You can go back into your own past and select material that makes it possible for you to explain your ideas with the accuracy and precision of immediate knowledge. If you draw on your own experience, you can select material that helps an audience to perceive your ideas in concrete form. Anyone who has worked on an assembly line has absorbed countless minute details that could never come secondhand. Vivid recollection of these details can supply material that would not be available from the most meticulous research.

II. SECONDARY EXPERIENCE

The knowledge gained from examining what others have thought and done can be called secondary experience. Such information is necessary because frequently people must speak on subjects with which they do not have direct personal experience. Many have not been Blacks, Jews, Catholics, forest rangers, United States senators, or social workers. Consequently, personal experience must be supplemented by examining the experience of others.

When you do not find in your own background some personal experience to lend vividness to your ideas, you can draw from what someone else has written or said an experience that *could* have happened to anyone, including every member of an audience. This kind of supporting material brings clarity to your ideas because it brings them within the comprehension of the listener. It adds interest to the speech because it has the immediacy of direct, personal experience.

Being dependent upon others for information, however, is always a potential danger. Some of the difficulties of audience acceptance that arise in using secondary experience as speech material have been discussed in the preceding chapter. The further point is to be made here that even when you choose speech materials carefully, the definitions, examples, statistics, and testimony you gather from sources outside your experience are always subject to bias. No matter how meticulous you may be in trying to maintain an objective attitude toward a subject (and this you will seldom be able to do), the external sources you consult are as susceptible as you are to personal bias.

It is extremely doubtful that all bias can be removed from any extended discourse. The very fact that you *select* the material you use, elect to use one datum and to dispense with another, automatically builds into a speech an inescapable bias. Even reports appearing in the news magazines and newspapers, theoretically intended to present an objective statement of newsworthy events, often demonstrate the editorial bias of the publication in which they appear. The evil in bias lies not in its being present but in its not being recognized. In order to detect the bias that will almost necessarily be present even in the writing and speaking of those who are concerned with what they say, study many sources of information.

Beyond the need to be on the lookout for the bias of any source of information you consult, using the experiences and ideas of others for speech material requires you to evaluate what you hear and read. You must learn to listen and read with maturity and judgment. To be ill-informed may be even worse than to be uninformed.

When they are thoughtfully evaluated and properly used, secondary materials will form a good basis for helping a listener to identify himself with your ideas. Remembering that secondary experience must have the vividness and the immediacy of direct personal experience, we present some of the ways in which this kind of supporting material can be found.

A. Conversations and Interviews

The conversations you have with friends will frequently provide material for a speech. Even the ideas with which you disagree can be useful; they may be examples of concepts prevalent in our society.

Frequently you will know of some expert, perhaps a faculty member or someone in the business community, who can help you to understand a more complex subject. You may be surprised to discover how willing people are to help you. Remember, their fields of specialization are important to them and they are usually pleased to know that they are of interest to others. Faculty members, for instance, feel a bit flattered when students ask for help in finding materials.

When you solicit information from others, however, it is wise to be sure you know what you want to ask. Begin thinking seriously about your subject sometime in advance. Do some reading before you approach the person you want to interview. Arrange an appointment. Say what you will need to know, and the limits of the subject you intend to speak about. Give the person you interview time to think about your questions. Then, when you have the interview, be prepared to ask specific questions. These will form the framework of the interview. You can expect to be disappointed with an interview that begins like this: "What can you tell me about electronics? I gotta give a speech tomorrow."

B. Radio, Television, and Lectures

Radio and television programs can be valuable sources of speech material. You will find, however, that gathering useful data from broadcasts is more difficult than gathering them from an interview. The major problem, of course, is that you can't ask questions. Accordingly, you must be more careful in listening and in taking any notes you may want to keep for future reference.

In many instances, radio and television programs offer data that would otherwise be unavailable. It is not likely that a college student could approach the U.S. president, for instance, and ask him for his views on the relations of this country with the Soviet Union, or federal aid to education, or government support of a program of medical care for aged citizens. Yet the president's views are often communicated to the nation at large over radio and television. Some statements made under these circumstances will not appear in print, since many newspapers do not report the complete text of speeches broadcast on radio or television.

To make the most of an opportunity to gather speech materials from broadcasts requires much the same kind of preplanning that is done for interviews. You may discover that the Egyptian ambassador is appearing on a public affairs broadcast. Because you are preparing a speech in which the background of Arab-Israeli conflict is pertinent, you will plan to listen. If you have some early planning in your speech, you will know the kinds of things to listen for.

Public lectures, not broadcast, are information sources less often available than broadcasts, but their content is often especially valuable. Even college lectures may supply excellent speech material.

Note taking is an important skill to acquire. Anyone who can write can take notes of one sort or another. Taking good notes requires not only the ability to listen well, but it also demands some general background in the subject at hand. Otherwise, it is difficult to make a proper distinction between what is essential and what is not. Indiscriminately made notes are either unnecessarily voluminous because they are filled with unimportant data, or they are too sketchy because the notetaker fails to put down important facts.

A pracice that is helpful in taking notes is to keep paper and pencil near at hand. Some people carry a notebook with them at all times so that they can jot down ideas as they occur. In this way, otherwise vagrant and fleeting thoughts, references, examples, and quotations can be captured and preserved.

C. The Library

By far the richest source of speech materials (indeed, of knowledge of all kinds) is a well-supplied library. Yet for many students a library is like a lost gold mine of fabulous wealth. They want the gold and are willing to work to dig it out, but they can't find the lode. A few nuggets fall into their hands by chance, but the real riches are never uncovered.

Each library has a systematic method of cataloguing and arranging materials, and these methods must become familiar to the one who uses the library. If you do not understand the card catalog, the use of indexes, or the numbering system in your library, ask a librarian to explain them to you. Librarians are glad to help. Remember that librarians are much more than persons who charge out books and collect fines when they are overdue. They are in a very real sense teachers and are professionally trained for their jobs. They will be glad to help you find specific pieces of information and to help you familiarize yourself with the resources of the library.

We make some general suggestions about how to find speech materials in the library. It would be virtually impossible to list every available source, but we can provide a functional classification of basic materials.

III. USING THE LIBRARY

A. The Card Catalog

Much of the material you will use in making speeches will be found in books. The card catalog is a device for locating these books. It is an alphabetically arranged collection of cards, listing such bibliographical data as title, author, publisher, date of publication, and other pertinent data. Every book is entered in the catalog with an author card. All but the most general are represented by a title card as well, and these cards will be alphabetically arranged. For nonfiction books, one or more subject entries will also be found.

When you use the card catalog and cannot immediately find what you want, look for additional cross references. If you wanted to explain why President Roosevelt kept the atomic bomb a secret from Vice-president Truman, you might look not only under such obvious headings as "Franklin D. Roosevelt," "Harry S. Truman," and "atomic bomb," but under such others as "World War—1939—1945," and "U.S. —Politics and Government."

B. Special Reference Tools

In addition to the general book collection, a library contains many other sources of information. Among these are standard reference works, magazines, newspapers, pamphlets, and government documents. You will probably find yourself using these sources in preparing speeches at least as much as you use the general book collection, but you may know less about them and their indexes than you do about using the card catalog for finding information in books. For this reason we have devised six main categories of information that student speakers usually need, and have provided brief explanations of where and how such information is most likely to be found.

1. For Basic Facts and Statistics

The *World Almanac*, the *Information Please Almanac*, and a number of other such volumes give a vast amount of specific information. The *Statistical Abstract of the United States* provides quantitative summary statistics (usually covering 15 to 20 years) on the political, social, and industrial organization of the United States. The *Statesman's Yearbook* gives statistics and facts on matters that concern the government. *Facts on File* is a weekly synopsis of world events which, with its index, becomes a ready reference for a variety of information. The *Congressional Quarterly* gives a synopsis of federal legislation and the voting records of senators and representatives.

2. For Brief Authoritative Articles

For an introductory discussion of a subject, you should go first to an encyclopedia. General encyclopedias such as the *Britannica* and the *Americana* give information on all phases of human knowledge, and their articles usually include bibliographies to suggest further study. The *Britannica* is widely considered the best general reference in the humanities, while the *Americana* is thought to be stronger in the areas of science and technology.

Specialized encyclopedias are available for more thorough treatment of a subject. To list a representative group, we may mention encyclopedias of *The Social Sciences, Religion and Ethics, World History, Banking and Finance,* and *The Arts and Sports*. Van Nostrand–Reinhold's *Scientific Encyclopedia*, Grove's *Dictionary of Music and Musicians*, and the *Dictionary of American History* supply information in the specific areas their titles name.

3. For More Extensively Developed Articles

Magazines will probably be your greatest source of current information. The most common index of such material is the *Reader's Guide to Periodical Literature*. It indexes a large number of popular periodicals from 1900 to the present. Its entries are arranged in much the same fashion as the card catalog.

Except for the card catalog, the *Reader's Guide* is probably the most used index in the library, but its limitations are too frequently overlooked. Because it indexes only popular magazines, it is of limited usefulness in investigating more specialized topics. There are too many specialized indexes to permit a complete enumeration here, but we list some that should prove useful. The *Social Science and Humanities Index* (formerly the *International Index*) is an author and subject index to the scholarly journals in the social sciences and humanities. The *Applied Science and Technology Index* (formerly part of the *Industrial Arts Index*) lists articles on business administration, public administration, and economics. The *Public Affairs Information Service* indexes a wide variety of books, periodicals, public documents, and mimeographed material in government, sociology, and business. The *Agricultural Index*, the *Education Index*, the *Art Index*, and the *Music Index* catalog periodical literature in their special fields.

The *New York Times* through its index is an especially useful source of information on current events. This paper prints complete texts of speeches and documents of public interest. Its treatment of news items is ordinarily more extensive than that found in other newspapers and in the news magazines. Most libraries subscribe to the paper and keep it on microfilm. The *New York Times Index* locates specific items in the paper and is an excellent reference tool.

4. For Biography

Current Biography is a publication that gives short useful biographies of living persons. A wide variety of *Who's Who* books give brief biographical sketches. Webster's *Biographical Dictionary* contains very brief biographies of a great number of distinguished persons of all times. The *Dictionary of American Biography* sketches the lives of prominent Americans, and the *Dictionary of National Biography* includes data on the lives of notable Englishmen. Moreover, all of the specialized encyclopedias mentioned earlier contain biographical studies.

The *Biographic Index* is helpful in locating more extended biographies. It is cross-referenced according to the profession or occupation as well as the name of the personages listed; it indexes biographical periodical articles as well as books.

5. For Dates

Dictionaries will supply many of the dates you will need. The *World Almanac* has a chronological listing of the events of the year previous to its publication. The *New York Times Index* provides the data of events reported in the newspapers.

6. For Quotations

John Bartlett's *Familiar Quotations* is the best-known source of short quotations. It is arranged chronologically by authors and has a fine index of topics as well. Another source of quotations, Burton E. Stevenson's *Home Book of Quotations,* contains a larger number of entries than Bartlett's book. It is arranged by topics.

IV. METHODS OF RECORDING MATERIAL

The information you wish to consider for your speech should be collected on cards or slips of paper, about 4×6 inches. It is perfectly satisfactory to cut 8½×11 sheets of paper into four pieces and use these, or you can buy cards at any bookstore. Four items of information should be entered on these cards: (1) a label to identify the material, (2) the author, (3) the information you wish to use, and (4) the necessary bibliographical data. If you prepare note cards carefully, you will need to check the original source only once.

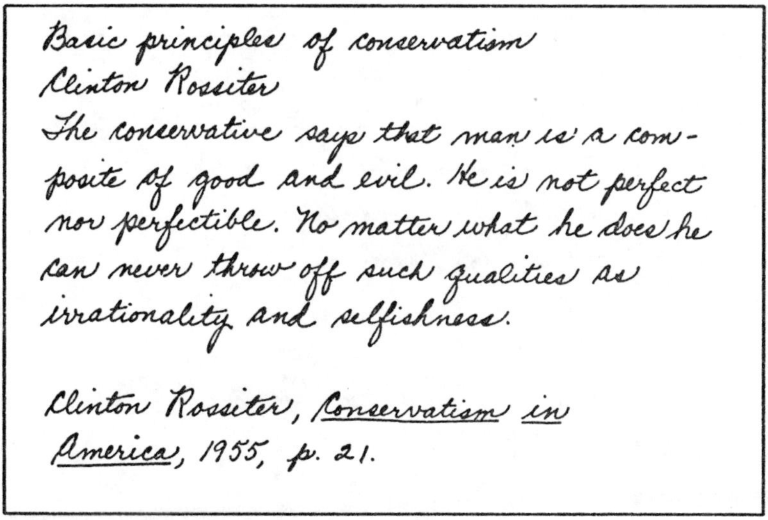

Basic principles of conservation
Clinton Rossiter
The conservative says that man is a composite of good and evil. He is not perfect nor perfectible. No matter what he does he can never throw off such qualities as irrationality and selfishness.

Clinton Rossiter, *Conservatism in America,* 1955, p. 21.

Figure 7.1. A note card to record an author's idea in words other than his.

141

Three useful kinds of cards are illustrated by examples as Figures 7.1, 7.2, and 7.3.

Because the information you gather from all the sources we have listed may eventually find its way into the outline of your speech, you

> Natural tendency of our economic life is to combination - Justice Oliver Wendell Holmes
> "It is plain from the slightest consideration of practical affairs, or the most superficial reading of industrial history, that free competition means combination, and that the organization of the world, now going on so fast, means an ever increasing might and scope of combination. It seems to me futile to set our faces against this tendency. (over)

> Whether beneficial on the whole, as I think it, or detrimental, it is inevitable, unless the fundamental axioms of society, and even the fundamental conditions of life, are to be changed."
>
> Catherine Drinker Bowen, Yankee from Olympus, 1945, p. 330.

Figure 7.2. A note card recording the exact words of the source material.

---

*Divorces in the United States from 1890 to 1972 per 1000
population, National Center for Health Statistics*

1890 – 0.5	1950 – 2.6
1900 – 0.7	1955 – 2.3
1910 – 0.9	1960 – 2.2
1920 – 1.6	1965 – 2.5
1930 – 1.6	1970 – 3.5
1940 – 2.0	1972 – 4.0
1945 – 3.5	

World Almanac, 1974, p. 1016

Figure 7.3. A note card recording factual data from the *World Almanac,*
a secondary source. The primary source is also recorded: The National
Center for Health Statistics. (Note that this is the card from which the bar
graph in Chapter 6 was made.)

will want to make it as easy as possible to handle. Putting each item
on a separate card makes it easy to rearrange the sequence of cards
without excessive rewriting or checking back to your notes. When the
rough draft of your outline has been prepared, you can decide where
the data on each card properly fit into the outline. When you use note
cards in this manner, much of the work in preparing an outline is done
automatically, painlessly, and easily.

SUMMARY

The supporting materials for a speech are found in one or the other
of two main sources of information: personal experience or the experience of others. The latter, also called secondary experience, comes
partly from talking with others in conversations and interviews, and
from listening to lectures or to programs on radio or television. By far
the most fruitful source of secondary speech material is the vast collection of data to be found in any good library. The card catalog, a great
variety of published indexes, and a large number of standard reference works, both general and special, offer an almost unlimited supply
of valuable material.

The items of information that you gather are entered on cards for ease of handling. From these, they may be transferred to the final outline of your speech. With the kind of material that will come to hand when you look diligently and prepare conscientiously, you can make sure that your speeches will show you know what you are talking about. Then you can claim the right to speak and can expect the respectful attention of an audience.

QUESTIONS

1. What is the value of your own experience as a source for supporting material?
2. What is secondary experience?
3. Can a speaker give an unbiased speech?
4. Explain how to go about setting up and conducting an interview.
5. On what basis are books classified in a card catalog?
6. Where would you go to learn basic facts and statistics?
7. What is the value of an encyclopedia?
8. Where are magazines indexed?
9. Draw up a sample note card that records an idea.

EXERCISES

1. Develop a 3- to 5-minute speech in which the supporting materials are based on personal experience.
2. Develop a 3- to 5-minute speech in which the supporting materials have been collected in interviews.
3. Answer the following questions using the sources available in the library:
   (a) Where does the following passage appear in the King James Bible? "He that is slow to anger is better than the mighty; and he that ruleth his spirit than he that taketh a city."
   (b) What are the title, publisher, and date of publication of a book about persuasion by Wallace C. Fotheringham?
   (c) What was the date of the first landing on the moon?
   (d) What was the population of Baltimore in the 1970 census?
   (e) Who said, "Error of opinion may be tolerated where reason is left free to combat it."
   (f) Whom did John Connally support for the presidency in 1972?

(g) Where did Edward Kennedy get his undergraduate education?

(h) What football team won the Rose Bowl game in 1973?

(i) How would you briefly describe the California condor?

I. Persuasion occurs on rational and extrarational grounds
II. Probability and proof
III. The structure of argument
    A. Deduction
    B. Induction
IV. The Aristotelian model of rhetorical argument
    A. Deduction in persuasion—enthymeme
       1. Argument from sign
       2. Argument from cause
       3. Distinguishing between sign and cause
    B. Induction in persuasion—example
       1. Argument by generalization
       2. Argument by analogy
V. The Toulmin model of substantive argument
VI. Avoiding errors in arguments
    A. Fallacies
    B. Refutation
       1. Testing sign relationships
       2. Testing causal relationships

Chapter 8

The Argumentative Dimension of Communication

Consider two men, neighbors, living side by side for years in friendship and harmony. Assume that these two men hold opinions which make them almost as different as men can be. One drives a Chevrolet; the other prefers a Ford. One is a Dodger fan; the other supports the Braves. The one is a Republican; the other a Democrat. They belong to different churches. One owns his own small business; the other works for wages and, at the place where he is employed, is a union shop steward.

In spite of their thoroughly differing views on these and many other subjects, two such persons might spend years in quite close contact as friends, neighbors, colleagues, or business associates without a word of controversy. The many differences between them will persist without being a source of controversy, however, only as long as neither of them is motivated to change an opinion of the other so that it agrees with his own. At whatever moment either of the two feels the necessity for concurrence between them, passive difference becomes active disagreement.

Noise, wrangling, and ill temper have come to be so closely associated with argument that it is frequently identified with quarreling. Certainly, the effort to resolve differences can be carried on in an atmosphere of harsh, angry words and raised voices, but these are not necessary to disagreement; they are not constituents of argument.

Arguing is what you do when you want to "prove" something, when you try to bring about concurrence with your views by stating and defending the position you hold. The expression you use to state your position is called a proposition. We have already discussed (Chapter II) the three kinds of propositions that may be advocated: propositions of fact, value, and policy. Each of these says what the speaker believes to be the proper answer to the corresponding kind of question. Each of them requires justification, for merely expressing an attitude or a belief does not always make it acceptable to others. The process of defending a proposition, of getting it accepted by an audience, is called *argumentation*. In order to create belief in a proposition, a speaker advances arguments to support it. An argument may be defined as *a statement or a group of statements intended to support a proposition*.

But let us say a word at this point about what it means to support a proposition. People often talk of "proving" propositions. But the word *prove* or *proof* can be misleading. To prove a mathematical theorem is something different from proving that the state of Indiana is a great place in which to live.

The difference between the two situations is best understood by distinguishing two different kinds of propositions: The first of these is called *analytic*. You could say, for example, that every angle of a triangle must be less than 180°. Whatever you may mean by such a statement must be understood in relation to what you mean by triangle. But the meanings you have for the word triangle (for example, that the sum of its angles is 180°) are such that if you understand the statement, you know it must be true. And that is what we mean by saying that a statement is analytic: To understand it is to know that it is true. To deny the truth of the statement would be a contradiction.

Other propositions are *synthetic*. These are not necessarily true; they need to be verified. "There are more registered Democrats than Republicans in California." "The quarterback is the most important member of a football team." And so on, to include any proposition that might normally be the subject of a controversy.

Now, notice the difference between these statements and the kind we have called analytic. To decide that we understand a synthetic statement does not require us to admit that it is true. If we understand that the sum of the angles of a triangle is 180°, we would contradict ourselves by denying that any one angle must be less than 180°. On the other hand, to affirm or deny the statement that the quarterback is the most valuable member of a football team may be either correct or incorrect; it may agree or disagree with whatever evidence exists or with whatever meanings we have for "quarterback," but nothing in the form of the statement makes a denial of it an inherent contradiction. From what we have said about analytic and synthetic statements, it is clear that the following statement is analytic: The propositions of persuasive speeches are synthetic.

Even though the propositions of persuasive speeches are synthetic (and, therefore, require justification), many propositions of policy, of value, and of fact cannot be evidenced as *true*. Many of these, nonetheless, are *believed*. What the arguments of persuasive communication are intended to do, then, is to *create belief*.

I. PERSUASION OCCURS ON RATIONAL AND EXTRARATIONAL GROUNDS

Suppose that you believe that segregationist attitudes are diminishing in the South, or that our deficit in the international balance of payments is the most serious economic problem America faces today, or that the United States should sponsor the creation of a World Energy Commission. If you set out to persuade others to agree with you, you would find in your audience beliefs, attitudes, and values that are in conflict with your own. These conflicting positions in the audience, however, are not based entirely upon rational grounds. The fact that we can believe a proposition which we cannot know is true, and the fact that we can be led to this belief by what someone else says, clearly indicate that there must be grounds for belief other than reason alone.

Human beings have needs, wants, and desires that significantly influence the decisions they make about what to do and the judgments they make about what is good or bad and true or false. But even though human beings do make decisions impulsively, led by their desires, by their prejudices, or by the persuasiveness of others, still they like to believe that their positions are "rational." For one thing, they have been taught that in our society it is proper, when considering serious matters, to be "logical" not "emotional." The arguments of persuasion, therefore, must meet the demand for satisfaction on both rational and extrarational grounds that seem to form the basis for most of what people believe and do: Arguments perform motivational as well as rational functions. Note carefully, however, that we are speaking not of what arguments *are* but of what they *do*. To think of one argument as rational and another as motivational, or to call one argument "logical" and another "emotional" is sheer nonsense. All arguments, in varying proportions, have both properties. It is a matter of *convenience* that we look at the argumentative and motivational dimensions of communication in separate chapters. Our purpose in the present chapter is to examine the argumentative dimension of human discourse.

II. PROBABILITY AND PROOF

Under ideal conditions the arguments you use to persuade would constitute conclusive proof of your proposition. Actual conditions are such, however, that conclusive proof is an unobtainable goal. If certainty were available, persuasion would not be needed, for investigation would bring knowledge and we cannot disbelieve what we know with certainty to be true. Thus the subjects of persuasive speeches will have at least two sides. Is a factual judgment true or false? Does a person or condition have an alleged merit or lack it? Should a proposed policy be adopted or rejected? Any answer to questions such as these is likely to be controversial. When it is, it will be because the evidence on both sides is so limited and so divided that clear-cut decision is difficult. Consequently, proof in persuasion will not have the force of logical or mathematical demonstration. That is to say, proof will not be absolute, for no matter how firmly a conviction may be held, there is always the possibility that it may be wrong.

But on the other hand, it is not enough to prove only that a proposition *can* be true. An audience may readily agree that a candidate elected from one political party *might* be more beneficial to the country in the presidency than the candidate from another. But an honestly concerned voter will usually want stronger grounds than "can" or "might" to vote for either candidate. Therefore, a speaker's efforts in persuasion are aimed at proving that a proposition is *probably* true. An audience looks at the two sides of a given proposition, recognizes that there is evidence and argument on both sides, and then gives its assent to the side that seems to have the weight of probability in its favor.

In demonstrating the probability of a proposition, "making a case for it," there is a wide range in the strength the case may have. The proposition can be made to seem only plausible; that is, the audience can agree that there is some reason to believe it might be true. A stronger case is one that shows that the proposition is likely to be true. The stronger the likelihood, the stronger the case. An audience is completely satisfied when a case is so strong that the proposition can be accepted as *true*. In these instances, listeners feel that the proposition is more than likely, that it has more than a good chance of being true. They are convinced; they believe: for them, the proposition is true. They may shift their position later, or new evidence may prove them wrong; but at the moment the decision is reached, they are convinced that the speaker's proposition is true.

To win such a reaction from an audience is a goal you should not hope to achieve on every occasion, from every audience, or from every member of any given audience. An audience's reactions are not dichotomous—it will not accept or reject your position in such a degree of black or white. Instead, listeners tend to respond along a continuum of shades of gray. That is to say, instead of expecting an audience to fall into two clearly distinguishable groups, those who agree and those who disagree, you must see that your task is to shift belief in the direction you advocate. Thus "possibility," "plausibility," "likelihood," and "assurance" are all reasonable goals for you to seek, depending on your particular audience. Consequently, when you face an audience hostile to your position, your speaking can be called successful if you produce only a measure of indecision in your listeners' devotion to their opposing point of view.

III. THE STRUCTURE OF ARGUMENT

It is not totally unreasonable to define logic in rhetorical arguments as anything that makes a listener think, "That's logical." And since proof is in the mind of the listener, the definition is indisputable. Thus arguments in rhetoric need to be perceived as valid because that will make them more persuasive. But rhetorical arguments are *substantive*. In evaluating the great bulk of them, the criterion of validity, in the formal and technical sense in which logicans use the term, simply does not apply. When the source of an argument makes a claim "certain" in the mind of a receiver, the receiver does not have *logical* certainty. Thus the danger that some crook may lead us astray with phoney arguments is an obvious reality. Perhaps most important for you to remember, then, is that your communication has effects. You are changing the way people view the world and you have no right to influence anyone without the highest qualifications. In our culture, this means having the strongest possible evidence and the most rigorous reason. Reasoning, therefore, is considered to be an important element of rhetorical discourse. It is artificial, futile and even destructive, however, to impose upon substantive human communication the rules that govern inference in formal analytic logic. Instead, the important question should be, "To what extent is logic an engine for helping you to help an audience to reach the same reasoned, thoughtful, reflective, 'proved' conclusion you have come to?"

The part that logic plays in rhetorical argument is suggested by Bertrand Russell. He says in *The Analysis of Mind* that logic is not interested in what people actually believe but only in the conditions that determine the truth or falsehood of what they might believe. But because so many of the propositions that people do in fact believe cannot be proved true or false, logic has severe limitations as an instrument for determining whether the beliefs of people are right or wrong.

When you advocate acceptance of a proposition, then, you will present *arguments*, which are, as we have said, statements or groups of statements purporting to *justify* your position by giving your listeners *reasons to believe* what you say is *true*. But there is a difference between a "good reason" for, or a "justification" of a proposition, and "proof" of it in an absolute sense. The part logic plays in the process is not to determine whether what you say is in fact true but rather to determine whether your arguments embody adequate *rational* grounds for believing them to be true.

Every argument in persuasion performs an identifiable operation: It presents (or suggests) evidence and specifies the implications of that evidence. The common practice is to speak of the evidence as the "premises." The implications are stated in what is called the "conclusion."

Traditionally, arguments are considered to be of two types: deductive and inductive. For both kinds of arguments the claim is made that their premises provide evidence for the conclusion, that the conclusion follows from the premises. Only in the case of deductive argument, however, is the claim made that the premises provide *conclusive* evidence. In a properly formulated deductive argument, the conclusion follows *necessarily* from the premises. Inductive arguments are those whose premises offer *some* evidence of the truth of the conclusion. The degree to which the premises of an inductive argument support the conclusion will vary with the amount and quality of the evidence. In no case, however, will an inductive argument provide conclusive proof of the conclusion. Here is a brief examination of the structure of these two kinds of argument.

A. Deduction

We have said that a deductive argument is one whose premises are claimed to provide conclusive proof of the conclusion. This is not to say, however, that the conclusion of any deductive argument is necessarily true. It means merely that in a valid (that is, a properly constructed) deductive argument, the conclusion is necessarily implied by the premises. The premises of the argument may be true or untrue, and the argument itself may be valid or invalid. Only when the premises are true and the argument is valid must the conclusion be true.

Deductive arguments take several forms, among them, the one most commonly used to illustrate deduction is the categorical syllogism. You have surely seen the classic example that has been appearing in textbooks for perhaps 20 centuries:

> All humans are mortal.
> Socrates is human.
> Therefore, Socrates is mortal.

To illustrate the relationship between the premises and the conclusion of this syllogism, we first draw a large circle to represent *all mortal beings*. The circle is intended to include not only humans but all animals, birds, trees, insects, fish, and anything else that lives and is subject to death. Next, we represent *human* beings with a smaller circle inside the large one. The smaller circle has to be inside the larger because inductive experience has shown that people, as a class, do die and therefore are a part of the larger group. Finally, we come to the specific instance in the form of the individual, *Socrates*, whom we represent by a third circle. Since Socrates belongs to the class of human beings, this third circle must be inside the one representing that class. Diagrammed, the syllogism looks like the structure in Figure 8.1.

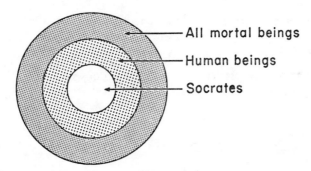

Figure 8.1. The categorical syllogism.

Immediately, it becomes evident that Socrates could not be classified as a human without at the same time being included in the group of mortals. It is easy to see why deduction is such an effective form of argument.

The categorical syllogism is only one of several forms the syllogism may have, and the syllogism is itself by no means the only form a deductive argument may take. Consequently, our discussion of deductive argument is merely illustrative. It is certainly not intended to be complete.

B. Induction

By inductive argument we mean this: From the fact that something is true of certain examined members of a class, the conclusion is drawn that the same thing will be true of unexamined members of that class also. The conclusion can be applied to an unlimited number of the unexamined members of the class. Thus induction is often a reasoning process that moves from particulars (or the less general) to the universal (or the more general). Another induction may extend the conclusion to a limited number of unexamined members of the class, for example, to the next one that appears. In this case, the induction moves from known particulars to a new unknown particular. The process of induction can be described as taking place in three steps:

1. *Isolated facts, conditions, or phenomena are experienced.* As an amateur entomologist, you collect various species of butterflies. The first butterfly you find proves to have a fine powder on its wings.

2. *Similarities appear among the specific instances that you examine.* Your second specimen is also seen to have a powdery substance on its wings. You observe that the same condition exists in all the butterflies that make up your collection.

3. *A conclusion is drawn.* You conclude that what has been true of all the butterflies you have found thus far will be true of butterflies in general, and that any butterfly you find in the future will have powder on its wings.

It is obvious that such a conclusion is no more than probable. Adding more and more evidence to support it does no more than increase the probability.

IV. THE ARISTOTELIAN MODEL OF RHETORICAL ARGUMENT

More than 2000 years ago, Aristotle observed that when speakers use arguments to prove a proposition, they use deductive and inductive reasoning in forms especially adapted to persuasion. To these forms he gave the names that students of rhetoric still use to label the different kinds of arguments found in persuasion. Rhetorical deductions he called *enthymemes*. Rhetorical inductions are termed *examples*. Here is a closer look at the way enthymemes (rhetorical deductions) and examples (rhetorical inductions) operate when they are used by a speaker to build proof.

A. Deduction in Persuasion—Enthymeme

When you use deductive inferences in persuasion, you may on occasion put your arguments into syllogistic form. Most often, you will not. Logically, a syllogism is an ordered structure of simple beauty, but stylistically, its formal and often stilted language leaves much to be desired. Speakers almost always put their arguments into the ordinary language of conversational speech. Instead of using complete syllogisms, you will state your deductions in an elided or abbreviated form. That is, you will omit whatever premises the audience can infer for itself and give only those parts of the argument that are necessary. The name "enthymeme" is given to deductive arguments that appear in this shortened form.

The reason for stating deductive arguments as enthymemes is mainly one of style. The attention and interest of an audience are so important and so elusive that you must do everything you can to retain both. If you force the audience to plod through every detailed step of your arguments, you will tire them, you will bore them, and often give the impression of talking down to them. Consequently, say only what must be said to make the argument clear. Whereas, however, speakers omit portions of arguments on *stylistic* grounds, listeners supply the missing premises for *rational* reasons. Thus a listener will supply whatever premise is needed to make an enthymeme seem rational.

According to Aristotle, who gave enthymemes their name, these arguments are not only abbreviated in structure but they have another very important characteristic: They are probable rather than certain proofs. Although it is true that the conclusion of a valid deductive argument follows necessarily from the premises, this says nothing about whether the conclusion is true. When speakers deliberate on policy decisions and on judgments of fact and value, the premises that provide evidence for their conclusions are themselves debatable. The conclusions of a deductive argument can never be more probable than the premises. The implication of this fact is illustrated by splendid clarity in Abraham Lincoln's refutation of an argument used by Stephen A. Douglas in one of their famous debates on the question of slavery in the United States. Lincoln said,

> Nothing in the constitution or laws of any state can destroy a right distinctly and expressly affirmed in the Constitution of the United States.
>
> The right of property in a slave is distinctly and expressly affirmed in the Constitution of the United States.
>
> Therefore, nothing in the Constitution or laws of any state can destroy the right of property in a slave.
>
> I believe that no fault can be pointed out in that argument; assuming the truth of the premises, the conclusion so far as I have capacity at all to understand it, follows inevitably. There is a fault in it as I think, but the fault is not in the reasoning; but the falsehood in fact is a falsehood of the premises. I believe that the right of property in a slave *is not* distinctly and expressly affirmed in the Constitution. . . .

Wendell Willkie, in his "Loyal Opposition" speech, delivered after his defeat for the presidency by Franklin Delano Roosevelt, defended the right of the minority to debate issues in those dangerous times just prior to World War II. Note that the premise upon which the argument depends, the assertion that any totalitarian idea should be rejected utterly, is not expressly stated. Instead, the speaker assumes that the audience will supply the missing assertion. Here is what Willkie said.

> It has been suggested that in order to present a united front to a threatening world, the minority should now surrender its convictions and join the majority. This would mean that in the United States of America there would be only one dominant party—only one economic philosophy—only one political philosophy of life. This is a totalitarian idea—it is a slave idea—it must be rejected utterly.

Willkie's argument not only illustrates the tendency of a speaker, for the sake of style, to elide deductive arguments, but it also exemplifies the second characteristic of the enthymeme: the fact that the proof it elicits is only probable. It is in no sense an absolute truth that any totalitarian idea should be rejected. Mr. Willkie could safely assume, however, that his audiences would accept the assertion as being probably true. Consequently, the argument was effective.

When you use deductive inferences in argumentation, they take the form of *argument from sign* or *argument from cause*.

1. Argument from Sign

In using argument from sign, you observe directly some fact or condition. Using this as evidence, you draw the conclusion that some other fact or condition, not immediately observable, is true. A good example of inference based on signs is medical diagnosis. In examining a patient, the doctor cannot directly observe the disease but, instead, looks for symptoms, a set of conditions that are directly observable. These symptoms are a set of signs from which the doctor can infer the presence of some disease.

Argument from sign may be thought of as deductive. It is always based on a generalization either explicit or implied, and can be put into syllogistic form. This generalization alleges a relationship between an observed sign and what it shows. It asserts that the observed phenomenon and the condition it signals always occur together, that the former does not occur without the latter. If the alleged relationship is accepted or believed by an audience, and if the condition taken as a sign is known or believed to exist, the conclusion follows without question.

Londoners of Shakespeare's day knew that they could see a play whenever a flag was raised over the Globe Theater. The presence of the flag was taken as a sign that a play would be presented. The conclusion is drawn from two premises: "A flag on the theater always signals the production of a play," and "The flag is flying." From these two propositions, the conclusion necessarily follows that a play is to be produced.

A student speaker, defending the proposition that the United States should continue to support UNESCO, contended that UNESCO has been instrumental in preserving art. In support of this contention, she offered these occurrences as signs that UNESCO has indeed labored to preserve works of art:

1. It advised the Austrian government on the restoration of a number of old paintings.
2. It helped Yugoslavia restore murals and frescos.
3. It advised Syria and Lebanon in their efforts to restore ancient monuments and archeological sites.
4. It helped Peru in the restoration of her historical monuments.

On December 8, 1941, the day after the Japanese attack on Pearl Harbor, Franklin Delano Roosevelt delivered the famous speech in which he asked the Congress to declare that a state of war existed between the United States and Japan. In that speech, the President said:

Yesterday, December 7, 1941—a date which will live in infamy—the United States of America was suddenly and deliberately attacked by naval and air forces of the Empire of Japan. . . .

Yesterday the Japanese Government also launched an attack against Malaya.

Last night Japanese forces attacked Hong Kong.

Last night Japanese forces attacked Guam.

Last night Japanese forces attacked the Philippine Islands.

Last night the Japanese attacked Wake Island.

This morning the Japanese attacked Midway Island.

Japan has, therefore, undertaken a surprise offensive extending throughout the Pacific area. The facts of yesterday speak for themselves.

The president was right—the signs of a Japanese surprise offensive were incontestable.

2. Argument from Cause

Every effect must have a cause, and no agent can properly be considered a cause unless it produces an effect. The two are inevitably associated. When an occurrence or condition is the direct result of an antecedent occurrence or condition, the relationship between them is said to be that of cause and effect. The one that exists prior in time and operates to bring about the other is said to be the cause. The one that exists as a direct result of the first is said to be the effect. Inferences based on causal reasoning appear either as arguments *from cause to effect* or as arguments *from effect to cause*.

1. *Cause to effect.* In a recent classroom speech, the speaker proposed that the state government should operate clinics to dispense narcotics at low cost to addicts. The speech contained these examples of argument from cause to effect: Lack of availability, plus the greed of peddlers, causes the price of narcotics to be high. High prices cause narcotics addiction to be very expensive. The expense of being an addict forces addicts to turn to crime for money to support their habit. The speaker argued further that the proposed clinics would reduce the cost of addiction, thus removing the cause of a large proportion of present-day crime, and would, at the same time, eliminate narcotics peddlers by removing their source of profit.

Do you remember Mark Antony's funeral oration over the body of Caesar? Shakespeare has Antony use this *cause-to-effect* argument.

It is not meet you know how Caesar loved you.
You are not wood, you are not stones, but men:
And, being men, hearing the will of Caesar
It will inflame you, it will make you mad.

Arguments of this kind move forward in time. That is, in reasoning from cause to effect, a speaker infers from one event or condition that a second event or condition will follow, the first being the cause, the second its result. This kind of reasoning is used to support an appeal for or against an increase in taxes, the choice of a person for public office, a program of disarmament, or any specified course of action.

2. *Effect to cause.* The second kind of argument from causal relation moves backward in time from a given condition and attempts to establish a probable cause. This kind of reasoning determines why the Roman Empire fell, why there has been a war, what causes juvenile delinquency, what causes a high divorce rate, or the cause of any other of the host of society's problems. Only an intelligent understanding of probable causes will permit more than temporary, symptomatic relief in any situation that demands improvement. Aspirin may stop a headache, but it will not stop the eyestrain that causes the headache. Not knowing that eyestrain is present may lead to effects even more serious than headaches.

In the British House of Commons, in 1780, Charles James Fox delivered a speech in which appears the following clear example of argument from effect to cause.

It is this cursed American war that has led us, step by step, into all our present misfortunes and national disgraces. What was the cause of our wasting forty millions of money, and sixty thousand lives? The American War! What was it that produced the French rescript and the French War? The American War! What was it that produced the Spanish Manifesto and Spanish War? The American War! What was it that armed forty thousand men in Ireland with arguments carried on the points of forty thousand bayonets? The American War! For what are we about to incur an additional debt of twelve or fourteen millions? This accursed, cruel, diabolical American War!

Patrick Henry used reasoning of this kind in the "Liberty or Death" speech that patriotic tradition attributes to him.

I ask . . ., sir, what means this martial array, if its purpose be not to force us to submission? Can gentlemen assign any other possible motive for it? Has Great Britain any enemy in this quarter of the world, to call for all this accumulation of navies and armies? No, sir, she has none. They are meant for us; they can be meant for no other.

3. Distinguishing Between Sign and Cause

Arguments from sign and from cause are often difficult to distinguish. For one reason, English has a limited number of logical connectives such as "because," "since," "hence," and "therefore." These or similar words are used to indicate argument and conclusions to argument regardless of whether you base your inferences on sign or on cause. Moreover, if argument from sign is to be effective, there must be some kind of causal relationship between two events when one is the sign of the other. Otherwise, signs are merely accidental.

An argument from sign is a way of knowing that a proposition is true. When you see a flock of geese pointing northward across the sky, you know that spring will soon be here. If a man buys a new car every year, wears expensive clothes, and lives in an exclusive section of town, you take these indications to mean he suffers no immediate lack of money. In each of these instances, the signs are interpreted to mean that the conclusion drawn from them *is* true. No attempt is made to say *why* it is true: why spring is coming or why the man in question is wealthy.

Arguments from cause, on the other hand, lend credibility to propositions by offering reasons that will explain *why* they are true. This kind of inference is a way of accounting for the existence of something.

The example of the physician's diagnosis helps to show the difference between these two forms of argument. When you are ill, the physician reasons from signs *that* you are ill. In order to know *why*, the doctor must look to the germ, virus, or condition that *caused* the illness. The major distinction, then, between arguments from sign and arguments from cause is in what they attempt to show. An argument from sign, making no use of causal relationships, attempts to show *that* a condition has existed, does exist, or will exist. An argument from cause assumes the condition and offers to explain *why* it is so.

B. Induction in Persuasion—Example

In describing the structure of inductive arguments, we said that their conclusions can be extended to either a limited or an unlimited number of unexamined members of a class. Each of these two possibilities serves as a basis for argument in persuasion. If the conclusion is unlimited in its extension, a generalization is made about the whole class. When you make such a generalization and offer evidence to sup-

160

port it, you use *argument by generalization.* When the conclusion to an induction is limited in its extension and is applied to some particular unexamined member of the class, you use *argument by analogy.*

1. Argument by Generalization

The generalizations you make in persuasion may be either true or false. For our purposes, it must be assumed that you yourself believe them to be true and that you would not otherwise bring them to bear in an argument. Many of the generalizations that are useful to you are propositions that an audience already holds to be true. Such propositions may vary widely, from the rashest kind of generalization to highly credible beliefs carefully distilled from intelligent interpretations of broad experience. But when an audience cannot be expected to know, understand, or readily accept propositions that are important because your arguments depend upon them, you may establish them inductively through argument by generalization.

Suppose that, in arguing against socialized medicine, you were to contend that the quality of medical service under such a system could always be expected to be poor. You might adduce a number of specific instances in which socialized medicine has afforded medical care of poor quality. On the basis of these specific instances, you would conclude that what is true of the known examples cited would be true of all other unexamined instances of socialized medicine, even those not yet in existence.

A large number of examples is not always necessary in effective rhetorical induction. It is quite possible that a single case in point might be sufficient to create belief in a proposition. In the example just cited, although there are several countries in which socialized medicine has been adopted as a policy, instead of listing a number of instances wherein the government pays the cost of medical care, you might develop an extended and detailed description of its failure in one specific place. It is evident that in drawing a universal conclusion from no more than one specific instance, there is grave danger of forming a hasty and untenable generalization. If such an argument is to have the desired persuasive force, it must be drawn from a carefully selected and well-developed example that an audience can easily accept as truly representative of the proposition it supports.

2. Argument by Analogy

Confusion sometimes arises over the term analogy because it is used in two ways: In the first sense, the word refers to the language device you may use to illustrate or clarify an unfamiliar idea by comparing it to a similar idea with which your audience is familiar. For example, you might say that the gills of a fish serve much the same purpose as the lungs of an animal, or that a world federation of nations would be quite like the United States in its political structure. An illustrative analogy has great merit not only for clarifying an idea, but also as a means of lending vividness to the idea. "We all know," said Emerson, "that as the human body can be nourished on any food, though it were boiled grass and the broth of shoes, so the human mind can be fed by any knowledge." To the extent that clarity and interest are necessary in any speech, an illustrative analogy may be useful in persuasion. It may also serve to create belief.

In a second sense, analogy is used to mean the reasoning process by which you argue that what is true of one specific instance will also be true of a similar specific instance. You need not learn to drive each of the makes of automobiles separately. Automobiles are enough alike in the way they operate for you to be able to move easily from one to another and drive it without learning how to operate each new one that comes along. Even if you learned to drive in a Chevrolet, and have driven only this one car, you know by analogy that you will be able to drive a Ford should the occasion arise.

An analogy draws a conclusion about two items, events, or conditions that belong to the same class. It is a prediction that because two things are alike in certain known respects, they can be expected to be alike in other respects where the similarity is as yet unknown. Using this kind of reasoning, you might argue that because socialized medicine has operated successfully in Great Britain it would operate successfully in the United States, or that since two cities are nearly equal in population, have similar kinds and amounts of industry, and are alike in other important respects, they may be expected to equal each other in say, wealth, or the number of children of school age, or some other point of comparison.

Franklin Delano Roosevelt used the following analogy in his "Arsenal of Democracy" speech, December 29, 1940.

Tonight, in the presence of a world crisis, my mind goes back eight years to a night in the midst of a domestic crisis. It was a time when . . . the whole banking system of our country had ceased to function. . . . I tried to convey to the great mass of American people what the banking crisis meant to them in their daily lives. Tonight I want to do the same thing, with the same people, in this crisis which faces America. We met the issue of 1933 with courage and realism. We face this new crisis—this new threat to the security of the nation—with the same courage and realism.

Suppose you were trying to prove that part-time students, taking all their classes at night, ought to meet the same rigorous standards set for day students. You might say: "Look at it this way. A swing-shift worker can't be any less capable and efficient than a fellow on the day shift. The work he turns out has to be just as good. What if you had a part-time job on the swing shift at Norco Aircraft? You wouldn't last a week if you did poor work there. If you ever told your boss the work you turn out shouldn't have to pass inspection because you're there only part time, how long do you think you'd last? Well, the same thing is true in school. The fact that you are a part-time student and take only late afternoon and evening classes doesn't mean you can get by with low quality work."

The chief benefit of drawing an inference by analogy is that it allows one to profit from experience; the chief danger lies in the fact that some important difference may have been overlooked in making the original comparison. The driver who has operated only late-model cars with automatic transmissions will not be able to drive a car with a standard shift solely on the basis of his earlier experience. The British system of socialized medicine can be expected to operate successfully in the United States only if the two countries are similar in respects that are important to government operation of a medical program.

It is clear, then, that an analogy is any argument of the form, "Event A is like Event B." One customarily hears the comment that all analogies are false. A more accurate appraisal would be that any analogy whatsoever may be true or false, but no one knows how to tell which is so. Any two events whatever have an infinite number of properties in common. To take two at random: Mariner XI and Miss America of 1975. What do these have in common? Among other things, both are more than 10 feet from the moon. Therefore, it is true to say that Mariner XI and Miss America of 1975 are alike (in this and an infinite number of other ways). But it is equally true to say that any two events are different in an infinite number of ways: Miss America of 1975 is, for example, closer to you than Mariner XI.

Consider the following as properties ascribed to two events:

Event A: $a\,b\,c\,.\,.\,j\,.\,.\,n$
Event B: $a\,b\,c\,.\,.\,.\,.\,.\,n$

Now pair the proper ties the two events have in common. It is reasoned that since Event A and Event B have properties *a, b, c, . . . n* in common, and since Event A has property *j*, then Event B has property *j* also. There is, however, no way of telling whether *j* is among the infinite number of properties the two events have in common or whether it is in the list of properties that Event A has and Event B lacks.

Now, someone is likely to say that it is silly to ascribe to Miss America the property of being more than 10 feet away from the moon. This statement is not so silly, however, as a property of Mariner XI. Nor does it seem so silly for Miss America to be closer to you than Mariner XI. The point is this: These are idiosyncratic judgments and are relative to the value system of the one who makes them. Hence an analogy says nothing about the events it compares but only about the person who makes it. Some similarities are significant; some are not. Some differences make a difference; some do not. The crucial problem in analogy, therefore, is in choosing events for comparison wherein you can specify a set of "significant" properties which the two have in common and whose differences are *not* "significant." Since this requires the judgment of some person, the probative value of any analogy depends upon the minds of the audience because they may regard what you consider to be significant similarities as trivial, or their few significant differences as important. Proof, as we have seen, is in the mind of the audience. A few years ago colleges were debating the topic of a guaranteed annual wage. A speaker used the following analogy to defend the contention that labor was unwise in demanding a guaranteed income.

The labor movement has made tremendous strides in this country since the pioneering days of Samuel Gompers. At the same time, labor has made many enemies who distrust unions as the weapon of the laboring man's greed. Right now, when the unions themselves are shot through with corruption, it would be foolish to demand a guaranteed annual wage. Do you remember the story of the dog with the bone? He saw his reflection in a pond. It looked to him as if the dog he saw had a bigger bone, so he dropped his bone to take the bigger one—and lost both. If the workingman insists upon reaching for the bigger bone of a guaranteed annual wage, he may lose many of the advances labor has made up to now.

Obviously, this analogy compares items that are not at all alike in any literal sense. The argument draws its force from the fact that it establishes an apparent or plausible ratio: The greed of the dog bears the same relationship to his loss of the bone that the laboring man's greed would bear to his loss of hard-won advances.

V The Toulmin Model of Substantive Argument

In the Cooper Institute address, Abraham Lincoln addressed a portion of his remarks to Southern politicians:

In [the] event [that a Republican President is elected], you say, you will destroy the Union; and then, you say, the great crime of having destroyed it will be upon us! That is cool. A highwayman holds a pistol to my ear, and mutters through his teeth, "Stand and deliver, or I shall kill you, and then you will be a murderer!"

In 1850, John C. Calhoun clashed in a debate with Henry Clay and Daniel Webster over the question of extending slavery into territory recently acquired from Mexico. The great call of Webster and Clay was for Union. Calhoun answered, "The cry of 'Union! Union! The glorious Union!' can no more prevent disunion than the cry of 'Health! Health! glorious Health!' on the part of a physician can save a patient lying dangerously ill."

A good analogy may be worth 10,000 syllogisms, much as a picture is worth 10,000 words.

V. THE TOULMIN MODEL OF SUBSTANTIVE ARGUMENT

In 1958, British philosopher Stephen Toulmin published *The Uses of Argument.** In that book, Toulmin is concerned with the question of whether the science of logic has any bearing on the assessment of the arguments people use in real life. As a theoretical study, logic has become something like pure mathematics. That is, it is a formal science, but one that has perhaps even less connection with rhetoric than pure physics has with the engineering of a bridge. As such, logic is not concerned with the kind of thinking people do in rhetorical situations. What Toulmin is looking for is a logical system useful for assessing the arguments people use in day-to-day communication: in jurisprudence, in science, psychology, sociology, politics, and the like. A logician is satisfied only when an argument is analytical, when its premises necessitate the truth of the conclusion.

An analytic argument is tautological. That is to say, its conclusion presents no information that is not inherent in the premises. To understand this better, look once again at the argument about Socrates above. If it is a *fact* that all human beings are mortal, the *statement* is

* Stephen Toulmin, *The Uses of Argument* (Cambridge, England: Cambridge University Press, 1958).

true. But that statement cannot be known true until *all* humans (including Socrates) have been investigated in this respect. Knowing that the statement is true, then, entails *prior* knowledge that Socrates is mortal. The conclusion, therefore, merely repeats something that is already inherent in the premises; it is tautological.

But such, of course, is not the case in rhetorical argumentation. The arguments you hear (and use) in support of a proposition are not "logical" in a sense that satisfies a logician, for they are not analytic. That is, arguments of this kind are not tautological. Their conclusions make inferential leaps to *new* information or positions. This movement, of course, is precisely what is required in rhetorical arguments. These arguments are not form without substance. Instead, they are *substantive;* they have content. Tautological arguments do not carry us beyond where we started and will not, therefore, help us to prove the proposition at the center of any rhetorical discourse because rhetorical discourse always involves the necessity of inferential leaps.

It is precisely this quality of movement that accounts for the probabilistic nature of substantive, rhetorical arguments. Since the arguments are not analytic, they are not "logical" in the formal sense. Their conclusions are not certainly true. They are at best probable in some degree.

At the same time, you see that people do argue in this fashion, that they claim to have *reasons* for what they believe and for what they assert, and that there ought to be a logical model of analysis for assessing the kinds of arguments people use in these rhetorical situations. To present such a model is what Toulmin purports to do. Let us look at his model now, keeping in mind at all times that what we give you is no more than a paraphrase of his significantly more sophisticated analysis.

Three terms are crucial in Toulmin's discussion of what takes place in an argument. These are *data* (D), *warrant* (W), and *claim* (C). Think of an argument as coming about this way: On the basis of *data* (earlier in this chapter we called the data "evidence" or "premises"), a *claim* (we have called this a "conclusion") is made. But some justification for moving from data to claim is required. Thus we need a *warrant*, a basis, a ground, or a justification for inferring (C) from (D). Diagrammed, the Toulmin model would look like this:

$$(D) \text{—————————} \text{ Therefore } (C)$$
$$\text{Since } (W)$$

But when you apply this model to an actual argument, you see that it, just like the Aristotelian model, will assess only an *analytical* argument. For example,

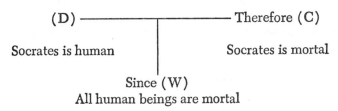

(D) ——————————— Therefore (C)

Socrates is human   Socrates is mortal

Since (W)
All human beings are mortal

But since we cannot know the warrant is true unless we have already examined *all* humans (including Socrates) with respect to mortality, we already know that Socrates will die. Moreover, we cannot know that Socrates is human unless we have applied to him all the criteria of being human—including the criterion of mortality. Therefore, Socrates is already known to be mortal. Thus this model is no more useful for assessing substantive arguments than the traditional analysis by Aristotelian logic. To make this quite clear, let's look once more at what is important about substantive arguments: They are not analytic; they are not tautological; their claims are not entailed in their data. There is an inferential leap from (D) to (C) that must be justified by (W). It is logical for you to argue "(D) therefore (C) because of (W)" only just in case (W) is a *relevant* warrant in that particular instance.

You can expect an audience to accept a claim only when that claim is adequately justified. This means the data must be sound and the warrant must be relevant. But, as we have said, one characteristic of arguments used in rhetoric is the omission of certain elements when the arguments are delivered.

Here's an example: In the wintry early months of 1974, there was considerable concern over a much discussed shortage of gasoline, one aspect of the energy crisis that bothered the greater part of the whole world. Often debated was the proposal to ration gasoline in much the same way it was rationed during World War II. One basic argument said: "We have a shortage of gasoline and that means we're going to have to institute a system of rationing." Even when an argument is phrased in this shortened form, it needs to be organized in the mind of a listener if it is to be assessed. That is to say, listeners will supply in their own minds whatever omitted data or warrant may be needed to make the argument operate *as if it were analytical.* They do this just as they supply the missing premises needed to put Aristotelian enthymemes into syllogistic form. In this case, a warrant has to be supplied, as shown in the following layout.

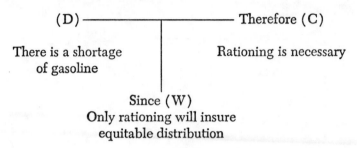

(D) ———————————— Therefore (C)

There is a shortage
of gasoline

Rationing is necessary

Since (W)
Only rationing will insure
equitable distribution

Surely, no one will call this argument *valid* in a technical, formal sense. Nonetheless, it is clearly *reasonable*. In order to analyze such an argument, Toulmin requires the use of three additional concepts in his model. All three of them point to the probabilistic nature of the argument. There is *backing* (B) to support the warrant, to show that (W) *is* relevant to the case at hand; there is a *rebuttal* (R) to designate circumstances under which the warrant would *not* be applicable, and there is a *qualifier* (Q) to indicate the probabilistic quality of the claim. Now add these to the argument in our example.

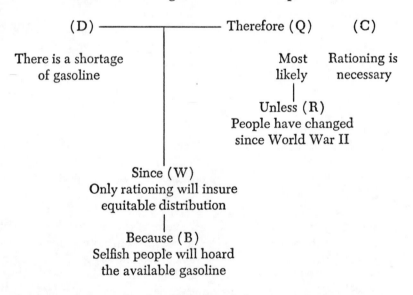

(D) ———————————— Therefore (Q)   (C)

There is a shortage
of gasoline

Most   Rationing is
likely   necessary

Unless (R)
People have changed
since World War II

Since (W)
Only rationing will insure
equitable distribution

Because (B)
Selfish people will hoard
the available gasoline

One further step in the development of this argument is not mentioned by Toulmin and is not an element in his model. This step is the addition of some reasonable backing or support for the data.

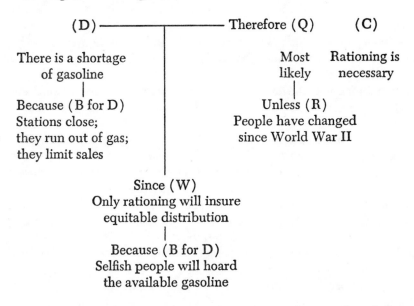

(D) ——————————————— Therefore (Q)   (C)

There is a shortage
of gasoline

Because (B for D)
Stations close;
they run out of gas;
they limit sales

Most   Rationing is
likely   necessary

Unless (R)
People have changed
since World War II

Since (W)
Only rationing will insure
equitable distribution

Because (B for D)
Selfish people will hoard
the available gasoline

Arguments are expected to be logical and this is the way their logicality can be tested in the mind of a listener: to organize the data in the form of a layout, to judge the truth of the data, to determine the relevance of the warrant, and to evaluate the backing for the data and the warrant and consider a possible rebuttal. On the basis of this kind of evaluation, the decision will be made whether to accept or reject the claim.

Because you can expect this critical behavior on the part of your listeners, you will want to lay out your arguments in advance; evaluate the data, warrants, and backing; and identify rebuttal conditions and the qualifier in accordance with Toulmin's model *and in the light of your audience analysis.* We do not know any better way to formulate rhetorically effective arguments.

VI. AVOIDING ERRORS IN ARGUMENTS

The whole purpose in laying out your arguments in this manner is to make them more effective. We have said unambiguously that we believe the Toulmin model will help you do this because it shows you how to assess arguments and by assessing them to discover whatever flaws they may have. Therefore, let's turn next to a consideration of these flaws or errors in arguments. That brings us to a brief discussion of fallacies (and some nonfallacies as well).

A. Fallacies

People often use the word "fallacy" to name *any* aspect of an argument they don't like: the mechanics of language, the mechanics of communication, the evidence, the reasoning, the appeal, or even the claim. Of course, anything that makes a listener reject a claim can be called an error in argument but not all errors in arguments are fallacies. In a more precise sense, the term is used to refer to *those arguments which are unsound but which are, nonetheless, likely to deceive.* For example, there may be many things "wrong" with the *expression* of an argument: the style, syntax, and grammar of the language; the pronunciation in oral arguments; and the spelling and punctuation in those that are written. None of these faults is intended or even likely to deceive. Consequently, while they may be criticized, and even though they may cause an argument to fail, they are not properly classified as fallacies. Further, to call an argument fallacious because the claim is unacceptable merely *rejects* the argument; it does not identify a fallacy.

A number of other aspects of argument are frequently referred to as fallacies when, as a matter of fact, they are not fallacies at all. We think some of these are worth mentioning. For example, it is a pious tendency of many textbooks to decry the use of motivational language. This is nonsense. Language has great power to motivate, and motivation is a very legitimate function of language. The responses language evokes are very useful because they help to create in an audience the belief the speaker wants the audience to have. (See the section on "Emotional Coloring" in Chapter 12.) There is nothing inherently evil or fallacious in the use of such language. A few examples will make clear what we mean.

Suppose you are told of a father who gave one of his kidneys to his son so that the boy might live and are then told that the boy's body rejected the organ and he died after all. Surely your pity would be aroused. If, as a result of this emotion, you made a substantial contribution to the Kidney Foundation, would you consider yourself to have been misled by a fraudulent appeal?

Professional golfer Johnny Miller is a superb player. Within the first month of the 1975 season he won two tournaments with combined purses of $70,000. Now, it is true that none of this makes him an authority on the design and manufacture of Sears and Roebuck sports clothes. Yet surely there is nothing *illogical* about his endorsing them. Even the gunman who threatens to kill a shopkeeper unless he hands over the money in the till should be accused of some fault other than fallacious argument. There is no need to press the issue. Arguments of this kind may be highly effective or they may be totally unpersuasive but, clearly, they are not inherently illogical. If they ever need to be condemned, it is when they are beside the point. But that is a different matter and one which we will consider below when we identify the fallacy of irrelevant conclusion.

The errors in argument that do concern us are indeed fallacies because they make arguments unsound. Therefore, you should be able to recognize them in the arguments of others and to avoid them in arguments of your own. The process for doing this is called refutation.

B. Refutation

Refutation is a necessary skill in communication for one very important reason: it protects against phoney arguments. Now, the only time one needs protection against a phoney argument is when the argument is persuasive in spite of being unsound. But since no one is going to be taken in by an argument that is obviously phoney, skill in refutation is really needed when the flaw in the argument is not readily discerned. We define refutation, therefore, as the disclosure of faults in either the form or the substance of arguments that make the arguments persuasive even though they are unsound. Let's see now what some of these errors in argument are.

Inductive arguments in rhetoric, you remember, are called arguments from example, and you use them in the form of generalizations or analogies. We need not discuss these at any great length because it is difficult if not impossible to talk about fallacies in inductive argument. Nonetheless, inductive arguments can go wrong. When they do, the fault invariably lies in the evidence from which the conclusion is drawn. In the case of generalizations, the evidence you use may fail to make the claim seem probable because the facts you adduce are judged by your audience to be inadequate. Analogies fail when the audience is not made to perceive the similarities between the analogs as more significant than their differences are. Avoid these problems and you will construct more effective arguments. To help you do this, it will be useful to review the parts of Chapter 6 that discuss the use of examples and statistics. To the extent that other forms of support (definitions, authorities, comparisons, and contrasts) are used in building inductive arguments, you will profit from reviewing also the advice given in the same chapter.

Deductive arguments seem to be susceptible to a greater number and variety of faults. Some of them have to do with the *form* into which the argument is cast. Others are the result of *material* flaws. The identification, definition, and discussion of formal error is the province of technical logic. By and large, then, we shall concern ourselves with helping you to understand and avoid some of the material errors in argument. Although an enthymeme is either an argument from sign or an argument from cause, we want to mention first two fallacies that are not exclusively associated with either of these two kinds of rhetorical deduction.

The first of these two fallacies is to *beg the question*. It occurs when an argument is circular: "I predict that before the snow flies we are going to have compulsory rationing of fuel oil in this country because as soon as it turns cold, the government is going to tell us all just how many gallons a month we can burn."

In other words, we are going to have rationing because we are going to have rationing. The "argument" is circular; it ends up exactly where it began. And it begs the question because it uses as a premise precisely the claim the argument is intended to prove.

Second, it is a fallacy to *ignore the issue* or, as it is sometimes called, the fallacy of *irrelevant conclusion*. It occurs when the claim supported by an argument is beside the point. For instance, there was a strange and gruesome law in ancient Greece that in murder trials the testimony of a slave could be accepted in court only if the testimony were given under torture. But if you wanted to attack capital punishment, wouldn't it be irrelevant to argue that capital punishment is bad because all civilized modern religions condemn the Greek practice? A variation of this fallacy occurs when a speaker thinks one thing has been proved but in reality something else has been proved (if indeed anything has been proved at all). You wouldn't try to defend capital punishment by arguing that Greek slaves were liars and had to be tortured to make them tell the truth. These two fallacies do occur in argumentation time and time again. The bulk of your problems can be avoided, however, by making sure that the sign relationships and the causal relationships that you use as warrants are dependable.

1. Testing Sign Relationships

In argument, the sign relationship you allege must be accepted by the audience. It is the crucial point in the argument. Consequently, before an argument from sign is used in persuasion, the reliability of the generalization upon which the argument depends must be examined in the light of three questions.

1. *Is there a reliable relationship between the observed fact and the conclusion drawn?* An accidental relationship is no sure basis for argument from sign. The conclusion you draw in such cases is likely to be a coincidence or just plain superstition.

A little boy, returning from an afternoon at the beach with his parents, sees another car on the street. He says, "Look, those people have been to the beach, too." He bases his inference on the fact that two long, pointed sticks protrude from the trunk of the other car. They look to him like poles for a pair of beach umbrellas. The basis for the inference is quite tenuous, because even if his supposition is correct, and the pointed sticks are a sign that there is a beach umbrella in the back of the car, their presence is by no means a certain sign that the people in the other car are returning from the beach.

There may be a splendid correlation between the number of smogless days in Los Angeles and the number of days of rain in Phoenix, Arizona, but a smogless day in Los Angeles is nonetheless a poor sign of rain in Phoenix. Perhaps you have heard it said that when more boys than girls are being born at any given time, the fact is a sign of impending war. Such a condition is about as trustworthy a sign of coming war as left-handedness is of superior intelligence.

2. *Do changed circumstances of time or place alter the relationship between sign and conclusion?* The reliability with which one condition can be taken as the sign of another condition can be altered by time and place. In the first half of the nineteenth century, the fact that a Southern farmer was a man of means would be a very reliable sign that he was a slaveowner. Today, no amount of wealth would be a sign that such a man owned slaves.

3. *Is the conclusion supported by the concurrence of other signs?* A single sign may often be insufficient evidence of the condition it seems to point to. Additional corroborating signs are frequently needed to support the conclusion of an argument from sign. Circumstantial evidence in a criminal case is an example. To say that a man is guilty of burglary because he was in the vicinity at the time the crime was committed is a weak argument. To show, in addition, that he was seen leaving the burglarized home and was arrested with stolen articles in his possession is to offer further and more substantial signs of his guilt.

In problems as complex as those that arise in human society, a single sign will seldom be a sure indication of a given fact or condition. Much more often than not, several are required to establish probability. Stock-market analysts make forecasts based on very tenuous data. What kinds of facts are such predictions based on? In July of one year, employment set a new record and unemployment dropped. For the second quarter of the year, the gross national product increased $5 billion over the first quarter. Personal income for the first seven months of the year is 1.06 times that for the same period in the year before. Now, do these facts *prove* that the overall economy is in a healthy state? They may justify the proposition for some; for others not. At any rate, the conditions described are *signs* that indicate something about the condition of business: From them, one can draw inferences about the present and future states of the economy.

2. Testing Causal Relationships

Arguments from cause, like arguments from sign, should be thought of as deductive. They, too, depend upon a stated or implied generalization—in this case, that in all instances a given event or set of circumstances can be expected to bring about a second event or condition as a direct result. Here again, as in the case of inference from sign, it is essential to the argument that the audience accept the premise that states the causal relationship upon which the speaker's conclusion depends. If the causal relationship stated or implied by the speaker is accepted by the audience, and if conditions described by the speaker are known or believed to exist, arguments from cause will be accepted as conclusive proof. In order to avoid the many dangers inherent in causal arguments, test their rhetorical soundness before you use them in persuasion.

1. *There must really be a causal relationship.* We have said that a cause always precedes its effect. That is, it comes earlier in time. This one characteristic is often an occasion of the fallacy called *post hoc, ergo propter hoc*—"after this, therefore on account of this." The fact that one event follows another does not mean that the second is the result of the first. Time sequence, then, does not constitute causal relationship. Superstitions are good examples of faulty causal reasoning of this sort. Either a causal faculty they do not possess is attributed to certain occurrences ("Oh, you broke a mirror. Seven years bad luck!") or, on the basis of coincidental time sequence, a causal connection that does not exist is alleged ("I sprained my ankle when I stepped off the curb because I walked under a ladder just before it happened.")

It is easy, but naïve, to allege a causal relationship where none really exists; many factors can intervene to destroy a neat chain of causal reasoning. You can be tempted to assert the truth of a conclusion on the basis of an event that you would expect to cause a certain result. You may fail to notice that other causal factors intervene. Having the engine in an automobile overhauled should result in improved performance and economy of the car. But if you try to economize further by using paint thinner for fuel, you introduce another factor that will completely prevent the engine overhaul from having the desired effect. By the same token, a fisherman plagued by mosquitoes can expect little help from an insect repellant if he washes it off because he doesn't like the smell.

2. *Avoid oversimplification in determining cause and effect.* Rarely, if ever, are cause and effect found in simple one-to-one ratio. Most often, an effect comes about through the operation of a whole series of contributing causes. It is quite simple to say that a president *caused* a depression or a war. It is also quite foolish to make such an assertion. The tremendously complex nature of social ills makes oversimplification both a temptation and a danger. If, however, you undertake to show that a president's policies made a substantial contribution to certain unfortunate events, you are on safer and also more reasonable ground.

More often than not, a cause generates, or at least influences, multiple effects. Any course of action, when put into operation, has results; that is, it becomes a cause operating to bring about effects that may be good, bad, or indifferent. If you argue that juvenile delinquency results from bad comic books (itself not a thoughtful analysis), you may conclude that censorship of reading materials would cause a reduction of juvenile delinquency. But censorship involves side effects that may be worse than any good it accomplishes.

Determining cause and effect is usually a complicated and difficult process. Yet causality may be the most important concept in the whole of argumentation.

SUMMARY

Controversies will arise for you when you are motivated to change opinions of others so that they agree with your own. In so doing, you use arguments to justify belief in your point of view. The arguments you use will be examples of either inductive or deductive inference. If the former, they will claim only to offer *some* evidence of the truth of the conclusion. Inductive arguments help to establish the probability of the conclusion drawn. Deductive arguments, on the other hand, are said to provide conclusive proof. That is, if the argument is valid, the conclusion is necessarily implied in the premises.

Although the conclusion of a valid deductive inference follows necessarily from the premises, this consequence says nothing about whether the conclusion is true. Only when the premises are certainly true *and* the argument is valid is the conclusion certainly true. But when speakers deliberate on proposed policies, judgments of value and allegedly factual conditions, the premises that provide evidence for their conclusions are only probable. Hence the proofs in persuasion are only probable. The arguments a speaker offers, then, are used to give a rational basis to belief. They do not constitute absolute proof.

There are two well-known models of argument that are informative and useful both in the construction and the assessment of rhetorical proofs. One is the Aristotelian analysis of rhetorical arguments. In the Aristotelian system, deductive arguments in rhetoric are either arguments from sign or arguments from cause. The first of these is a method of knowing *that* some statement is true. An argument from cause provides a reason to explain *why* a statement is true.

Inductive arguments in persuasion either make generalizations or draw analogies. In making generalizations, a speaker presents evidence to justify the belief that what is true of the instances cited will be true of all unexamined instances of the same phenomenon. An argument by analogy does not use its premises as evidence that exemplifies something about a whole class. Instead it concludes that what is true of examined instances will be true of a particular other instance of the same class of phenomena.

The second model is the Toulmin analysis of substantive arguments. In this system a claim is inferred from given data on the justification of a warrant. "(D), therefore, (C), since (W)." The probabilistic nature of substantive argument in Toulmin's model is made clear by the use of backing for the data and the warrant, the identification of rebuttal conditions that specify the applicability of the warrant, and a qualifier to indicate the degree of dependability of the claim.

Arguments are subject to error. Many people call all of these errors fallacies, but, more precisely, a fallacy is an argument that is persuasive even though its claim is a *non sequitur*. The process of pointing out such flaws in arguments is called refutation.

QUESTIONS

1. What conditions set up an occasion for persuasive speaking?
2. What is an argument?
3. Why are analytic statements not propositions for rhetorical argument?

4. Why are your efforts in persuasion aimed at proving that your proposition is probably true?

5. Explain the two grounds upon which persuasion occurs.

6. What two systems of analysis may be used for the assessment of arguments?

7. What is an enthymeme?

8. Differentiate between arguments from sign and arguments from cause.

9. What differences do you see between the systems of Aristotle and Toulmin?

10. What are the merits of the Toulmin system?

11. Explain the elements of the Toulmin model.

12. What are fallacies?

13. Explain what it is to beg the question and to ignore the issue.

14. What is refutation? When is it useful?

EXERCISES

1. Write a short essay (no more than three double-spaced type-written pages) in which you explain how the principle of probability is applied to some problem in your major field of study. You need not go into extensive detail. Write the paper so that it reflects the general understanding of experts in the field. The following topics might suggest the kind of subject you should choose:

    a. Can history predict future events?

    b. What is the nature of probability theory in genetics?

    c. How much do intelligence tests and intelligence quotients tell elementary-school teachers about their students?

    d. To what extent does chemistry provide absolute truths?

    e. What is the theory behind minority rights in a democracy?

    f. In what sense is human personality predictable?

    g. Is mathematics an absolute science?

    h. How do economists know when a country is in a depression?

2. Examine the texts of several speeches delivered in the last presidential campaign. (See the *New York Times, Vital Speeches of the Day,* or *Representative American Speeches* for texts of many of these

speeches.) Find examples of generalization and analogy which the writer uses in developing his case. Evaluate these examples. If you reject them, explain why.

3. In the editorials of news magazines or in newspapers, find samples of argument from sign and argument from cause. Lay the arguments out in the format of the Toulmin model. Supply any missing parts and assess the arguments.

4. Collect examples of arguments you hear in conversation and evaluate them as in Exercise 3. Here are some samples of what you might listen for:

   a. "I didn't think you were at home. I didn't see your car in the driveway."
   b. "My eyes are bothering me. I must have been studying too much."
   c. "Don't make so much noise; you'll wake your mother."
   d. "All the best television-viewing times are filled with westerns. Look at Saturday night's schedule."

Tell what kind of argument is used in each of the examples given in this exercise. Using the Toulmin model, explain how you would counter each of these arguments if you disagreed.

5. Find examples of specific arguments in the following speech. Analyze the arguments according to the Aristotelian model and according to the Toulmin model. Evaluate the arguments in terms of the criteria of the two models.

THE PUBLIC MUST BE HEARD FROM*

Arthur R. Taylor

One cannot be in Arizona today, December 7, without being reminded of American history and another December 7, to whose memory the battleship Arizona remains in eternal memorial at Pearl Harbor. But this day, happily, is also to be remembered for another major moment of history, the ratification of the U.S. Constitution by the first state, Delaware.

Speaking to this convention of Arizona broadcasters, I find it hard to contemplate what might have happened to broadcasting without the Constitution—how communication would have developed without the

* Mr. Taylor is president of the Columbia Broadcasting System, Inc. The speech was delivered to the Arizona Broadcasters Association in Phoenix on Dec. 7, 1973. Reprinted by permission from *Vital Speeches of the Day*, **40** (Jan. 15, 1974), pp. 199–202.

safeguards it provides for an independent press and the right of free speech and, above all, how healthy competition among communicators would have developed or been maintained.

A broadcaster, like any other businessman, is in business to earn a profit. But he can only earn that profit by presenting a program service attuned to the needs and desires of the public, and offered to the public in competition with the programs of other broadcasters. The most successful broadcaster is the one most responsive to this public, and the greater the competition among broadcasters for the attention of that public, the better the public itself is served.

This is nothing new. From the invention of movable type to the development of television, every potential advance in communications has had to offer its services in the marketplace of ideas. The ones that have succeeded have always represented a broadening of service, either by providing new forms of information and entertainment, or by introducing techniques for wider distribution, or simply by reducing the cost to the point where more people could afford the service. The most successful of all communications media in this nation's history, television, meets all these criteria.

Today we are confronted with another self-proclaimed revolution in communications that meets none of the criteria. It is not providing new forms of information and entertainment, it is not expanding the total audience for those communications and, far from decreasing the cost, it is seeking to raise the cost while decreasing the audience.

The proposition I speak of is called pay cable television and, as I will demonstrate, it is sheltered from the normal American standards of fair competition. As a result, there is a real possibility that millions of American families will be denied the movies, sports events and other television attractions that now form an integral part of their lives. Millions of others will be allowed to view these attractions only at the expense of a large and continual drain on their family finances.

What we are speaking of, in short, is less a revolution than a sneak attack on the family pocketbook. The basic notion of pay cable television, as it is now developing, is nothing more than that the average television viewer should pay for the programs that he now receives free. The effect of this change on the free broadcasting industry would be an incalcuable disservice to the American viewing public.

Let us agree at the outset that we have no quarrel with the growth of cable television in its original form. We welcome it for the two real contributions it was intended to make to our society. The first is obvious. Because of remoteness, mountains, skyscrapers and the like, broadcast television cannot promise every viewer a perfect picture at every moment. Cable television very often can promise and deliver better reception of local, over-the-air signals to its subscribers.

Cable television systems have already been built in most places where they are necessary to provide a good television signal. Now that industry

179

is turning toward larger cities where television reception is, by and large, rather good. To attract subscribers in these cities, cable operators must offer another service.

This brings us to cable television's second potential contribution. There are only so many channels on the broadcast television dial. Broadcasters are charged with serving mass audiences; there is simply not enough time in the day to offer all the programs for which small, specialized audiences exist. Cable television offers an abundance of channels—24 or 40 in many places, with reports that the number may someday rise to 100. Thus, cable television can bring to the public a wide variety of services that broadcast television does not offer at this time, ranging from presently untelevised cultural events to new services like shopping-by-television. Perhaps most important, cable's multiplicity of channels promises access to a vital medium of special communication to such groups as doctors, educators, local governments and community organizations.

Cable television's founders consistently said that they would develop new programs and services. However, most cable systems have never originated programs of their own. A number of others which did so at one time in anticipation of rules that would require origination halted their origination activities after it became clear the rules would not immediately be implemented. Instead, the industry's current leaders have announced their intention to concentrate their efforts on the presentation, for a price, of exactly the same type of movies and sporting events people presently see on free television.

If pay cable television service were entirely separate and independent of over-the-air television, it would be a legitimate competitor. We broadcasters would meet it in the marketplace, just as we meet newspapers and movie theaters and other media. The public would choose between the services each of us offered.

Cable television, however, is not this sort of competitor. The programs that it uses to gain entry into the American household for its wires and its tuning box are not its own, but those of free television. Once it has gained that entry, cable television proposes to add more charges.

To put this proposition in its simplest form, consider the football fan who subscribes to a cable service in the hopes of improving his television reception of football games (or any other program) broadcast by CBS. For this improved picture he contracts to pay a fixed monthly fee. This football fan then brings the cable television wires and tuning box into his living room. As the cable service adds subscribers by promising to deliver better reception of free television programs it is creating an asset—a distribution system.

The fees cable television has received for distributing free broadcast television programs (for which privilege incidentally it has paid nothing to the free broadcaster who originated and paid for the programs to begin with) have allowed the cable system to gain access to an audience which is exclusively its own. The cable system can then proceed to approach the distributors of programs now seen on free television, calculating that by charging its subscribers an additional fee for the exclusive right to see certain programs, it can generate sufficient revenues to outbid CBS for the rights to football games or movies or other forms of entertainment. Cable television systems can do this right now under existing regulations. All the cable system has to do is include the games in its locally approved general monthly charge to its subscribers.

Now our friend the football fan must pay more to see the football games be used to see free, or he must do without the games. His friends who had not subscribed to cable television would not be able to see the games at all. If our fan had not wanted to see free television broadcasts of football games more clearly he would never have subscribed to the cable system, but it is his very subscription to this system which could permit the cable system to take these games off free television and to increase his monthly subscription charges.

It is important to understand the several meanings of the phrase "pay television." In the most basic sense, all cable television is pay television. Every subscriber must pay for the privilege of receiving what is furnished on the cable. But cable subscribers may also pay, either separately or as part of their regular monthly charge, for other programs. Some of those programs lack the mass audiences needed to justify their appearance on free television. It is a legitimate goal for pay television to bring these specialized attractions into homes that otherwise would be denied them.

The form of pay television to which we are specifically opposed is that by which free television's attractions are to be diverted to pay cable television. We use the term "siphoning" to describe this process. It is a descriptive term and an apt one. When gasoline is siphoned from one car to another, the car that receives the fuel may work beautifully, but the other is at a severe disadvantage.

The economic logic of siphoning was never better illustrated than when Joe Frazier fought Muhammad Ali for the heavyweight boxing title in 1971. About 1.5 million people paid more than $16 million to see the fight on closed-circuit television in auditoriums in the United States and Canada. Overseas, hundreds of millions of people saw the fight on free television, but returned only a fraction as much revenue to the promoters. That sort of lesson is easy for a promoter to remember.

What benefits a promoter, however, doesn't always benefit the public. Throughout the country there are innumerable areas where families are so isolated that it is uneconomic for cable operators to build systems. These predominantly rural families depend on television as virtually their sole source of entertainment. They would be denied many of television's most popular attractions—no matter how much money they were willing to pay —if those attractions were siphoned off to pay cable television simply because no cable system existed in their areas.

The situation would hardly be better for families in areas where cable television systems did exist. For the first time, the amount and kind of television they could watch would be determined by their financial situation. *TV Guide* has already found families paying more than $20 a month for a very limited pay television schedule. With the addition of a full line of sporting events and movies to the schedule, many families could have to pay $30 or more every month for the program features they now receive free.

Even for the affluent, this is a needless cost. But how many less affluent families can afford at all that large an inroad into their limited spending power? The burden would be a heavy one for young couples just starting to build a family, and for older ones living on fixed pensions and Social Security benefits. The burden would be heavier still in communities where unemployment and poverty are widespread; and I need not remind you that many of our citizens live under exactly these conditions. The effect of siphoning would be to make these minorities second-class citizens in terms of their access to their basic source of entertainment and information.

One in every four American families has an income under $5000 a year; but the best information available to us indicates that only one in eight families that subscribes to cable television has an income below that level. More than one family in every three has an income under $7000; but among families that buy original sports and movies on cable television, only one in nine has an income under $7000. These comparisons suggest that the economic discrimination inherent in pay television has already begun.

This discrimination is a matter of public concern, because cable television, like broadcast television, is a public communications medium. Acting through the Congress, our nation has determined that these media should be used in the public interest. It is hard to imagine how the public interest would be served if millions of viewers were denied access to television entertainment and information programming, while millions of others were compelled to pay for programs they now receive free. We are determined that this must not happen.

Based on its performance to date, if pay television sports and movies were offered to each of the nation's 7.8 million cable television subscribers, about a fourth would sign up. If each of those homes paid the modest fee of one dollar for a movie, and if the cable television operator split that dollar 50-50 with the movie producer, the movie producer could receive about a million dollars for the pay television rights to his movie. Free television presently pays about $750,000 to show a typical movie two or three times on a national network. In other words, without adding a single new subscriber, cable television already possesses the bargaining potential to buy almost any movie it wants. We could perform the same calculation for the rights to sporting events; the conclusion would be the same.

The Federal Communicaitons Commission has rules intended to protect the public from this siphoning of popular free television attractions. They provide in part that most movies can be shown on pay television only if less than two years, or more than 10 years (under certain limitations), have elapsed since their first theatrical release, and that sporting events may be shown only if they have not appeared on free television within the previous two years. Series-type programs may not be siphoned at all. But the Commission is presently being asked to weaken these rules, which even in their present form, as I noted in the football example, contain loopholes so great they offer grossly inadequate protection to both broadcasters and their public.

To cite a prominent example, a cable television system can circumvent the rules entirely by integrating its pay television charges into the basic locally approved monthly price for its subscribers, rather than charging for pay television attractions on a per-program or per-channel basis. In New York the cable television systems serving Manhattan offer New York Rangers and Knickerbockers home games as part of the basic monthly charge; recently the cable operators asked the city for a 33⅓ percent increase in that basic monthly charge. If siphoning is permitted, that is the pattern we are likely to see.

Even though keeping major attractions free and available to the entire public would seem obviously to be in the public interest, some FCC commissioners appear to look favorably on pay cable television as a means to further the Commission's stated intention to "get cable going." No one disputes the goal because the social value of the diversity cable television might offer the public is incontestable. But there are two flaws in the notion that siphoning is needed to get cable going. The first is the growth cable has already achieved. It has today enrolled one out of every nine television homes in the United States, compared with one out of every 700 twenty years ago; it is estimated that in another 10 years, cable will claim at least one out of every five homes, and perhaps as many as three out of every five.

Second, if a cable operator can earn huge profits by diverting the attractions of free television to his own use, what incentive has he to develop diverse new programming? Cable operators often argue that siphoning is necessary, because the resultant profits would support this new programming especially in the public service area. That argument startled Congressman Torbert Macdonald, Chairman of the House Subcommittee on Communications and Power, who recently told the industry, "When the cable industry promised the country a great diversity of programs and services, they never mentioned that it could be attained only by doubling the admission fee."

We have always believed that public service is a specific obligation of any broadcaster, not a favor to be granted in return for profitable concessions by governmental entities. However, if that is to become the battleground, let us note that free television's profits have supported a vast range of public service programs of very material social value. Television's news coverage of elections, moon landings and wars have touched the lives of hundreds of millions of people, while its spectrum of public affairs, cultural, educational and religious programs has in a quieter way also contributed much to the worth of our society.

Pay television advocates often argue that free television isn't really free because the cost of the advertising is added to the cost of the products viewers purchase. To the contrary, most advertisers believe and can demonstrate that their advertising makes possible mass distribution that brings down the cost of products. When advertisers are denied commercial time on television, they do not reduce their prices; they spend their money on other media or marketing techniques. But when they do advertise on television, their expenditures allow the public to receive their preferred forms of entertainment and information without cost.

Representative Macdonald has emphasized "the cardinal principle that what is now being offered to TV audiences at no extra charge won't be forced off the air into a coin box in the home, and thus restricted to those who can and will pay for it." In this society, our first hope would be that this principle could have been implemented through the free competition for program attractions between two separate, independent media—broadcast television and cable television. As we have seen, the institutional structure which presently governs the relationship of these two media make any genuine competition impossible.

If the present structure is maintained, only government regulation will protect the public from having to pay for those attractions. Even with the most obvious loopholes plugged, we do not believe the present anti-siphoning rules provide sufficient protection for the public. But they do contain sound principles that belong in any overall effort to protect the public interest in its favorite attractions. There are three specific additional steps that warrant very serious consideration as protections of the public interest.

First, cable television's liabilities under the copyright laws must be clearly defined. This definition may be provided by cases now before the courts, or specific legislation may be required. In either case the principle must be established that cable television, like every other entertainment medium, may transmit a program to an audience only when it has obtained permission of that program's copyright owner.

Second, pay cable television should not be permitted to siphon any program that has appeared on free television in the past five years. That is the standard the FCC has imposed upon over-the-air pay television for sports programs, and we believe it is equally appropriate to pay cable television. By pay cable, we mean any form of cable television that offers programs otherwise unavailable to its audience, whether the audience is required to pay for the programs by the event, by the channel or by the calendar period.

Third, before the owners of programs that have not appeared on free television in the past five years may sell those programs exclusively to pay cable systems that also carry free television's broadcasts, the programs must be offered to over-the-air free television. Such offers must be at a cost that is equitable and consistent with what free television pays for comparable attractions. There are difficult questions inherent in such a rule, but there is no reason a standard cannot be formulated that fairly balances public and private interests. Once implemented, such a rule would ensure that, no matter how public tastes might change, the most popular attractions would be accessible free to every television viewer, no matter where he might live or what he might earn.

But as we discuss means to safeguard the public interest, let us remember that the public, too, must be heard from. Broadcasters and cable operators, theater owners and movie producers are quite able to make their positions known. But it is the public that will be most affected if its favorite attractions are diverted from free television to pay cable television, and it is the public's willingness or unwillingness for that to happen which must be communicated to legislators and regulators, in Washington and closer to home.

I. Identification
II. The logic of motivation
III. The nature of motivation
    A. A hierarchy of motivation
    B. Significance of the hierarchy
    C. Building motivation into the speech
        1. By direct argument
        2. By building the need
        3. By the choice of examples
        4. By the choice of words
IV. Using motivation
    A. Make the motivation a product of the ideas of the speech and not an end in themselves.
    B. Choose the motivation that is best adapted to the audience.
    C. Use multiple motivations where appropriate.
    D. Keep the motivation consistent.
    E. Let the materials of the speech develop the motivation.
    F. Avoid overusing motivation.

Chapter 9

The Motivational Dimension of Communication

To study motivation is to study what causes people to act as they do. That is the primary concern of this chapter. We shall be interested in the factors of motivation and some of the principles by which such motivation can be applied to purposive communication.

Since this book has as its primary purpose helping speakers to be more effective communicators, it would be easy to lose track of the fact that there is much more to effective communication than what is deliberately designed by the speaker. In our discussion of attention and communication (Chapter 5) we noted that certain preestablished conditions in the audience influence the extent to which listeners will attend to a particular message. We saw how an audience's habits, set values, suggestibility, and tendency to project would influence its attention to a topic. In the chapter on audience analysis (Chapter 4) we looked more carefully at the nature of audiences, how they set preconditions to which any speaker must adapt, based on values, and salient beliefs and attitudes.

Preconditions will influence the extent to which an argument is judged reasonable by a listener; supporting material is clear and interesting; the source is credible; and language and organization are adequate. Thus your listeners have a particular orientation and that orientation predetermines much of your effectiveness. When you are unsuccessful in informing or persuading an audience, you should not feel that this is necessarily a personal failure. In some situations (and to some extent in virtually all situations), your objectives cannot be attained.

Aristotle's definition of rhetoric as the faculty of "finding all the *available* means of persuasion" is still a good one. You are interested only in the *available* motivation and that means only that motivation which you can *find* in a listener.

I. IDENTIFICATION

Recall the term "identification," which we discussed in Chapter 4. Identification helps to explain this listener-related sense of communication. You identify your proposal with what is already in an audience; you do not forcibly change it. In 1973, James Reston of the *New York Times* could address the graduates of the University of Utah in terms that would be effective only if they were concerned about the events in government at the time, the moral values he espoused, and their own future. Only then would there be identification between listener and message.

Washington is full of people these days with new bills to reform campaign spending, combat official secrecy, limit the power of the presidency and do a lot of other good things, but the new bills are not as important as the old rules of decent human conduct. We are in deep trouble today simply because people have not been telling the truth, because they have been cheating and chiseling and asquiescing in things they knew were wrong.

If I had said this a year ago at Commencement, you would have said—and maybe you are still saying—who needs these kindergarten moralities, but now we know. The government needs them and so do we. You can talk all you like about generation gaps, and the silly sermons of porky old geezers like me, but the lesson is in the newspaper headlines and on TV.*

James Reston could not be sure of the exact impact of his message on his listeners. No speaker can control all the factors. There is a

---

* James Reston, "1973 University of Utah Commencement Address," June 2, 1973, privately printed by the University of Utah, Salt Lake City, Utah.

"partially 'unconscious' factor in appeal," says literary critic Kenneth Burke.* Thus there is some mystery to every communication situation. No speaker or receiver understands fully what is going on. Some of the unknowns in the communication transaction will be resolved by the interpersonal relations established between listener and speaker as communication takes place. That is, the more you communicate with someone and genuinely seek to understand that person's motivation, the more successful you should be in identifying with that person's motivation.

II. THE LOGIC OF MOTIVATION

In Chapter 8 we said that proofs in persuasion are only probable, and that the audience determines what is probable and what is not. Even so, a listener's door to objective reality is no more open than is yours. You know the world only as you perceive it. Your perceptions of what is probable are colored by all your experiences: by the set of values you gained from your parents; the impressions you received while growing to maturity; and your reactions to contact with other people in the streets, in schools, in the army, or on athletic teams. All these experiences influence your perception and lead you to conclusions about life which have not undergone the tests of rigorous logic but which, nonetheless, are firmly held convictions.

The convictions you have about people in general, about groups, about events, and about yourself may be called assumptions. When people sit as members of an audience, their own assumptions are rarely up for debate. Instead, they serve as measures of the acceptability of your ideas and arguments. In order to persuade an audience, therefore, you must argue within the framework of the assumptions of the audience. This does not mean that persuasion is nonlogical; its logic, however, must operate within the framework of the attitudes, beliefs, and values of the listener.

Perhaps it would be well to begin by saying that the extent to which your behavior is consistent with your perceptions of the world around you is the extent to which you are logical. For you to "know" that smoking is injurious to your health and still smoke is not illogical. This behavior merely indicates that you are not subject to motivation alone. You may regard the "pleasure" of smoking as greater than the

* Kenneth Burke, "Rhetoric—Old and New," *The Journal of General Education,* 5 (April 1951), p. 203.

"harmfulness." You may consider smoking a sign of sophistication. Or, you may even evade the issue entirely: "Other people may get cancer from smoking but not me." Although the probabilities of scientific evidence make it seem "illogical" to think that you are somehow biologically resistant to disease because of your greater will power, it is not illogical if you *reason* that because of your resistance you can smoke without harm to yourself. You may be wrong or you may be foolish and you may even die because of this reasoning, but you are not *illogical*.

An audience has, therefore, a consistency (a logic, if you will), but to understand it you must understand what motivates listeners. In Chapter 4 we examined the factors that tend to make audiences what they are and to respond as they do, and in Chapter 8 we examined the structures of reasoning that systematize the process of argument and inquiry. This chapter is concerned with the elements of the speaking situation whereby you can effect some changes in an audience by identifying your proposal with what motivates your listeners.

III. THE NATURE OF MOTIVATION

Motivation is a basic element in human activity. You can have several needs that demand satisfaction at one and the same time. One or another of these needs may be more salient than the others and, therefore, motivate you to ignore the others and attend to it. As soon as that need is satisfied, you can turn your attention to other needs, which become, in their turn, more salient. For example, if you are quite hungry you are probably much less conscious that you crave companionship or want a clearer picture of how you should lead your life. When you have eaten and the hunger need is removed, however, the other needs become more pressing. They may seem to develop at the moment, but they were actually there all the time although they were overshadowed by the severity of the need for food.

When you want an audience to respond to an argument, search for the needs of the audience. Through argument, support, language, and delivery, identify your proposal with them. You may use the needs of the audience to build either positive or negative motivations. That is, you may show your listeners that they can achieve the satisfactions of their needs through your proposal or you may move them to reject some idea because it threatens to thwart their motivations.

III The Nature of Motivation

A. A Hierarchy of Motivation

Abraham Maslow has postulated what he calls a "hierarchy of needs.* His theory essentially is this: There is a hierarchy of needs from the physiological to the social, and the lower needs must be satisfied in order for the others to be operative. A starving person, for instance, is not likely to be much concerned about reading a book. Look now at a hierarchy of needs adapted from Maslow. It will be our purpose to show you how to adapt these needs to your own persuasive ends by using them as a basis for motivating audiences to respond as you wish.†

1. *Physiological needs.* These needs include hunger, thirst, sex, and so forth.
2. *Safety needs.* This group ranges in scope from physiological safety, as in the protection of life, to a social safety need for the security of job, possessions, and personal feeling.
3. *Belongingness and love needs.* Human relations of both giving and receiving acceptance and affection are included in this group.
4. *Esteem needs.* Included in these needs are a feeling of strength, achievement, competence, self-respect, self-esteem, and the feeling that others who matter have the same esteem for us.
5. *Self-actualization needs.* In this group is a feeling of self-fulfillment of doing that for which one is best fitted.
6. *Freedom needs.* In order to meet any of the other needs, one must feel the ability to act to meet those needs. Also included here are the freedom to speak, to act, and to defend oneself.
7. *Aesthetic needs.* A sense of beauty, proportion, and form.

B. Significance of the Hierarchy

When Maslow posits his list of needs as a hierarchy of motivation, it is important to understand the sense in which he does this. If all the needs are unsatisfied, then the physiological needs, he says, which are most prepotent, are likely to dominate. Thus one who is beset by

* Abraham Maslow, *Motivation and Personality* (New York: Harper & Row, 1954), pp. 80–106. Much of the discussion of this section is adapted from Maslow.
† Maslow is rather confusing on number six and on number seven. He does not list them as basic needs, but he does call the aesthetic need a need. The freedom need he calls a "precondition for basic need satisfaction." (Maslow, op. cit., p. 92) It serves our purpose to treat them all as needs.

severe hunger has little interest in anything else. Therefore, when the physiological needs are met, the safety needs and, after safety needs, belongingness needs, and so forth, become most important. But this principle applies only in the abstract or general sense. When you speak, social motivations are far more important than physiological. For one reason, you rarely speak to people who are in a situation of severe physiological deprivation. In the second place, social needs will frequently be more important than physiological needs. You wait for others to be served at the table because it is the socially acceptable thing to do even if you are hungry. What you often think of as hunger is more like appetite, a social drive. Even sex may sometimes be considered more a matter of self-esteem or belongingness and love than it is a physiological phenomenon. Sociologist Kenneth Boulding has even questioned whether "survival" needs, as he calls physiological and safety needs, are "the highest value in the biological world."[*]

As a speaker, you are much more likely to be telling your listeners which foods are safest for them, which persons love them more, which activities will build their self-esteem or make them feel self-actualized than you are to persuade them on the ground that something or someone can fill physiological needs. The question of which motivation in the hierarchy you should use will be a function, not so much of its place in the hierarchy but of its place in the consciousness of the listener.

C. Building Motivation into the Speech

Once you have determined a basis of motivation that best relates both to your audience's needs and to your proposition, you must identify for the audience the proposition with the motivation. There are four major ways of doing this: (1) by direct argument, (2) by reinforcing the need, (3) by the examples used, and (4) by the choice of words.

1. By Direct Argument

Frequently, speakers will use indirect means to relate the proposition to the individual listener. Others will be much more blunt. Here is Governor George C. Wallace of Alabama at a convention of law enforcement officers. In order to enlarge his audience's sense of self-

---

[*] Kenneth E. Boulding, *The Image* (Ann Arbor: University of Michigan Press, 1961), p. 72.

esteem and identify that self-esteem with his thesis that law enforcement is a local responsibility, Wallace uses arguments that are at the very center of the self-image of the audience.

These are a few of the fundamental principles of our government from which federal government has departed.

We are suffering the unhappy consequences.

On the far-flung outposts of our freedom, patriotic American citizens are defending the principles of our heritage at the risk of their lives. On the home front, it is you who are on the front line, defending the same principles.

It is you to whom we look for securing the peace and tranquility and protection of life and property.

Yours is a thin line between law and anarchy. It is a responsibility that demands the most in character, courage and devotion to duty.

Your task is made immeasurably more difficult, if not impossible, when government refuses to be bound in its actions by the fundamental principles from which we derive stability and certainty in law, and thus, the security essential to a free and orderly society.

You are doing a magnificent job.

I salute you.*

2. By Building the Need

Even when the audience has a need of one sort or another it will frequently not generate a motivation strong enough to provide a basis of identification. In such a case the need must be enlarged in the minds of the audience. In Chapter 17 we look at the "problem-to-solution" method of organization, wherein a major factor is the emphasis put upon the severity of the problem in order to provide greater motivation for a change.

Here is Gloria Steinem speaking on the women's revolution to a mostly female graduating class at Vassar College. She believes that part of her job is to show these women how their self-actualization has been thwarted:

With women, the whole system reinforces this feeling of being a mere appendage. It's hard for a man to realize just how full of self-doubt we become as a result. Locked into suburban homes with the intellectual companionship of three-year-olds; locked into bad jobs, watching less-qualified men get promoted above us; trapped into poverty by a system

* Quoted by permission.

193

that supposes our only identity is motherhood—no wonder we become pathetically grateful for small favors.*

3. By the Choice of Examples

Here, by selecting his examples, Malcolm X appeals to the safety motivation at the Organization of African Unity.

The American government is either unable or unwilling to protect the lives and property of your 22 million African-American brothers and sisters. We stand defenseless, at the mercy of American racists who murder us at will for no reason other than we are black and of African descent.

Two black bodies were found in the Mississippi River this week; last week an unarmed African-American educator was murdered in cold blood in Georgia; a few days before that three civil-rights workers disappeared completely, perhaps murdered also, only because they were teaching our people in Mississippi how to vote and how to secure their political rights.

Our problems are your problems. We have lived for over 300 years in that American den of racist wolves in constant fear of losing life and limb. Recently, three students from Kenya were mistaken for American Negroes and were brutally beaten by New York police. Shortly after that, two diplomats from Uganda were also beaten by the New York City police, who mistook them for American Negroes.

If Africans are brutally beaten while only visiting in America, imagine the physical and psychological suffering received by your brothers and sisters who have lived there for over 300 years.†

4. By the Choice of Words

The intensity of the language in which you encode the motivation you use to support a proposal will influence the audience to perceive your conviction to be more intense.‡ Such intensity, if not overdone,

* Quoted by permission.

† Malcolm X, "An Appeal to African Heads of State," *Malcolm X Speaks*, George Breitman, ed. (New York: Grove Press, 1966), p. 74. Reprinted by permission of Pathfinder Press, Inc. Copyright © 1965 by Merit Publishers and Mrs. Betty Shabazz.

‡ There is considerable research on this phenomenon. John Basehart, "Message Opinionation and Approval—Dependence as Determinants of Receiver Attitude Change and Recall," *Speech Monographs*, 38 (Nov. 1971), pp. 302–310; John W. Bowers, "Some Correlates of Language Intensity," *Quarterly Journal of Speech*, 50 (Dec. 1964), pp. 415–420; Michael Burgoon and Lawrence J. Chase, "The Effects of Differential Linquistic Patterns in Messages Attempting to Induce Resistance to Persuasion," *Speech Monographs*, 40 (March 1973), pp. 1–7; Carl W.
Footnote continued next page

will tend to make the listeners more conscious of their motivation and its relation to your proposal.

There is no doubt that the words you choose can reinforce a motivation you want to develop in an audience. Notice how Billy Graham uses intense negative words such as "friction," "conflict," and "warfare" and reinforces them by repetition as he builds in his predominantly Christian audience motivations centering in the "esteem" needs. Although his argument says that Christians must live with friction and conflict, they and they alone have a greater role to play in society.

And the Bible indicates that the Christian life is a life of conflict and warfare. There are some people who promise that faith in God will remove all troubles and difficulties. This is not true. God had never promised to remove all our troubles, problems, and difficulties. In fact, sometimes I think the truly committed Christian is in conflict with the society around him more than any other person. Society is going one direction, and he is going the opposite direction. This brings about friction and conflict. But God has promised, in the midst of trouble and conflict, a genuine peace, a sense of assurance and security that the worldly person never knows (John 16:33). God has also promised new recources, new strength, through the indwelling of his Holy Spirit. However, millions of people, including some Christians, harbor anxieties and worries.*

IV. USING MOTIVATION

The following six principles are helpful in selecting motivation.

1. Make the motivations a product of the ideas of the speech and not an end in themselves.

Carmichael and Gary Lynn Cronkhite, "Frustration and Language Intensity," *Speech Monographs*, 32 (June 1965), pp. 107–111; William J. McEwen and Bradley S. Greenberg, "The Effect of Message Intensity on Receiver Evaluations of Source, Message, and Topic," *Journal of Communication*, 20 (Dec. 1970), pp. 340–50; R. Samuel Mehrley and James C. McCroskey, "Opinionated Statements and Attitude Intensity as Predictors of Attitude Change and Source Credibility," *Speech Monographs*, 37 (March 1970), pp. 47–52; Gerald R. Miller and John Basehart, "Source Trustworthiness, Opiniated Statements, and Response to Persuasive Communication," *Speech Monographs*, 36 (March 1969), pp. 1–7; Gerald R. Miller and J. Lobe, "Opinionated Language, Open- and Closed-mindedness and Response to Persuasive Communication," *Journal of Communication*, 17 (Dec. 1967), pp. 333–341.

* Billy Graham, "The Cure for Anxiety," text distributed by the Billy Graham Evangelistic Association.

2. Choose the motivation that is best adapted to the audience.
3. Use multiple motivations where appropriate.
4. Keep the motivations consistent.
5. Let the materials of the speech develop the motivations.
6. Avoid overusing motivation.

A. Make the Motivations a Product of the Ideas of the Speech and Not an End in Themselves

We have noted that people's motivations are excited when they are under stress. Stress occurs when an audience becomes aware that some desired end is frustrated or unfulfilled. In such a state the audience will try to relieve the stress. If the audience is made to realize, for example, that its own safety is involved in whatever policies America develops toward air pollution, it will feel a need to find some means to alleviate this stress. If, in fact, such a motivation is aroused, then any proposal you recommend must be consistent with that motivation; the audience must perceive it as a means of relieving the stress brought about by the threat to its well-being. For this reason you must be sure that you provide motivation that grows out of your own particular solution to a problem. If a motivation merely creates stress, the audience may choose a solution that is quite different from the one you advocate. Arousing fear of air pollution, for instance, without directing that fear toward a specific goal may result in the decision to stop all cars and close all factories when you would have cautioned restraint. The motivation must, therefore, be developed not only in terms of exciting the audience's concern but also in directing it toward an acceptable solution. When you cause an audience to perceive a need, you motivate it to seek a solution to that need. But if you don't offer a specific proposal for action, the audience is disorganized and its behavior is not predictable. If, for example, you arouse feelings toward injustice without showing a means for the relief of injustice you may, in extreme cases, inadvertently be producing a riot.

Furthermore, society will usually judge you unkindly when you put the desire to motivate an audience above a concern for ideas that help to resolve problems. You are then in danger of being labeled a "rabble-rouser," and eventually your views may be ignored.

A final point is perhaps one of ethics rather than of rhetoric. Your first responsibility is to tell the truth as you see it, not to pursue the false god of temporary success. Above all, be honest with your audiences and true to yourself. Don't be like the student who truly believed in capital punishment but elected to argue against it because the instructor and the class opposed it.

B. Choose the Motivation That Is Best Adapted to the Audience

A representative of the police department speaking on highway safety to a high-school audience might appeal to the need for safety. Frequently, however, adults have lectured teenagers on such a subject only to discover that this appeal had no effect. Why? Because young people don't have the same fears of death that adults have. The solemn warnings of adults seem to teenagers to be pretended fears intended to thwart youth's natural independence and interest in adventure. The motivation of self-esteem might be more meaningful to an audience of young people. The speaker would better say, in essence:

No doubt about it, you are old enough to make your own decisions on what you should do. Adults have already put a lot of responsibilities on you, and in return we should be willing to give you some deserved privileges. Everyone should be allowed to clown a little, but you can see that too much fooling around in cars can be dangerous.

It's up to you to police yourselves. Tell the guy who goes too far and endangers others that he is not the kind of person you want to associate with. It is the few of that kind who make it tough on the great majority of drivers who are a real credit to themselves.

This argument bases its motivation on an appeal that is more likely to move the audience. Too many speakers use motivations they think *should* be effective. But if an audience is not religious, or patriotic, or acquisitive, then it will not respond to those motives. Build appeals on the motivations your listeners *actually* feel. You can do so only when you have made an accurate evaluation of what an audience thinks and feels about the subject of your speech. Here again the importance of audience analysis becomes clear.

C. Use Multiple Motivations Where Appropriate

You may wish to tell a group at a service club that support for the Children's Camping Fund will benefit the community and at the same time increase the stature of the club and its members. Thus you use both social and personal appeals to influence their self-esteem and win their support.

Multiple motivations are useful in meeting the problem of possible differences within audiences. There may be in an audience people who have an emotional concern for the community and at the same time others who, although they are impervious to this appeal, are susceptible to personal self-esteem. One appeal reaches one listener and a second reaches another, and so both may be persuaded. Indeed, Maslow states that motivations are usually multiple.*

D. Keep the Motivation Consistent

The fact that motivations may be or usually are plural does not mean that multiple motivation may be used indiscriminately. Unless the motivations compliment one another, a discordant note will be given to the speech and you will appear to be inconsistent. So, when you use two or more appeals, be sure that they are compatible. It is compatible to support a camping fund by offering the good of the community and enhancement of the listener's self-esteem as motivations because the listener fulfills self-esteem needs by doing what is "right" for the community (belongingness). But suppose you were to urge the retention of capital punishment on the grounds that it protects the listeners against murderers (physiological, safety) and also saves them tax money by eliminating the cost of keeping convicted murderers in prison (for most, a mild safety need). These motivations are not particularly compatible because the second motivation for many people runs precisely counter to the same antipathy toward taking human life that gives the first motivation its appeal. If you were to use an inconsistent double appeal of this sort, you would counter your own motivation. In essence, you expect the listener to respond to an appeal to self-preservation (a notion of the value of life) and also to a second appeal which, if accepted, denies the significance of life at least as compared with money. Motivation must be activated in the audience without establishing grounds for arousing those same emotions *against* the proposition.

When multiple motivation is appealed to, be sure that the consistency among the appeals is clear. Allow them to develop together so that they become, in a sense, parts of one motivation. Do not jump from one appeal to another.

* Abraham Maslow, *Motivation and Personality* (New York: Harper & Row, 1954), p. 68.

E. Let the Materials of the Speech Develop the Motivation

You will find it inadvisable to tell an audience straight out what motivation you want them to perceive as salient. You should not say, "And I tell you this for your own safety," or "You should feel love for these people," or "Do this because it will give you greater self-esteem." Most frequently, effective appeal is developed through the details of the speech, not by pointing it out. The old literary dictum applies well here: "Show, don't tell." Words have persuasive force only because they call up meanings that excite the motivations of a listener. If you wanted to arouse someone to some action concerning an automobile accident, which of the following would you do?

1. Discuss the emotion of those who give speeches about auto accidents?
2. Discuss the emotion of those who view auto accidents?
3. Discuss the emotions of those who are in auto accidents?
4. Show a picture of an auto accident?
5. Show a picture of an auto accident in which someone dear to the viewer was injured?

This list obviously moves from the less to the more personal. At the same time it moves from what is less concrete to what is more concrete. The more personal and the more concrete an idea, the greater is its capacity to stir up the motivations of an audience. To be successful as a speaker, you must select those examples, statistics, and comparisons and contrasts with which your listeners can identify their motivations.

F. Avoid Overusing Motivation

In one sense this principle is a contradiction in terms because an overused motivation is no motivation at all. The member of the college club or fraternity who sees all small crises as major catastrophies or the politician who sees every occasion as a time to defend "home, flag, and mother" lose effectiveness because listeners learn to discount what they say. At a time when the case demands powerful motivation, such speakers, like the boy who cried "wolf," will be ignored.

There is quite a bit of research on fear appeals, and the evidence is mixed as to their effectiveness when used in strong doses.* But it

* For a summary of the findings of this research, see Gary Cronkhite, *Persuasion: Speech and Behavioral Change* (Indianapolis: Bobbs Merrill, 1969), pp. 179–85.

is quite clear from the research, and common sense would confirm it, that with many people, strong fear appeals will have a boomerang effect. They will cause a receiver to avoid the problem presented by the message and perhaps become less interested in it than before.

What is the overuse of motivation? The answer to that question is determined by the audience. The history of oratory is resplendent with examples of great speeches with highly developed motivation by such men as Demosthenes, Cicero, John Donne, Daniel Webster, Abraham Lincoln, Woodrow Wilson, Franklin D. Roosevelt, Martin Luther King, or John F. Kennedy. One can also find great speeches with considerably more modified appeal, frequently by the same men. The key to the greatness of an orator is the ability to adapt to an audience.

SUMMARY

Motivation is found in people; it is not imposed upon them by a speaker. To be an effective speaker, you must identify your proposal with a motivation that the listener already possesses. There is a logic about motivation because the audience, starting from its own assumptions, is led by your speech through a rational progression to conclusions that are consistent with its view of the world. Because of its motivations, which are stirred up by what you say, the audience can identify with your proposal. Motivation must, therefore, be seen as a part of the listener's logic.

There is a hierarchy of need that establishes a basis for defining areas of motivation. The following one is developed from the ideas of psychologist Abraham Maslow:

1. Physiological needs
2. Safety needs
3. Belongingness and love needs
4. Esteem needs
5. Self-actualization needs
6. Freedom needs
7. Aesthetic needs

Although it is difficult for a person to consider more refined social needs when under strong physiological pressure, the social needs are the most important for a speaker.

Motivation is incorporated into the speech by using direct argument, by the building of the need, by the choice of examples, and by the choice of words.

In using motivation, follow these principles: The appeals should be a product of the ideas of the speech and not an end in themselves. The motivation should be consistent throughout the speech, even when motivation is multiple. The motivations used should be compatible with one another to insure consistency of effect. The materials of the speech should carry the motivation; you should avoid overusing motivation.

QUESTIONS

1. Which kinds of motivation do you suppose are most often effective with college students? Why?

2. How legitimate is the hierarchy?

3. What is the danger of using a large number of different motivations in a speech?

4. How can multiple motivation be effective?

5. How obvious should you be in identifying for your audience the motivation you use?

6. Give an example of overused motivation.

EXERCISES

1. Examine one of the speeches at the end of Chapter 17 and prepare a short written report showing what motivation the speaker uses and what specific techniques are used to develop that motivation.

2. Conduct a class discussion using one of the speeches at the end of Chapter 17. Discuss the kind of motivation used and the extent to which you would think it effective with two different audiences you identify.

3. Give a short oral report on the motivation you believe would be most effective on a specific subject to an audience of people like you.

I. The nature of credibility
   A. Credibility and *ethos*
   B. Credibility and ethics
II. Kinds of credibility
   A. Direct credibility
   B. Secondary credibility
   C. Indirect credibility
   D. Reputation
III. Factors of credibility
   A. Trustworthiness
   B. Competence
   C. Dynamism
   D. Audience and subject dependence of factors
IV. Developing credibility
   A. Be temperate in showing trustworthiness, competence, and dynamism.
   B. Build credibility indirectly.
   C. Use the credibility of others to support your own.
   D. Sometimes use candor to disarm a hostile audience.
   E. Use a chairperson's introduction to build credibility.

Chapter 10

The Credibility Dimension
of Communication

Credibility is a measure of the degree to which an audience accepts a message because of the trust the audience places in the source of the message. Perhaps no area of the study of communication has been so thoroughly researched as that of credibility. Consequently, there is more discussion about how it works than about such other factors of communication as evidence, argument, motivation, and language. It has also been viewed by some students of communication as a "dominant factor in persuasive communication."* It cannot be said to what extent it is a truly dominant factor or, instead, one that absorbs characteristics of other factors and merely appears to be dominant.† There can be no doubt, however, that the tradition of communication theory,

* James C. McCroskey, *An Introduction to Rhetorical Communication* (Englewoods Cliffs, N.J.: Prentice Hall, 1972), p. 63.

† James C. McCroskey and Robert E. Dunham, "Ethos: A Confounding Element in Communication Research," *Speech Monographs*, 33 (Nov. 1966), pp. 456–63; Paul D. Holtzman, "Confirmation of Ethos as a Confounding Element in Communication Research," *Speech Monographs*, 33 (Nov. 1966), pp. 464–66.

behavioral research, and popular lore all point to the perceived credibility of the speaker as an important factor in communication.

I. THE NATURE OF CREDIBILITY

Every time you believe something because it comes to you by the 6 o'clock news, you are giving credibility to the newscaster and the news team. Chances are when you accept what a professor tells you or you believe what is found in a book, you are accepting the ideas because you trust the source from which they came. And when you reject an idea because it comes from someone you don't trust, credibility is at the base of your negative judgment.

Most frequently, such credibility is mixed with other factors. That is, the source you trust also uses arguments you find reasonable and motivates you by using the beliefs, attitudes, and values that you already hold. And the process is self-supporting. You tend to see as most credible those persons whose values are the same as yours. So, over time, the credibility of a message source will be affected by your attitude toward the message as will the message be affected by the credibility of the source.

A. Credibility and Ethos

Aristotle used the term *ethos* to name the kind of proof that is provided by the character of a speaker. The concept of *ethos* is frequently associated with credibility. However, it applied only to what Aristotle called the "artistic" proofs; that is, those which were provided by the speaker in his design of the message.* Obviously, ethos is still a useful term, but it is only one part of credibility; other factors, those which Aristotle called "nonartistic," also must be considered. Credibility, therefore, includes more than what is designed by the speaker. Audience assumptions prior to the speech, as we shall see, are also important in affecting persuasion.

B. Credibility and Ethics

Because *ethos* has been translated by some writers as "ethical proof" and "the character of the speaker," it has often been associated with

* *The Rhetoric of Aristotle,* trans. by Lane Cooper (New York: Appleton-Century-Crofts, 1932), p. 8.

ethics. But although it is often true that a credible speaker does meet some religious, humanistic, or general societal standard of ethics and morals, credibility is assigned by an audience. It is not an ideal characteristic lodged in a person. In the extreme sense, a cutthroat has great credibility for a band of pirates. Even though people should give credibility only to those they consider to have the highest ethical sense, they do not automatically do so. It is true, in general, that societies tend to have identifiable value systems which apply in most cases, but individuals and groups within the society will vary the emphasis they place on different segments of the societal value system. It is important in understanding credibility not to assume that it has a necessary ethical component.

II. KINDS OF CREDIBILITY

Let's look at four kinds of statements by speakers that may be given credibility by a listener: direct credibility, secondary credibility, indirect credibility, and reputation. Let us remind you again that although, from time to time we will speak of credibility as if it resided in the speaker, it is the credibility *which audiences give to speakers* that we are interested in.

A. Direct Credibility

Some speakers will make direct references to themselves in an attempt to gain credibility. They will tell their listeners about aspects of their character that should make them believable: "Listen, I wouldn't cheat you," "you ask Sam, he will tell you I'm a right guy," "I promise you I will do everything in my power to see that you are happy."

Here is Shirley Chisholm, congresswoman from New York, using direct credibility as she announces her candidacy for president on January 25, 1972:

I stand before you today as a candidate for the Democratic nomination for the Presidency of the United States.

I am not the candidate of Black America, although I am Black and proud.

I am not the candidate of the Women's Movement of this country, although I am a woman, and I am equally proud of that.

I am not the candidate of any political bosses or special interests.

I stand here now—without endorsements from any big name politicians or celebrities or any other kind of prop. I do not intend to offer you the tired and glib clichés which have for too long been an accepted part of our political life. I am the candidate of the people, and my presence before you now symbolizes a new era in American political history.*

B. Secondary Credibility

Secondary credibility is somewhat like direct credibility in that the source of credibility is identified directly but depends for its strength on the credibility an audience will give to someone else whom the speaker associates with his proposal. All testimony has favorable secondary credibility or it is worthless. You would surely never quote someone your audience had no confidence in, or worse still, distrusted.

In the following excerpt, Phyllis Jones Springen addressed the Danforth Associates on "The Dimensions of the Oppression of Women" in 1971, using the secondary credibility of Swedish sociologist Gunnar Myrdal to support her own views about women:

Gunnar Myrdal added an appendix to his *American Dilemma* entitled, "A Parallel to the Negro Problem." He traced the emancipation of both the slave and the woman with the economic changes of the Industrial Revolution. He went on to say that as in the Negro problem, most men had accepted as self-evident the doctrine that women had inferior endowments in most of those respects which carry prestige and power in society. (About the only thing not said about women is that they all have rhythm.)

Myrdal continued that as the Negro had his "place," so there was a "woman's place." The myth of the contented woman who did not want suffrage or civil rights had the same social function as the myth of the "contented Negro."

Her education was first neglected, then changed to a special type to fit her for her "place." He went on to say that the most important disabilities affecting a woman's status were those barring her attempt to earn a living and attain promotion in her work.

The same cycle Myrdal described is still present in 1970. A woman is not expected to earn a living. Laws still on the books treat her as an inferior creature. And the woman who does work—no matter how well qualified—

Shirley Chisholm, "Statement of Candidacy," released by Shirley Chisholm for President Headquarters, Cambridge, Mass., Jan. 25, 1972.

often works for far less than the male—even the Negro male who is known to be the victim of discrimination.*

C. Indirect Credibility

Unlike the previously mentioned two forms of credibility, where speakers directly associate their proposal with their own or someone else's qualifications, there is a third kind which is indirect.

In this sense every statement has credibility to the extent that it identifies the speaker with arguments, motivation, values, and salient beliefs in which the audience has confidence. Even the use of language the audience admires or delivery techniques that impress it add to this kind of credibility. In Chapter 19, "Criticizing Speeches," you will find an example of two contrasting statements by former President Richard Nixon that illustrates the difference between direct and indirect credibility.

D. Reputation

In a very real sense, the three forms of credibility we have just discussed (direct, secondary, and indirect) are all parts of what Aristotle called *ethos*, the artistic actions of the speaker to which the listener may give credibility. Reputation refers to that credibility which speakers have before they begin to speak, based on their past actions. Reputation may be altered by the other forms of credibility but only over time. At the beginning of a communication act, speakers are stuck with their reputation—and it can have a great effect on their effectiveness.

The problem of reputation has a special problem for the inexperienced speaker. For instance, as you address your class, chances are you don't have a reputation to draw on. There are probably groups in which you are known, where you can draw on your reputation. Perhaps your high school club, church group, or small group of close friends will accept what you say because your reputation is good with them. Individuals in your class may give you credibility because they know you. But for many people in the class you have no reputation, and for them you will need to build other forms of credibility.

* Phyllis Jones Springen, "The Dimensions of the Oppression of Women," *Vital Speeches of the Day,* 37 (Feb. 15, 1971), p. 266.

III. FACTORS OF CREDIBILITY

There has been considerable research in recent years to identify those factors to which audiences give credibility.* That research has produced a variety of factors but two which have been with us since Aristotle first defined the factors of *ethos,* emerge on all scales: trustworthiness and competence.

A. Trustworthiness

Trustworthiness as a factor of credibility tells us that listeners tend to give credibility to people they feel can be trusted. Obviously, what characteristics are signs of trustworthiness will vary with audience and subject.

B. Competence

Judgments of competence may vary from one audience to another. One audience may find competent the person who engages in manual labor, while another sees competence as a function of higher education. However, any audience must perceive you to be competent, however it may define the term, before it will consider you a credible source.

C. Dynamism

A third factor has been identified by a number of researchers: dynamism. Dynamism, that is, greater intensity of language and voice and greater physical activity, seems to serve as an intensifier. How-

* Kenneth Andersen and Theodore Clevenger, Jr., "A Summary of Experimental Research in Ethos," *Speech Monographs,* **30** (June 1963), pp. 59–78; Kenneth Andersen, *Persuasion: Theory and Practice* (Boston: Allyn and Bacon, 1971), pp. 217–63; Kim Giffin, "The Contribution of Studies of Source Credibility to a Theory of Interpersonal Trust in the Communication Process," *Psychological Bulletin,* **68** (Aug. 1967), pp. 104–20; James C. McCroskey, *An Introduction to Rhetorical Communication,* pp. 63–81; David Markham, "The Dimensions of Source Credibility of Television Newscasters," *Journal of Communication,* **18** (1968), pp. 57–64; and Jack L. Whitehead, "Factors of Source Credibility," *Quarterly Journal of Speech,* **54** (Feb. 1968), pp. 59–63; Carl I. Hovland, Irving L. Janis, and Harold H. Kelly, *Communication and Persuasion,* (New Haven, Conn.: Yale University Press, 1953).

ever, it does not always show up on the scales and, unlike trustworthiness and competence, it can be viewed as negative.* What may be dynamic to one person is too "pushy," "brassy," or "loud" to another. The overly aggressive salesman is a good example of the negative quality of dynamism. Although it is difficult to imagine someone's saying, "I didn't like him because he was too trustworthy," or "She's competent, so she must be wrong," it is not strange at all to think of a remark like "I don't trust him, he's too pushy."

D. Audience and Subject Dependence of Factors

We have already mentioned this point earlier, but before we look at some ideas about how to develop credibility for a speech, we should remind ourselves again that these characteristics are audience-defined. Thus, although everyone will want a speaker to be competent, different people define competence differently. Business men put greater trust in those who have "met a payroll"; tradesmen see competence in those who work with their hands. Frequently, we see speakers who have to tell their audiences about past experiences in order to build credibility. The politician who says to a group of farmers, "I was a farm boy myself," is building credibility. Credibility is also subject-related.† The skilled machinist may see competence lodged mostly in his own kind until his child is ill or he has to go to court. Then the physician or the lawyer seems most competent.

In addition to variety in the ways people define each of the factors, there is a dynamism about the relation among the factors. Suppose an audience finds you highly trustworthy but not particularly competent, or vice versa. These are not unusual situations, which illus-

* W. Barnett Pearce, "The Effect of Vocal Cues on Credibility and Attitude Change," *Western Speech*, 35 (Summer 1971), pp. 176–84; McCroskey, *An Introduction to Rhetorical Communication*, op. cit., p. 75; William McEwen and Bradley S. Greenberg, "The Effects of Message Intensity on Receiver Evaluations of Source, Message and Topic," *Journal of Communication*, 20 (Dec. 1970), pp. 340–50; Gerald R. Miller and John Basehart, "Source Trustworthiness, Opinionated Statements and Responses to Persuasive Communication," *Speech Monographs*, 36 (March 1969), pp. 1–7; Gerald Miller and J. Lobe, "Opinionated Language, Open- and Closed-Mindedness and Response to Persuasive Communication," *Journal of Communication*, 17 (Dec. 1967), pp. 333–41; Velma J. (Wenzlaff) Lashbrook, "Source Credibility: A Summary of Experimental Research," Paper presented to the Speech Communication Association Convention, San Francisco, Dec. 1971, p. 8.

† Milton Rokeach and Gilbert Rothman, "The Principles of Belief Congruence and the Congruity Principle as a Model of Cognitive Interaction," *Psychological Review*, 72 (March 1965), pp. 128–42.

trates again the complexity of credibility. In addition, impressions of competence and trustworthiness may change as the communication act takes place. Thus reputation is only a starting place.

There is also some evidence to show that low credibility is not the opposite of high credibility in a particular situation but may involve a quite different factor.*

IV. DEVELOPING CREDIBILITY

Five principles may help you to use credibility in a speech.

1. Be temperate in showing trustworthiness, competence, and dynamism.
2. Build credibility indirectly.
3. Use the credibility of others to support your own.
4. Sometimes use candor to disarm a hostile audience.
5. Use a chairman's introduction to build credibility.

A. Be Temperate in Showing Trustworthiness, Competence, and Dynamism

Although you must show your listeners that you are worth listening to, you have the potential for injuring your credibility if you create the impression that you are too self-centered. It is generally agreed, however, that if direct statements about credibility are introduced in a not too obvious way, they tend to increase the listener's willingness to believe what you say.† Frequently, you can avoid the problem of political injury by specifically downgrading your experience humor-

---

* Don Schweitzer and Gerald P. Ginsburg, "Factors of Communication Credibility," in Carl W. Backman and Paul F. Secord, *Problems in Social Psychology* (New York: McGraw-Hill, 1966), pp. 94–102. See also Elliot Aronson and Burton W. Golden, "The Effects of Relevant and Irrelevant Aspects of Communicator Credibility on Opinion Change," *Journal of Personality*, 30 (June 1962), pp. 135–46; Jean S. Kerrick, "The Effect of Relevant and Nonrelevant Sources on Attitude Change," *Journal of Social Psychology*, 47 (1958), pp. 15–20; J. W. Koehler, J. C. McCroskey, and W. E. Arnold, "The Effect of Receivers Constancy Expectations in Persuasive Communication," Research Monograph, Department of Speech, Pennsylvania State University, University Park, Pa., 1966.

† Kenneth Andersen, *Persuasion: Theory and Practice* (Boston: Allyn and Bacon, 1971), p. 228; Terry H. Ostermeier, "Effects of Type and Frequency of Self-Reference upon Perceived Source Credibility and Attitude Change," *Speech Monographs*, 34 (June 1967), pp. 137–44.

ously. Here is a professor of economics speaking before a business-man's club.

I appreciate your introduction, Mr. Trautman, and I am pleased to be here to give you some of my observations of the problems of the small businessman during cyclical changes. I have spent many years sutdying this problem. I was also foolish enough to write a book on business cycles a few years back. I'm sometimes afraid that the more I study the less I know, and I'm sure you're all aware of the old saying that if all the economists in the world were placed end to end they wouldn't reach a conclusion.

Direct, heavy-handed attempts to impress listeners with one's own qualifications, to speak like the salesman who keeps insisting that he has no personal reason for making a sale, when the customer knows that he does, can be injurious.

The research evidence clearly supports the common sense notion that you should avoid any statements which communicate to your listeners that you mean to manipulate them.*

B. Build Credibility Indirectly

Much of your credibility is built by the fact that you show through your thoroughness, accuracy, and careful thought that you are competent rather than by *telling* listeners that you are competent.

In a very real sense, all the factors of the speaking situation go together. Credibility helps to make argument, evidence† and motivation more believable and thus more persuasive. Conversely, when you organize, support, and use ideas and language well you strengthen your credibility.

C. Use the Credibility of Others to Support Your Own

To a large extent, quotations from sources that rank high in the estimation of your listener help to make you more believable. By

---

* Carl I. Hovland, Irving L. Janis, and Harold H. Kelly, *Communication and Persuasion* (New Haven, Conn.: Yale University Press, 1953), p. 86.

† The use of supporting material has been shown to strengthen credibility particularly of a speaker with low credibility and particularly if the evidence is not known to the listener. James C. McCroskey, "A Summary of Experimental Research on the Effects of Evidence in Persuasive Communication," *Quarterly Journal of Speech*, 55 (April 1969), p. 175.

adding this secondary credibility to your own, you can make your messages more believable.*

D. Sometimes Use Candor to Disarm a Hostile Audience

So much emphasis is placed on not offending hostile listeners that you may think it is always best to hide your true views from such an audience. But many speakers are so successful through candor that that technique cannot be ignored. Several years ago an assemblyman in California spoke to a regional meeting of the California State Employees' Association and said in effect, "There is no need to disguise the truth many of you know. I voted against your pay raises this year, and it's only fair to tell you that I will do it again if I feel that they are against the interests of the state." Persons who were at that meeting still comment on his statement and remark, "He may not agree with you, but at least he's a man who isn't afraid to tell you where he stands." Candor in that case built credibility contradicting the all-too-prevalent notion that a politician is one who skirts issues. There are grave dangers in hiding your biases. When a receiver discovers that there is covert bias, that is the time when the most damage is done to your credibility.†

E. Use a Chairperson's Introduction to Build Credibility

The chairperson's introduction can build the credibility of a speaker by giving relevant facts that will be significant to the audience. A chairperson who is better known to the audience than you are can fre-

---

* Kenneth Andersen and Theodore Clevenger, Jr., "A Summary of Experimental Research in Ethos," *Speech Monographs*, 30 (June, 1963), p. 71; Robert S. Cathcart, "An Experimental Study of the Relative Effectiveness of Four Methods of Presenting Evidence," *Speech Monographs*, 22 (Aug. 1955), 227–33; Terry H. Ostermeier, "Effects of Type and Frequency of Self-Reference upon Perceived Source Credibility and Attitude Change, *Speech Monographs*, 34 (June 1967), pp. 137–44; Irving D. Warren, "The Effect of Credibility in Sources of Testimony on Audience Attitudes Toward Speaker and Message," *Speech Monographs*, 36 (Nov. 1969), pp. 456–58; M. Myers and A. Goldberg, "Group Credibility and Opinion Change," *Journal of Communication*, 20 (June 1970), pp. 174–179.

† Judson Mills and Elliot Aronson, "Opinion Change as a Function of a Communicator's Attractiveness and Desire to Influence," *Journal of Personality and Social Psychology*, 1 (1965), pp. 173–77.

quently do a better job of building credibility for you than you yourself can.* Remember this situation when you are called upon to chair a meeting and plan your introductions carefully with it in mind.

SUMMARY

Credibility is an important factor in persuasion. Listeners attribute it to you on the basis, primarily, of the extent to which they feel that, on a given subject, you are competent and trustworthy. In some cases it is given because of dynamism on your part. Credibility is broader than the term *ethos* because it includes the reputation you have before a speech, not merely what you do within the speech. It should not be confused with ethics. Some persons who might be considered unethical when measured by general community standards will have great credibility among their peers.

There are four kinds of credibility. Direct credibility is what a speaker seeks when making direct statements about credibility. Secondary credibility involves the process of identifying other credible sources with one's own self and message. Indirect credibility is that built by the strength of the argument, motivation, evidence, and the like.

Credibility may be consciously developed by observing five principles: Be temperate in direct credibility, build indirect credibility, use the credibility of others, sometimes be candid, and use a chairman's introduction to build credibility.

QUESTIONS

1. What is credibility?
2. What is *ethos*? How do credibility and ethos differ?
3. How does credibility differ from ethics?
4. What are the two clear characteristics that you must evidence in order to win credibility?
5. Which rules for developing credibility seem most universal?

* Kenneth Andersen and Theodore Clevenger, Jr., "A Summary of Experimental Research in Ethos," *Speech Monographs*, 30 (June 1963), p. 64; Franklin Haiman, "An Experimental Study of the Effect of Ethos on Public Speaking," *Speech Monographs*, 16 (Aug. 1949), pp. 190–202.

EXERCISES

1. Consider some prominent public speaker you have heard recently. What did you know about his reputation before you heard his speech that affected your reception of his ideas? What did his speech do to confirm or deny your opinion of him? Write a short paper explaining your reactions.

2. Which do you consider more important to a speaker's effectiveness, motivation or credibility? Why?

3. Examine two of the three speeches following Chapter 17. How well does the speaker develop credibility according to the principles discussed in this chapter?

I. The purpose of the outline
II. Types of outlines
   A. The scratch outline
   B. The brief
   C. The rhetorical outline
      1. The complete sentence outline
      2. The topic outline
III. Techniques of outlining
   A. Parts of the outline
      1. Introduction
      2. Body
      3. Conclusion
   B. Subordination and coordination
      1. Subordinate ideas
      2. Coordinate ideas
      3. Symbols of subordination and coordination
   C. Number of headings
   D. Checking the outline
      1. Logical consistency
      2. Formal correctness
      3. Content completeness of informative speech outlines
IV. Important technical principles
   A. Each heading an assertion
   B. Each heading a single idea
   C. No more than one symbol for any one heading
   D. Headings discrete
   E. Usually at least two coordinate headings at each level
V. Revising the outline

Chapter 11

Outlining

A clearly evident characteristic of any instance of human communication is the presence of order. That is to say, any message whatsoever will (and must) have structure of some kind. This follows, of course, from the fact that there cannot be substance of any sort without form. The two are inseparable in the sense that the one cannot exist without the other. Every painting must have composition; every statue must have shape; every verbal message must have some kind of structure. And form is an essential factor in determining how substance is perceived. How verbal communications are understood, then, is partly but importantly determined by the order a speaker imposes upon the materials of a speech. We can, for our purposes, define order in a speech as the sensible, intelligible structure that enforms its substance.

Even though some kind of structure is necessary (in the sense that it is inescapable), no particular structure will necessarily be the right one, the best one, or the most useful. The random throwing of a pair of dice will produce an order of a kind. When the dice stop rolling, they will be in some spatial relationship to each other and the numbers that show on their faces will be in some numerical relationship to each other. But to create order in this fashion is willy-nilly. Apply this notion to speaking: No matter how badly a communicator garbles a message, it will still communicate *something* to an audience. Indeed, it is even possible that an audience will interpret a jumbled message to mean what the speaker intends to say. But because so much of this outcome is the result of chance, the outcome is inherently unpredictable. Human communication of the sort we are concerned with aims at influencing mental and physical behavior in a precise and predetermined manner. When you speak, you want to be as sure as possible that a message will get the response you want. But the ideas and materials of a speech usually come to you in a helter-skelter fashion. You gather information, evidence, and arguments as they come to light. Common sense strongly suggests, therefore, that if an audience must grasp, in perhaps 5 minutes, a message that you may have had 5 days or even 5 weeks to prepare, a reasonable sequence and form will improve the audience's chances of understanding your message *accurately*.

Moreover, the efficiency of communication will certainly be increased because the audience requires less effort to understand what you mean when ideas are presented in a coherent order. The greater the ease with which an audience can listen and understand, the greater the chance its interest will be maintained and the greater the chance that it will be willing to listen at all. For these reasons, you will certainly profit from presenting the otherwise isolated and random elements of a speech in coherent and orderly sequence and form.

Look now at the utility of being well-ordered from a related but somewhat different point of view. Human beings will not, with ease, long tolerate chaos. Randomness in events makes the events unpredictable, and the ability to make predictions that are at least hopefully dependable is a necessity for mental comfort. Thus people instinctively look for order in their world. They will certainly look for it in the messages communicated to them by other people. Organization, therefore, is necessary because it is *expected*. To achieve your goals in speaking, you must meet the expectations of your audience. In listening, these expectations become needs that you must fulfill if they are to give you the response you want. Everything you do, then, is aimed at fulfilling the needs of your listeners. If this is done, the listeners will accept what is said. If not, they will very likely reject it, or quite possibly fail to perceive the meanings you are trying to convey. Neither of these latter two outcomes will be a happy one.

We have been talking to this point not about any particular organization a speaker may use other than to say that hopefully it will be a good one. In Chapters 15, 16, 17, and 18 we shall discuss and describe particular methods of organizing the message under consideration in each chapter. It will be clear when you look at these that we think of organization as a wholly active process, wherein speakers make and carry out decisions about the structure they will impose on their speech materials. In this chapter it is our purpose to talk about the written manifestation of the organization of a speech. This is called an outline. Outlining is a significant aspect of speech preparation because outlines are related to organization; because good organization brings desirable order to a speech and because, as we have seen, a reasonable order is an important help toward success. This chapter, therefore, shows you how to make a good outline for a speech.

I. THE PURPOSE OF THE OUTLINE

The basic function of the speech outline is to make visible to your eye the relationships your mind sees among the elements of the speech. It represents on paper the division of ideas suggested by your analysis of the subject; it suggests by the manner in which it groups related materials the logical connections among them; it manifests the coherence, sequence, and form that your sense of rhetorical effectiveness imposes upon the ideas and materials encompassed by the subject and the purpose of your speech. In addition to helping organize a speech, the outline is helpful in delivering it. Since the outline is a plan of what you intend to say, carefully arranged in advance, it helps to insure you against the danger of omitting anything significant. At the same time, it helps to insure against any temptation to ramble, to bring in notions that are unnecessary, unrelated, and extraneous. The outline is the blueprint for the speech.

II. TYPES OF OUTLINES

A. The Scratch Outline

Almost any group of comments can be jotted down on paper and called an outline. Such a *scratch* outline might be helpful in beginning to think about a topic, but it would serve only poorly as a final means of organizing a speech. More often than not, probably, the parts of such an outline will first occur in the form of questions. These questions identify such things as the information areas you must investigate and the general blocks of information or argument that must be developed for the audience in order to fulfill their expectations and achieve your goals. Let's take an example. Suppose you want to talk about the problem of slums in American cities. First off, you might raise such questions as, "What do we mean by slums?" "What causes them?" "Where are they?" "Who lives in them?" "Why?" When you write these questions down (if you do), you have what may be called a scratch outline of some of the general notions that will be covered in the speech. If your purpose is persuasive and you want to argue in defense of a proposition (say, for example, to support Federal slum clearance legislation), you may identify some obvious issues and jot down some arguments that come easily to mind.

Such uses of scratch outlines are, as we say, helpful. Others are frequently less so. Instead of representing a planned structuring of ideas, they are "laundry lists" of random notions only vaguely related to each other and to the central topic of the speech. To begin thinking about a topic this way isn't necessarily all bad. Unfortunately, however, many outlines are never developed beyond this level because the speaker has taken the easy way out. In general, the result will be an outline representative of poor topic analysis, inadequate development of the subject, and a set of speaking notes of precious little help in delivery.

B. The Brief

At the other extreme from the almost inevitably inadequate scratch outline is the brief. The most elaborate of all outline forms, the most thorough in its preparation, and the most inclusive in its content, is called, paradoxically, a *brief*. The brief is an argumentative outline and contains *all* of the arguments that a speaker can discover both *for* and *against* a proposition. It takes its name from the compilation of arguments presented to a court by an attorney. Ideally, the brief is a complete storehouse of arguments on both sides of a debatable proposition. Each item in a brief is a complete sentence. The usefulness of a brief is apparent, especially in situations like debate, where speakers are likely to be confronted with many of the opposing arguments included in the brief. Moreover, preparing a brief helps to assure complete analysis of a proposition.

C. The Rhetorical Outline

Despite its usefulness in analysis, and despite its value as a store-house of detailed information on both sides of a controversy, the length of a brief makes it unsatisfactory as an outline for a persuasive speech. Moreover, because the materials of the brief are not oriented toward a specific audience, it suffers, in a somewhat different sense, from a problem of the scratch outline; that is, because of its all-inclusiveness, it is a sophisticated sort of laundry list. When you want to argue for or against a proposition, select from the brief only those materials which will help to prove a case for a specific audience and then organize them into a useful outline. Indeed, the brief itself need not ever exist. When you have finished analyzing the proposition, however, you have examined the materials you would use if a brief were to be made.

The materials selected for use in a speech are put into a *rhetorical* outline. The rhetorical outline has the same general structure as the longer, more detailed brief. As we have said, however, it is unlike the brief in the essential respect that instead of being a compilation of all the available information on a given subject, it contains only those materials and ideas which will be needed to accomplish the purpose of a specific speaking situation. The rhetorical outline is by far the most useful at all stages of preparation and in delivery of the speech.

1. The Complete Sentence Outline

In writing a rhetorical outline, we frequently meet the temptation to state each idea as a grammatically complete sentence. The reason may be that we tend to write the outline of a speech as if we were talking. The temptation should be overcome, because a complete sentence outline, whether we want it to happen or not, will almost inevitably result in a manuscript of the speech or, at any rate, a document that in delivery needs only the addition of a transition here and there. Such a practice, however, will give strong impetus to speaking from the manuscript, or from memory, and as you can see from Chapter 13, each of these modes of delivery has serious limitations. We want to help you develop skill in *extemporaneous* communication.

2. The Topic Outline

A better form of the rhetorical outline, and the one we consider best for outlining effective extemporaneous speeches, is the *topic* outline.

The logical structure of the topic outline is identical with that of the complete sentence rhetorical outline. The essential difference is that instead of presenting complete ideas throughout, the topic outline uses key phrases intended to help identify the idea that belongs in a given heading. To make this difference clear, let's go back to the example of slums in American cities. A speaker, advocating passage of a Federal slum clearance bill, was demonstrating the seriousness of the problem. One section of the speech will help to compare the complete sentence outline with the topic outline.

Complete Sentence Outline	*Topic Outline*
I. Slums are a serious problem in American cities.	I. Slums a serious American problem
A. Decay has occurred in major American cities.	A. Decay
1. Areas of more than 40 years of age have become decay spots.	1. In spots 40 years old
2. 27 percent of non-farm homes do not meet Federal standards of structure and sanitation.	2. 27 percent unsound, unsanitary
B. There is an insufficient number of dwellings for the population.	B. Insufficient dwellings
1. More than 1.5 persons per room is considered by sociologists to be overcrowding.	1. Overcrowding at 1.5 per room
2. Of America's dwelling places, 6 percent house more than 1.5 persons per room.	2. 6 percent hold more than 1.5
C. Slum areas create financial problems: 15 percent of Los Angeles live in slum areas.	C. Financial problems: Los Angeles, 15 percent in slums

1. They contribute less than 3 percent of the city's tax income.	1. Less than 3 percent of tax income
2. They consume 33 percent of the city Health Department's budget.	2. 33 percent of Health Department's budget
3. They require more than 33 percent of the city's law-enforcement budget.	3. More than 33 percent of law-enforcement budget.
II. . . . (and so on)	II. . . . (and so on)

The column on the left is a well-developed rhetorical outline that clearly communicates the intention of the speaker. In its entirety, such an outline will reconstruct for its readers the substance of the speech, even if they were not to hear it delivered. The topic outline, on the other hand, shows an identical organization and contains precisely the same supporting detail. At the same time, despite its economy of language, the topic outline will be quite clear to the speaker and allow greater flexibility in language and detail. This type of outline will be most useful in the great majority of public speaking situations active, effective citizens meet.

III. TECHNIQUES OF OUTLINING

All speeches that are substantive in content and substantial in length, have three identifiable parts: a beginning, a middle, and an end. Outlines for speeches mirror these three essential parts in what are called, respectively, an introduction, a body, and a conclusion. A speaker uses each of these three parts for its appropriate function.

A. Parts of the Outline

Although people may hear you speak, they do not inevitably listen. But since you cannot be an effective speaker until you gain your hearers' attention, your first job is to make them listen.

1. Introduction

The devices used to catch your audience's attention and arouse their interest, the things said to make them listen, are included in the first part of the speech and the outline, called the introduction. Included also are the subject sentence indicating the purpose of the speech, and any necessary background material.

2. Body

After the introduction, the specific purpose is developed in the body of the speech. Here the speaker either informs, persuades, or entertains the audience in accordance with the speech purpose.

3. Conclusion

Th conclusion summarizes the speech or rounds it out in some appropriate manner. The following example illustrates the general format of the outline and its parts.

INTRODUCTION

I. Attention and interest material
II. Subject sentence of the speech
III. Background material (if necessary)

BODY

I. First main point
II. Second main point
III. Third main point
(And so on)

CONCLUSION

I. Brief summary of the main points
II. Restatement of the subject sentence
III. Remarks that will bring the speech to a graceful close

B. Subordination and Coordination

The symbol (I, II, 1, 2, A, B, a, b, or the like) that marks each main head and subhead shows the relationship of that heading to others in the outline. The symbols used, and also the degree to which a heading in an outline is indented, indicate the superior, subordinate, or coordinate rank of the heading.

1. Subordinate Ideas

If one idea is used to explain, or prove, or otherwise support another, it is said to be *subordinate* to the other.

> I. A main head is superior to its subheads.
> A. Subheads are subordinate to their main heads.

The indenting of the subhead and the use of a different symbol series indicates the subordination to the eye. In the outline, subordinate heads *always follow* the main head. (Note: When substantive examples of outlining techniques are given in the following illustrations, they will often appear in complete sentences. This is not because we are unmindful of our advice to use key phrases and a topic outline format. It is because the examples are taken out of their context and therefore might not otherwise be meaningful.)

> *Wrong:* I. Evidence or supporting material, (therefore)
>
>   A. Main idea
>
> *Right:* I. Main idea, (which we understand because)
>   A. Evidence or supporting material

> I. 27 percent of nonfarm homes do not meet Federal standards of structure and sanitation, (therefore)
>   A. Decay has occurred in major American cities
>
> I. Decay has occurred in major American cities, (which we understand because)
>
>   A. 27 percent of nonfarm homes do not meet Federal standards of structure and sanitation

This same principle holds true at no matter what level of subordination you are outlining. If, for example, the subhead in the illustration just above were itself in need of further explanation or support, the material used to support it would be placed after A, indented from it, and labeled with a different symbol series to indicate subordination:

> I. First main head
>   A. Support for explanation for I
>   1. Support or explanation for A

For persuasive effect *in delivery*, you may wish to develop an idea by presenting first the support and then the main head. But if you tried to outline the material in this manner, you would create the danger of becoming lost in detail and causing the audience to overlook the main head. If, in order to achieve some rhetorical effect (say, for example, climax), you decide to present some portion of the materials in this way, you should not materially change from the conventional outline. A change in outline form might be confusing to the eye. Note in the following example the confusion when only a change in a letter, not any change in symbol series or indentation, marks the movement from one main idea to another.

I. First main head	I. Decay has occuurred in major American cities.
A. Support for I	A. Areas of more than 40 years of age have been allowed to become decay spots.
B. Further support for I	B. 27 percent of nonfarm homes do not meet Federal standards of structure and sanitation.
A. Support for II	A. More than 1.5 persons per room is considered by sociologists to be overcrowding.
B. Further support for II	B. Of America's dwelling places, 6 percent house more than 1.5 persons per room.
II. Second main head	II. There is an insufficient number of dwellings for the population.
III. Third main head (And so on)	III. Slum areas create financial problems. (And so on)

The outline is clearer and easier to control if you keep it in conventional form and add an arrow to the margin of the paper to remind yourself that the sequence of delivery is to be reversed.

I. First main head	I. Decay has occurred in major American cities.
A. Support for I	A. Areas of more than 40 years of age have been allowed to become decay spots.
B. Further support for I	B. 27 percent of non-farm homes do not meet Federal standards of structure and sanitation.
II. Second main head	II. There is an insufficient number of dwellings for the population.
A. Support for II	A. More than 1.5 persons per room is considered by sociologists to be overcrowding.
B. Further support for II	B. Of America's dwelling places, 6 percent house more than 1.5 persons per room.
III. Third main head (And so on)	III. Slum areas create financial problems. (And so on)

2. Coordinate Ideas

If two or more headings in the outline support the same larger heading, they are said to be coordinate. In the outline illustration just given, headings A and B under I are coordinate with each other and, by the same token, A and B under II are coordinate with each other. Note also that I, II, and III are coordinate. The larger heading they coordinately support is the proposition of the speech itself. In every instance, all coordinate ideas under the same heading are given an equal degree of indentation and are labeled with consecutive symbols in the same series.

3. Symbols of Subordination and Coordination

The symbols used to show subordination and coordination are purely arbitrary, but custom has established a fairly general usage. Main heads are designated with Roman numerals, first-level subheads with capital letters; then follow Arabic numerals and lower-case letters in that order for further subordination. Any intelligible system of symbols is perfectly satisfactory, provided that they are consistent for all of the ideas in a coordinated series, and provided that they distinguish subordinate from coordinate ideas. The sequence may be as follows:

I. First main heading
   A. Clarification or proof of I
      1. Clarification or proof of A
         a. Clarification or proof of 1
            (1) Clarification or proof of a
               (a) Clarification or proof of (1)
               (b) Further clarification or proof of (1)
            (2) Further clarification or proof of a
         b. Further clarification or proof of 1
      2. Further clarification or proof of A
   B. Further clarification or proof of I
II. Second main heading
   [And so on]

C. Number of Headings

The process of arranging the materials of a speech into a series of main heads and subheads that show proper coordination and subordination will raise the question as to how many headings may be used at any given level of subordination. There is no definite answer beyond saying that the number of headings depends entirely upon what a speaker thinks will accomplish his purpose. For the main heads this number will usually be somewhere between two and five. It is quite possible, however, for a very brief speech to develop a single main head to explain one aspect of a subject in informative speaking, or to develop a single argument in persuasive speaking. Using more than five main headings will ordinarily make it difficult for an audience to remember very many details of what the speaker has said.

D. Checking the Oultine

As the outline develops, it should be checked for logical consistency, formal correctness, and (in the case of informative speeches) content completeness.

1. Logical Consistency

Since the major purpose of outlining materials is to blueprint a speech and to put order into ideas, logical consistency is an absolute requirement for the outline itself. It is met by making sure that the coordination and subordination indicated by the outline are present in the ideas themselves. Suppose, for example, that a speaker arguing for the creation of a metropolitan transit authority were to organize a section of the speech outline thus:

> I. Residents of Los Angeles are facing a crisis in transportation.
>   A. Responsible and informed citizens agree something must be done.
>   1. The mayor made this a central issue in his campaign for reelection.
>   2. The City Council has established a commission to study the problem.
>   B. Traffic congestion is at a breakdown point.
>   1. Approximately 600,000 automobiles enter and leave the downtown area of Los Angeles every 24 hours.
>   a. Most cars carry only 1 person: the average is 1.4 persons per car.
>   b. More than half come and go between 7 and 9 A.M. and 4 and 6 P.M.
>   c. Rush-hour traffic is mainly one way.
>   (1) Morning traffic is mostly inbound.
>   (2) Evening traffic is mostly outbound.
>   d. Cars are expensive to operate.
>   2. Adequate parking facilities are unavailable.

This format would have told us that "d" is subordinate to "1" and thus that idea "d" helps to support or clarify idea "1." Clearly, though, the idea that cars are expensive to operate has no direct connection with how many automobilies enter and leave downtown Los Angeles every day. Nor does the idea that driving a car is expensive help to explain or to prove the idea (b) that traffic congestion is at a breakdown point. In no logical sense, then, is "d" subordinate to either "1" or "B." Instead, the idea that cars are expensive to operate much more directly supports the idea in the main head (I). Its logical purpose in the speech is to help show the urgency and magnitude of the problem itself—its place in the outline should correspond. Since it has the same purpose as "A" (agreed citizenry) and "B" (traffic congestion), subhead "d" under "1" is really coordinate with "A" and "B" and should become "C" in the outline. The corrected outline would then look like this:

I. Residents of Los Angeles are facing a crisis in transportation.
    A. Responsible and informed citizens agree that something must be done.
        1. The mayor made this a central issue in his campaign for reelection.
        2. The City Council has established a commission to study the problem.
    B. Traffic congestion is at a breakdown point.
        1. Approximately 600,000 automobiles enter and leave the downtown area of Los Angeles every 24 hours.
            a. Most cars carry only one person: The average is 1.4 persons per car.
            b. More than half come and go between 7 and 9 A.M. and 4 and 6 P.M.
            c. Rush-hour traffic is mainly one way.
                (1) Morning traffic is mostly inbound.
                (2) Evening traffic is mostly outbound.
        2. Adequate parking facilities are unavailable.
    C. Cars are expensive to operate.

2. Formal Correctness

Many of the problems of logical consistency can be eliminated in the process of making the speech outline formally correct; they can be, that is, if the techniques of outlining are properly used. And the formal correctness of all speech outlines can be checked effectively by a simple and mechanical method.

To see how, begin by observing and reviewing the organization of the persuasive speech. The purpose of the speech is to build acceptance of a proposition. In the outline, main ideas are listed as main heads and are followed by supporting subheads. Main heads (I, II, and so on) are subordinate to the proposition itself. All coordinate divisions of the outline, taken together, should prove the heading to which they are in common subordinate. To illustrate:

The speaker's proposition should be accepted *for*
I. The first main argument supports it. [The first main argument I is true] *for*
   A. The first subhead supports I. [The first subhead A in turn is true] *for*
      1. This piece of evidence supports A, *and* [A is true also because]
      2. This piece of evidence likewise supports A, *and* [I is true also because]
   B. The second subhead supports I. [The second subhead B in turn is true] *for*
      1. This piece of evidence supports B, *and* [B is true also because]
      2. This piece of evidence likewise supports B, *and* [the speaker's proposition is true also because]
II. The second main argument supports it. [The second main argument II is true] *for*
   [And so on]

Thus, to check the outline of a persuasive speech, add the word *for* to the end of each heading in the outline *that is followed immediately by a subordinate point*. Add the word *and* to the end of each heading in the outline *that is followed immediately by a coordinate point or by a larger heading*. The skeleton looks like this:

The proposition should be accepted	*for*
I. Helps to prove the proposition	*for*
A. Helps to prove I	*for*
1. Helps to prove A	*and*
2. Also helps to prove A	*and*
B. Helps to prove I	*for*
1. Helps to prove B	*and*
2. Also helps to prove B	*and*
II. Helps to prove the proposition	*for*
[And so on]	

The word *for* signifies the various expressions associated with the logical relation of subordinate points to their superior head. If *for* seems incongruous when it is applied as a test, apply one of these other expressions: *because, for instance, in the same way that, as is shown by,* or *as authorities agree.*

Checking an outline by this *for-and* method is relatively simple. If the speaker cited in the section just presented used it to check the outline of the speech supporting creation of a metropolitan transit authority, common sense would have said immediately that something was wrong. On the one hand, it makes very good sense to say:

> B. Traffic congestion is at a breakdown point (*for* the reason that)
>   1. Approximately 600,000 automobiles enter and leave every 24 hours (*and* for the reason that)
>   2. Parking facilities are inadequate.

But within the context of this argument, there is no meaningful way to claim that:

> 1. 600,000 automobiles enter and leave (*for* the reason that)
>   a. ....
>   b. ....
>   c. ....
>   d. Cars are expensive to operate.

The outline of an informative speech can be tested for formal correctness by mentally adding in front of subordinate points such connective phrases as *for example* and *that is to say*. In coordinate positions use such words as *moreover, furthermore,* and *in addition*. Since the outline of any speech, informative or persuasive, will be in topic outline form, the complete ideas must be imagined.

3. Content Completeness of Informative Speech Outlines

The outline of an informative speech can also be tested by a system of adding ideas. The coordinate headings taken together should add up to no more and no less than their superior head. Consider the following:

> *Specific Purpose*
> I. ....
>   A. ....
>   B. ....
>   1. ....
>   2. ....
> II. ....
>   A. ....
>   B. ....

Now, "add up" the ideas contained in each of the headings:

I. B. 1 + I. B. 2 = I. B.
I. A. + I. B. = I.
II. A. + II. B. = II.
I. + II. = Specific purpose

The following outline would be found faulty because it has more in it than the specific purpose sets forth:

Specific purpose: To inform the audience of the species of trout in the Sierra Nevada Mountains.

I. My trip to the Sierra last summer
II. How to fish for trout
III. Rainbow trout
IV. Brook trout
V. Brown trout
VI. Golden trout

The first two points, although they may be interesting, are pieces of major material that make the six points, when added, total to more than the specific purpose.

The body of the same speech might be so divided that it would total to less than the specific purpose.

I. Rainbow trout
II. Brook trout
III. Brown trout
IV. Golden trout

This outline does not include enough: Lacking such items as "cut-throat trout" (among several others), it totals only to "*some* species of trout," not to "*the* species of trout."

The speaker may have reason for not discussing the omitted point. It could well be the lack of speaking time. But where time or other conditions force a speaker to exclude a point, this fact should be accounted for in the background material or by a narrowed subject sentence.

Unless a speaker uses this system of testing by addition, he may also produce an outline that contains both too much and too little, in that it includes extraneous items and omits others that are essential:

Specific purpose: To inform the audience of the species of trout in the Sierra Nevada Mountains.

   I. How to fish for trout
  II. Rainbow trout
 III. Brook trout
 IV. Brown trout

The examples given here are of main points as they relate to the specific purpose. The same principle applies to lower levels of subordination.

IV. IMPORTANT TECHNICAL PRINCIPLES

A. Each Heading an Assertion

Each of the headings in an outline, both main heads and subheads, should identify an assertion. Do not use a question as an outline heading. The major fault with questions in the outline is that there can be no clear relationship between a question and either a superior or a subordinate point. Because a question makes no definite claim, it cannot be proved and it cannot be used as supporting material to clarify or to prove. Moreover, if a heading is phrased as a question, none of the suggested methods of testing the outline can be applied. The injunction against questions *in the outline* does not mean that you should avoid rhetorical questions *in the delivery of your speech.* An outline, however, shows the logical structure of a speech. As such, it should answer questions, not ask them.

> WRONG: How serious is traffic congestion in Los Angeles?
> RIGHT: Traffic congestion in Los Angeles is at a breakdown point.

B. Each Heading a Single Idea

Each of the headings in an outline should contain a single idea. An outline is not an essay with numbered paragraphs. Moreover, the purpose of the outline is to show the logical relationships among the individual ideas. These relationships are not properly shown if more than one idea is put into a single heading.

WRONG:
1. A 6-year traffic survey in Los Angeles demonstrates an interesting paradox. Although approximately the same number of persons daily come in and out of the downtown area, traffic has increased 20 percent.

WRONG:
1. A 6-year-traffic survey in Los Angeles demonstrates the interesting paradox that approximately the same number of persons daily come in and out of the downtown area, but that traffic has increased 20 percent.

RIGHT:
1. A 6-year traffic survey in Los Angeles demonstrates an interesting paradox.
   a. Approximately the same number of people daily come in and out of the downtown area.
   b. Traffic has increased 20 percent.

C. No More Than One Symbol for Any One Heading

To label a single item in the outline as both I and A or both A and 1 is illogical. It suggests that a subordinate point is its own main head, which is, of course, impossible. When a double symbol is used, it ordinarily means that the writer of the outline has a series of subordinate points and senses that they need a head but has not devised it.

WRONG:
I. A. Decay has occurred in major American cities.
   B. 27 percent of nonfarm homes do not meet Federal standards of structure and sanitation.

RIGHT:
I. Slums are a serious problem in American cities.
   A. Decay has occurred in major American cities.
   B. 27 percent of nonfarm homes do not meet Federal standards of structure and sanitation.

WRONG:
I. Los Angeles faces a crisis in transportation.
   A. 1. 600,000 autos enter and leave every day.

RIGHT:
I. Los Angeles faces a crisis in transportation.
   A. Traffic congestion is at a breakdown point.

2. Adequate parking
   is unavailable.
B. Citizens agree that
   something must be
   done.

1. 600,000 autos enter
   and leave every day.
2. Adequate parking
   is unavailable.
B. Citizens agree that
   something must be
   done.

D. Headings Discrete

There should be no overlapping among the divisions of an outline. Advocating the repeal of child-labor laws, one speaker argued that other cities in the nation might derive the benefits Philadelphia got from its work-school program initiated to combat the labor shortage of the Second World War. Here is a part of the argument:

I. The wartime work-school program was of great value in Philadelphia.
   A. The program helped reduce the number of drop-outs from school.
   B. The program taught initiative and responsibility.
   C. Young people gained a new sense of importance from contributing to the family's resources.
   D. Discipline problems at home and at school diminished.

Notice that subpoint B overlaps both C and D. These two points (C and D), instead of being coordinate with B, are really pieces of evidence to show that B is true. They are effects of B. They should be subpoints 1 and 2 subordinated *under* B.

E. Usually at Least Two Coordinate Headings at Each Level

The purpose of subordinate headings in an outline is to break down the idea contained in the main head, to show its parts or to show how it was arrived at. When an outline contains a single subheading, it is not usually a true logical division of the idea to which it is subordinated. Instead, it is most often a restatement of the same idea with greater specification of detail.

236

WRONG:

A. The president threatened to veto the bill increasing
   social-security payments if the increase was too big.
   1. He said the increase must not be more than 7
      percent.

RIGHT:

A. The president threatened to veto the bill increasing
   social-security payments if the increase was more
   than 7 percent.

The general exclusion of one-point subordinations does not necessitate exclusion of evidence. You may want to furnish a single piece of evidence or supporting material, an example, or a statistic. By all means do so. In such instances it is quite proper to use a one-point subhead.

RIGHT:

A. Most cars on the freeways in Los Angeles carry
   only 1 person:
   1. The average is 1.4 persons per car.

RIGHT:

A. Americans are often chauvinistic:
   1. American tourists frequently belittle the cus-
      toms of the countries they visit.

Illustrations used earlier in this chapter suggest another acceptable method of including in the outline material that might otherwise constitute a one-point subhead:

RIGHT:

A. Most cars on the freeways in Los Angeles carry
   only one person: The average is 1.4 persons per car.

RIGHT:

A. Slum areas create financial problems: 15 percent of
   the population of Los Angeles lives in slum areas.

V. REVISING THE OUTLINE

The first outline of a speech is usually weak. Often it is little more than the scratch outline mentioned earlier. Usually, when you begin to think about a topic, you lack detailed information and often fail to see the ideas in clear perspective. Moreover, as you gather information and as your ideas develop, you see that relationships you first perceived do not exist. New ideas come into the picture and less useful ones are discarded. As your knowledge and understanding develop, you see the need for revision of the outline, both for clarity and for forcefulness of presentation. A constant examination of the outline will be necessary, even to the actual moment of speaking.

SUMMARY

In outlining, keep the following points in mind:

1. A rhetorical topic outline is preferable.

2. Partition the main ideas into a series of distinct, coordinate headings.

3. Use statements, not questions, to express ideas.

4. Use proper indentations and symbols to show coordination and subordination accurately. Use one symbol per idea, one idea per symbol.

5. Check the outline for logical consistency and formal correctness.

6. Check the informative outline for completeness by applying the test of addition.

7. Revise the outline as necessary for greater clarity and force.

QUESTIONS

1. What is the purpose of an outline?

2. Give the general format of a speech showing what is included in the introduction, the body, and the conclusion.

3. Explain subordination and coordination.

4. How should the speaker mark his outline to help him when he wants to deliver the evidence before stating the idea it supports?

5. What is the customary order of subordination in which the various symbols are used?

6. How many main headings should a speech have? Why?

7. How can the outline be tested by a system of adding ideas?

8. The text gives five technical principles for outline development. Explain the three you think are the most important.

EXERCISES

1. Using the following points, make an outline for the body of a speech showing subordination and coordination by the use of correct

symbols and indentations. First find your main heads (there are two of them); then look for the subheads; and then proceed to further levels of subordination.

Specific purpose: To inform the audience about the major activities open to students on a college campus
  1. Students attend classes
  2. Pamphlets
  3. There are extracurricular activities
  4. Plays
  5. Students plan and attend their own social events
  6. College football team
  7. College fencing team
  8. Volleyball
  9. They take tests
  10. Periodicals
  11. Students have a variety of cultural activities outside the classroom
  12. College track team
  13. Art exhibits
  14. Softball
  15. Dances
  16. College basketball team
  17. The primary activities on a college campus are curricular
  18. Books
  19. College wrestling team
  20. Golf club
  21. Parties
  22. College baseball team
  23. Students use the library as a source of information
  24. Clubs and fraternities have a league
  25. They write papers and deliver speeches
  26. Maps
  27. Touch football
  28. Concert series
  29. Tennis club
  30. They listen to lectures by the instructor
  31. Students attend athletic events as spectators and participants
  32. Swimming club
  33. Intercollegiate athletics

34. Lecture series
35. Minor sports
36. They engage in class discussions
37. Major sports
38. After-school sports are available
39. Intramural athletics

2. State the specific purpose of the following speech and then outline it. This speech was delivered by Senator Edward M. Kennedy to the United States Senate on December 6, 1973 (Edward M. Kennedy, "Energy in Foreign Policy," *Vital Speeches of The Day*, 40 (Jan. 1, 1974), pp. 162–66).

ENERGY IN FOREIGN POLICY

Edward M. Kennedy

Twice in the past month, on November 7 and again on November 15, President Nixon has spoken to the nation on the growing emergency that the United States faces over the supply of energy. He has stressed both the short-term problems facing us in the next few months, and the long-term problems in ensuring that sufficient supplies of energy will be available to fuel our industries, heat our homes, provide our transportation, and serve as the lifeblood of our economy in the years to come.

The Senate has now passed emergency legislation containing a number of proposals advanced by the President, and other measures supported or initiated by Congress. I commend the distinguished Senator from Washington, Senator Jackson, for his leadership in this effort. And I strongly support effective efforts now, both to meet the immediate domestic energy emergency and to plan for the future.

But there is one area of the energy issue that has so far received too little attention. And that is the foreign policy role which the United States should be playing in a variety of areas to encourage international cooperation to ease the crisis and to develop new long-term relations among all nations in matters relating to energy.

During the past few weeks, we have had dramatic evidence that the foreign policy dimensions of energy are critical to our future. First, there was the embargo of oil shipments to this country from Arab states, and the overall curtailment of oil production. Second, there was the onset of one of the worst diplomatic crises in the history of the Atlantic Alliance, brought on by Europe's great dependence on Arab oil.

I regard the foreign policy dimensions of the energy crisis as equal in severity to the domestic dimensions of the crisis. My purpose in speaking today is to suggest some specific steps that the United States should take, both now and in the future to deal with this dimension of the crisis. These steps are designed to insure that the United States plays its proper role in the world economy, and to promote cooperation rather than conflict among nations in this vital area.

The present crisis may have exploded upon us in recent weeks, but it was hardly unforeseen. The United States was facing a domestic energy emergency this winter, long before the Arab oil embargo was imposed. And long after the embargo is lifted, we will continue to reap the harvest of the Administration's past failures to act to alleviate the worsening domestic fuel shortage before it became an emergency.

For at least three years, for example, from February 1970 until April 1973, the recommendation of the President's own Cabinet Task Force for increased oil imports was allowed to gather dust. At the time, foreign oil was cheap and readily available, and domestic oil could and should have been stockpiled against the present emergency. Instead, we continued a policy of artificially boosting domestic oil prices, simultaneously expending as many barrels of domestic oil as we could pump from the ground. Now, we are paying for our shortsightedness and belatedly recognizing our failure to conserve domestic reserves and our failure to preserve emergency stockpiles of oil.

Now, President Nixon has suggested that the United States undertake "Project Independence," to enable us to become independent of foregin sources of energy by 1980. This is a significant and ambitious proposal that implies major changes in the way we live our lives, in the way that we do business in America, and in the way we conduct our foreign policy. Before we embark on a proposal of such enormous magnitude, we must consider very carefully what it will mean. We must define our objectives in energy, and assess the alternatives that exist and the price the nation is willing to pay to achieve its goals in energy. And in those calculations, the international role of energy must be carefully assessed.

There are five main issues to be considered in this respect: (1) the facts of foreign energy dependence; (2) oil as a political weapon; (3) the economics of dependence on Arab oil; (4) the role of Europe and Japan; and (5) worldwide cooperation in energy.

In the past, the United States has traditionally relied upon its own supplies of energy. But increasingly in recent years, we have had to turn to the outside world to meet our need. From a net exporter of energy in the 1940's, we have now become a net importer. The change has been dramatic. In 1970, we imported a full 25 per cent of our oil, mostly from Canada and the Caribbean. Earlier this year, our dependence on the outside world for oil reached 33 per cent of our total consumption. Before the current crisis, we expected by 1980 to import 50 per cent or more of our oil consumption.

At the same time, the share of our total imports from the Middle East and North Africa has risen. For many years, it averaged about 10 per cent.

Before the current embargo this year, it was running about 33 per cent. And this share of our imports had been expected to rise to about 60 per cent by the end of the decade.

As long as we import large and growing quantities of oil, our increasing dependence on the Middle East and North Africa is virutally inevitable. For many reasons, oil resources in Canada, Latin America, Nigeria, Indonesia and elsewhere outside the Middle East and North Africa will simply not be available in sufficient quantities to offset our growing dependence on that region.

If we decide to reduce our dependence on the Middle East, therefore, we must either increase our own domestic supplies of energy or reduce our domestic demand. As a nation, we are now considering appropriate courses that will in time increase our domestic supplies. A major and urgent effort is clearly needed to end this winter's emergency in fuel oil. And an equally substantial effort is needed to develop the technology that can increase production of clean fuel for the future, whether or not we seek to be totally self-sufficient in energy.

But it will be many years before these new supplies are available in substantial quantities. Even if we are prepared to reduce significantly the controls on the pollution of our environment and to change our way of life, it will be very difficult for us during this decade to produce enough energy to meet our domestic demands entirely from sources outside the Middle East and North Africa, much less to become totally self-sufficient. And at current and projected rates of U.S. demand for energy, becoming truly self-sufficient in the 1980's would impose high costs in investment and in damage to our environment that might well be regarded as unacceptable by large segments of the American people.

As a result of these facts, we have finally begun to focus more attention on limiting our demand for energy. This winter's oil emergency requires it. And so does the Arab embargo, whose impact means the loss of more than two million barrels of oil a day, or more than 10 per cent of our daily consumption.

It is unfortunate that the Administration refused to recognize the impending shortage when it was first apparent nearly a year ago, and opposed early steps such as mandatory allocation legislation designed to alleviate that shortage. Certainly, a wiser policy when the danger signs were clear so many months ago could have spared the nation the worst effects of the current emergency precipitated by the Arab oil embargo, and might well also have spared the nation the unwanted ordeal of rationing that now appears to be the only realistic way out of the immediate crisis.

Beyond our current difficulties, however, we must also consider carefully whether it will be necessary to launch a program of long-term fuel rationing, as a more or less permanent part of our national policy, in order to become fully self-sufficient in energy.

Because the estimates and forecasts are so unclear, the degree to which the crisis can be met by less drastic long-term steps is by no means certain. By changing our most wasteful habits of energy use, including an end to the manufacture of large and inefficient automobiles, we can do much to solve the problem.

What is certain is that the era of gigantic American energy waste is over. By now, there is virtually unanimous recognition that we can no longer accept a situation in which the United States, with 6 per cent of the world's people, uses nearly one-third of the world's energy, at a per capita rate more than twice that of the next leading user, except for Canada.

But limiting consumption of energy too much could also mean an end to America's economic growth. Already, we face the danger that the current short-run energy emergency may bring on a recession in 1974, with its threat to jobs, to profits, and to our standard of living.

Beyond the short-run emergency, however, we also face the much more dismal prospect of a prolonged economic depression, comparable to the period of the early 1930's, with all the profound consequences that such a result would entail for America and the world. Each year, the controls might have to become tighter, as demand increases, until, sometime in the late 1970's or early 1980's, new sources of energy hopefully will become available in quantities large enough to ease the crisis and restore the nation to an even keel on energy.

Because the domestic path we may be obliged to follow poses such drastic and possibly unacceptable consequences, it is all the more important for us to explore every possible avenue of international cooperation in order to achieve the most appropriate blend of policies.

In essence, there are two tiers of the problem of Arab oil and its solution. First, there is the use of oil as a weapon in the Arab-Israeli conflict, with the impact this threat has on the security of the world's energy supply. Second, there is the economic dimension of energy supply, and the readiness of oil-exporting states to fulfill the energy demands of the oil-importing states.

There is now a concerted effort by the Arab producer states to change our policy during the Middle East crisis, by withholding oil from us and by restricting the supplies available to our Allies. This challenge is more serious than it was in 1967, when we imported far less oil from the Arab states. And in the future, increasing imports of oil from the Arab world could make the challenge even more serious.

Regardless of the strength of the oil weapon, however, our course as a nation is clear: we must never give into this kind of pressure. This would be against our interests; against the faith placed in American commitments; against our principles as a nation; and against our concern for action in the pursuit of peace.

During the current embargo, therefore, we must be prepared to do without Arab oil, as we have been doing in recent weeks. And we must be prepared in the future to sustain any embargo of oil shipments undertaken by any nation as a political weapon. To resist such pressure, we can adopt a number of specific policies:

—We must be prepared to ration fuel on short notice, and to allocate fuel for priority users;

—Whenever possible, we must build up our stockpiles of fuel in the United States;

—We must begin long-range efforts to limit consumption of energy;

—We must try to work out energy-sharing arrangements with other oil-importing countries; and

—We must undertake a long-range effort to seek new sources and increased quantities of energy from areas outside the Arab world, and maintain controls on the growth of our imports of this oil.

Yet, for any major industrial nation today, maintaining "energy independence" does not mean withdrawing completely from the outside world. Even if this were possible, it would not be necessary in order to gain protection against external threats like the oil embargo. For we must remember, the economic interdependence of nations is a two-way street. Every nation that exports goods must also find markets for them. Every nation that wishes to benefit from the stability and growth of international trade must be bound by the same rules of international behavior that bind every other trading nation. No nation can defy the rules of international commerce without provoking strong reaction that will cause it damage in return.

The United States is not a "pitiful, helpless giant," either in the Middle East or elsewhere. We remain the world's foremost economic power, and retain significant ability to shape events beyond our shores.

Nor is this lesson lost on the Arab states. They, too, must decide how far they can proceed in the use of their oil weapon, without incurring unacceptable consequences, related primarily to the future role they will be able to play in the international economic world. Already, the current embargo is provoking a reaction in the United States that is helping us to overcome current difficulties, and that will make us better able to meet such challenges in the future.

This statement of policy is not unique in international commerce. It applies wherever there is a danger of too much dependence. In the give and take of trading relations, those nations gain benefits and avoid losses by having the wisdom to act within the limits of their power, mindful both of the power of other nations and of their mutual economic dependence.

There is another factor to be considered. It remains in the interests of the United States, and of all nations, to see an end to the conflict between Israel and its Arab neighbors. Once that conflict is finally, fully, and forever over, we shall be able to put behind us our concern that Arab oil will be used as a political weapon against Israel or ourselves as an exacerbating element in that troubled area.

V   Revising the Outline

The loss to all nations of continued conflict in the Middle East has now been amply demonstrated. We must hope that this lesson has now been learned by the nations involved most directly and indirectly in that conflict. A solution can and must be found. And we in the Senate should pledge our support for every effort to bring this conflict from the battlefield to the conference table, and to move from there in the direction of a just and lasting peace.

The second tier to the problem of depending on oil from the Middle East and North Africa, and the second tier of the policies we should adopt, is the economic dimension.

Even if the Arab-Israeli conflict is settled—even if the threat of oil as a political weapon in the conflict is removed—there will still be no guarantee that oil from the Middle East will flow in the quantities that importing countries will require for their economies. To be sure, rapidly developing nations like Iran may pump as much oil as possible to finance their own mushrooming economic development. But three of the largest producers —Saudi Arabia, Kuwait, and Abu Dhabi—have so much oil and so few people that they have little incentive to increase production. In fact, recent price increases will permit their income to go up, while oil production actually goes down.

This economic glut also helps support the current embargo on Arab oil shipments to the United States and the overall reductions in oil output. Without it, oil would be far less appealing as a political weapon for any state dependent upon income from oil to run its economy.

If these conditions continue, oil production will not increase, and the world will face the risk of a mad rush for limited oil supplies by all importing nations. Prices will continue to rise; the United States, Western Europe, and Japan may come into serious economic rivalry with one another; and, the world's developing nations may bear the heaviest burden.

In time, of course, rising prices will also reduce demand and make other sources of energy more economical, but it will also take time to make these sources available. For the quantities of energy needed, that means the 1980's.

It is therefore important once the present Arab boycott has ended, once the current Middle East crisis has been resolved, and once we are looking forward to an era of more stable relationships in the Middle East, for all oil-importing nations to help increase the economic and financial incentives for the Arab world to increase its oil production. This means action by the industrial states in several areas, such as:

—providing technical assistance for rapid economic development in the producing states themselves;

—lending support for diversification of their economies;

—encouraging a generalized expansion of trade between the oil producers and the United States and other industrialized nations;

—helping the producers to find attractive ways to invest their oil revenues in the industrialized nations, whether in energy industries or elsewhere; and

—encouraging the producers to lend large amounts of funds for economic development, both in other Middle East nations and in the developing world as a whole. The need for such funds is manifest. And for the
oil-producing states to make it available—either directly or through sub-
scriptions to the World Bank—would be an immense contribution to the
future of the developing countries and a political credit to the producers
themselves.

Yet these economic steps—and others like them—may not alone be
enough to encourage significant increases in production by the wealthy,
but sparsely populated oil-producing states. In the long run the oil-
importing states must also begin to recognize that the new wealth and
economic power of the producer nations require a more prominent role
for them in the international economy. Once the current bitter confrontation eases, it may well be desirable that the producer states be given not
only economic incentives to produce their oil, but political incentives as
well—a sense of involvement in, and a shared responsibility for, the structure and the workings of the world economy as a whole.

Eventually, as accommodation replaces confrontation, the United States
and other oil-importing nations are likely to provide a substantially
greater role to the oil-producing states in negotiations on international
trade and monetary reform. There will be an increase in high level
exchanges of visits by the leaders of both exporting and importing states.
And as greater harmony and cooperation develops, the oil-importing
nations will begin to treat the oil-exporting states with the attention and
respect in economic matters that their economic power now demands and
deserves.

It is in our interest, through steps like these, to promise responsible and
cooperative attitudes among the oil-producing states. As has been true
in the East and West since the Second World War, such attitudes can
help reduce conflict in international economic, political, and even military
relations. They can increase a sense of mutual interdependence. And they
can help reduce incentives to use economic power as a political weapon,
where such use will cause reduced confidence in stable and productive
economic relations.

The two-tiered approach that I have presented here today with regard
to the flow of Arab oil is no panacea for the foreign policy problems that
the United States now faces. But this two-tiered approach—firm resolve
and a vigorous search for peace in matters of politics; and accommodation
and cooperation in matters of economics—can make the problems for us
less difficult and the choices we face less burdensome. It may well enable
us to maintain our essential energy independence, without resort to the

extreme of total self-sufficiency that would be required if we must give up all imports of oil from the Arab world and elsewhere.

So far, I have discussed energy from the standpoint of the United States. Yet, it is clear that the problems are not ours alone. They face all oil-importing nations. Europe and Japan are several times more dependent than the United States on oil imports, especially imports from the Arab world, and consequently their current energy crisis is several times more serious.

Unlike us, Europe and Japan do not have sufficient reserves of coal or untapped oil to adopt their own "Project Independence," even if they decided to accept the cost of a policy of total national self-sufficiency in matters relating to energy. Inevitably, like it or not, the other major nations of the world will seek new international alternatives to solve their own energy crises, and the United States cannot afford to ignore their efforts or abdicate its responsibility to participate in the search for such alternatives.

The world's developing countries are also hard hit by the energy crisis. For example, because of recent price rises in oil, India faces an annual increase in its foreign exchange costs of several hundred million dollars— money that India simply does not have. The difficulties for Europe and Japan may be severe; for India and other developing countries, they could be catastrophic. That is why I have proposed that we encourage the producer states to make capital available to the rest of the developing world.

Recently, we have been deeply concerned with the serious breach in relations between the United States and our Allies in Western Europe. None of us here could welcome the general lack of European backing for America's efforts to support Israel, to limit the involvement of the Soviet Union, and to bring an end to fighting in the Middle East. But whether we like it or not, we must understand that the abrasive factors that led our principal Allies to act as they did will cause continuing problems for all of us in the Atlantic Alliance, until the underlying difficulties in energy relations are solved.

There will be similar difficulties in our relations—and those of Europe— with Japan, which has also been putting its concern for oil first during the current crisis. Japan now fears for the future growth of its economy because of oil production limits. She predicts a 50 per cent rise in her imports bill for energy next year, because of price rises that have already taken place.

Because competition for oil from the Middle East and North Africa will grow, even after the oil embargo ends, it is now imperative for the United States, Western Europe, and Japan to begin real cooperation in energy matters. We are all in this together; and together we will either meet the energy challenge, or watch it drive us apart in a vicious scramble for scarce energy supplies.

For many years, there have been half-hearted attempts to cooperate on energy matters in the Organization for Economic Cooperation and Development—OECD. But despite the claims of President Nixon in two energy messages to Congress this year, these efforts have failed. The states of the European Community have not been able to agree among themselves. The Japanese have so far elected to go it alone. And our own vital interest in cooperation has not received the high-level commitment in the administration that is needed to stimulate an adequate response from our Allies.

The draft of the new Atlantic Charter, offered by the United States on September 29, contains only passing reference to these critical energy problems. And more than two months after the confirmation of Dr. Kissinger as Secretary of State, he has still not honored his pledge to fill all our ambassadorial vacancies within that time—including the year-old vacancy at the OECD. These attitudes and practices demonstrate the inadequacy of our commitment to real cooperation. They also show a continuing failure to grasp the urgency of the situation now facing all oil-importing states.

Energy cooperation between the United States, Canada, Europe, and Japan can take several forms. I propose today a six-part effort:

—*First*, joint research and development, both in new forms of energy and in new uses of fossil fuels like coal, which the United States possesses in abundant supply;

—*Second*, joint commitment to increased investment in sources of energy outside the Middle East;

—*Third*, joint planning on stockpiling, limiting consumption, and standby rationing. Here, the United States has a special responsibility and a special opportunity to reduce pressure on world energy markets by reducing its inflated rate of energy consumption;

—*Fourth*, joint, open and thorough investigation of the role played by the international oil companies, in order to settle the controversy over their power once and for all;

—*Fifth*, arrangements to share energy resources in time of scarcity on an equitable basis, to insure that no nation suffers too drastically from the crisis. Only in this way can the United States, Europe, and Japan avoid the cutthroat competition that will inevitably materialize in the race to obtain scarce oil supplies. Only in this way can they hope to prevent relations among themselves—as well as relations within the European community—from being seriously damaged by brutal competition over energy. Such damage could not be limited to energy relations, but would extend to trade and monetary relations as well. And if any one of the three areas is damaged, all would suffer; and

—*Sixth*, most important of all, there must be a political commitment by all three great industrial areas to seek answers to energy problems in common, and not separately. None of us can afford to make unilateral decisions about energy without taking into account the needs and interests of the others. As we have found in so many other areas affecting our security and the international economy, serving the interests of all nations is the only way to serve the interests of any one of them.

And so, I urge President Nixon today to commit the United States, seriously and forthrightly, to cooperation with the European community and Japan on energy issues. I urge him to appoint an Ambassador to the OECD now. And I urge him to use his best offices to encourage the European Community and Japan to act in concert and to join us in a common effort.

This is no time for generalities. It is a time for specific negotiations and concrete acts that together can create an "International Charter of Energy" that will be written in the daily successes of growing cooperation among the major nations of the world.

Even this effort, however, will not be enough. Energy cooperation must not shut out other industrial states, or the oil-producing nations, or the developing countries of the world. Our interest in promoting new institutions of economic relations on energy demands that all oil-importing and oil-producing states be vitally involved in cooperation with one another. Our concern to see a world that is increasingly just demands that we not turn our backs in this area on the have-not nations of the world.

Thus, there is a further effort needed to deal with energy problems in an orderly and coordinated way. This involves the role to be played in world energy markets by the oil-exporting states, themselves.

If our initial efforts to increase other supplies of energy and to limit consumption begin to succeed, the nature of the world economy can begin to change. When these efforts begin to moderate the rising pressure of demand for oil from the Middle East and North Africa, there will be a rising self-interest in these producer countries for stability in world energy markets. Even in the near future, it is possible that concern for stability, for economic development, for productive investments, and for the future of the international economy will create areas of common interests between producers and consumers of oil. This could happen now, despite today's strong bargaining position of the producers and the current political motivations of the Arab states.

It is time, therefore, to consider the energy problems of both exporting and importing countries together. It is time to search for areas of common agreement. And it is time to begin looking systematically at the worldwide dimensions of energy affairs.

I believe that there should be an international effort to explore all dimensions of energy in the international economy—wherever the energy comes from, wherever it goes, whatever form it takes.

There are obvious precedents for such an effort in the great institutions of the world economy. There is GATT, the General Agreement on Tariffs and Trade, which provides the framework for the orderly growth of trade and for trade negotiations. There is IMF, the International Monetary Fund, which provides greater certainty in monetary relations and a focus for monetary reform. And there is the World Bank, which plays such an important role in promoting economic development in many areas of the world.

But there is no institution—no body of agreed rules and procedures—to provide a framework for energy relations or a forum for reconciling divergent energy interests.

I propose, therefore, that the United States take the lead in working for the creation of a World Energy Commission, a worldwide institution on energy, with a set of agreed rules and principles governing international energy research, production, and trade. Today, I am submitting a resolution for the consideration of the Senate, urging the President to propose the convening by the United Nations General Assembly of a World Energy Conference, to include all nations. The UN has convened similar conferences in the past in other areas where there are shared interests among nations but no effective way to cope with shared problems, and the UN should do so now on energy.

The World Energy Conference should be designed to find areas of long-term common economic agreement among energy-exporting and importing states, to focus on specific areas of energy research, and to lay the groundwork for permanent international institutions and arrangements on energy matters.

This World Energy Conference could become a "Bretton Woods" on energy, like the conference in 1944 that produced the IMF and the World Bank. Thanks to the foresight of the leaders who gathered at Bretton Woods, thirty years ago, we mapped a plan that guided us out of the shattering consequences of World War II and set the course of international economic affairs for a generation. The time has come to do the same for energy, and Bretton Woods can be our model.

In sum, the United States cannot afford to ignore the international dimensions of the energy crisis. Just as we are now vigorously debating and developing programs to meet our domestic need, so we must also respond to the international need that so clearly exists.

The efforts I have proposed—technological, economic, and political—will help the United States to cope with current problems and master future difficulties. These efforts can help us resolve the dilemmas that otherwise will face us—and that also will face Europe and Japan—as we seek to escape from our present crisis.

They can help us avoid ever having to choose between oil and Israel—or any other country. They can help us to reconcile our interests in secure energy supplies with adequate protection for our environment. They can begin stimulating cooperation with other oil-importing nations. And they can begin to shape a larger international framework for considering energy problems, a framework that will benefit all countries.

There is no magic answer to energy problems, but there is hope in careful thought and timely action. The overall lesson is clear: the United

States is now deeply involved in the world economy, and will become increasingly involved as years go by. In addition, the line between foreign and domestic policy is no longer a clear one. What we do at home in energy will vitally affect our foreign policy, and our foreign policy in energy will vitally affect the way we live at home.

We do not need to fear these developments, or react in panic, anger, or misunderstanding. Nor do we need to cut ourselves off from the international community in our struggle to solve the crisis. We can no more become a Fortress America on energy than we could do so militarily a generation ago.

Rather we must make our increasing interdependence with other nations work to our advantage, and to the mutual advantage of all countries willing to share with us the common benefits and responsibilities of international economic relations. Our attitudes are critical. We can lose the moment, and pay a heavy price in the future. Or we can seize it, and help to shape the world energy economy in ways that will benefit all people everywhere.

I. How language works
   A. Symbolism
   B. Meaning
      1. Denotation
      2. Connotation
      3. Syntax
      4. Context
   C. Emotional coloring
II. Style
   A. Written style and spoken style
   B. Characteristics of good oral style
      1. Propriety
         a. Shoptalk
         b. Slang
         c. Taboos
         d. Formal English
         e. Informal English
      2. Precision
         a. Accuracy
            (1) Avoid exaggeration
            (2) Avoid ambiguity
         b. Concreteness and specificity
            (1) Avoid meaningless qualifiers
            (2) Avoid abstract terms
            (3) Avoid general terms
      3. Simplicity
      4. Directness
      5. Originality
   C. Making style vivid
      1. Figures of speech
      2. Parallel structure
      3. Antithesis
      4. Rhetorical questions
III. Improving language and style
   A. Become aware of your own use
      of language
   B. Be curious about words
   C. Study the language of others
   D. Practice writing and speaking

Chapter 12

Language and Oral Style

The outline of a speech has on occasion been likened to the skeleton of a human body. The comparison is useful insofar as it suggests the relationship of parts to whole in functional order. Moreover, if outline is to speech as skeleton is to body, it is clear that a speech is not wholly represented by its outline. In much the same sense that the human skeleton requires ligaments, muscles, and nerves to function, a speech becomes a complete and living thing only when the sinews and flesh of language are added.

At least one further comparison can be made. The muscles of the human body are either weak or strong, flabby or firm. Language, too, is either weak and flabby or firm and strong. In this chapter, we shall consider how language is used to give movement and strength to a speech by adding to the skeleton of the outline the firm, strong muscles of effective oral style.

I. HOW LANGUAGE WORKS

When you address an audience, the understanding you want your listeners to have or the proposition you want them to accept cannot be transplanted directly from your mind into theirs. Instead, you must use some medium of transmission. Language is instrumental in formulating such a medium.

A. Symbolism

Language may be defined as a system of visual and audible symbols, verbal and nonverbal, which you use to encode a message. Such a message is transmitted to an audience in order to evoke meanings in your listeners. But not just any meanings. You want to evoke meanings which are similar enough to your own that it may be said your audience understands what you intend to say.

The use of language as a means of communication is an enormous feat of symbol making. To cite a fairly simple instance, the word *and* is widely symbolized by the mark "&" (and has been ever since 63 B.C.). The mark itself is called an ampersand, and this is a further verbal symbolization. So you see that you can not only devise things which stand for other things, but you can also devise words that are names for these new things.

Words may be represented by graphic signs in writing or by combinations of sounds in speaking. Whether the set of graphic signs looks like

W. Va.   or   West Virginia,

it is represented by roughly the same combination of sounds when put into speech. We say "roughly" because the sound signs, too, may undergo some variation, depending on the accent and dialect of the speaker. But despite differences in spelling (British *kerb* vs. American *curb*) or in spoken renderings (*tomayto* vs. *tomahto*), verbal symbols are created to describe or refer to the things they name.

Not all language is verbal. Certain kinds of communication dispense with words: A skull and crossbones on the label wrapped around a bottle will tell you something important about the contents as quickly as the verbal symbol *Poison*. The cross and the star of David are almost universally known symbols, but neither of them is verbal language. Shaking a clenched fist communicates something quite clearly to a large part of the world's population, but it is not a word. Verbal language, however, is the primary means by which human beings have

254

recorded and transmitted the accumulated experience and wisdom of the past. And, for the most part, you depend on verbal symbols to communicate ideas. You use language to tell your listeners what is in your mind. Since the language is not the ideas, but only stands for them, an enormous part of the effectiveness of your communication depends upon your ability to use language well. The problem in using language is to choose the right symbols to evoke the intended response.

B. Meaning

Because word symbols stand for things and ideas, we tend to think that words are the basic units of meaning, but words in themselves have no meaning. The answer to the apparently simple question, "What does *slip* (or *hand* or *sack* or *pool*) mean?" is, equally simply, "Nothing!" The meanings, that is, the various senses in which these or any other words are used, are never in the words themselves. They exist only in the people who use and receive them. But the meanings for the one who hears words are never precisely the same as the meanings for the one who speaks them.

The point is that all meaning is idiosyncratic; it is only in somebody's mind and it is peculiar to the person who has it. Hence the exact duplication of meaning, the evocation of the same meanings by a verbal stimulus in two people, could occur only if their two brains were identical, cell for cell, synapse for synapse, nerve for nerve. In addition, each of the two people would have to have had identical experiences with the phenomenon that the verbal symbol names. These conditions cannot be met. Consequently, the meanings evoked in two people by the same symbol must be different. However, since people who have words which they use in common also have overlapping meanings for these words, communication is impaired only to the extent that the dissimilarities in their meanings create confusion. A couple of examples will suggest the kinds of differences that cause confusion.

If someone proposes to tell a group how to make raisin cookies, each person in the audience will have somewhat different meanings for "raisin." The object that the name "raisin" denotes to each member of the audience is, however, likely to be pretty much the same sort of thing. It could happen that one might buy muscat raisins and another white raisins so that their cookies would not be exactly alike, but that difference isn't very serious.

In other cases different meanings create confusion. The superintendent of a highway construction crew says, "Make sure that everyone is out of the area before you set off the dynamite." In this message situation, the superintendent is likely to take pains to satisfy himself that both he and the dynamite crew have very much the same meaning for the term, "Make sure."

In view of the fact that meanings are in people, not in words, you can readily see, despite popular misconceptions to the contrary, that the dictionary does not govern the language. The function of a dictionary is not to *define* any given word, but merely to *record* the many senses in which people have used the word to express their meanings in various contexts at various times.

Theoretically, you may define a word in any way you choose and then use it in that sense. If this use of the word fails to stir up overlapping meanings in the one who hears it, or if it runs too far counter to his meanings for the word, communication suffers. Here's an example of what we mean.

In this book, the word *proposition* is used to name a statement that expresses a judgment concerning fact, value, or policy. This is an ordinary use of the term in rhetoric. In logic, however, the word is used in quite a different sense. To avoid possible confusion, we thought we might use the word *conclusion* instead of *proposition*. After all, your proposition is the conclusion of your line of argument and it is the conclusion at which you want your listeners to arrive. The word *conclusion* was abandoned, however, after one of us tried to define it in class one day. A student objected to the definition quite vigorously, saying, "You can't use the word *conclusion* that way. It really means something else." This student must have felt as Alice did when talking with Humpty Dumpty.

"There's glory for you!"

"I don't know what you mean by 'glory,'" Alice said.

Humpty Dumpty smiled contemptuously. "Of course you don't—till I tell you. I mean 'there's a nice knock-down argument for you!"

"But 'glory' doesn't mean 'a nice knock-down argument,'" Alice objected.

"When *I* use a word," Humpty Dumpty said, in rather a scornful tone, "it means just what I choose it to mean—neither more nor less."

"The question is," said Alice, "whether you *can* make words mean so many different things."

Somewhere between the rigid confusion of Alice, who tries to make *words* (instead of people) "mean" something (and then always mean the same thing), and the arbitrary nonsense of Humpty Dumpty, who should not hope to be easily understood, lies a way of using words to let someone know what you have in mind.

To understand something about the way language works, consider for a moment some of the relationships among words and reality and people. Four important notions are involved in this consideration: *denotation, connotation, syntax,* and *context.*

1. Denotation

The denotation of a word is the object, event, or concept that it names. When people think and talk, they need some way of pointing to or signifying things they can't carry around in their hands. Words, then, are used as symbols that stand for, that *denote,* the things people want to refer to in conversation. An "automobile," a "monarchy," and a "unicorn" are, in varying degrees, difficult to designate by pointing out. Yet, for one reason or another, you may want to talk about them. The word used to name each thus becomes a way of pointing to the thing it names. Other events, such as those named by words like "speak," "take," or "be," are named by words that are intended to denote the event. Denotation may be said to name the relationship between a word and the world outside your head. Words become necessary in communication directly in proportion to the difficulty one would have in pointing to the object, event, or concept they are used to name. But what about "unicorn?" Can that word be used to refer to anything outside the user's mind? The answer is, "Yes, the word unicorn denotes a small, horselike animal with a single horn in the center of its forehead."

"Show me one."

"I can't. I don't think there ever has been, is now, or will be a single instance of a unicorn in the whole world. If there ever were to be one, that one, or any other like it, would be what the word would denote."

2. Connotation

Not only do people have denotative meanings for words, which, as we have seen, grow out of the relationships words have with objective reality, but, in addition, they develop connotative meanings for the words as well. These latter meanings do not develop as a result of the relationship between the words and *reality,* as in the case of denotations; instead they result from the relationships *people* have with words and what the words name.

It is possible for two users of the same language to have very much the same understanding of the objects, events, or concepts which words in that language are used to name, such as "socialized medicine," "guaranteed annual wage," or "federal aid to education." But in addition to this denotative meaning, each individual has other meanings that cannot be shared with any other person. These meanings are internalized, personalized, attitudinalized. They result from the fact that every experience you have with a word, whether you use it yourself or someone else does and every experience you have with what the word is used to name, adds to and changes your meanings for the word by changing your attitude toward the thing. These meanings, which develop from the relationships among people, words, and things, are called connotations.

To say it another way: Denotative meanings are externalized; they are unaffective (unemotionalized), impersonal, and, for the most part, common among all the users of a language. Connotative meanings, on the other hand, may be thought of as internalized; they are affective, personal, and particularly idiosyncratic.

3. Syntax

Words may also elicit meanings in a third manner. This way results from the relationships words bear to other words when they are used in accordance with the grammatical customs of a language. That is, the *syntax* you use, the way in which you structure your sentences, gives clues to what you mean. Consequenty, you ought to follow the grammatical practices accepted in the language and expected by your audience. If you do not, you run a double risk: You are likely to lose credibility (have the audience think less well of you, think you less worth listening to), and you are less likely to be understood in the sense you intend.

4. Context

A fourth and final dimension of meaning is found in context. Syntactical meaning has to do with the way words elicit meaning by virtue of their placement in a sentence. It is a function of grammar, of the relationship of words to other words. Contextual meaning refers to the meaning words evoke by virtue of the subject matter that surrounds them. We said earlier in this chapter that words are not the basic units of meaning. With few exceptions they are ambiguous; they can be taken in any of several senses. Even when they are formulated into syntactically correct sentences, they often fail to encode a speaker's meaning in such a way that it will be accurately understood. Have you ever seen a dog run? Of course! But are you sure? Sometimes the word "run" denotes an enclosure within which domestic animals may range about. So we ask again whether you have ever seen a dog run. Perhaps and perhaps not. This example helps to explain the difference between syntactical meaning and contextual meaning. At the same time, it helps to show how the context within which a word appears gives clues to what you mean to say. The question we asked about the dog run was phrased in perfectly acceptable syntax. Yet that syntax points to one set of meanings, while the question was intended to elicit another. Only when the question is surrounded by other words, put into a context, will it say what the user intends.

C. Emotional Coloring

Language serves not only to transmit fact and opinion to an audience but also to communicate affective attitudes as well. In some instances, it is useful to report facts with as little emotional coloration as possible. Informative speaking, for instance, is intended to communicate an idea in such a way that it will be *understood* and *remembered*. Consequently, the language should be objective. To the extent that the language is also interesting and clear, it will serve you even better.

At other times, understanding and retention are only part of your goal. In persuasive speaking particularly, language has the additional function of creating attitude. On these occasions, you could deliberately choose emotive or attitudinal language—language intended to influence the emotional reactions of your audience regarding the ideas you discuss, for language has great power to evoke emotional response. The affective responses language evokes are instrumental in shifting an audience's meanings toward your own and thereby help to create in the audience the attitudes, opinions, and beliefs you want it to have.

Language, however, also has great power to lie or to deceive because it encapsulates a whole complex of attitudes and reactions into a single word. When that word is honorific, it is called a euphemism; when the word is pejorative, its use is said to be name-calling. Both euphemism and name-calling have bad reputations and, for the most part, rightly so. They are two widely used substitutes for adequate evidence and sound argument. And herein lies the danger of emotive language. When attitudes and feelings are separated from evidence and reasoning, the results are frequently to the disadvantage of both speaker and audience as well.

The names that people apply to things always tell more about the people than about the things. Professor Felix Cohen, noted philosopher of law, once remarked that if he were to be called an unbeliever, an infidel, and a Gentile, he would know that the people using these terms would be, respectively, a Christian, a Mohammedan, and a Mormon. When someone argues against the extension of social security to include hospitalization and health benefits by referring to such a proposal as "socialized medicine," we know more about the speaker's attitude than about the proposal.

But there is a proper use for emotive language. Once you are convinced that you have a clear and correct understanding of your subject, then your language becomes a tool for communicating that understanding to others. Since your attitudes are a part of the truth as you see it, you cannot properly be denied the use of whatever language will accurately and efficiently communicate those attitudes, as part of your thinking, to others. Neither moral laxity nor intellectual fuzziness is involved when you take advantage of the emotive connotations of words to supplement the logical elements of your proof.

To put the whole matter briefly, attitudinal and connotative language is frequently a necessary and desirable tool of effective public speaking. It helps to communicate ideas and attitudes clearly, vividly, and interestingly. And this is precisely what a speaker tries to do.

We add, almost (but not entirely) parenthetically, the well-intentioned advice that although the history of oratory offers many examples of speakers who have used language to create bias, who have given emotional coloration to subjects requiring objective treatment, and who have substituted additudinal language for evidence and sound argument, nonetheless *you*, following the tradition and the example of the just and honorable speakers of all time, should use the powerful weapon of language in a manner acceptable to your own conscience and to the ethical dictates of society as well.

II. STYLE

Any number of speakers may talk on the same subject. They may use the same sources of material, indeed the same materials. Further, they may organize their materials and ideas in the same manner. Yet when these speakers deliver their talks, no two speeches will be alike in every detail. Ignoring differences in voice, in physical appearance, and in such visual aspects of delivery as posture, stance, and gesture, there will still be one noticeable and substantial difference among the several speeches. This difference will be in the use of language. No two speakers will choose the same words to express what may be essentially the same idea. That variety in language which distinguishes one expression of an idea from another may be called style.

Style is defined in a variety of ways. Put simply, it is the choice of words you make to communicate what is in your mind. To use language well is to clothe the speech in suitable garments. Good oral style is that use of language which meets the intellectual and emotional demands of speaker, speech, audience, and occasion. In the following portion of this chapter, it will be our purpose to identify, as clearly as we can in brief treatment, those elements of style that make for an effective use of language in speaking. As a first step toward understanding the style of oral communication, let's see how it differs from written discourse.

A. Written Style and Spoken Style

In writing, the expression of ideas is directed toward the eye. Some importance is ordinarily attached to the ability to comprehend a passage of writing quickly and easily. In general, however, there is relatively little demand on you to grasp an idea instantly when it is presented in written form. Under ordinary circumstances, you may examine a page at leisure. Whenever you wish, you may pause to reflect on what you have read, to think about the ideas, and to absorb them at any comfortable rate. You can reread a passage any number of times understanding requires and interest allows. In short, the goal of a writer is to make ideas ultimately intelligible to a reader.

A listening audience, on the other hand, has no such opportunity for leisurely consideration of the ideas presented to it. Listeners cannot go back to rehear. If they pause to reflect, they break the tightly woven chain of the speaker's organization, lose connection with the speaker's development, and are left behind. Often, they are completely lost as listeners. Consequently, whereas writers must be ultimately intelligible to readers, speakers must be instantly intelligible to listeners.

B. Characteristics of Good Oral Style

In the use of language, as in all other aspects of speaking, clarity and interest are indispensable qualities. That is to say, the task of language in a speech is to make ideas instantly, clearly, and accurately intelligible, and to do so in a manner that engages the continuing attention of the audience. The language usage that best attains this end constitutes good oral style. It will display these characteristics: propriety, precision, simplicity, directness, and originality.

1. Propriety

Style is appropriate to the extent that language is adapted to your audience and to the occasion of your speech. As a matter of fact, in daily life you constantly adjust your speech practices to different audiences without ever thinking of the process. During the course of a day, you talk to your colleagues, your boss, your neighbors, casual acquaintances, total strangers, old friends: No two listeners are exactly alike. In each of these situations the process of audience analysis automatically and unconsciously precedes your selection of vocabulary, sentence structure, and figure of speech. A political orator speaking to members of his own party will use one kind of language and even certain terms that he will take pains to avoid when addressing an audience which also includes people of another political persuasion. That a man would address his wife in the same way he addresses the salesman who tries to sell him an insurance policy is highly unlikely. A man who is signaling an S.O.S. doesn't use scientific or technical terminology, nor does he use the language of the *Congressional Record* when making love.

The choice of language, then, is habitually determined by the audience and the occasion. One of the hallmarks of ineffective communication is the inability to adapt one's language to these two elements of the speaking situation. Linguistically ill-equipped, such a speaker is as handicapped as an automobile that can travel in one gear only.

a. Shoptalk. The phenomenon of "shoptalk" illustrates one aspect of language propriety. Many occupations and activities have what amounts to a private system of language signals, a jargon incomprehensible to all but those participating in the activity.

Shoptalk sometimes provides speakers with useful verbal shortcuts that immediately identify them with an audience. Used thus, it may gain a vital psychological advantage. The limitations of such language usage are apparent. The jargon of the trade is useful only for talking to the trade.

b. Slang. Other language forms have even more limited usefulness than shoptalk. These forms should be considered totally inappropriate. Among them is slang. There is nothing wrong with the motive that generates slang. It grows out of the attempt to find a fresh, colorful, sharp, or humorous expression of an idea. Usually, however, slang is shortlived. If it does last, either it becomes a part of standard speech and is no longer slang, or it becomes the hackneyed, impoverished language of the speaker who is illiterate or too lazy to find language that says what he really means. You may justify using slang on the ground that it adds vividness to your expression, but you run the danger that it will add a jarring note to what you say.

c. Taboos. Even more to be avoided than slang is language that violates the taboos of the speaker's audience. These are many. Among them are profanity, vulgarity, and obscenity. Language of this sort may communicate very effectively—profanity, for example, is notoriously expressive!—but it is not socially acceptable.

Linguistic taboos are more often applied to what are considered improper word forms or improper occasions than they are to subject matter. Certain tribes avoid naming their gods for fear of offending them, but they will use circumlocution to talk about the gods. Two terms with the same denotation will often flourish side by side because one of them has connotations that make it taboo and improper in public discourse. Examples are certain words that refer to the functions of reproduction and excretion. Whatever the taboos of an audience, if you violate them you will expose yourself to reproof and a consequent loss of effectiveness.

d. Formal English. At another extreme from shoptalk, slang, and linguistic taboos is a language style which a subject, audience, and occasion sometimes require. It is called *formal* English. This term is used to denote the variety of language used for communicating with people who demand precise expression either because they are exacting in their language usage or because the matter communicated is highly important. The language used in a Supreme Court proceeding, for example, must be formal in tone and precise in meaning—informality or flippancy would be highly inappropriate, imprecision a source of confusion. The English of a United Nations debate or report needs to be formal because formal English will come closest to evoking the same meanings in all the people who use English for communication—a few being the Australians, Canadians, Ceylonese, Ghanaians, Indians, Irish, Jamaicans, Maltese, Pakistanis, and delegates from the United States. Moreover, formal English is better suited than colloquial English for accurate translation into French, Russian, Chinese, and the other languages used at the United Nations. Although relatively few situations call for a strictly formal usage, it is to your advantage to know how to operate at this level, for certainly in college you will be expected to write (and even to deliver orally) academic reports, reference papers, and, at the graduate level, seminar papers and theses. All of these situations customarily require formal English.

e. Informal English. All the styles of language we have been examining are of limited usefulness for public speaking: Shoptalk is for specialists only; slang is normally inappropriate; linguistic taboos must not be violated; and formal English is used in the kind of speaking that is rarely heard in the course of ordinary life. What style of English, then, is widely and generally appropriate?

Stephen Leacock described it in his remark about the use of "English" for literature and "American" for speaking. Conversation is conducted in "American" or informal English. Informal English admits many words and sentence constructions that formal English excludes, words and forms customarily found in the casual speaking of educated people. Since such people are at ease in this language, a speaker may well use it in addressing them. Compilers of dictionaries label some of its words "colloquial," as indeed they are. But "colloquial" need not suggest inferiority or incorrectness; it is merely a descriptive label. Colloquial language is not necessarily incorrect and may be highly appropriate.

Informal English includes that large body of words and expressions employed by educated people in carrying on the public and private business of the contemporary world. This language is found in communications aimed at general listeners and readers: speeches, magazine articles, newspaper columns, and the like. This is the language that will be appropriate in the majority of speeches you will be called upon to make while in college and after graduation.

2. Precision

For all his bumbling speech, Polonius knew well the functions of language. It was clear to him that Hamlet was reading *more* than "Words, words, words." Polonius understood that words are used to communicate meaning, or, as he put it, "matter." You may smile at his clumsiness, but you should admire the old man's efforts to be clear and precise in what he said.

To be precise in language is to choose the right words for expressing an idea. The right words are those that say clearly what you have in mind. They put your ideas sharply into focus and minimize the chance of confusion on the part of a listener.

We have said that good oral style is designed to make ideas instantly intelligible. But you will be able to say clearly only what you have clearly in mind. Consequently, the first requirement for clear language is a clear idea. Assuming, though, that you know what you want to say, your problem is to say it well.

Language must have two major characteristics to be precise (and thus clear). The first of these is accuracy; the second is concreteness.

a. **Accuracy.** The two most important obstacles to accuracy in speaking are exaggeration and ambiguity.

(1) Avoid exaggeration. Hyperbole is the name given to the kind of exaggeration that is used for dramatic effect. This sort of exaggeration is an acceptable figure of speech and is not likely to cause confusion or lack of clarity. When you say, "My car is as old as the hills," no one will take the statement literally. Such deliberate and intentional inaccuracies in language add vividness to expression. But this use of hyperbole is noticeably different from what happens when a grossly exaggerated statement is expected to be literally taken. This sort of exaggeration introduces unnecessary and thoughtless imprecision into what should be an accurate statement of fact.

The advertising vocabulary contains obvious offenses in using the kind of exaggeration that robs a statement of accuracy. "Big" isn't *big* enough, so advertisers use, in progression, "gigantic," "colossal," and, not even ultimately, "supercolossal." This kind of thinking leads toothpaste manufacturers to identify as their "large" size the smallest tube of toothpaste available through retail channels. When the supersuperlatives have been exhausted, what next?

To exaggerate for emphasis has been called an American trait. It is more nearly universal. But exaggeration fails to achieve its effect when it is used unceasingly, as the habit of using too much spice makes normally seasoned food seem flat.

(2) Avoid ambiguity. Ambiguity is found in contexts, not in words. A statement is ambiguous when either of two meanings is possible and the context does not make clear which is intended. Grammatical ambiguity (often called *amphiboly* or *amphibology*) results from an uncertain grammatical construction. Newspapers offer frequent examples of amphiboly. More amusing than confusing, it is, nonetheless, an example of inaccuracy in the use of language:

"Throw the horse over the fence some hay."

"I like teaching more than my wife."

"Her hair was pulled back in a bun while at her throat which complemented her navy-blue tailored dress was a multistrand of beads."

"The restaurant is famous for *paté de foie gras* made from goose livers and its fine chef."

News notes about members of a woman's club: "We are sorry to report that our Past President, Mrs. Gertrude Sturtevant, is at home recuperating from an operation."

A headline: "Drowning dampens spirits at beach party."

Story on a society page: "A few youths swam in the chill night air."

A second kind of ambiguity grows out of the fact that a word may evoke a number of potential meanings and the context fails to make clear which of these is intended. The lawyer who phoned his wife to say he would be late for dinner because he was delayed by a bar meeting was guilty of (deliberate?) ambiguity.

b. Concreteness and specificity. The greatest enemy of precision in language, other than a lack of accuracy, is vagueness. It resides in the words, not in their contexts. Once your meaning for a word is determined within a context, ambiguity is removed and your meaning is usually clear. A vague word, on the other hand, is one so broad that no matter what its context, left unaided, it will tend to be imprecise. We will mention three classes of words that lead to vagueness; meaningless qualifiers, abstract terms, and general terms. The implication is that you avoid using them whenever possible.

(1) Avoid meaningless qualifiers. Many words give the impression of qualifying or quantifying when really they don't. What do you mean, for example, when you say that a man is "fat," "thin," "tall," "short," "middle-aged," or "old"? The terms are so relative that they require reference to some scale or some exact criterion. The images listeners get from such terms as these will vary widely and also differ widely from what a speaker intends to convey. How many is "some," "few," "several"? How much is "lots," or "very"? Whenever you can (and this will be nearly always) give precise information.

(2) Avoid abstract terms. An abstract term is one that names a quality apart from any material instance of it. By their very nature, abstract terms must be vague because they refer to no tangible object. Abstract terms, like other vague words, lack precision because they can mean so many things. You can hardly avoid talking about such abstractions as *justice, honesty, democracy, virtue,* and the like, but to do so without definition or without clear examples that convey a precise image is to be vague.

Abstract terms are tempting for several reasons. Most obvious of these is the fact that it is easier to use an abstract term than it is to make clear distinctions among a number of borderline cases, all of which are comfortably covered by the abstract term. You could condemn "gambling" but avoid mentioning or thinking about church bingo parties. You could denounce "undemocratic nations," and let your hearers put the government of Transcisalpuria into that category if they wish. You could deplore "corruption" in "unions"; You need not then stigmatize Local 4321 of International XYZ. This is not good communication.

Another reason abstract terms are tempting is that they make it possible to avoid definite commitments. When governments "rattle sabers," they do not make blunt threats but rather veil the threatened consequences in vague language. No government would say, "Stop putting missile bases in the countries around our border or we'll knock your head off." Instead, the language of diplomacy leaves enough room for doubt so that maneuvering is possible and backtracking causes no loss of face. "Inconsistent with national safety," "will strongly oppose any attempt," "lead to serious consequences." Analyses of conditions and forecasts of trends made by stockmarket analysts are splendid examples of precisely this sort of vagueness.

(3) Avoid general terms. The use of general terms is a third cause of vagueness in expression. A comedian, whose name we have forgotten, makes fun of the practice of using what he calls the "vague specific." Good examples of the "vague specific" are found in several of the phrases student speakers seem to like to use: "Authorities agree . . ."; "In my research I found that . . ."; "In an article I read . . ."; and "Statistics show. . . ." Other examples of general terms: "a large midwestern city," "noted chemist (physicist, theologian, or whatever)," and "government sources."

The solution to problems of vagueness in language is to make the language as precise as possible. The way to do this is to use concrete rather than abstract terms, to use specific rather than general terms, to formulate meaningful definitions, and to give clear examples.

Developing a sensitivity to language will make you aware of the subtle shadings in idea and emotional coloration that may be achieved in your use of words. Moreover, it will make you intensely aware of the linguistic practices that exist in your own speaking. Begin to strive for the word or phrase that carries the exact shade of meaning that you intend. Do not be content with one that is only a near approximation.

3. Simplicity

A naïve but common assumption is that "big" words are somehow better because they are more impressive than their ordinary and familiar counterparts. Acting on this assumption, speakers often sound pompous when they mean to be dignified. Nothing is more damaging to one's purpose than feeble elegance. Henry David Thoreau, whose own style is marked by economy and simplicity, commented that long words had a paralysis in their tails. (Thoreau said that he went for walks along the river not on riparian excursions.) Far from being an elevated variety of English, self-conscious formality is pretentious and unnatural.

Former Representative Maury Maverick coined the term "gobbledygook" as a label for writing or speaking that is pompous, wordy, involved, and full of long, Latinized terms. Gobbledygook is almost totally destructive of clarity. What did the college administrator mean who listed these aims for education?

> . . . the development of intellectual consistency, the creation of aesthetic awareness, the liberation of the personality, the awakening of nonverbal and nonrational sensibilities to amplify adult experience, and the structure of an insight into the eternality of human aspiration and frustration.

Multisyllabic words from Latin and Greek roots may seem impressive to the one who uses them, but for English-speaking listeners one- and two-syllable words of Anglo-Saxon origin are better. As we recall it was Thomas Aquinas who said that simplicity is the essence of beauty. Impressiveness in style is a part of its beauty, but pomposity is too easily mistaken for impressiveness.

Lack of simplicity often robs style of propriety and precision. First, propriety suffers when language is too technical. The doctor who warns a patient of "an incipient carcinomatous condition in the duodenum immediately inferior to the pylorus" would be much clearer (to the layman) if he spoke of "the first stages of cancer at the upper end of the small intestine." Second, an attempt to use "impressive" language can often lead to embarrassing mistakes in accuracy. In Sheridan's play, *The Rivals*, the now famous Mrs. Malaprop gave her name ("malapropism") to this kind of mistake:

> Observe me, Sir Anthony.—I would by no means wish a daughter of mine to be a progeny of learning; I don't think so much learning becomes a young woman; for instance, I would never let her meddle with Greek, or Hebrew, or Algebra, or Simony, or Fluxions, or Paradoxes, or such inflammatory branches of learning—neither would it be necessary for her to handle any of your mathematical, astronomical, diabolical instruments: —But, Sir Anthony, I would send her, at nine years old, to a boarding-school, in order to learn a little ingenuity and artifice. Then, sir, she should have a

supercilious knowledge in accounts;—and as she grew up, I would have her instructed in geometry, that she might know something of the contagious countries;—but above all, Sir Anthony, she should be a mistress of orthodoxy, that she might not misspell, and mispronounce words so shamefully as girls usually do; and likewise that she might reprehend the true meaning of what she is saying. This, Sir Anthony, is what I would have a woman know;—and I don't think there is a superstitious article in it.

To achieve simplicity, use not only short, forceful words, but also as few words as possible to accomplish your purpose. Notice we say *to accomplish your purpose*, and not just to be understood, because your purpose includes being understood in a certain way.

4. Directness

The style of public address is much more direct and personal than written style. A speaker uses first and second person pronouns "I," "you," "we," to a much greater extent than a writer. On July 26, 1952, Adlai E. Stevenson accepted the Democratic party's nomination to run for the presidency. In the following excerpt from his acceptance speech, observe not only the directness and personal quality of his style, but the simplicity as well.

Mr. President, Ladies and Gentlemen of the Convention, my Fellow Citizens:
I accept your nomination—and your program.
I should have preferred to hear those words uttered by a stronger, a wiser, a better man than myself. But after listening to the President's speech I even feel better about myself.
None of you, my friends, can wholly appreciate what is in my heart. I can only hope that you understand my words. They will be few.*

5. Originality

Change of pace is as important in speaking as it is in pitching a ball game. Nothing destroys interest or dulls attention as effectively as monotony. You remember that in Chapter 9 we identified change as being one of the characteristics of a stimulus that make it attract attention. Originality in style is a form of skillful change, one that helps to avoid monotony in language. Instead of using trite expressions, try to bring freshness and vigor to your speaking through saying what you

* Adlai E. Stevenson, *Major Campaign Addresses of Adlai E. Stevenson* (New York: Random House, 1953), p. 7.

have to say without the use of clichés, hackneyed phrases, and figures of speech that are tired from overuse.

William H. Whyte, Jr., constructed a composite business speech built out of 60 badly overused expressions and constructions. It is an example of what Whyte says can be called *reverse* gobbledygook which "lends a powerful straight-from-the-shoulder effect to ambiguity and equivocation." Look at the style of that speech,

"COOPERATION—AN OPPORTUNITY AND A CHALLENGE."*

It is a pleasure and a privilege to be here with you today. These great annual meetings are always an inspiration to me, and doubly so today. After that glowing introduction by our toastmaster, I must confess, however, that I'd like to turn the tables and tell a little story on Chuck. When I say it's about the nineteenth hole and a certain gentleman whose baritone was cracked, those of you who were at the Atlanta conference last year will know what I mean. But I won't tell it. Chuck Forbes is too good a friend of mine and, seriously, I know full well we all realize what a tower of strength his yeoman service has been to the association in these trying times.

Yes, gentlemen, trying times. So you'll pardon me if I cast aside the glib reverberation of glittering generalities and the soothing syrup of sugar-coated platitudes and put it to you the only way I can: straight English.

We're losing the battle!

From every corner the people are being weaned from the doctrines of the Founding Fathers. They are being detoured from the high-speed highways of progress by the utopian highwaymen.

Now, the man in the street is a pretty savvy fellow. Don't sell him short. Joe Doakes may be fooled for a while, but in the end he wants no part of the mumbo jumbo the global saboteurs are trying to sell him. After all, he is an American.

But he has to be told.

And we're not telling him!

Now let me say that I do not wish to turn the clock back. None of us do. All forward-looking businessmen see themselves as partners in a team in which the worker is a full-fledged member. I regard our employees as our greatest business asset, and I am sure, mindful as I am of the towering potentials of purposeful energy in this group of clear-sighted leaders, that in the final analysis, it is the rock foundation of your policies, too.

But the team can't put the ball across for a first down just by wishing it. The guards and the tackles can't do their job if the quarterback doesn't let them in on the play. And we, the quarterbacks, are muffing the ball.

How are we to go over for a touchdown? My friends, this is the $64

* William H. Whyte, Jr., "The Language of Business," *Fortune*, 42 (Nov. 1950), p. 114.

question. I don't know the answers. I am just a plain-spoken businessman. I am not a soothsayer. I have no secret crystal ball. But I do know one thing: before we round the curve into the homestretch, we have a job to do. It will not be easy. I offer no panaceas or nostrums. Instead I would like to suggest that the real key to our problem lies in the application of the three E's.

What are the three E's?

Enterprise! Endeavor! Effort!

Each and every one of us must appoint himself a salesman—yes, a missionary, if you will—and get out and do some real grass roots selling. And when we hit the dirt, let's not forget the customers—the greatest asset any business has.

Now, much has been done already. But let's not fool ourselves: the surface, as our chairman has so wisely said, has hardly been scratched. The program is still in its infancy. So let me give it to you straight from the shoulder. The full implementation, gentlement, depends on *us*.

So let's get on the beam! In cracker-barrel fashion, let's get down to earth. In good plain talk the man in the street can understand, let's remind Joe Doakes that the best helping hand we will ever find is the one at the end of his own shirt sleeve.

We have the know-how.

With sights set high, let's go over the top!

C. Making Style Vivid

The most important function of style in language is to give vividness to the ideas language conveys. Language brings clarity and interest to a speech only if the style makes ideas not only instantly intelligible but also vividlv perceptible. Language that has the good qualities already discussed in this chapter will do much to make expression vivid. We now turn our attention to a number of special devices that you may use to reinforce the effectiveness of the language you use.

1. Figures of Speech

Figurative language uses words to convey meanings beyond the literal. It makes some change in the use of a word and thereby adds color and vividness to expression. The language of everyday conversation is abundantly sprinkled with figures of speech.

The most common figures are *metaphor* and *simile*. Both are formed by comparing one object with another. A simile makes a comparison between two things, ordinarily indicating the comparison with such a word as *like* or *as*. When a sports broadcaster told how spectators left a stadium during a dust storm, he said the event "looked like a mob scene being sandblasted off a billboard." This kind of comparison of the two events constitutes a simile.

If the things compared are closely alike, a simile is not vivid. If the broadcaster had compared the dust-driven spectators to people running indoors from a rain, he would have had a dull simile.

Senator Henry M. Jackson spoke to the Senate on December 4, 1973. He used this occasion as an opportunity to submit to his colleagues his proposals regarding agreements between the United States and the Soviet Union on the limitation of strategic arms. At one point he said, "Today our monopoly in MIRV technology has vanished like last year's snow. . . ." A bit later in the same speech, however, the Senator was somewhat more imaginative when he said,

If the interim agreement ever represented interim equality, it is because it was like a stand-off between an American lightweight at the top of his form and a Soviet heavyweight, ill-trained and out of condition.

Note, however, that every speaker on occasion faces the temptation to carry an image too far. Jackson continued,

The interim agreement has provided for 5 years of training in which the sluggish Soviet heavyweight can get into shape while we remain, however agile, lightweight by comparison. It is here that politics—call it psychology if you will—is affected by strategic strength; for no lightweight in his right mind would ever enter the ring under such circumstances, so that the match could easily go by default.*

A metaphor, like a simile, is based on comparison. But whereas in a simile the comparison is explicit, a metaphor is an implied comparison. The difference between the two figures is that while simile says one thing is *like* another, the metaphor says that one thing *is* another. In October 1896, Robert G. Ingersoll used this metaphor in a speech: "I know that labor is the Atlas on whose shoulders rests the great superstructure of civilization and the great dome of science adorned with all there is of art." Henry Clay said that the Union formed by the Constitution was "a marriage that no human authority can dissolve the parties from."

Here is a more recent example of a speaker's use of metaphor. On November 1, 1973, James D. Koerner, speaking in Milwaukee on the subject of "Changing Education," told his audience,

* *Congressional Record*, Dec. 4, 1973, p. S21758.

We have built a system in which we, if you will permit me a different and rather extended metaphor, cram everybody onto the same school bus. Students, teachers, administrators, and yes, parents, all are sentenced to a 12-year ride in the same vehicle.°

After extending the metaphor for *several* paragraphs, Dr. Koerner says, "I will now mercifully forgo this metaphor which, like all metaphors, can be pushed too far."† Even if we believed his metaphor were not pushed too far, we would agree with him that any metaphor easily can be.

Similes and metaphors, used intelligently, can add greatly to the vividness of a speech. They will detract from it, however, when they are abused. Trite similes and far-fetched metaphors are fatal to effective expression.

Trite expressions in the speech of others are much more noticeable than are those you use yourself. Examples of tired speech abound. Here are a few instances of the sort of similes and metaphors that fail to interest because they have been used too much.

Mad as a wet hen
Nervous as a cat
Slow as molasses in January
White as a sheet
To stick like a leech
To be a bookworm
Good as gold
Fat as a pig

Unfortunately, unlike old slang, clichés never seem either to work their way into the standard language or to go quietly away. Instead, it seems, they prefer to hang around and just go on being clichés. Avoid them. Language is like a flashlight battery—it illuminates better when it is fresh.

Overstatement, understatement, and *irony* (identified as forms of humor in Chapter 18) are used also as figures of speech to heighten the vividness of an idea without seeking to arouse laughter. Overstatement has already been referred to in this chapter under the name of hyperbole. It consists in using a stronger word than is necessary to convey an idea. The result of this usage is to exaggerate, but for vividness, not deception. Observe the several examples of overstatement in

° *Vital Speeches of the Day,* **40** (Jan. 1, 1974), p. 178.
† *Vital Speeches of the Day,* **40** (Jan. 1, 1974), p. 179.

the following excerpts from a single paragraph in a lecture by Adlai Stevenson.

I am not a historian, but I doubt if anyone will dispute the *incomparably* dramatic qualities of the twentieth century. . . . In 50 years, distance has been *obliterated* by a technological revolution that has brought *all mankind* cheek to jowl, and that has released the creative and obliterative power of the atom. . . . National independence and democracy have scored *spectacular* victories and suffered *shocking* defeats. . . . Two new *colossi*, the United States and the Soviet Union, have *suddenly* emerged. Ideas, on which the West has had an export *monopoly* for centuries, are now also flowing out of the East and colliding everywhere with our Western ideas.*

In Chapter 13 you will find vitality identified as a desirable characteristic of effective speech delivery. In a perhaps figurative sense, the *language* of a speech can infuse some of this vitality or energy into the encoding of a message. When this happens, the resulting style may sometimes appear to be overstatement. The following example will make this clear. In it, notice the directness with which the speaker approaches the audience. Note also the energy and vitality of composition. Finally, keeping in mind the fact that the one who makes the speech might not agree that what is said ought to be called overstatement, decide what you think about this particular case.

On October 31, 1973, Dr. L. M. Skamser spoke to the Northeastern Poultry Producers Council, Hershey, Pennsylvania. He said,

Things will never be the same for you. The fast-changing events of the past 12 months have left everyone gasping in surprise. Shortages everywhere. Devaluation. Price controls. Record-shattering prices for grain. A farm bill to encourage production. And no one knows what happens next.

Things are changing and the changes are radical. . . .

We are living in a world of radicalism. Bombarded by headlines, our society and our government make extreme moves on partial or inadequate information. Fictional, earthshaking problems are solved in 27 minutes on television shows, and the 27-minute solution is being sought for all problems, real or fictional.†

Understatement‡ is the opposite of exaggeration. It deliberately says less than what might be said and thus calls attention to an idea. To say

---

* Adlai E. Stevenson, *Call to Greatness* (New York: Harper & Row, 1954), p. 109. Italics added.
† *Vital Speeches of the Day*, **40** (Jan. 1, 1974), p. 188.
‡ See Chapter 18.

of a man one considers thoroughly dishonest "He is not the most scrupulous person I know," is to understate the case.

Irony* uses language to say one thing but to imply quite another. It is often found in the same context with either exaggeration or understatement. Note the combination of irony, understatement, and overstatement in the following passage. The speaker, Robert G. Ingersoll, is arguing *in favor of* the demonetization of silver.

In 1816 Great Britain demonetized silver, and that wretched old government has had nothing but gold from that day to this as a standard. And to show you the frightful results of that demonetization, that government does not now own above one-third of the globe, and all the winds are busy floating her flags.

There is no question that figures of speech add vividness to the expression of a speaker's ideas. But a word of caution: Figures of speech can be used to excess. When they are, the style becomes not vivid but flamboyant, flowery, and weak. Here, in a press release from the office of a congressman, is an example of what can happen.

If we throw stones of criticism we will break the glass houses and the idols with feet of clay will be toppled from their pedestals of self-exaltation by the angry winds created by the righteous indignation of Americans sacrificed on the cross of gold by selfish, greedy men and their stooges in high places.

Another example of the overuse of figures of speech is a portion of a letter written to the editor of a newspaper:

If the country's listing ideal isn't soon righted people will someday find that an even keel is so far out from underneath that no counterweight thrown against a rotten ship of state can vindicate the cause of freedom without rending permanently some plank in the bulwark that this society has always taken for granted as being there, being somewhere, but which won't exist at all once debasement gives way to disjunction, and a bright hope born in 1776 founders and becomes part of the memory of that mass of other toppled nations which spell in grotesque form the failure of man to govern himself.†

---

* See Chapter 18.

† From a letter to the editor of the Bernardsville (New Jersey) *News*, quoted in *The New Yorker*, 41 (Dec. 25, 1965), p. 50.

2. Parallel Structure

Another method of making ideas vivid is to repeat phrases of identical or similar construction. The effect of the repetition is to draw the attention of the audience to the speaker's ideas. A well-known example appears in Lincoln's Gettysburg Address. "Government of the people, by the people, for the people." In his first inaugural address, President Franklin Delano Roosevelt used this parallel structure.

Our greatest primary task is to put people to work. . . .
The task can be helped by definite efforts to raise the values of agricultural products and with this the power to purchase the output of our cities.

It can be helped by preventing realistically the tragedy of the growing loss, through foreclosure, of our small homes and our farms.

It can be helped by insistence that the Federal, State and local governments act forthwith on the demand that their cost be drastically reduced.

It can be helped by the unifying of relief activities which today are often scattered, uneconomical and unequal. It can be helped by national planning for a supervision of all forms of transportation and of communications and other utilities which have a definite public character.

And in his second inaugural address, President Roosevelt said:

I see millions of families trying to live on incomes so meager that the pall of family disaster hangs over them day by day.

I see millions whose daily lives in city and on farm continue under conditions labeled indecent by a so-called polite society half a century ago.

I see millions denied education, recreation and the opporutnity to better their lot and the lot of their children.

I see millions lacking the means to buy the products of farm and factory and by their poverty denying work and productiveness to many other millions.

I see one-third of a nation ill-housed, ill-clad, ill-nourished.

Senator Edward M. Kenndy, in a speech on the problem of energy in foreign policy delivered to the Senate on December 6, 1973, said to his fellow Senators,

During the current embargo . . . we must be prepared to do without Arab oil, as we have been doing in recent weeks. And we must be prepared in the future to sustain any embargo of oil shipments undertaken by any nation as a political weapon. To resist such pressure, we can adopt a number of specific policies:

We must be prepared to ration fuel on short notice, and to allocate fuel for priority users;

Wherever possible, we must build up our stockpiles of fuel in the United States;

We must begin long-range efforts to limit consumption of energy;

We must try to work out energy-sharing arrangements with other oil importing countries; and

We must undertake a long-range effort to seek new sources and increased quantities of energy from areas outside the Arab world, and maintain controls on the growth of our imports of this oil.*

3. Antithesis

Antithesis is the opposing or contrasting of ideas. Not only is antithesis widely and commonly used, but it is also among the oldest of the consciously practiced rhetorical techniques. (Incidentally, the familiar English construction "Not only . . . but also . . ." used in the preceding sentence and often throughout the book is a famliar example of antithesis.) Antithesis was a favorite stylistic device among the orators of ancient Greece. Listen to the magnificent language of Demosthenes, considered by many to be the finest speaker the world has ever known. In his speech *On the Chersonese* he gives us a splendid example of antithesis, combines it with parallel structure and, as he balances idea against idea and clause with clause, he builds toward the climax of a passage of exceptional power and grace.

It was not safe in Olynthus to speak in behalf of Philip until the fruits of his capture of Potidaea had been bestowed on the Olynthian people; it was not safe in Thessaly to speak in behalf of Philip until the mass of the Thessalians had been helped by Philip's expulsion of their tyrants, and his restoration of the Pylaca to them; it was not safe in Thebes, until he had restored to them Boeotia and uprooted the Phocians; but at Athens, when Philip has not only robbed us of Amphipolis and the Cardian land, but is preparing Euboea as a rampart against you, and is now moving on to Byzantium, it is safe to speak in behalf of Philip.

Perhaps the most famous instance of antithesis in the oratory of modern times is in John Fitzgerald Kennedy's inaugural address: "Ask not what your country can do for you. Ask what you can do for your country."

4. Rhetorical Questions

A question is "rhetorical" when you expect no direct answer to it from your audience. You know the answer; you use the question not to

* *Congressional Record*, Dec. 6, 1973, p. S21982.

elicit an overt response but to add vividness to the expression of your ideas. A direct question, even one that requires no answer from a listener, engages immediate, personal attention to a degree that statement often will not.

In his famous "Compromise Speech," delivered to the Senate in February 1850, Henry Clay used rhetorical questions as a method of forcing his listeners to formulate explicit (but silent) answers to his questions. In the paragraph quoted below, Clay refers to the first of eight resolutions he had proposed as a compromise between North and South over the question of slavery.

The first resolution, Mr. President, as you are aware, relates to California, and it declares that California, with suitable limits, ought to be admitted as a member of this Union, without the imposition of any restriction either to interdict or introduce slavery within her limits. Well now, is there any concession in this resolution by either party to the other? I know that gentlemen who come from slaveholding States say the North gets all that it desires; but by whom does it get it? Does it get it by any action of Congress? If slavery be interdicted within the limits of California, has it been done by Congress—by this government? No sir. That interdiction is imposed by California herself. And has it not been the doctrine of all parties that when a State is about to be admitted into the Union, the State has a right to decide for itself whether it will or will not have slavery within its limits?

A rhetorical question may be used to summarize a point developed by a line of argument. "What better way, then, is there to destroy peace than by preparing for war?" The answers to these kinds of questions are obvious.

President Franklin Delano Roosevelt used rhetorical questions very effectively. In a campaign speech, delivered in Chicago on October 14, 1936, the president said,

To [the business men of America] I say:
Do you have a deposit in the bank? It is safer today than it has ever been in our history. It is guaranteed. Last October first marked the end of the first full year in 55 years without a single failure of a national bank in the United States. Isn't that on the credit side of the government's account with you?
Are you an investor? Your stocks and bonds are up to a five and six year high level.
Are you a merchant? Your markets have the precious life-blood of purchasing power. Your customers on the farms have better incomes and smaller debts. Your customers in the cities have more jobs, surer jobs, better jobs. Didn't your government have something to do with this?

Are you in industry? Industrial earnings, industrial profits are the highest in four, six, or even seven years! Bankruptcies are at a new low. Your government takes some credit for that.

Are you in railroads? Freight loadings are steadily going up and so are passenger receipts because, for one reason, your government made the railroads cut rates and make money.

Are you a middleman in the great stream of farm products? The meat and grain that move through your yards and elevators have a steadier supply, a steadier demand and steadier prices than you have known for years.

In his annual Message to Congress, January 3, 1936, this same master of style put rhetorical questions into combination with the device of parallel structure to achieve a striking effect:

Shall we say that values are restored and that the Congress will, therefore, repeal the laws under which we have been bringing them back? Shall we say that because national income has grown with rising prosperity, we shall repeal existing taxes and thereby put off the day of approaching a balanced budget and of starting to reduce the national debt?

Shall we abandon the reasonable support and regulation of banking? Shall we restore the dollar to its former gold content?

Shall we say to the farmer—"The prices for your product are in part restored, now go and hoe your own row"? Shall we say to the home owners—"We have reduced your rates of interest—we have no further concern with how you keep your home or what you pay for your money, that is your affair"?

Shall we say to the several millions of unemployed citizens who face the very problem of existence—yes, of getting enough to eat—"We will withdraw from giving you work, we will turn you back to the charity of your communities and to those men of selfish power who tell you that perhaps they will employ you if the government leaves them strictly alone"?

Shall we say to the needy unemployed—"Your problem is a local one, except that perhaps the Federal Government, as an act of mere generosity, will be willing to pay to your city or to your country a few grudging dollars to help maintain your soup kitchens"?

Shall we say to the children who have worked all day—"Child labor is a local issue and so are your starvation wages; something to be solved or left unsolved by the jurisdictions of forty-eight states"?

Shall we say to the laborer—"Your right to organize, your relations with your employer have nothing to do with the public interest; if your employer will not meet with you to discuss your problems and his, that is none of our affair"?

Shall we say to the unemployed and the aged—"Social security lies not within the province of the Federal Government, you must seek relief elsewhere"? Shall we say to the men and women who live in conditions of squalor in country and in city—"The health and the happiness of you and your children are no concern of ours"?

Shall we expose our population once more by the repeal of laws to protect them against the loss of their honest investments and against the manipulations of dishonest speculators?

Shall we abandon the splendid efforts of the Federal Government to raise the health standards of the nation and to give youth a decent opportunity through such means as the Civilian Conservation Corps?

III. IMPROVING LANGUAGE AND STYLE

Facility in language and felicity in style increase the fidelity of communication. Neither of these is innate, and neither of them is easy to achieve. Your style will be what it becomes over the years, and it will be what *you* make it. We offer here a few suggestions to guide you in doing what every speaker must do—build your own style through the experience of years. But start now!

A. Become Aware of Your Own Use of Language

Listen to yourself. Record your speeches whenever you can. Instead of forgetting about a speech once you have delivered it, use it for practice material. Your primary concern in preparing a speech is with the ideas it conveys, and with the organization and materials that will make the ideas interesting and clear. In delivering the speech, with the ideas firmly at hand, and with notes to refresh your memory, you are free to give consideration to the language you use. This is the essence of extemporaneous speaking.

B. Be Curious about Words

As you read and listen, never let an unknown word pass you by. Make it identify itself. Examine its etymology and its usage. Then add it to your vocabulary. A good dictionary is one of the most valuable reference books you can own. But to keep a word in your vocabulary, you have to use it. If you do not, you will soon lose the word.

C. Study the Language of Others

Listening carefully to the speeches you hear in class is one good way of making a start toward being habitually aware of the language others use. An even better procedure is to read printed texts of speeches, to study them thoughtfully, to examine their structure and their materials and to analyze the speaker's use of language.

D. Practice Writing and Speaking

No matter how much you may learn about style, your own use of words will improve little without practice. The speaking you do in class is, of course, only a beginning. The most significant progress comes through experience. Through practice in both writing and speaking you can work toward developing an artistic use of language that functions with the ease of habit.

SUMMARY

The ideas you communicate are not a material substance that can be passed from hand to hand like money, nor can they be poured into a listener's head like water from a cup. Instead, ideas are "stirred up" in an audience by the symbols you use to *stand for the ideas.* Almost all word symbols can convey many different ideas; that is, each one can elicit many potential meanings. The meanings a word will actually elicit are determined by four relationships:

1. Denotation—the relationship of words to *reality.*
2. Connotation—the relationship of *people* to words and the objects, events, and concepts the words are used to name.
3. Syntax—the relationship of words to *other words* in grammatical structures.
4. Context—the relationship of words to the *passage* or *discourse* in which they are used.

Style in language is the way words are put together to express thought. Oral style differs from that of written discourse mainly in that the language of a speaker must make ideas instantly, clearly, and accurately intelligible.

Good oral style has these distinguishable characteristics: propriety, precision, simplicity, directness, and originality. Language is appropriate when it is properly suited to the audience and the occasion of a speech. Informal English, as it is normally used by educated people in the majority of their writing and speaking, is the most widely appropriate. To be precise, language should be both accurate and concrete. Exaggeration, ambiguity, and vagueness are the natural enemies of precision in language.

Simplicity in style is best achieved by avoiding flowery, impressive-sounding language in favor of short, forceful words of Anglo-Saxon origin. Simplicity also demands brevity, using as few words as possible to say accurately what is meant.

In their everyday communication, audiences use a liberal sprinkling of personal pronouns, contractions, and direct quotations. Their ears are attuned, therefore, to the relaxed idiom of informal conversation. You can lend directness to your style by using this same kind of informality and personal quality in your language.

Clichés, trite expressions, and hackneyed, overused phrases rob a speaker's style of originality. Originality in style is best achieved by avoiding tired words and phrases in favor of language with freshness and variety.

The most successful style is that which makes your ideas come alive for your audience. We have mentioned only four of the several devices that give style the vividness effective speaking requires: figurative language, parallel structure, antithesis, and rhetorical questions. There are many others you should know and use.

To improve the style of your speeches, do these four things:

Become aware of your own use of words.
Be curious about words.
Study the language of others.
Practice writing and speaking.

As a critical and responsible speaker, understand that words may be weapons, not to be used without full knowledge of the consequences of their being uttered. Understand clearly the linguistic implements at your disposal. Neither use them unscrupulously to make points easily nor be mastered by them—Be always in firm control.

QUESTIONS

1. Define language.
2. What kind of language is the primary means of human communication?
3. How do words communicate?
4. What is denotation? Connotation?
5. How do syntax and context give clues to a speaker's meaning?

6. Under what conditions can a speaker be criticized for the improper use of attitudinal and connotative language?

7. What is style?

8. What are some of the differences between written style and oral style?

9. What usefulness is there in shoptalk?

10. When is exaggeration used improperly?

11. What three classes of words lead to vagueness? Give examples.

12. What is a malapropism? Give examples.

13. What is parallel structure? Give examples.

14. How does antithesis make more vivid the expression of an idea?

15. What is a rhetorical question? How is it used?

16. What should you do to improve your style?

EXERCISES

1. Construct a sample vocabulary of the jargon used in at least one occupation. Translate each word or phrase into language appropriate for a general audience.

2. Select an essay written in "formal" English style and convert one or more paragraphs into acceptable, informal, oral style.

3. Find the mistakes in Mrs. Malaprop's comment and suggest a more accurate word for each.

4. Note examples of vague terms used in classroom speeches (meaningless modifiers, abstract words, general words) and show how they may be made more precise through illustration and definition.

5. Write down trite expressions in one round of classroom speeches and suggest a phrase that expresses each idea more vividly.

6. This chapter considers only a few of the many widely used figures of speech. Make a list of several figures not mentioned and find examples of each in printed texts of speeches. For example: metonymy, synecdoche, personification, and apostrophe.

7. Record a brief extemporaneous speech. Transcribe it and then polish the style.

I. Psychological elements of delivery
   A. Communication and catharsis
      1. Cathartic elements of speech
      2. Communicative elements of speech
   B. Factors affecting adjustment to a speaking situation
      1. Culture
      2. Past experience
      3. Conditioning
      4. Person addressed
   C. The conflict of cathartic and communicative elements
   D. Some practical suggestions
      1. Don't blame yourself.
      2. Adopt a conversational attitude.
      3. Realize the importance of experience.
      4. Prepare thoroughly.
      5. Practice consciously the positive aspects of the speech role.
II. Vocal elements
   A. Voice production
      1. Pronunciation
      2. Articulation
   B. Elements of voice
      1. Pitch
      2. Force
      3. Time
      4. Quality
   C. Using your voice to communicate meaning
      1. Emphasize the important words.
      2. Make clear distinctions among the ideas.
      3. Make words sound like what you mean.
      4. Speak in a conversational manner.
III. Physical action in delivery
   A. Eye contact
   B. Posture
   C. Movement
   D. Gesture
IV. Delivering the speech
   A. Modes of delivery
      1. Speaking from manuscript
      2. Speaking from memory
      3. Speaking impromptu
      4. Speaking extemporaneously
   B. Characteristics of good delivery
      1. Directness
      2. Spontaneity
      3. Involvement
      4. Vitality
      5. Intelligibility

Chapter 13

Delivery

Speaking demands your immediate physical presence in a way that writing, painting, sculpture, and other forms of communication do not. The ideas, organization, and supporting details in any given instance of written or spoken communication can be the same. Except for some few differences in style (the way language is used), what most distinguishes writing from speaking is that a speech must be delivered. Indeed, it doesn't become a speech until the moment of delivery. Even more to the point is the way in which your presence affects the audience. Consequently, good delivery makes a significant contribution to effectiveness in speaking. It is the vital, physical means by which messages are transmitted to a listener.

The importance of solid content in a speech is not diminished, however, by saying that good communictaion demands good delivery. For a listener, delivery is not only the vehicle for communication but also an important determinant of your credibility and the significance of your ideas.

Our purpose in this chapter is twofold. First, because skillful delivery implies an understanding of its psychological, vocal, and physical elements, we shall examine these. Second, with that discussion as background, we shall look at the modes and characteristics of delivery.

I. PSYCHOLOGICAL ELEMENTS OF DELIVERY

One important determinant of the effectiveness of your delivery and, therefore, the precision with which you convey your message accurately to your audience, is the attitude you have toward the speaking situation. This section of the chapter will consider the relationship between these attitudes and your effectiveness as a speaker.

A. Communication and Catharsis

Speech is a human behavior, one of the behaviors that people perform to bring their environments and themselves into equilibrium. The fact that the audience is clearly a part of your environment explains your desire to minimize the entirely natural anxiety you feel about the reactions of your listeners. Such anxiety springs from the fact that communication, whether in private conversation or formal public speaking, is an eminently personal ego-involving situation. The act of speaking satisfies two different needs: cathartic needs and communicative needs.

1. Cathartic Elements of Speech

Some speaking serves to meet your personal needs alone. On such occasions you are not concerned about what reaction you will get from others; you want to express your emotions as a way of eliminating them: to experience a catharsis. You have had the experience of talking to yourself, have had thoughts that you must express if you are to maintain satisfying emotional equilibrium. For example, you make sure you are alone and then "tell off" the wise guy in the political science class, saying the things that social training would not allow anyone to say to the wise guy's face: how obnoxious he is, how he disrupts the class with useless questions, how he insults people with whom he disagrees. Having vented your spleen through cathartic speech, you achieve a personal satisfaction. The next time you meet your obnoxious acquaintance face to face, you can smile and say, "Good morning."

Although such speech does influence the attitudes and conduct of others, you do not intend it to, even when it is not addressed to your self. The principle of catharsis has long been recognized as a valuable psychological experience both by religious leaders and by psychotherapists. It is an essential part of everyone's life. You often tell your feelings to a friend not because you feel that the friend can do something about them, but because you have the need to express your feelings to someone—to get them out.

Feelings that invite catharsis evidently arise from problems that reside in the speaker rather than in the listener—audience, psychologist, confidant, or friend. Other feelings that reside in speakers are anxiety over being ridiculous, embarrassment, and worries about clothes or haircut or facial contours. All speakers have these feelings in some measure.

2. Communicative Elements of Speech

In this book we are less interested in cathartic elements of speech than in speaking that communicates something else, the kind of speaking which serves as a means of gaining a socially significant response from a listener. It is a social act; both speaker and listeners are involved. Cathartic speech, in contrast, is not social; it is personal, often individual.

B. Factors Affecting Adjustment to a Speaking Situation

The total speaking situation—an interaction of speaker, speech, audience, and occasion—is a transaction in much the same sense that what happens between a merchant and a customer is a transaction. Speakers not only change the audience but the audience also changes them. The relationship between speaker and audience is more than one in which the speaker initiates a stimulus to which the listener responds. As soon as a speaker begins to initiate stimuli, the listener begins to respond; this response in turn stimulates the speaker. A dynamic circular relationship involving a large number of variables is set up. There are so many factors in the total speech situation that any attempt to decipher individual patterns of stimulus and response would be quite useless. There are, however, several general social factors that affect your attitude toward the act of speech and your perceptions of audience reactions.

1. Culture

Your ability to cope with a listener's reactions are determined in part by the subculture from which you come. Some cultural and subcultural groups emphasize the ability to use language in a sophisticated way and thus demand of their members a level of success that puts pressure on them. Even when parents in our society do not make specific demands on their children, the children whose parents' professions generally require a high degree of language skill, such as lawyers, ministers, and teachers, feel that they are under pressure to develop language skills.

Certainly,the general American culture, committed to solving society's problems through persuasion, puts a high priority on effective communication at all levels of the society. The tremendous success of Dale Carnegie courses and Toastmaster and Toastmistress clubs testifies to the significance of communication in our society. Some will respond favorably to the influence whereas others will seek to avoid the speaking situation or search for easy ways to satisfy its requirements.

2. Past Experience

Past experience has an important influence on your attitudes. This is the reason that satisfactory experiences in communication should be provided for students in the elementary schools. This is not the time to define good elementary school experiences, but we may certainly say that unfortunate experiences in the past affect one's response to the present. We can all understand the problem of the awkward junior high school boy who is called upon to recite in class and forgets his memorized poem. If he is treated unsympathetically by his teacher and is laughed at by his classmates, he may remember that experience and avoid all other speaking situations whenever he can.

The influence of past experience is not limited to the schoolroom. All your experience with language, all the responses you receive from listeners, parents, teachers, and friends can affect your approach to any new speaking situation.

3. Conditioning

The process of conditioning can make the speaking situation more difficult. Anxiety arises when you see a difference between what you expect to happen and what you perceive actually happens. Thus, whenever you perceive that you do not meet a standard you have set for yourself, you will take a different path the next time you speak. You will keep trying something new until your behavior is reinforced —until you get satisfaction from the experience—until your expectations and perceptions are the same. From then on you will tend to do those same things so long as your receive the reinforcement. Thus you are conditioned to a particular way of preparing and delivering a speech.

When, on consecutive occasions, you attempt some new way of meeting the situation, each time without success, you become increasingly frustrated and your anxiety increases. Finally, a new kind of conditioning sets in and you find that the only way to escape the frustration and anxiety is to avoid the experience altogether. When compelled by circumstances to give a speech, you would be quite anxious in the situation.

4. The Person Addressed

Another social influence that affects adjustment to the speaking situation is the amount of anxiety aroused in you by the person spoken to. Many teachers who are very nervous before an audience of adults have no difficulty whatsoever when speaking before their classes. They have learned to expect favorable responses from children but not from adults. Sometimes a speech class poses a problem because you know you will be graded by the instructor and evaluated by the other students in the class. Your classmates, when the instructor is absent, do not constitute a threat and, therefore, are not the source of concern that they are when they are in the classroom situation.

Culture, past experience, conditioning, and the person being addressed are by no means the only elements that affect the attitude you will have toward a speaking situation. Many other social influences affect you. We have discussed these four to point up the fact that although each experience is unique, the social elements in a situation cause you to generalize about your experiences, frequently to your own disadvantage. They teach you to expect success or failure and thus establish attitudes toward the speaking situation before it is ever confronted.

C. The Conflict of Cathartic and Communicative Elements

One of the most annoying reactions you can have to a speaking situation is fear. The outward signs of this fear and anxiety are called "stage fright." In its milder form it is known as "nervousness." It may involve stumbling over words, vocalizing pauses (the injection of "uh" and "er" without regard to meaning), trembling hands and knees, or the inability to look directly at members of the audience. The type and extent of the symptoms differ from person to person. Regardless of the form the symptoms take, the fear reaction can be said to result from the fact that cathartic elements in the speaking situation are interfering with the communicative purpose of the speech.

Obviously, if you care only about fulfilling your expressive (non-communicative) needs in public speaking, you have a problem that a speech class cannot hope to cure. It is highly doubtful that if you were such a person you would remain long in a speech class. The notion that such a person might exist, however, helps to show what is behind fear reactions. Each fear reaction indicates a tendency to be concerned with personal ego needs rather than with the effectiveness of the talk, to worry not about how well your listeners understand your ideas, nor how persuasive your arguments are, nor how much the audience enjoys your humor. Instead, stage fright shows the tendency to fret about how an audience will evaluate you, how you look, and whether they are laughing *at* you rather than *with* you. In short, your anticipations about the audience are reinforced by a glance, a whispered comment in the back of the room, or a cough. In most situations the audience is not making such an evaluation. You should not come before an audience feeling that you are to be judged on such personal grounds. You come to share an idea with the listeners. We might say that your anxiety and fear are proportional to the extent to which you question your personal acceptability rather than the acceptability of the idea you espouse.

Needless to say, you can never entirely separate your person from your attempt to persuade. Nor should you try. No one has ever been a speaking machine. Personal involvement with the ideas of a speech is essential to the kind of enthusiasm which helps build satisfactory audience response. For this reason, even the most experienced speakers are anxious about the speaking situation. A competent speaker expects such anxiety, uses it by designing the speech so as to clear away as much anxiety as possible and lives with the remnant of anxiety that no speaker can eliminate.

D. Some Practical Suggestions

Understanding why fear and anxiety are present in a speaking situation will help you to develop proper attitudes toward speaking in public. Here are some practical suggestions to help you put this knowledge to work.

1. Don't Blame Yourself

Speakers who find themselves subject to some of the physical reactions of fear and anxiety will frequently enlarge the problem by becoming angry with themselves. But stage-fright reactions cannot really be voluntarily controlled. If you understand how powerless you are, you may be able to stop blaming yourself and thus reduce the psychic feedback. You cannot will away the anxiety no matter how much pressure you put on yourself. Speakers who learn to live with that anxiety have gone a long way toward freeing themselves of fear.

2. Adopt a Conversational Attitude

One of the most helpful attitudes to develop is the idea that public speaking is an expanded and frequently somewhat formalized version of conversation. People speaking to a group of friends in informal surroundings have little difficulty in saying what they want to say. If you think of public speaking as something enormously greater and more formal than private conversation, you burden yourself with pressures that are not a part of the informal situation. The more you can think of public speaking as conversation, the easier public speaking will be. The same direct, friendly, enthusiastic kind of communication that is so enjoyable in a friendly get-together is what makes public speaking effective.

3. Realize the Importance of Experience

Just as unhappy experiences can condition you to fear public speaking, so also can favorable experiences condition you to enjoy it. To attain this goal, you must banish from your ideas about speaking as much of the mystery as possible: You must know what good speech is and must study the methods of organizing speeches, supporting them, and delivering them. You must also realize that in the cafeteria, the hallway, or at the dinner table you are continually making speeches and that it is your perception of a speaking situation, rather than the actual situation, which makes it threatening. When you see that making a good speech has no requirements that you cannot master, and that an effective speaker is an intelligent artisan rather than a miracle worker, you can begin to have the kind of experiences which build confidence. Each favorable experience will reinforce the others.

4. Prepare Thoroughly

It seems obvious that anxiety will attack you if you aren't sure of what you want your speech to do or whether the speech will do it. In the presence of these uncertainties, you are insecure about how the audience will react. Careful preparation is the only realistic solution to this problem. Study your speech subject well. Be sure to understand the limited topic on which you will speak and build a broad circle of information around it.

There are certain laxities that effective speaking does not allow: "I'm not too sure about this, but I think you understand what I mean." "I think it is pronounced . . ." "I understand that Professor Kernaghan has a different view on this, but I couldn't find his book in our library." "I had to work late last night, so I didn't have a chance to check all the facts." These and similar statements merely say that you are not expert on the subject. Listeners ask, "Why should I listen?" Confidence in speaking grows out of knowing that you are well prepared and out of seeing that your audience realizes you are qualified to speak on your subject.

5. Practice Consciously the Positive Aspects of the Speech Role

There is much value in deliberately adopting the pose of good adjustment to the speaking situation. Psychologists tolerate the view that the acceptance of a role makes a person do things which are compatible with it. You may feel more composure because you adopt the body set and delivery of one who is composed. Actors have long recognized that audiences tend to do and feel what they see being done and felt. When they see someone in pain on the stage, they "feel" pain. When the actor is happy, they "feel" happy. This reaction is called *empathy*. Empathy is useful to a public speaker. If listeners perceive an alert speaker, they will tend to be alert. The speaker, seeing a favorable audience response, tends to become more confident.

Here are a few specific actions you can practice to help give you the appearance of emotional control.

Walk briskly to the platform. Walk directly and resolutely to the rostrum and put down your notes. Don't slouch or shuffle along the way. Don't glance nervously at the audience or fumble with your papers or clothing.

Look directly at the audience. When you reach the rostrum and have assembled your notes before you, look directly at the audience for a brief time before beginning your speech. Think of this as a moment when you "meet" the audience and make your first friendly contact with them. During the speech, concentrate on looking directly at the members of the audience. Speakers who seem unable to look directly at their listeners give a sure sign of anxiety. Eye contact is perhaps the most important factor in good delivery. It will be discussed in more detail among the visual elements of delivery later in this chapter.

Use a good attention factor in your introduction. Your introduction may set the tone for the reactions you will get to the rest of the speech.

For this reason, you will want to get off to a good start. Make sure to plan an opening that will arouse the interest of the audience; then deliver it as you planned it. Don't let any anxiety you feel make you rush into the main body of the speech and so slide over the interest-gaining use of the attention factor. Attention factors have been discussed in Chapter 5, and further discussion appears in Chapter 16 under the heading "Gaining Attention."

Control the rate of delivery. When nervous fear strikes you, your first reaction is to get the unpleasant experience over with as soon as possible. This reaction is understandable because the human organism always tries to avoid unpleasant stimuli. Your effectiveness can be hurt by the perfectly normal desire to escape an unpleasant situation. To avoid this reaction, measure the rate of your delivery. Talk more slowly than you might be inclined to, especially at the beginning of the speech.

Keep your nervousness to yourself. No matter what happens, don't tell your audience that you are nervous. Far too many speakers do this, as a defense. They try to break the ice by saying something like, "Well, I hope you're more relaxed about this speech than I am." Or, when they fumble with words or have muscle spasms, they look self-conscious or apologize or giggle. You might be able to gain sympathy this way, but you won't win respect.

If you tell listeners about your troubles, they may give you sympathy, but they will withhold the very important goal you seek—support for your ideas. Audiences can feel sympathy for a speaker in distress, but they will not follow one who finds it necessary to lean on the audience.

If you are obviously nervous, your listeners know it without having to be told. When you have difficulty, empathy makes the audience suffer with you. Furthermore, there is some reason to believe that feeling sympathetic makes an audience uncomfortable. This discomfort can very easily turn to annoyance directed at a speaker who makes the request for sympathy. If you fight out the problem your audience will react favorably to your perseverance. Many will admire you for doing what they feel they cannot do.

II. VOCAL ELEMENTS

One important means of making and keeping contact with the world is the sense of hearing. Through it comes a large proportion of the stimuli that influence thought and action. These stimuli come to the ear in the form of sound. As far as the ear is concerned, all sound is made up of four elements: pitch, force, time, and quality. It is these elements that the ear hears and transmits to the brain, where they are interpreted and thus stir up meanings. The ear hears voice in terms of these same four elements and is capable of distinguishing a wide range of variation in the pitch, force, time, and quality of the voices it hears. Consequently, these elements are basic considerations if you want to use your voice effectively, for all judgments about your voice are limited by the ears of your hearers. To understand the function of these elements in the production of good speech, remember how speech is brought about.

A. Voice Production

A stream of air, forced from your lungs under pressure by the muscles of exhalation, vibrates your vocal folds, causing sound. Speaking requires greater muscular activity than does quiet breathing. Otherwise, the stream of air will not be under enough pressure to vibrate the vocal folds strongly enough to produce a sound of desirable quality and sufficient strength. This sound is resonated in the various chambers of your throat, mouth, and nose, thereby giving the characteristics that make it your voice as it is heard by others. Once this has been done, you have (literally at the tip of your tongue) the raw material of speech. But vocal sound does not become speech until you have modified the vocal tone through pronunciation and articulation into the sounds that make up whatever dialect you speak. Pronunciation and articulation, then, are significant in the production of good speech.

1. Pronunciation

Pronunciation is the sum of all the audible characteristics of the word: the individual sounds, the order in which they occur, their duration, the stress given to syllables, and so on. Good pronunciation is achieved when the sounds you articulate are acceptable in the standard version of the dialect you speak. In other words, it is quite possible for you to have very precise articulation and still be guilty of poor pronunciation. If, for example, you pronounce the word *can't* as "cain't," even though your articulation of each sound in the word is quite accurate and precise, and although the word is clearly understood by all who hear you, your pronunciation of this word should be considered poor because it is not the one accepted by the vast majority of educated Americans. ·

Dictionaries are the most obvious authoritative source of information about the accepted or agreed pronunciation of words. Notice, though, that we do not speak of "correct" pronunciation. As long as a language is spoken, it changes. Dictionaries can only report what is current usage at the time they are printed, and printing a word does not freeze its pronunciation for all time. But since language changes occur slowly, a dictionary's report of standard pronunciation may be safely accepted.

English is spoken in a large number of dialects throughout the world. Speakers from England, Canada, Australia, New Zealand, and other parts of the English-speaking world are clearly distinguishable one from the other. Persons who learn English as a second language will also ordinarily use a distinguishable pronunciation.

Not only will English be pronounced differently in different parts of the world, but within the borders of one country a variety of dialects will be heard.

In the United States, there are many dialect regions. Three of these include a large enough portion of the population to be considered the major dialect regions of this country. The three major dialects of the United States are Eastern, Southern, and General American English. Each of these is recognized as a "standard" dialect, and is considered to be preferable to any other speech pattern in the area in which it is used. Deviations from the standard dialect of the region in which a speaker lives are generally considered "substandard" and ought to be avoided.

2. Articulation

Articulation is the process by which the individual sounds are formed and connected into speech. The primary articulators of the human voice are the tongue, lips, teeth, upper gum ridge, palate, and the vocal folds themselves.

Think for a moment about the total physiological process of voice production. Muscles of the chest and abdomen must be tensed and relaxed at the proper moment and for just the right sustained period of time to provide air at just the proper pressure. The vocal folds must be lengthened and shortened, tensed and relaxed with great speed and precision to produce desired pitches. The resonating cavities must be modified in shape by the articulators at a rapid rate and at precisely the right moment to form accurately the different sounds of speech.

The fact that intelligible speech can occur at all seems almost miraculous.

Actually, this complex mechanism works so rapidly and each part is so thoroughly integrated with every other that an attempt to isolate and improve any single part of the process should be guided by a highly skilled professional. A knowledge of the physiology of the vocal mechanism is of value in the classroom primarily in order to dispel some of the untrue notions about speech. It is easy to see that a speaker seriously oversimplifies the process when he looks for the solution to speech problems in "diaphragmatic breathing," "lower pitch," or "more careful articulation." In a public speaking class, only the most general problems can be solved.

B. Elements of Voice

In talking about the voice in isolation from other factors in delivery, it is perhaps best to think of the vocal mechanism not only as a means of producing sound, but also as an instrument admirably suited to controlling variation of pitch, force, time, and quality in the sounds it produces. Let us examine each of these elements in order to define it and to discover the part it plays in effective communication.

1. Pitch

When an elastic system is set into vibration by some outside force, sound results. The rate at which the vibrations occur (number of vibrations per second) is called the frequency. It is the frequency of vibration that is interpreted by the ear as pitch. To produce the pitch A above middle C, the sound source must vibrate 440 times per second. The faster the sound source vibrates (that is, the higher the frequency), the higher the pitch sounds. As the frequency increases or decreases, the pitch rises and falls. Pitch can be defined as the relative highness or lowness of a sound in terms of some musical scale. By using the muscles in the larynx, a speaker controls the length and tension of the vocal folds in order to produce variations in pitch.

For a sound to be audible to the normal ear, the frequency must be within certain limits. If there are too few or too many vibrations per second, the human ear cannot hear the sound. This principle is utilized in "silent" whistles that are used for signaling to dogs. These are so high in pitch that a man cannot hear them, but a dog's ears respond to such high pitches that the whistle is plainly audible.

2. Force

Perhaps the easiest element of voice to understand is force. For our purposes, we can use this term to refer simply to the loudness of a sound. When the stream of air that vibrates the vocal folds is not strong, the vocal folds move but little and only relatively slight disturbances are set up in the air that transmits the sound to the ear. Consequently, the ear is not strongly stimulated and the sound is heard as a soft tone. When the breath is more strongly expelled from the lungs and the vocal folds are caused to vibrate more vigorously, greater disturbances are set up in the air. These strike the ear more forcibly, and the ear records the sound as being loud. There is no necessary connection between force and pitch—each can vary independently of the other. There is a tendency, however, for pitch to rise as force increases.

3. Time

There are three ways the ear recognizes time in speech. The first of these is through *duration*. This term refers to the length of time any given sound is made to last. For an example, look at the two words *leap* and *gleam*. The letters *ea* are used to spell the same vowel sound in both words. The vowel is quite short in the word *leap*, but in *gleam* the vowel lasts a noticeably greater length of time.

The second factor of time is *rate*, or the number of words spoken per minute. There is no necessary connection between rate and duration any more than there is between pitch and force. The two are independent of each other. That is, the rate of speech can be slow, even though the individual sounds are given short duration. The result is a choppy, staccato delivery. On the other hand, when rate is slow and duration is long, a form of drawl results. By the same token, the duration of individual sounds can be long or short when the rate is fast.

The third factor of time is *pause*: the moments when sound ceases. Pauses are an essential part of speaking: You must breathe, you must rethink your ideas, and you must allow the audience to grasp what you have said before you go on. The most efficient use of pauses takes place when you make all three of these objectives coincide. That is, you should pause to breathe and to think at points where it will most benefit your listeners to have an interval for assimilating an idea.

Frequently nervousness will interfere with an effective use of pauses. When you rush ahead to get the speech over with in the shortest possible time, none of your pauses, whether for breathing, for thought, or for audience assimilation, will make much sense.

Often you may feel that if you aren't talking all the time, the audience's impression of your fluency will suffer. Many speakers, oppressed by this notion, will fill what should be pauses with meaningless vocalization, a continued nervous insertion of "er" and "uh" that not only distract from what is being said but also make them appear to be at a loss for ideas and words.

The length of a pause can indicate the importance of a point you have made. In a sense, it tells the listeners how long you want them to "think that one over." By pausing when you have completed a main point, you can tell the listeners how important the point is, at the same time letting them think the idea over. You can also think about what you are going to say next and draw in a good breath of air before continuing. When pauses are properly used, they do much to clarify the phrasing in a sentence; they add emphasis to ideas; and they contribute greatly to the audience's impression of you as a mature, thoughtful, and secure person.

4. Quality

There is a wide variety in the sounds produced by different kinds of vibrating bodies. Among musical instruments, for example, it is easy to distinguish one from another because no two different kinds of instruments sound exactly alike. It is not necessary to know the name of a marimba or a glockenspiel to tell them apart even when they play the same notes. The difference lies in the quality of the sounds they produce. Similar quality differentiations can be made among human voices. Even over the telephone, an instrument designed for intelligibility of transmission rather than fidelity, a voice can usually be recognized. Characteristic articulations as well as pitch and time patterns help to identify it, but its unique quality also helps to single it out.

C. Using Your Voice To Communciate Meaning

When you speak, you must make your ideas immediately intelligible. Listeners cannot stop to mull over what you say as they might reexamine an obscure paragraph in an essay. Discourse cannot be meaningful in the sense you intend or compelling to the degree you want it to be without the kind of delivery that brings your ideas sharply and immediately into focus. Here are some of the ways in which you can use your voice to give clarity to your ideas.

1. Emphasize the Important Words

In speaking, you give up the writer's advantage of allowing a reader to understand ideas at leisure. Nonetheless, you have an advantage that a writer lacks. You can use your voice to say instantly what you mean. You do not have to depend on such crude symbols as commas, periods, exclamation points, and question marks to carry shades of meaning. If you have good control of your voice, you can give a whole complex of different emphases to a single phrase.

In almost any sentence some words are more important than others; thus the less important ones can often be omitted without loss of the basic meaning. Because reader time and newspaper space are both at a premium, newspaper headlines are usually telescoped to the shortest form the writer thinks can still accurately communicate meaning. Sometimes an obvious verb will be left out. "Legislative Session Near Close." Such words as *a, and, the* are seldom used. "Clouds, Fog Lift for Pleasant Day." To say more is unnecessary; to say less would destroy intelligibility.

Even in the case of newspaper headlines, however, the words that remain are not of equal importance. A news item may be headed "Pilgrims for Holy Week Come to Old Jerusalem." While all of the words may be needed, some carry a larger burden of the communication than do others. The word *Pilgrims*, for instance, not only cannot be omitted, but it is obviously more important than the words *for* and *to*. If this headline is read aloud, the word *Pilgrims*, then, must be given somewhat greater stress than either *for* or *to*. The phrase *for Holy Week* refers not to just any week in the year but to a very particular one. Thus the word *Holy* would be given more stress than either of the other two words. Further, the word *Week* is of greater relative importance than *to*. In terms of emphasis, then, the words in the headline call for something like the following degrees of relative emphasis: "PILGRIMS for HOLY Week Come to OLD JERUSALEM."

In the most rudimentary sort of language use, nouns and verbs do the real work. As ideas become more complex, other kinds of words are used to add subtlety to the meaning. You are the only one who knows exactly what you mean; you are the one who must decide which of your words carry the burden of your meaning. In every case, you must select these important words that carry your meaning and give emphasis to them.

Emphasis is likely to be identified at first thought with loudness. One way to let an audience know what is important is to make it loud.

This is the parent's tried and true method with young children. When Mother says, "Come at once," children will frequently wait until the call becomes loud enough to indicate that Mother means business. However, sophisticated people soon learn that loudness is the simplest form of stress. The most effective emphasis is created through *variety*, in *all* the elements of vocal delivery: pitch, force, time, and quality.

2. Make Clear Distinctions Among the Ideas

"Catholics make up approximately 5 percent of the population in West Virginia compared with 30 percent in Wisconsin." In this sentence there are at least two and possibly three opposing sets of ideas that must be made separate and distinct. Clearly, 5 percent is different from 30 percent, and this difference should be made clear by the voice. Moreover, West Virginia is not to be confused with Wisconsin. A distinction is also implied between Catholics and non-Catholics among the populations of the two states. Variety in pitch, force, time, and quality must make audible for the listeners such distinctions among the speaker's ideas.

The same principle applies not only to words that communicate a contrast, but also to those that express ideas in a series. A lack of vocal variety can make them all sound alike. In a West Coast area the Weather Bureau once made a most unfelicitous assignment of a representative to read the midday forecast. He was well aware of the different words for meteorological phenomena, but his voice patterns prevented his listeners from hearing these words clearly. Through its lack of variety, his voice made *clouds, fog, rain, clear, warm,* sound the same; by all these words he might almost as well have *meant* the same. Because his meanings for these words were not the same, variation in pitch, force, time, and quality should have been used to suggest that each of the words in this series was to be distinguished from the others.

3. Make Words Sound Like What You Mean

There are many words that are an imitation of the sound they name (called onomatopoeia). This is true, for example, in naming the sounds made by birds: ducks quack, geese hiss, sparrows chirp, hens cluck, and so on. Insects buzz and hum. The word *boom* imitates the sound it names. The fact that words often imitate sounds can add color to speech.

The imitation of the sound indicated by a word, however, is only a part of what we are talking about when we say that you should make words sound like what you mean. One of the major functions of words is to communicate not only the factual and logical notions you have in mind, but an emotive qualitative content as well. You can convey attitudes toward the ideas you discuss more clearly if you use your voice to carry to listeners the emotional qualities you want in your words. By vocal quality, you can make *war* sound heroic or unpleasant, *peace* sound pleasant or weak. Your voice can help to show the goodness or badness you impute to ideas, their rightness or wrongness, their beauty or ugliness, their merit or lack of it.

4. Speak in a Conversational Manner

Probably nothing in speaking contributes more importantly to effective delivery than a conversational style. You can conceivably use unacceptable pronunciation or grammar, yet if your delivery is spontaneous, direct, and conversational, your chances of effective communication are better than if you had beautiful pronunciation and perfect grammar but lacked a conversational delivery.

Most Americans do not, as a rule, read aloud very often or at any great length. When they do, they sound much like the child first learning to read. Even when they read fluently, the words of inexperienced or untrained readers will most likely sound crated for delivery, boxed in with a variety of stiff patterns, repetitions of pitch cadences, an unvaried tempo, an unchanging degree of force, and a dull quality of monotony that destroys much of the meaning the reader wants to convey. Reading patterns often attach themselves to the speaking of memorized words as well. One mark of a poor actor is the inability to speak in a spontaneous, conversational mode.

Good speakers use all the means of emphasis at their command, and the amount of emphasis they can create through variety is enormous. Considering this fact, it is amazing that so many speakers talk as if they were reading a series of words from a paper. Through monotony and dullness they throw away one of the most important advantages a speaker has over a writer—the ability to give instantaneous clarity to ideas through variety in the elements of speech.

III. PHYSICAL ACTION IN DELIVERY

Everything you do, in public or private address, helps to communicate something. "Everything" includes not only the language you use, but in addition, whatever you transmit to your listeners by the way you use your voice and the "silent language" you transmit with your body.

Each of these media of communication, the linguistic, the vocal, and the physical, is a language and is therefore interpreted by the audience as having some bearing on what you are trying to say. The more of these languages you put to use at the same time, the more channels you use simultaneously to carry your message, the more likely the message is to get through. It is quite apparent that all the languages must be saying the same thing, that all the channels must be carrying the same message. Otherwise, not only will they fail to help you make clear to the audience what you want it to understand you to mean, but they will actively hinder you by counteracting and contradicting each other. You want to make sure that your words, voice, and physical actions—all of the visible and audible cues you give the audience about your meaning—are saying the same thing at the same time. Therefore, it is up to you to see to it that the communication of your ideas is not hampered by the way in which you use your body when you speak.

A. Eye Contact

When you speak, *look directly at the audience*. This means something more than not looking at the floor, at the walls, out the window, or head-down into your notes. It means more than sweeping the audience with an occasional glance. It means looking directly and personally into the faces of individual members of the audience, moving the look from person to person in the group, and making personal eye contact with everyone to whom you speak. Now, when you address a very large crowd, or speak in a large auditorium where you are removed from the audience at some distance, looking directly into the eyes of each listener becomes difficult or impossible. You must nevertheless give the impression as well as you can that you are doing just that.

Your own experience will tell you that listeners do not respond well to a speaker in public or private who does not look at them. Some people are not aware of this reaction because their own habits of eye contact are poor. But you have met people who avoided your glance. What was your reaction to them? There is no point in trying to make a case for the notion that someone who refuses to look you in the eye is shifty or untrustworthy; the important idea here is that you react to the one who does.

There is one more important reason for you to look directly at your listeners. You should take advantage of every bit of help you can get.

The audience itself is an important source of help. As a rule, people respond to what they see and hear, and their responses tell you what effect you have on them. It would be extravagant not to use to advantage the feedback the audience gives you in reaction to your speech. Only by making direct visual contact with individual members of the group can you tell who is alert and friendly, who is bored, who is unconcerned, or who is just not listening.

B. Posture

An audience's response to you as a person is the most significant factor that determines its response to your ideas. Indeed, it is futile to distinguish between you and your ideas. Posture is one determinant of an audience's response to you as a person. Consequently, you should stand before your audience in a manner that indicates stability and assurance. Your posture should be poised but not stiff, relaxed but not sloppy.

Experienced speakers sometimes lean on a speaking stand, put their hands in their pockets, or even sit on the edge of a table. Whether such posture is acceptable depends more on the degree of formality in the speaking situation than it does on "rules" of public speaking. Such obvious casualness is likely to work to the disadvantage of a beginning speaker, for many audiences tend to expect speakers to treat them with a kind of formal respect. Correctly or incorrectly, they consider the speaker whose posture is too relaxed to be taking liberties with them. A second and perhaps more important reason for not being too casual is that you are likely to dramatize your relaxation in the effort to dispel or disguise stage fright. Instead of covering up your nervousness, you emphasize it, which detracts from your effectiveness.

Even so, you can achieve and communicate assurance through control over your body and its posture. Though you may not control the trembling in your muscles, you can control what you do to try to hide it. If you have any such need, stand straight, balance your weight on both feet, and look directly at your audience. The results will be far better than anything you can do by way of draping yourself over the lectern, crossing your ankles, slouching with your hands in your pockets, sitting on the edge of a desk, or pacing back and forth in front of your audience. Granted, this posture won't do much to keep your hands and legs from quivering, but it will help keep your nervousness from interfering with your communication. You may not think so, but your audience will. And that is the important point. Put the stress where the stress belongs. Remember that you are there to *talk*, to talk about *ideas*, not to model clothes or make a pretty picture for the audience.

C. Movement

In general, avoid making any movement that is not necessary. Moving from one place to another in the room, pacing back and forth on the platform, are seldom necessary. Many an anxious speaker has used such wandering as a means of working off some of the excess energy that builds up before a speech. But when there is nothing in the *speech* to motivate the pacing, when the motivation is in the *nervousness of the speaker*, walking around during the speech serves no real purpose as far as the audience is concerned and is therefore only distracting.

A highly important detail of movement is the manner of getting to your designated speaking position and back to your seat when you have finished. An audience will consider these acts a part of your speech and will hold you responsible for everything you do from the time you leave your seat until you sit down again. Your speech begins not when you utter your first words but when you first stand up. Similarly, your speech is not over with your conclusion; it goes on until the attention of the audience is no longer on you. It is quite conceivable that you will hold the attention of your listeners even after you sit down and until something actually distracts them from you.

Under these conditions it is only reasonable to conduct yourself in a manner that will not detract from the general effectiveness of your speech. Walk to and from the platform with firmness and poise. A large part of the credibility discussed in Chapter 10 comes from your giving the audience the impression that you are prepared to speak and that you welcome the opportunity. Preserve your dignity by neither racing nor shuffling to the front of the room. When you have finished speaking, maintain the atmosphere of competence and authority you have built up by returning to your seat quietly and deliberately.

D. Gesture

Another kind of bodily activity in speech is gesture. Gesture is distinguished from the kind of movement just discussed by the fact that it involves the hands, arms, and head but does not carry a speaker from one part of the room to another.

If they are to be effective, gestures must appear to be natural and spontaneous. When speakers are criticized for lack of physical activity, they will often comment that gesturing is not "natural" for them. More often than not, the very remark will be accompanied by an emphatic and decisive gesture. The point is that gesture is quite *natural*, but it is not *habitual* for the beginner in a formal speaking situation. The solution to the problem is to carry over into public speech the same freedom of movement you normally give to hands, arms, and head, and the same mobility of facial expression you use in private speech. Obviously, some speakers quite naturally gesture more than others. But all speakers should use gestures at least as extensively as they do in private conversation. Those rare persons who do not gesture at all, even in private speech, should maintain the poise of private speech even in public. They should have no difficulty in finding a place to put their hands. The usual experience has been, however, that most speakers have some movement of the hands and arms, but these movements are choppy and incomplete. Beginning speakers frequently have slight movement of the hands as their hands rest at their sides or on the rostrum. In such cases they feel the need for movement but are inhibited from making gestures consistent with the meaning they intend their words to convey. If involuntary or inhibited gesturing is your problem, give some conscious attention to making your gestures deliberate, complete, and forceful.

Gestures made with the hands and arms are of two kinds: those that are used to point up ideas by giving emphasis to the words that carry the ideas, and those that are used for description. There is no set vocabulary of gestures. You may emphasize an idea with your finger or pound a word home with your fist. You may spread your hands to show size or extend your arm to show place. You will find that when you are enthusiastic about your own ideas and when you have the will to communicate those ideas, your own personal speaking habits will supply you with a spontaneous and varied group of gestures that belong to you.

Facial expression is as significant in delivery as gestures made with the hands and arms. When you speak, your face gives your listeners very clear cues on your own reactions to what you are saying. Audiences tend to read your face as closely as they listen to your words. Therefore, it is up to you to give them accurate cues. A lively mobility of facial expression is such a natural part of spontaneous oral communication that even though you may be thoroughly engaged in what you are saying, if you have a stiff, deadpan face, the audience will tend to interpret your lack of facial expression as a lack of enthusiasm for your own ideas.

IV. DELIVERING THE SPEECH

The psychological, vocal, and physical elements of speaking are, in a sense, the raw materials out of which you make effective speech delivery.

A. Modes of Delivery

Four different methods of delivering a speech are commonly recognized. These four modes of delivery differ from each other according to the kind of preparation the speaker makes for the delivery. If the language of the speech is thoroughly prepared in advance, the speech can be delivered either from a *manuscript* or from *memory*. On the other hand, when the specific language that will be used in the speech is not chosen before the moment of delivery, the speech will be either *impromptu* or *extemporaneous*.

1. Speaking from Manuscript

There are three kinds of speaking occasions that may legitimately call for a speech to be read from manuscript.

The first of these is the making, by a person in a position of responsibility, of a statement so important that mistakes must not be permitted to occur. When the president of the United States speaks for this country to the world, even a simple slip of the tongue or a momentary lapse of control over his own emotions might have far-reaching and serious consequences. Similarly, an ambassador to the United Nations will almost always deliver a prepared statement from manuscript.

An occasion of great formality may demand a polish in the speech that cannot be expected through complete preparation of language beforehand.

The third kind of occasion that may make use of a manuscript desirable occurs whenever there are strict time limits put upon a speaker. The length of time a speech will last is much more easily determined when the speech is in manuscript, and the time can much more easily be adhered to when the speech is delivered from manuscript. The most common instances of this sort can be observed in broadcasts over radio and television. The very strict time schedules of these broadcast media require a speaker to meet a specific time limit.

Apart from these kinds of occasions, however, a manuscript ought not to be used. It is totally unlikely that such demands for precision in wording will arise in a public speaking class or, for that matter, in any of the speaking that all but a few will be called upon to do in the future.

Besides being on most occasions unnecessary, manuscript speaking has certain quite definite disadvantages. William Jennings Bryan, commented on these in connection with his Madison Square Garden speech in 1896, accepting the nomination as Democratic presidential candidate:

I was compelled to choose between an extemporaneous speech, which would be less concise and comprehensive, and a speech which, because read from manuscript, would disappoint the audience. I knew, too, that in order to secure an accurate report of the speech in the daily papers it would be necessary to furnish a copy in advance of delivery, and I knew that if delivered from memory it would be taken down in shorthand and compared with the copy furnished to the press. After weighing the relative advantages of, and objections to, the two modes of delivery, I concluded that it was the part of wisdom to disappoint the few thousands who would be in the hall in order to reach the hundreds of thousands who would read it in print. Having decided to use my manuscript it was necessary to make the speech as brief as possible because the crime of reading a speech increases in heinousness in proportion to its length.

Judgments about what is required for an effective speech are a function of the audience. It is extremely difficult, therefore, for you to determine in advance of the speaking situation itself precisely how your message ought to be structured. You have a much better chance of accomplishing your purpose when you speak in simple, direct, straightforward language to an audience with whom you are making close visual and psychological contact. With this kind of delivery, it is much easier for you to make the necessary adaptations to the occasion and the idiosyncrasies of the audience. When you use a manuscript you tie yourself to a set pattern of words and deny yourself any opportunity for adapting to your audience during the course of a speech. For these reasons, unless it is absolutely necessary to do so, a speech should not be delivered from a manuscript.

Should the occasion make it necessary to use a manuscript, your delivery should have the qualities that characterize any good delivery. These characteristics will be described later in this chapter.

2. Speaking from Memory

In preparing a speech to be delivered from memory, you would ordinarily write out a manuscript, practice from it until you know it by heart, and then deliver the speech from memory. This kind of speaking has few of the advantages but carries with it all of the disadvantages of the manuscript mode of delivery. Unless you are a reasonably accomplished actor, you will find it difficult to deliver a talk from memory and to maintain close contact with the audience at the same time. Even if you are a good actor, or recite well, you will be burdened with the same lack of flexibility from which a manuscript speaker suffers. There is, moreover, another disadavantage to speaking from memory. If you forget, you are lost. We say, categorically, *never* memorize a speech. If the occasion demands that kind of preparation, prepare a manuscript and use it instead.

3. Speaking Impromptu

An impromptu speech may be defined as one for which no immediate preparation has been made. One is called upon to speak unexpectedly and says things on the spur of the moment. We have all, at one time or another, imagined ourselves in a speaking situation wherein we were required to "think on our feet," and (since we always see ourselves as the hero of our own daydreams) have come through admirably, swaying masses of people, crushing opposition, the epitome of impromptu eloquence. The picture is unrealistic.

We are not saying that such skill is undesirable or impossible to attain. It is, however, hard to come by. Henry Ward Beecher, after delivering a splendid talk that seemed to be completely impromptu, was asked how long he had prepared for it. He answered that he had been preparing for the talk for 40 years.

Except when you are given no warning, you should never speak impromptu. Take every opportunity to prepare as thoroughly as time will allow. If called upon to speak with no preparation, remember that the same principles of organization and support apply to all speaking. If at all possible, take a few moments to think through what you will say and perhaps to jot down a few notes. Even if you must react at once, remember that the major function of a speech is to introduce an idea, develop it, and finish discussing it. In this way, even the most hastily prepared talk can be given the quality of order.

4. Speaking Extemporaneously

Under ideal circumstances, all public address would be extemporaneous. In this mode of delivery, the ideas, organization, and supporting material of a speech are thoroughly prepared in advance. Moreover, the delivery of the speech is practiced as well. The only part of such a speech that is *ex tempore* (that is, grows "out of the time" or comes at the actual moment of delivery) is the *language*. This is chosen in much the same manner as the language of an impromptu speech. The difference between impromptu speaking and extemporaneous delivery, other than the thorough preparation of the content of the latter, is in the fact that the extemporaneous speech has been "talked through" several times. You do not write the speech in full (although you may, and usually will, use an outline as speaking notes), nor do you make any effort to memorize the language you will use in delivery. Indeed, each time you practice the speech, you will use different language and work toward a more precise and clear statement of your ideas. When finally you deliver the speech, you are so thoroughly familiar with what you intend to say that you can in a very real sense "ad lib" the language that will be more effective for the audience, the subject, and the occasion of the speech.

It is apparent that extemporaneous delivery has the greatest number of advantages and the fewest disadvantages of all the four modes of delivery. It lends itself to direct visual and psychological contact with the audience. It can have all the spontaneity and immediacy of casual conversation without the disorganization that often characterizes conversation. It affords you great flexibility in meeting the specific and yet shifting demands of your audience. Extemporaneous speaking is the principal concern of this book and all of what is said in it is most directly applicable to this mode of delivery.

B. Characteristics of Good Delivery

A highly communicative pattern of language and delivery appears in the everyday conversational speech of a large number of persons who do not carry over this quality into public speaking experiences. This fact is unfortunate, for good delivery, even in formal situations, needs all the best qualities of good conversational speech.

1. Directness

Good conversational delivery is *direct*. Talk to your audience. Choose words that your listeners will understand. Look directly at them. Don't look over their heads, or out the window, or through them as if they were not there. Recognize that they *are* there and talk to them with much the same delivery and language you would use if they were guests in your home.

2. Spontaneity

Good conversational delivery appears to be *spontaneous*. This does not mean that you sound as if you were fumbling through the ideas of the speech for the first time. It contributes much more to your credibility to give the impression that you are delivering a well-thought-out, clearly developed, and carefully built speech. Spontaneity in speaking gives the delivery freshness and immediacy. It puts you *in the presence of the audience*. Lacking spontaneity, delivery is dull and rotelike, much as if someone had turned on a tape recorder and left it unattended.

3. Involvement

Good conversational delivery clearly manifests your personal involvement in what you are saying. Your own intellectual and emotional interest in the subject are vivid cues to the audience about the significance of what you have to say and your desire to say it to *this* audience. If the audience judges you to be uninterested in your subject, there is certainly no reason why it should be interested.

4. Vitality

Good conversational delivery has *vitality*. It usually involves variety in voice and bodily action that provide cues to the audience about the relative importance of the materials in a speech. Vitality in delivery demands the kind of gesture and movement that you would naturally use to emphasize a point in ordinary conversation. Some people, it is true, do not gesture very much. But we all gesture more than we realize. As an experiment, pay some attention to what you and others do in everyday speaking situations. You may be surprised to see how much gesturing is done.

5. Intelligibility

Good conversational delivery is readily *intelligible*. Nothing you say will make much sense if it is difficult for your audience to hear. But to make the members of an audience "hear," you must make them *listen*. Doing so requires that your voice be more than merely audible. A speaker's voice should be loud enough not only to be heard, but also to command attention in spite of the many normal distractions to be expected. To hold the attention of an audience, you must be able to contend with such competitors as a noisy air conditioner in the rear of the room or with a group of small boys playing ball outside an open window.

Besides *audibility*, a good speech has other qualities that contribute to the intelligibility of delivery: *Articulation* (the formulation of individual sounds) should be clear and precise without being stilted. *Pronunciation* should be acceptable; it should follow the standard usage of the educated members of the speaker's community.

SUMMARY

Speech is used, often at one and the same time, to communicate an idea to someone, to elicit a response, and to fulfill personal needs without concern for a response.

Many factors influence the way each speaker adjusts to a speaking situation, but all cases of poor adjustment come about because cathartic elements break through into the social or communicative purposes of the speech. For this reason you must do all you can to concentrate on the social purpose of speaking and not on personal needs.

Speech classes are not designed to resolve feelings of insecurity. If those feelings are relatively insignificant, a course in speech may be the means whereby they can be resolved. The practical suggestions offered in this chapter make no pretense toward performing psychotherapy. They are designed to help speakers learn how to control the disruptive interference of their personal needs so that the speaking they do will fulfill its primarily social aim. Students do learn to speak well in spite of the perfectly normal anxieties that assail all speakers.

Speech is brought about when vocal sound is resonated by the cavities of the throat, mouth, and head to give each voice its characteristic quality. The indeterminate vocal sound is transformed into speech by the articulators: lips, teeth, tongue, palate, upper gum ridge, and vocal folds.

Speech is heard by the ear in terms of its four variable characteristics: pitch, force, time, and quality. By controlled variation of these elements, you can give emphasis to your ideas and help bring clarity to any speech.

In using your voice, you should be guided by four principles:

1. Emphasize the important words.
2. Make clear distinctions among the ideas.
3. Make words sound like what you mean.
4. Speak in a conversational manner.

Physical action is as much a part of a speech as ideas or vocal delivery. An audience judges you and your ideas by what it sees almost as much as by what it hears. Consequently, controlled physical action is an important part of effective delivery. Perhaps the most significant visual aspect of communication is eye contact; look directly at your audience. Stand before the audience with a relaxed yet not too casual posture. The way you move to and from the speaking position helps to manifest your vitality, but you should not pace around the room during your speech. Gestures should be full and complete rather than choppy and underdeveloped, definite rather than vague.

You must make decisions about the mode of delivery to use. Among them (speaking from manuscript or memory, speaking impromptu or extemporaneously), extemporaneous delivery is by far the best choice in any except extraordinary circumstances. In any case, your delivery should have these characteristics: directness, spontaneity, involvement, vitality, and intelligibility.

QUESTIONS

1. Differentiate between a speaker's cathartic and communicative needs.
2. What do you consider to be your greatest source of anxiety in the speaking situation?
3. What is conditioning? How is it significant to a speaker?
4. What false emphasis is the basis of fear reactions in a speaker?
5. The text mentions some practical suggestionss that will help alleviate nervousness. Which two do you consider most important? Why?
6. Would you agree that a person with good articulation would have good pronunciation?
7. How it acceptable pronunciation determined?
8. Should a Southern dialect be considered a substandard form of American speech?
9. What are the four elements of sound that the ear hears?
10. Discuss how the pause is used in effective speech.
11. What must the speaker substitute in his speech for the punctuation marks used in writing?

12. What is the significance of the conversational mode in speech?
13. Why is eye contact important?
14. How much should a speaker gesture?

EXERCISES

1. There are many opportunities to observe, analyze, and evaluate the part vocal behavior plays in communication: the public platform, the pulpit, the theater, legislative assemblies, and the like. Observe one of these instances of communication and write a 500-word paper analyzing and evaluating the effectiveness of the part played by the use of voice in helping the speaker or performer communicate.

2. Analyze and evaluate the effectiveness of the part played by physical action in helping a speaker, actor, dancer, or pantomimist to communicate.

I. Methods of adapting to interaction
   A. Vicarious learning
   B. Response inhibition
   C. Covert communication
      1. Spatial aspects
      2. Motion aspects
      3. Paralinguistic aspects
II. Group norms
III. Group Roles
   A. Group task roles
   B. Group building and maintenance roles
   C. Individual roles
IV. Leadership

Chapter 14

Interpersonal Interaction

Communication, as we have said, is a transaction in which the messages transmitted affect both the sender and the receiver to some degree. When you watch the president of the United States on television explaining his view of the state of the economy, interpersonal interaction occurs which affects you; and you, although he doesn't know you personally, also affect him.

When we speak of interpersonal interaction, remember that all the circumstances of the transaction influence it, or just the individuals themselves. Thus the setting of the communication affects the interaction. Consider the differences among a religious rally, a company board meeting, a class session, or a group meeting at an ice cream parlor; they surely influence the interaction as does the subject under discussion. The very fact that you "know" the president of the United States by television and not face-to-face has considerable influence on you. We can complicate that problem more by saying that you probably "know" him as a result of a secondhand report—a friend who saw him on TV tells you what he said.

The persons who view it with you, the nature of the room in which you watch, the two-dimensional nature of the picture, the color; all these and more have an effect on the transaction. And each of these will have an effect that is a product of your past experiences with the person speaking, the medium, and the circumstances of viewing. These factors can influence the transaction as much as the words that are used.

This interaction among the parties occurs in all kinds of communication, but nowhere is it more clear than in small-group decision making. There conscious and active interaction is an essential ingredient to success, and there the group is assembled to interact as a means of completing a specific task.

The communicative transaction is, therefore, a product of the integration of the participants with all their past experiences, the circumstances under which the communication takes place and the task of the group. What we say in this chapter is appropriate to any communication transaction, but we shall focus on the interaction that takes place in small-group decision making.

I. METHODS OF ADAPTING TO INTERACTION

When people communicate with one another, they do so both consciously and without awareness. Any common sense observation would confirm that in a transaction you learn things about people from what they *do not* tell you as well as from what they *do* tell you. By thousands of little signs which they, and probably you, are not aware of, people communicate with you.

Three communicative factors take place, for the most part without your being aware of them. These factors, which influence the communicative transaction, are vicarious learning, response inhibition, and covert communication.*

One caution is necessary before we begin. You must be very careful not to mistake what is communicated with what is truth. Shifty eyes may *communicate* to your grandmother that you stole the cookies, but they don't necessarily mean that you are guilty. It is important to know what you communicate and work to improve your communication so that you will communicate what you *want* to say. To do this, you must look at factors below your normal consciousness level which you may

* This section is adapted substantially from Mark Abrahamson, *Interpersonal Accommodation* (New York: Van Nostrand–Reinhold, 1966), pp. 13–62.

not mean to communicate and lift them to the conscious level for correction and improved communication.

A. Vicarious Learning

Much of what you learn about how to behave around others or how to communicate in groups you learn vicariously. You see how others behave and how they are treated and you respond accordingly. If you are continually rewarded for certain kinds of behavior and punished for others, you will, to maintain a position in the group, adopt the rewarded behavior.

In many groups you will be rewarded for friendliness toward the other members, for seeming to appreciate what they say, and for non-antagonistic behavior. But a group of college debaters get their interaction rewards from winning arguments, and football players are rewarded for aggressiveness of the most physical kind. Aggressive talk is good talk, in the locker room. Without even realizing it, members who want to remain a part of the group frequently adapt their behavior toward what is rewarded in the group. In a single day you are a part of a number of groups and your communication is adapted to each: the chemistry laboratory group, the lunch group, the athletic group, and the review-for-a-test group.

B. Response Inhibition

In part as products of vicarious learning, but also because of other factors, the responses you make are inhibited. In any situation there is, as a matter of fact, an infinite number of responses available in any situation. However, you learn to restrict the number of possible responses to a few. When asked what time of day it is, you do not normally go get a glass of water, stand on your head, or say "15 apples and 27 oranges."

Even among the limited number of responses that would normally be available in such a circumstance, there are restrictions. You learn to respond in certain ways at certain times. Some roles are easy to play, others are not. Therefore, you will tend to choose a response that is most comfortable. There is some evidence that the process of response selection is based on a kind of comparison among responses. The comparison is made as a result of past experience with similar responses and perceived alternatives. In short, your response is at least in part a product of how it compares in reward with what can be gained from a different response.

C. Covert Communication

A good deal of what you communicate about yourself and subjects you talk about, as we have noted earlier, you communicate without the awareness of yourself or those in the group with whom you interact. Unfortunately, much of the popular attention given this phenomenon has resulted in a lot of psychoanalytic nonsense on the subject. Some writers claim that you can tell what someone is thinking by a series of specific physical and vocal cues that always mean the same thing. But you cannot tell what a girl is thinking by the direction in which she crosses her legs. Communication is far more complex than parlor game psychoanalysis would imply.

Nonetheless, covert communication does exist and (if you put proper restraints on your imagination), it will help you better understand the interpersonal interaction that takes place in communication. We shall look at three types of covert communication: spatial, motion, and paralinguistic.

1. Spatial Aspects

Any time two or more persons are together they are communicating. One "cannot say nothing."* Even the spatial relationships among people communicate. For instance, the distance you stand from a person tells something about the relationship the two of you have. These relationships are different from one culture to another. Latin Americans stand closer together in ordinary communication than North Americans do. In the United States, if someone stood as close to you as Latin Americans stand to one another, you would probably feel hostile, or you might feel that a sexual relationship was being set up. When an American is confronted by a person from such a culture, the American frequently backs up and the Latin interprets this as aloofness.†

Similarly, there are distances beyond which we find ourselves no

---

* Erving Goffman, *Behavior in Public Places* (New York: Free Press, 1963), p. 14.

† Edward Hall, *The Silent Language* (Greenwich, Conn.: Fawcett Publications, 1959), p. 164.

longer engaged in small-group interaction. If the room in which a small decision-making group is meeting is arranged in such a way as to separate the chairperson from the other members of the group, it will communicate to them that something other than a decision-making group is being set up. A classroom in which the teacher stands at the front and everyone else looks at that one identifiable authority figure indicates an interpersonal interaction much different from a living room, where all are on the same level and in relatively the same spatial relationship, one to another. Although persons perceived as authority figures will be treated differently from other members of the group regardless of the spatial arrangement, groups who wish to encourage equal contributions from members should arrange the seating on the basis of equal spatial relationships or as nearly equal as possible.

2. Motion Aspects

Although there is a lot of mysticism about the ways in which facial expressions and movements communicate, there is no doubt that they do communicate, and experimental evidence indicates that people can, at least in broad ways, interpret such actions. In Chapter 13 we discussed some of the ways in which gesture is used to facilitate the accurate transfer of meaning.

Frequently, the most sophisticated members of groups will dominate groups, not because they talk more than others (they frequently talk less) but because they do not waste time talking as much as the others about matters that are extraneous to the task. More important to our discussion of motion, they also give many cues by the way they move, stand, and use facial expression that convey more meaning than others about the direction they feel the group should go.

3. Paralinguistic Aspects

Also in Chapter 13 we discussed some of the paralinguistic aspects of communication. You communicate to others not merely through the words you use and motions you make but through the voice quality and inflections of your speech. Again, your speech may not reveal the real you, but if you speak in a monotone or a whine or mumble, you communicate something to other people that you probably don't want communicated. As people know you better, such voice quality characteristics are less likely to be a problem, but, at least on first meeting someone, they can create an unfortunate impression and interfere with communication.

II. GROUP NORMS

While you have personal methods of adapting to interaction situations through vicarious learning, response inhibition, and covert communication, you also respond to certain social factors that constitute the norms of the group. Each group develops certain "shared expectations of right action that bind members of a group and result in guiding and regulating their behavior."*

That norms of behavior differ from one culture to another is obvious to all of us. Earlier we said that Latins stand closer to people in conversation than do Americans. We know of the greater polite formality of speech and action that constitutes the norm for Oriental behavior. In our more informal society, such an approach to interaction would seem strange.

Within our society there are wide varieties of group norms. The teenage "gang" is quite different in the way it communicates from the adult cocktail party. The basketball team members interact with one another in ways quite different from the members of a business conference.

In some groups, where the members know one another rather well, the norms are clearly established from the beginning. In other situations, norms develop as the group moves along through group punishment and reward. Most groups will be less productive in terms of systematic decision making, precisely because the early part of the discussion requires an "orientation phase," when the group socializes and eliminates the tension that is built up because of the strangeness of the situation.†

During the discussion the members of the group must also learn about the environment in which they function. They must learn the constraints that are placed on their decision making by the outside forces which must approve their decision.‡ No decision-making group functions alone. It must always be concerned about the way its decisions and resultant behavior will be received by outsiders. The members might choose to ignore some of the views of outsiders. A gang of thugs might decide to violate the law, but still they cannot ignore the police.

* Ernest G. Bormann, *Discussion and Group Methods* (New York: Harper & Row, 1969), p. 261.

† B. Aubrey Fisher, *Small Group Decision Making: Communication and the Group Process* (New York: McGraw-Hill, 1974), p. 140.

‡ Ernest G. Borman, *Discussion and Group Methods* (New York: Harper & Row, 1969), p. 262.

There is no list of norms that one can learn as a step toward better group interaction. You know a good deal about the norms of the groups you participate in and, by moving tentatively at first, chances are that you can "size up" new groups. In this move into new groups, reciprocity is the most important principle to utilize. B. Aubrey Fisher says that if there is a universal social norm, it is reciprocity.[*]

The norm of reciprocity is that others will respond well to you if you respond well to them. If you try to help them, they will try to help you. If you show you like them, they will tend to like you more. It is not a new idea—remember "Do unto others as you would have others do unto you"?

Thus far in our discussion of norms we have spoken only of ways in which general norms cause group members to behave in similar ways. But that is not the entire case. One of the functions of norms, in addition to identifying behavior in which all are expected to engage, is to establish a variety of roles for the different members of the group and for different times in the decision-making process.

III. GROUP ROLES

In order that a group may function satisfactorily, a number of roles must be assumed by the members. All of the possible roles may not be necessary in any given decision-making group, but a wide variety of them is necessary for most groups. One person may take a role and hold it for the whole discussion or may change roles as the task changes, perhaps many times.

It has been popular to talk of two roles in decision making: the leader and the participant. This point of view implies that there are certain conditions inherent in the individual that makes one person a leader and others followers. But, as we examine the variety of roles available, you will see that particular ones will, at particular times, with particular tasks, make one person more prominent in the decision making than another. In a small group your importance to the discussion will in part be a product of your personality, but it will also be determined by the role that the group norms impose on you.

In some situations the most physically assertive person may find himself the leader, while at other times the most conciliatory person will. In short, any of the list of roles discovered in small-group deci-

[*] B. Aubrey Fisher, *Small Group Decision Making: Communication and the Group Process* (New York: McGraw-Hill, 1974), p. 56.

sion making by the First National Training Laboratory in Group Development in 1947, still regarded as a satisfactory list, may be a characteristic of leadership at a particular time. The labels are self-explanatory.

A. Group Task Roles

1. Initiator–contributor
2. Information seeker
3. Opinion seeker
4. Information giver
5. Opinion giver
6. Elaborator
7. Coordinator
8. Orientor
9. Evaluator–critic
10. Energizer
11. Procedural technician
12. Recorder

B. Group Building and Maintenance Roles

1. Encourager
2. Harmonizer
3. Compromiser
4. Gate-keeper and expediter
5. Standard setter or ego ideal
6. Group observer and commentator
7. Follower

C. Individual Roles

1. Aggressor
2. Blocker
3. Recognition seeker
4. Self-confessor
5. Playboy
6. Dominator
7. Help seeker
8. Special interest pleader.*

* Kenneth D. Benne and Paul Sheats, "Functional Role of Group Members," *The Journal of Social Issues*, 4 (Spring 1948), pp. 41–49.

In Chapter 15, where we discuss various patterns of group decision making, you will see how discussions go through stages. It will be easy for you to see how certain roles are particularly useful to the task of the group at particular points. There are times when someone who takes the role of information seeker is most useful. Other times require a coordinator or a compromiser. Your ability to know which role is needed and which you are called upon to take as the decision-making process moves along, will in large measure represent your success at interpersonal interaction.

IV. LEADERSHIP

In Chapter 15 we shall discuss ways in which you can do a better job as chairperson if you are assigned to that task by an outsider or by the group. But avoid confusing the occupancy of the chair with leadership.

It is usual to think of a chairperson, the person in charge of procedure, as *the* leader of the group. In fact, however, such a person may not be the leader at all. Assigned to control the group, some people become mere figureheads, not leading the group but following the procedural and substantive suggestions of some other member. This other member is the real leader. In short, unless the appointed chairperson guides the discussion procedure or the substance of discussion, or both, that person is not the leader.

The leadership role is a function of the group; that is, the members decide who will direct their thought. Leadership may change hands as the attitudes of the group or the area of discussion changes. The members of a decision-making group may accept the leadership of one person on one topic, or on one phase of a problem, and at another time turn for leadership to another member. The group decides not only whom they will follow, but also how much authority they will give and how long they will accept the leader.

Should your group launch into discussion without a designated leader, every member of the group must be prepared to assume the responsibilities of the chair. If you note, for example, that the group should move on to another phase of the discussion, you do not wait more than briefly for someone else to make the suggestion; you make it yourself. Perhaps someone else will emerge as leader, and thus you will not need to take upon yourself the procedural initiative. But every member must be prepared to act if the need for leadership arises.

A struggle for power may develop among those who want to assume leadership. Power struggles can develop even when a leader has been assigned by an outside authority. But people in discussion are generally less likely to challenge a properly constituted authority, and the best possible authority for leadership is a mandate from the group. *Emerging* leadership is more likely to produce the *real* leaders of the group—the leaders of procedure and substance that the members acknowledge. When it does so, profitable discussion is more likely to result.

Think of situations within your own experience. When you sit with a group of friends in the college cafeteria and discuss some campus problem, you do not elect a leader or call upon the student body president to appoint one. Despite the lack of a formally appointed chairperson, someone will emerge as leader of the discussion. Discussions do not fail because no leader is assigned. They may fail because the participants have insufficient knowledge, or because they don't think analytically about the subject, or because they don't really want to engage in serious exploration of a problem. The success or failure of a group is not determined by whether the leader is appointed or allowed to emerge but from the way in which each person accepts the most useful roles.

SUMMARY

Because communication is a transaction in which messages are transmitted that affect both the sender and the receiver, the conditions of interpersonal interaction are important to it. The existence of interpersonal interaction is most obvious in small-group decision making, but it is important as well in all kinds of public communication.

There are three principal means by which you adapt personally to the interaction of communication. You apply these means both consciously and without awareness but you are most likely to apply them without being aware of them.

The first of these is vicarious learning, wherein you observe how others are punished or rewarded by a group for their behavior and then you adapt your behavior to suit. Rewarded behavior will vary from group to group and from time to time, and people learn to adapt to the standards of the particular group or search for other groups with standards more like their own.

A second means of adaptation is response inhibition. Over a period of time you learn, in part vicariously, to inhibit certain responses on the basis of a kind of comparison system. That is, you compare the rewards and punishment of one possible response with the potential reward and punishment of other responses.

A third means of adapting to interpersonal interaction is covert communication. You adapt because something about the spatial relations among persons; the nature of their movements, gestures, and facial expressions; and their inflections and voice quality communicate to you.

In addition to these personal means of adaptation, there are social norms that you learn to perceive. They vary from group to group and from task to task. These norms help people to relate to one another and to the environment around them. If there is a universal norm, it is probably reciprocity: People tend to give what they get.

Group norms not only establish individual standards of behavior, but they also determine the roles individuals must take in given situations. A number of roles have been classified under three general headings: (1) group task roles, (2) group building and maintenance roles, and (3) individual roles. The roles you might play will vary with the situation, even within a single discussion.

Leadership is not a single role. It is a function of the group. It cannot usually be assigned by an outsider; it must emerge from the group. Its nature and the person exercising it will vary from time to time. It may be shared at one time, held by one person, or passed around, depending upon the people involved, the situation, and the task.

QUESTIONS

1. Is interpersonal interaction limited to small-group decision making?

2. What factors go to make up the communication transaction?

3. How are vicarious learning and response inhibition related?

4. What spatial aspects of communication have you observed among your classmates?

5. Do the more productive members of groups talk more than the other members?

6. Which principle of interaction is a universal norm if there is one?

7. Do norms remain constant in a particular decision-making group?

8. What roles are available?

9. Which roles are for leaders and which for followers?

10. Are there advantages to emerging leadership?

EXERCISES

1. Observe a small group of people engaged in conversation. What examples of covert communictaion can you see? Discuss with your class the extent to which you think you can determine what people really mean by such signs.

2. Write a short paper on the norms you have observed in some group to which you belong.

3. With a small group of people engage in a role-playing discussion. Each of you take an assigned role and discuss a subject for a half hour. Then exchange roles for another half hour. Discuss with the class the problems you experienced in role playing.

4. In your class, observe what happens in a discussion in which the chairperson is assigned. Did that person act as leader or did someone else? If leadership changed hands, try to record what seems to have been the cause for the change. Discuss these observations with others in the class.

I. Small-group decision making defined
II. Patterns of group decision making
   A. The Dewey pattern of reflective thinking
      1. Locating and defining the problem
      2. Analyzing the problem
      3. Establishing goals
      4. Finding the best possible decision
      5. Putting the new policy into operation
   B. Other reflective thinking patterns
   C. Argumentative decision-making patterns
   D. Negotiation
III. The chairperson's responsibilities
   A. Getting the discussion started
   B. Keeping the discussion going
   C. Bringing the discussion to a close

Chapter 15

Small-Group Decision Making

Many of the decisions you make are made in small groups. Much of the national congressional decision-making activity is the product of unpublicized committee work. A business conference is not public speaking in the usual sense, but it is an essential and probably the most prevalent kind of oral business communication. Juries engage in small-group decision making. At every level of society small groups function as decision-making units.

I. SMALL-GROUP DECISION MAKING DEFINED

In order to define better what we mean by small-group decision making, let us look at some of its constituents. The most obvious is that we are talking about a group that is limited in size. Groups may be as small as two, as when two people try to decide what movie to go to on a Friday evening or when to have lunch; there is some point of maximum size where they are no longer a small group. We could set a number (perhaps 10), but the number is not the most important factor.

A group is a group not only for the reason that it is limited in size; it is also interactive. All the members of the group must be able to participate in the decision making in an active way. That is, each must serve as speaker, listener, and decision maker. Thus a group could have no more than 10 members and yet be a public speaking audience wherein one person speaks to them—as when only a few people show up at a public lecture.

Similarly, intercollegiate debaters in a tournament interact with one another and are few in number, but a judge makes the only significant decision. Also, a symposium wherein each of four to six speakers explains some phase of a single problem is not a small group making a decision. The participants do not make a decision and theirs is merely a series of public speeches; they are not interacting with one another.

Therapy groups have become popular in recent years. We do not question the validity of such groups, but their interests are not ours because, although they are limited in size and the participants interact, they do not make decisions on questions reaching outside the individual. Our discussion excludes them from consideration.

Thus we may say that *small-group decision making is a process that involves a limited number of people interacting with one another about a problem of interest to them all in a situation where the group has the power to make effective decisions.*

The decisions groups can make cover a variety of questions. There is no limit. They are not restricted to problem solving on questions of policy. Juries make decisions on questions of fact: Is he innocent? Church groups make decisions on questions of value: What modes of conduct does our religion tell us are the best for the relation of the races? Sexual mores? The role of women?

For such group communications to be productive of useful decisions and to do so in the minimum amount of time, decision making must be as systematic as possible without preventing the essential interaction of the parties. To do this, we must look at some of the possible patterns that might be followed by the group.

II. PATTERNS OF GROUP DECISION MAKING

Some patterns of decision making are advanced by those who believe them to be "natural"; that is, what actually happens in group process when people are left alone. Others, although recognized by their authors as not being natural, are advocated as the most systematic way of finding a decision. Our interest here is in introducing you to a representative group of patterns. We believe that for your purposes you should be interested in them as systematic patterns from which you can choose, depending upon the nature of your group and the question addressed.

We shall divide them into two basic groups based upon the way in which they see the relation of the analysis of the situation to the actual decision making: the reflective and the argumentative. Reflective patterns of decision making, regardless of their complexity, always attempt to make an investigation of the circumstances before advancing a decision. Argumentative patterns advance tentative decisions first and then engage in the analysis of the situation to test them.

A. The Dewey Pattern of Reflective Thinking

Over a half century ago, philosopher John Dewey attempted to define a systematic method by which an individual should think in order to arrive at better decisions.* Others have taken the pattern he advocated and applied it to the group situation. Because it has been the basis of much of the thinking on group decision making for the past 30 years and because it is the most thoroughly developed pattern, we shall look at it here in some detail. It has been interpreted in a number of ways with minor variations. The following is our own adaptation to group decision making. We shall consider the group discussion process as developing through the following five steps: (1) locating and defining the problem, (2) analyzing the problem, (3) establishing goals, (4) determining the best solution, and (5) putting the solution into operation.

1. Locating and Defining the Problem

The way you think about problems is conditioned by your needs and desires. The universal motivation to remove the stresses that arise from a felt difficulty makes it easy to seize upon the most obvious answer to a problem rather than to engage yourself in a rational evaluation of possible solutions. Subjectivity is, therefore, a danger; emotionalism, a peril. But to engage in the discussion of a subject with which you have no identification is dull. To pretend complete objec-

* John Dewey, *How We Think* (New York: D. C. Death, 1910).

tivity on a subject of great concern is foolish. The desirable approach to problems is on some middle ground; not to dehumanize a discussion, only to introduce order and direction into it.

"Feeling" a difficulty, in most instances, means becoming irritated by something in the environment. The very irritation obstructs thinking and thus may hinder the finding of a sound solution unless the irritant is first located and defined.

Imagine (and perhaps you don't need to imagine) a university parking lot that fills up early and, even though you have paid your parking fee, when you arrive for your 9 o'clock class at 8:45, either you can't get into the lot or you have to search so long for a place that you are late for class. You might respond with rage, demand that someone be fired, or kick the parking lot gate. You might also change your habits and come at 6:30 to be sure of finding a place. Both of these are decisions, but they are not reflective. Reflective decision making requires careful analysis of the situation.

The inadequacy of language creates the second difficulty that makes the location and definition of problems necessary. Different people use the same words to mean different things. Joe, in a delayed car, may remark to Fred, "Well, I guess this traffic is too much for our cops to handle." Joe intends to express compassion for a police force faced with an insoluble problem; Fred hears the remark as a too-temperate complaint against inexcusable inefficiency. Even among homogeneous groups, a problem never presents itself with such clarity that there is immediate and common understanding of its nature. A group of people talking on any subject will think about the topic from differing points of view. When you talk with others about any set of circumstances, communication often suffers for lack of common ground. Failure to clear away at the outset as many of the obstacles to communication as possible will do much to destroy a potenially good discussion. Consequently, locating the problem is necessary.

The various methods of definition are discussed in Chapter 6. The method to use is the one that will best specify, through clarification of words and phrases, the nature of the problem under consideration. It is important that the participants in a group recognize that they are searching for agreement and, therefore, that a series of dictionary definitions of words in the statement of the problem may be useless, even misleading. It is through the meeting of minds that the subject will be limited and defined. Since the members of the group have the "felt difficulty," only they can appraise or agree on the statement of the problem. And at the conclusion of this step of location and definition, the group should be in agreement about the specific subject under discussion and be prepared to analyze it with a minimum of confusion.

2. Analyzing the Problem

Analysis is the second step in the problem-solving process. Its function is to find the cause of the difficulty. The thoroughness with which this essential step is conducted determines as much as any other factor the effectiveness of the group in establishing desirable policy.

The first step in analysis is a review of existing conditions. When a doctor sees a patient for the first time, he needs to make a thorough examination. He takes the patient's history. Then he examines and questions the patient for symptoms, the patient's "felt difficulty." From history and symptoms, he endeavors to determine causes. This determination of causes is the important step in the process. The group discussing a policy question can be compared to a group of doctors in consultation. Both analyses require a thorough investigation of facts, a familiarity wtih conditions past and present, in order that the consultants may penetrate to the causes of the problem.

The causes determined must be sufficient; that is, they must account for all the symptoms and all the history. It is a common mistake to stop looking for causes while some significant symptoms remain unexplained. This mistake can arise from overlooking the symptom or from ignoring it when proposing the possible cause. It is a type of mistake easily made when considering research material from various sources. One member of a group might have studied material, for example, in a Department of Health, Education, and Welfare report on urban blight. This report would note and list various symptoms and perhaps submit several surmises or propose a single opinion as to their cause. Another might have studied an article on urban blight from *Harper's* magazine, likewise mentioning symptoms and submitting surmises or opinions about causes. If the two sources were in only partial agreement and if the group accepted symptoms from one and causes from another, the analysis would be foolish. The group must be sure the causes account for the symptoms.

3. Establishing Goals

Before determining what solution will best meet a problem situation, a person or a group must have some standard for judging or testing a proposed solution. For example, when you go to the store to buy a pair of socks, you may be thinking, "I want them to go with my blue pants, and I want the cheapest all-wool pair I can find." By these standards you evaluate the many different pairs of socks from which you can choose. That is, you determine the goals you want your specific choice to help you attain: three goals—socks to match the blue pants, socks to be inexpensive, socks to be made of wool. Your decision is to buy a specific pair of socks. At another time, you might want a pair of socks that would be long-wearing. This would be a new goal and might, therefore, cause you to select a different pair, that is, to arrive at a different decision.

A more complicated set of goals would guide you in exploring serious social questions and the need for determining them would be more apparent. Your decision about the socks is based on an analysis, perhaps almost unconscious, of an existing need and its causes. Decisions about a social problem are similarly based on analysis.

In the same sense that the basis for determining the causes of a problem is an examination of symptoms, the goals of a discussion group are based on what analysis shows the nature of the problem to be. Once established, the goals serve as standards of judgment for evaluating potential solutions. Indeed, this is the reason the symptoms and the causes are explored in the first place—to know better what kind of solution to look for. Through analysis of the problem, the group distills the principles which will tell what a good solution must be.

Determining goals is frequently a difficult step in discussion because goals are not always made explicit outside of discussion. When you are asked why you bought a certain pair of socks, aren't you likely to say, "Because I liked them"? Likewise you may support a certain political party, believe in stricter law enforcement, or want more government intervention to help our older citizens without clearly spelling out why. But there is a why—a goal or set of goals—and if someone insists, you can usually explain. However, if you are to be systematic in your personal and group decisions, you must identify goals *before* you propose solutions.

To determine goals, then, is to develop a yardstick to measure the many possible courses of action that will be recognized. If the analysis of the problem has been thorough, the goals will be more easily determined. The more thorough and realistic the goals of a group are, the better are the chances of its choosing the most desirable solution to a problem.

4. Finding the Best Possible Decision

Determining the best policy requires an examination of the advantages and disadvantages of each possible course of action. Each is compared with the others to see which will come closest to achieving the goals that have been established. If these goals are realistic, the best decision is the one that most closely fits their specifications; it is the one that most effectively cures the causes of the problem, and thus eliminates its undesirable symptoms.

All reasonable possibilities should be considered. That is to say, it is quite possible that the policy in force at the time the group meets (the status quo) might prove to be the most desirable. It is quite possible, in other words, that any proposed change would be for the worse. At any rate, the status quo should always be evaluated in comparison with the alleged advantages of any proposed change in policy.

5. Putting the New Policy into Operation

The final step in the pattern of reflective thinking is implementation of any new policy. In this part of the discussion, the group examines the newly concluded policy to see what must be done in such areas as legislation, financing, public education, and the like, in order to put it into action. The problem-solving group must find the most practical way, in the light of its criteria, to implement the solution.

In summary, then, the reflective thinking pattern of group decision making develops through the following steps:

    I. Location and Definition of the Problem
       Clarify the limits of the problem and define all vague, ambiguous, or unfamiliar terms to the satisfaction of al the members of the group.
    II. Analysis of the Problem
       A. Symptoms
          Examine the specific details and the status quo and the pertinent history leading to it, to find evidence of the nature of the problem and its severity.
       B. Causes
          Examine the symptoms and history to determine what cause or causes produced the undesirable elements of the situation.
    III. Goals
       Develop standards of judgment for the group. That is, phrase the specifications that enumerate the requirements for a good solution.
    IV. Appraisal of Possible Solutions
       A. List the reasonable courses of action.

B. Evaluate each to see how well it attains the stated goals of the group.

C. Select the course of action that most closely achieves the goals.

V. Procedure for Putting the Solution into Operation

B. Other Reflective Thinking Patterns

It should be clear that the Dewey reflective thinking pattern is concerned with finding decisions on questions of policy. It is thought of by most as a problem-solution procedure. Although this is not the only possible objective, it tends to be the one most emphasized. Other simpler models are less wedded to the problem-solution format and better adapted to answering questions of fact or value. One such simpler pattern postulates three stages in group decision making.

1. Orientation (when the group decides what the nature of the situation is).

2. Evaluation (when the group decides what attitude to have toward the situation).

3. Control (when the group decides what to do about the situation).°

The important point to observe about this pattern, as is the case in the Dewey pattern and in similar patterns others have advanced,† is the emphasis on evaluating the nature of the situation *before* possible decisions are advanced. Many people prefer to use reflective patterns for making decisions because they feel that unless they carefully examine the problem before they examine the possible answers, their decisions will not be based on solid enough knowledge.

C. Argumentative Decision-Making Patterns

In contrast to the reflective pattern of decision making (situation analysis-before-decision-suggestion) there is some research and considerable experience to recommend using a pattern which we shall call argumentative decision making. Groups using one of the reflec-

° Robert F. Bales and Fred L. Strodtbeck, "Phases in Group Problem-Solving," *Journal of Abnormal and Social Psychology*, 46 (1951), pp. 485–95.

† Warren G. Bennis and Herbert A. Shepard, "A Theory of Group Development," *Human Relations*, 9 (1956), pp. 415–37; Bruce W. Tuckman, "Developmental Sequence in Small Groups," *Psychological Bulletin*, 63 (1965), pp. 384–99.

tive patterns are oriented toward analyzing a problem before making decisions. In the argumentative method, on the other hand, potential decisions are advanced tentatively and then tested by the members of the group. Each testing permits the members of the group to understand one another better and so to advance new decisions that are additions to, or modifications of, the original proposal. In this way group decisions are built a piece at a time but they begin from a proposal for decision, not with an analysis of the problem. This method may not be desirable for complex problems, but it is surely a common method you use in your everyday life. A guy says to his date, "Let's go see 'True Grit' at the movie tonight." "No," she says, "I don't like westerns." "But this isn't an ordinary western." And so on. This model has been described as a "spiral." When one person advances a decision, it is tested and altered until all have agreed upon it. It is then fixed and used as a basis for determining decisions about other questions.°

Although this pattern is less tightly organized than the reflective thinking method, it is still systematic. It involves "reach testing" a proposed step forward from an agreed-upon position. If the step is agreed to an advance is made; if not, the group returns to the earlier position and "reach tests" another idea.†

A more general argumentative pattern is described by B. Aubrey Fisher, whose research revealed that decisions are made by groups in four steps.

1. *Orientation.* Participants are tentative in advancing proposals and stating disagreement with others. They seem to be determining their positions in the group.

2. *Conflict.* There is strong ideational conflict among members of the group. They seem to have established their social positions and the most vigorous testing takes place.

3. *Emergence.* Argument tends to dissipate and movement toward consensus of opinion begins. There is some tendency to be more ambiguous, as in the orientation stage, because members who expressed strong opinions in the conflict stage are in the process of accepting the consensus.

4. *Reinforcement.* Although the group has actually made a decision its members need to reinforce the views which reflect their unity of opinion.‡

° Thomas M. Scheidel and Laura Crowell, "Idea Development in Small Groups," *Quarterly Journal of Speech,* 50 (April 1964), pp. 140–45.

† B. Aubrey Fisher, *Small Group Decision-Making* (New York: McGraw Hill 1974), p. 138.

‡ B. Aubrey Fisher, "Decision Emergence: Phases in Group Decision-Making," *Speech Monographs,* 37 (March 1970), pp. 53–66.

Although it would probably be too complex a process for most groups, the pattern for analyzing argument explained in Chapter 3, "Analyzing the Proposition," could also be used as a basis for group decision making.

D. Negotiation

Negotiation is a form of argumentative decision making. However, it functions so often in our society as a special kind of decision making that it is worth examining briefly. Negotiation is a form of decision making that occurs in a situation where two or more parties (usually two) have differing points of view over which they desire to reach a decision. Such a decision will require them to compromise but in a situation where *some* compromises are not as acceptable as no decision. In a sense, then, each party is in an antagonist position with respect to the other and has drawn a line beyond which further retreat is unacceptable. Each first advances a strong maximal demand, and the area of disagreement becomes the area of negotiation. Each party then advances possible concessions in exchange for concessions from the other side until an agreement is made or until the negotiations break down.

The main goal of the participants is to find out what the minimum acceptable level of the opponent is without revealing their own. Then they advance proposals as close to that as possible while advancing arguments to show that the proposal should be accepted because the opponent can expect no better.

Although negotiation is carried on in private, an "audience" is frequently involved. Any decision will be made public. In the case of labor management negotiations, for instance, the membership of the union and the corporate board must approve the decision. This creates another pressure on the negotiators.

III. THE CHAIRPERSON'S RESPONSIBILITIES

Many groups quickly assign a chairperson or have one assigned for them by some outside authority. You may be elected chairperson by your social club; your teacher may assign you the job in class; or the group may say when they convene, "You be the chairperson."

As we observed in Chapter 14, just being "in the chair" does not make you a leader, but having been selected, by whatever means, gives you some authority and, of course, responsibility. The following are some practical suggestions that may help you to fulfill the repsonsibility.

A. Getting the Discussion Started

The first of your three responsibilities, getting the discussion off to a good start, is probably the most difficult. Once it has been started and the group is functioning, the discussion tends to move along. Your introduction of the question should be clear, brief, and interesting. You may give a short résumé of the history and background of the problem, or you may show briefly the nature and importance of the question. This sort of beginning, if you choose it, is only to permit the participants a moment to collect their thoughts. No one needs or wants a long speech from you. Under no circumstances should you take the responsibility of analyzing the problem. If necessary you should introduce the members of the group to one another by name. This much is easy. It is a set of functions that must be performed but is not the vital problem in getting the discussion started.

Any serious fumbling by the chair tends to occur in beginning the analysis of the problem. Visualize a situation in which an inexperienced chairperson, having finished the introductions, assumes that the discussion will proceed spontaneously. It will not; the members of the group are still waiting for some kind of starting gun. Hence the chairperson may try to push the discussion off with the question, "Well, who wants to begin?" This will almost inevitably fail to get the discussion started efficiently.

It is true that some groups are eager to rush on; these may need to be held back. Most groups, however, have to be led into useful and worthwhile discussion. There are several ways of helping these less vocal groups to get under way.

You might ask a question, carefully designed to elicit an intelligent response, which can be a useful device for getting started. This opening question should ordinarily be directed to the group rather than to an individual. It would probably be unwise to put any particular participant "on the spot" this early in the discussion. Moreover, the question should be general rather than specific. It may require a specific piece of information which no one has at his fingertips.

A useful maneuver is for you to quote some statement referring to the problem at hand and ask the group for comment. You can cite some specific instance or illustration of the problem and ask for comment on it. If the topic is a broad one, you may want to ask for some specification or limitation. In each of these cases, any member of the panel should be able to give a reasonable comment.

B. Keeping the Discussion Going

Once started, a well-informed group will usually move along quite briskly with a minimum of prodding. Once you get the discussion started, your major functions are to encourage general participation, to keep the discussion on the track, and to guide the group away from hasty, unrealistic action.

One of the main problems you face is that of keeping at least a reasonable balance in the amount of participation from each member of the group. There is, more often than not among student groups, at least one person who is too talkative and at least one who is too reticent. It is your job as chairperson to see that everyone participates, and that no one monopolizes the time of the group. If several speakers try to speak at the same time, the one who has spoken less frequently up to that point should be given the opportunity to speak first. Sometimes real diplomacy is necessary to keep the discussion from becoming one-sided. Because no chairperson should be a dictator, you should use tact, geniality, and good humor.

There are two dangers to be avoided. In curbing the overly talkative speaker, you must be very careful not to offend the person. To do so is to stand a good chance of losing an effective contribution from a potentially valuable member of the group. On the other hand, in the effort to get some contribution from a timid person, you may be tempted to ask a direct question requiring specific information. As we said earlier, this tactic is dangerous; the respondent, lacking the necessary data, will, in all probability, be even less inclined to speak thereafter. It is usually safe to ask for a comment or an opinion regarding an idea, a contribution, or data already advanced by another member of the group.

It is a great temptation in group discussion, because of the informality of the situation, and because of the group's easy familiarity with the detailed information it involves, to wander around the topic and to digress at length. Since these digressions can be valuable in bringing out ideas and interpretations of data, you must determine when the digression is worthwhile and when it is a waste of time. The safest, and perhaps most efficient, way to avoid wasting time in interesting but unnecessary and fruitless digressions is to guide the group tactfully and courteously, but firmly, through some discussion pattern. This will require, early in the discussion, some careful assessment of which

340

pattern is best fitted for the subject and the inclination of the group.

One of your most useful devices is frequent, brief summary of what the group has accomplished up to the point of summary. Then, to help keep the group on the track between summaries, it is advisable to make very short paraphrases of significant contributions as they are made. Such paraphrases are especially helpful if someone has made a comparatively lengthy statement. Brief summaries and even briefer paraphrases of individual remarks serve a triple purpose. They help to avoid needless repetition. They help to keep the discussion on the track. They point out areas of agreement and disagreement, and thus indicate the precise status of the discussion at any given moment.

Probably your most important function as chairperson in group decision making is to see to it that the group makes a thorough investigation of the problem at hand. More than this, it is important that there be a clear understanding of the areas of agreement and disagreement. To accomplish these functions, you must see to it that all important points are heard.

Not only must these points be heard; they must also be examined critically and clearly. Both evidence and reasoning must be submitted to rigorous test. It is your responsibility as chairperson to see that the testing is done. Since you do not want to be involved directly in argument, this guarantee of testing can best be accomplished through the use of guiding questions. By means of such questions, you can accomplish several ends: (1) make sure that all important facets of the problem are viewed; (2) require the members of the group to consider and comment on the evidence and reasoning of others. It is best to avoid using questions that can be answered Yes or No. Instead, raise the all-important questions of fact and value that must be clearly thrashed out before any group conclusion can be of real worth.

Ideally, the goal of any small-group discussion is consensus, general agreement among the members of the group on what the best decision is. Remember, of course, that consensus is not always possible. A discussion comes about in the first place because there is conflict, an honest difference of opinion as to what decision should be adopted. There is nothing in the nature of small-group communication that inherently assures success in the effort to eliminate these areas of disagreement. No matter how conscientious a group is, no matter how impartially and reasonably its members investigate available data, there may still remain honest differences of opinion at the end of the discussion. No outcome of group exploration is more useless than a contrived or forced consensus. Differences of opinion are not to be strangled. You will want to point out and stress the areas of agreement

341

that do exist, but it is also important that the differences be brought out; otherwise, they can never be eliminated. Consensus is valuable only when it results from a realistic adjustment of honest differences.

C. Bringing the Discussion to a Close

Any deliberation will eventually end, especially in class discussions where the bell rings at the end of the period. The type of conclusion the chairperson will use is determined largely by the results achieved. If the group has reached an agreement, summary is in order. When no conclusion is reached because still existing issues need further discussion, you can put your concluding comments into the form of a progress report, summarizing the agreement and disagreement.

SUMMARY

Many decisions are made in small groups, where there is no audience-speaker relationship per se but where each person in the group functions as both speaker and listener. Small-group decision making of the sort we are discussing involves a limited number of people (at least two) interacting with one another about a problem of mutual interest in a situation where they can make a decision.

In such interactive communication, groups have been observed to move through patterns of decision making. In this chapter we observed three such patterns. The first was the reflective thinking type wherein groups engage in extensive definition and analysis before identifying and testing solutions. The second pattern was argumentative decision making in which decisions (or partial decisions) are suggested early and tested, with each point of agreement being used as a basis from which to move forward to another potential decision. The third method, negotiation, is a kind of argumentative pattern but one in which clearly opposed sides are defined from the beginning and minimum and maximum concession levels are probed in search of a point of consensus.

Although leadership and other roles vital to understanding the interpersonal interaction of group decision making were discussed in Chapter 14, there are a number of practical suggestions that will be helpful when you are assigned to chair a small-group discussion. In general, as chairperson your responsibilities are to get the group started, to keep the discussion moving along, and to bring it to a close.

QUESTIONS

1. What is small-group decision making?
2. What are the steps in reflective thinking?
3. Why must symptoms be considered in determining causes?
4. Why is the establishment of goals so difficult?
5. Why must the status quo be examined as a possible solution?
6. What is the essential difference between reflective thinking and argumentative patterns of decision making?
7. What is meant by "reach testing"? "Spiral" model?
8. What is the main goal of participants in negotiation?
9. How should a chairperson go about getting a discussion started?
10. How does the chairperson put a stop to a discussion when no definite conclusion has been reached?
11. How does the chairperson use the technique of summary?

EXERCISES

1. Make an analysis of some personal problem, using reflective thinking: How worthwhile do you find this method? What alternate possibilities do you think would be as effective? More effective? Why?

2. With four or five other members of your class form a discussion group. Select a problem to discuss. Word it. Come to some basic understanding about what the terms of the question mean. Let each member of the group gather material and make an outline. Present the group discussion in class a week after you have chosen the topic.

3. With several other members of the class, set up a mock negotiation situation, perhaps with your instructor over grading procedures, and conduct a negotiation session. Then let the rest of the class discuss the effectiveness of each side and the reasons for success or failure.

4. Observe the chairperson of some group to which you belong. Write a short paper explaining what techniques the chairperson used and how successfully they worked.

I. Determining the specific subject of the speech
   A. Limiting the subject
      1. Narrowing the scope to limit a subject
         a. Limit the subject in time
         b. Limit the subject in space
         c. Narrow the subject to a subproblem
         d. Discuss a portion of a process
      2. Treating a series of narrowed aspects of a subject
   B. Formulating a statement of purpose
II. Organizing the body of the speech
   A. Patterns of arrangement
      1. Chronological pattern
      2. Geographical or spatial pattern
      3. Topical pattern
      4. Pattern of definition
      5. Pattern of comparison and contrast
      6. Pattern of cause and effect
   B. Using multiple patterns of arrangement
   C. Number of points in the body of the speech
III. Adding supporting detail
IV. Preparing the conclusion
V. Preparing the introduction
   A. Gaining attention
   B. The subject sentence
   C. Background material
VI. Practicing the delivery

Chapter 16

Speaking To Inform

We made the point earlier that the ancients were not concerned with a theory for informative communication. For them, the function of rhetoric was to find proofs, to guide the composition of *argumentative* discourse. We have also seen that because all communication is affective it should, therefore, be considered at least to some degree to be persuasive.

Nonetheless, one fact of contemporary life is the startling rate at which knowledge is increasing. Bombs and populations are not the only things that explode. We are living in a period of "information explosion." There is so much information available that it is even difficult to store it. And information retrieval is a major problem for anyone interested in using the knowledge that is available. No one, of course, has more than an infinitesimal fraction of universal knowledge. All the knowledge in the world is useless, then, unless you can get it. Obviously, therefore, there is inescapable need for transmitting information. That is why such an enormous part of all the talking that goes on in the world is done to accomplish such ends as clarifying ideas, transmitting facts, or giving instructions. At home, at school, and at work, as well as on the public platform, much communication has as its purpose giving information to others. Clearly, the ability to communicate information effectively is an important skill. To be effective, informative communication must be interesting and clear. This chapter is intended to help you make it so.

In every case, what an audience understands you to say, rather than what you intend to say, is the significant criterion of what, in fact, you have said. If a message is to be transmitted with clarity, therefore, it must be prepared in such a manner that you can best hope it will be received with accuracy. To accomplish this end, prepare an informative speech using the following six steps:

1. Determine the specific subject of the speech.
2. Organize the body of the speech.
3. Add supporting materials.
4. Prepare the conclusion.
5. Prepare the introduction..
6. Practice the delivery.

I. DETERMINING THE SPECIFIC SUBJECT OF THE SPEECH

Before you can make an outline, and even before you can begin to gather materials, you must do two things: first, you determine the scope or breadth of your subject and, second, you formulate a precise statement of what your specific subject will be.

A. Limiting the Subject

1. Narrowing the Scope to Limit a Subject

More often than not, determining the scope of a speech means limiting or narrowing the subject so that you can develop your ideas in sufficient detail within the time limit of your speech. Here again, as in every other aspect of speaking, the influence of the audience is paramount. What it wants or needs to know determines in large measure the extent to which, and the methods by which, you fix the scope of your subject.

Speech instructors frequently hear the complaint that an adequately limited subject isn't broad enough. On the contrary, industrious and imaginative research will discover a variety of instructive ideas in the most narrowly restricted subject. The truth of the matter is that it's easy to get a little lazy sometimes and to think about subjects in a broad, inadequately defined fashion is lazy. But because every speech must ultimately end, even if the only limitation is the physical endurance of the speaker, no matter how spooky, or even suicidal, the project may seem, you have to limit the subject so that the ideas may be developed in whatever detail is warranted. What you will discover is that you haven't blocked yourself out of a speech topic after all. Instead, if you go about the job of speech preparation in the right way, although you may begin by thinking the subject is too narrow, you are likely to appear on the day you are to speak with the concern that you have too much material. There are several means of narrowing a topic:

a. **Limit the subject in time.** Such a general subject as "American presidential elections" might be narrowed to a discussion of "The disputed election of 1876," or "The wartime elections of 1864 and 1944." The subject of music could be limited to the period of the baroque masters. A discussion on art could be limited to the period of "dadaism."

b. **Limit the subject in space.** American foreign trade is far too broad a subject for a single speech. It can be the source of a successful speech subject, however, if you limit your discussion, for instance, to a consideration of trade with a selected country or to the most significant foreign products that enter the United States through the Port of New York.

c. **Narrow the subject to a subproblem.** Select as the specific topic of the speech a part of some larger question or controversy. Instead of discussing the general question of labor–management relations, for example, isolate the subproblem of the struggle between rival unions competing to represent farm workers in California agriculture.

d. **Discuss a portion of a process.** A prelaw student, who was also a Vietnam veteran and wanted to talk about the administration of justice, selected a limited subject in this area relevant to both his military experience and his interest in the law. He made a very interesting talk on the subject "The uniform code of military justice."

The kind of limitation you give to a subject must first be decided in terms of the subject itself and then be modified by what the audience needs and wants to know; choose the narrowing principle that will best clarify the ideas. While you might use no more than one of these methods in limiting many subjects, in restricting others you will want to use more than one. It is not necessary to narrow a subject by all of these methods, but here is what might be done with a single topic, using all four methods of limitation.

> GENERAL SUBJECT: International diplomacy
> NARROWED IN TIME: Spring 1974
> NARROWED IN SPACE: Mid-East
> NARROWED TO A SUBPROBLEM: The Arab-Israeli conflict
> NARROWED TO A PORTION OF A PROCESS: The role of the U.S. State Department

2. Treating a Series of Narrowed Aspects of a Subject

Sometimes, however, an audience or occasion can prevent you from narrowing your subject in the conventional manner just described. You might not want to restrict the scope of your talk by any of the four methods suggested. Nevertheless, the same demands for clear exposition must be met in these circumstances as in those that permit subjects to be narrower in scope.

When you must cover a broad subject, you can do it successfully by putting together a series of treatment of *narrow aspects* of the broader subject. An example will help to clarify the distinction between the two methods of limitation. A student who planned to go to the seminary after graduation to study for the priesthood wanted to select a topic from the general subject of the Catholic Church. Using conventional methods of narrowing the scope' of his subject, he might have arrived at this topic: "The rites of ordination to the priesthood of the Catholic Church." Instead, this speaker chose to present the Church in a much broader aspect. In his speech he maintained the overall broadness of view of the general subject, but he selected three specific points which he felt would not only increase his audience's knowledge of the Church, but would also be of interest to a group of non-Catholic listeners: the Mass as the central act of worship, the practice of confession, and the doctrine of papal infallibility.

B. Formulating a Statement of Purpose

Before you can begin to organize the speech, and even before you begin to gather materials, you must make for yourself a clear statement of precisely what response you want from your audience. The most common procedure for making such a statement is to formulate an infinitive phrase which, at one and the same time, identifies your purpose in speaking, specifies the subject of the speech, and sets its precise scope. The resulting expression of what you intend to accomplish in your speech is called a statement of specific purpose or, more simply, a statement of purpose. It identifies for you exactly what idea you want to clarify for your audience. Going back for a moment to the subject of international diplomacy as it was limited in the example just above, here is the statement of purpose for a speech on that topic:

> To inform the audience about the "shuttle" diplomacy of Secretary of State Henry Kissinger during the Spring 1974 crises in Arab–Israeli relations.

The statement of purpose should be put in writing so that you can refer to it as a guide for your speech. It will serve as a test to help you decide what material belongs in the speech and what does not. You can always find many interesting ideas and tempting pieces of material to put into a speech. The great problem is one of selection: admitting those items which are essential to the specific purpose and rejecting those which are not. Sometimes, even the most interesting material must be omitted if the essential unity of the speech is to be preserved. To be useful, speech materials must be more than interesting; they must be directly related to the central idea of the speech as expressed in the statement of purpose and they must serve to make the idea clear. Once it is formed, the statement of purpose should be used as a rigorous standard by which to eliminate unneeded materials.

Recently, a student gave a speech with the specific purpose of informing the audience about the basic teachings of Siddhartha Gautama, founder of the religion now known as Buddhism. The speech was developed through four main points: (1) Hindu influence, (2) the "Four Noble Truths" that explain the cause and cure of human suffering, (3) the "Noble Eight-Fold Path" by which the cure of human suffering can be established, and (4) the concept of Nirvana. Unfortunately, in the course of the speech the speaker drifted into a lengthy discussion of Gautama Buddha's life. Now, without doubt a close connection exists between a religious-philosophical system and the life history of its founder. Nonetheless, in this instance it was apparent that the speaker included this material because it was *interesting* and not because it was *necessary* to accomplish the specific purpose of the speech. The speaker could have formulated the statement of purpose in a manner to justify a discussion of the life of Buddha. In this instance, however, the statement of purpose failed to serve as a guide to the selection of materials in the way it should have.

II. ORGANIZING THE BODY OF THE SPEECH

The earliest writers on public speaking recognized order as an essential ingredient in good communication. Note that we say "good" communication. No matter how badly you may jumble your ideas and materials, you will still communicate something. You have very little assurance, however, that what you mean and what your audience thinks you mean will bear much resemblance to each other. If a speech is to make the impression you want, its parts should be so related that the speech as a whole is easy to understand and easy to remember.

All the essential material implied in the statement of purpose is contained in the body of the speech. The introduction and the conclusion help the audience to perceive accurately what is in the body of the speech. Since the body is the essential part of a speech, it is organized first.

A. Patterns of Arrangement

The process of organizing the body of a speech may be looked at from two points of view. The first of these is analytical. You examine your subject to determine what kind of logical division or partition you can impose upon it. Dividing the subject into parts is necessary (as we saw in Chapter 2) because the whole of the subject cannot be communicated at once. The component ideas must be given to the audience one at a time. It is the function of the analytic process to determine what these components are.

A part of the analytic process in the organization of an informative speech is directed toward making decisions about what we may call the rhetorical requirements of the speaking situation. This means that you must not only decide what kind of partition the subject demands, you must also make judgments about what kinds of information are needed to satisfy audience demands. Journalists long ago developed a rule of thumb to test the completeness of a news story. If the opening paragraph does not answer the questions Who? What? When? Where? Why? and How? the writing is considered faulty. When you make an informative speech, you will profit from examining the content of your speech with a journalistic eye.

In the discussion of outlining (Chapter 11) the comment was made that the main points of an informative speech should "add up" to the subject proposed by the statement of purpose. The notion involved here is somewhat similar but includes the additional dimension that you may partition your speech adequately with respect to the subject and yet fail to meet the demands of the audience. For example, it is not uncommon to hear a quite competent discussion of a complex operation, procedure, concept, or piece of machinery. The question "How?" is satisfactorily answered, yet the speech is unsatisfying because nothing is done to relate the idea, action, or object described to any function or purpose. The "Why?" is ignored. No suggestion is made here that every informative speech will demand attention to all of the who-what-when-where-why-how questions. In any instance, one or several of these may be totally irrelevant. Our advice is simply to be aware of them, to consider them, and to make a judgment about how many of them must be answered to make what you want to say interesting and clear to your audience.

The second aspect of organization is the process of synthesis. You decide how to arrange the parts of the subject into a pattern which you think will best meet the expectations aroused in the audience by the subject sentence of the speech and by the attention factor you have used to enlist the interest of the audience.

In deciding what will be the main points in the body of your speech, look for the organizational pattern that will best help your audience understand and remember what you say. There are several methods of arranging an informative speech to achieve clarity and retention. We shall comment on the chronological pattern, the geographical or spatial pattern, the topical pattern, the pattern of definition, the pattern of comparison and contrast, and the pattern of cause and effect. Select for your speech the pattern that best fits your subject and best meets the expectations of the audience.

1. Chronological Pattern

Many subjects will yield easily to a historical or chronological sequence of presentation. In the following example, the basic steps in the development of the table of atomic weights are clarified by using a chronological partition as the means of ordering the main ideas.

> STATEMENT OF PURPOSE: To inform the audience about the basic steps in the development of the periodic table
> I. Scientists observed certain similarities in the behavior of groups of elements
> II. Mendelyeev found that the elements could be arranged in an order of increasing atomic weight to bring the elements of these groups into columns

III. Ramsey completed the organization by assigning atomic numbers

IV. Later atomic chemists related the atomic numbers to the distribution of electrons in the shells of the various atoms

2. Geographical or Spatial Pattern

Another common pattern of arrangement is by location. Such an order provides the opportunity to develop a subject in terms of the relation of one point to another in space. Geographical order in this case is virtually essential. A speech on the subject of the pollution in America's rivers might be organized into (a) rivers of the East, (2) rivers of the Midwest, (3) rivers of the West. Such an organization, however, would not be the best for understanding the problem of pollution. Geographical order is useful only when the essential ideas are best divided and best understood on that basis. The following outline explains the parallel between latitudinal life zones by using a geographical pattern of arrangement. This example is particularly interesting from two points of view; first, two geographical principles actually are at work in one speech and, second, no better pattern or organization is immediately apparent for this subject.

> STATEMENT OF PURPOSE: To inform the audience of the parallel relationship between the plant life of a region and the region's altitude and distance from the equator
>
> I. Tropical forests flourish near sea level and near the equator
>   A. Climatic conditions
>   B. Typical plants
> II. Deciduous forests occur in temperature zones at low altitudes
>   A. Climatic conditions
>   B. Typical plants
> III. Coniferous forests grow at higher altitudes and far from the equator
>   A. Climatic conditions
>   B. Typical plants
> IV. Mosses, lichens, and low herbaceous growths are characteristic of the far north and areas above timber line
>   A. Climatic conditions
>   B. Typical plants

V. Ice and snow caps the highest mountains and both
   polar regions
   A. Climatic conditions
   B. Typical plants

3. Topical Pattern

Any method of partitioning that divides a subject into its component
parts can be called a topical pattern. In this sense, both the chronological and the geographical patterns or organizations are forms of
topical arrangement. The latter is considered as a separate method of
organization to accommodate natural or traditional classifications that
are neither chronological nor geographical. Many such classifications
are familiar to you: animal, vegetable, and mineral; political, social,
and economic; strings, percussion, woodwinds, and brass. Any subject
that can be analyzed into component parts can be organized by the
method of typical arrangement. Here is an example of topical partition.

> STATEMENT OF PURPOSE: To inform the audience of the
> sources of energy required for generating electrical power.
> I. Fossil fuel
> II. Water power
> III. Atomic energy
> IV. Solar energy
> IV. Geothermal energy

Although it is not necessarily evident and the outlines makes no
point of it, the fact that the main headings come in a generally accurate chronological order, relative to the sequence in which the various
power sources have been widely exploited, will not harm the clarity of
the speech and might even help. We shall have more to say about the
use of multiple patterns of arrangement later in this chapter.

4. Pattern of Definition

A fourth method of division is definition. Speeches intended to
answer such questions as "What is radioactivity?" or "What is a depression?" or "What is a Socialist?" can often be made meaningful by
using as main heads methods of definition selected from among those
discussed in Chapter 6. One may properly ask whether this pattern of
organization is clearly distinguishable from others, such as the topical
arrangement or that by comparison and contrast. Nonetheless, it is
easy to see how it gets its name and how it can be profitably used.

STATEMENT OF PURPOSE: To inform the audience of the essential nature of jazz
I. Jazz is a form of popular music indigenous to the United States
   A. Jazz originated in New Orleans
   B. Jazz began just after World War I
II. Jazz differs from other popular music
   A. It differs from spirituals
   B. It differs from western music
   C. It differs from folk music of the hill country
III. Jazz takes several forms
   A. Dixieland
   B. Blues
   C. Progressive jazz

5. Pattern of Comparison and Contrast

Speakers frequently make use of the similarities and differences between two items or concepts when an audience is familiar with one of them and not familiar with the other. Comparison and contrast are not only rhetorical forms of definition and forms of supporting material (see Chapter 6) but they can also serve as organizational principles for an informative speech.

STATEMENT OF PURPOSE: To inform the audience of the characteristics of a good teacher
I. A good salesman must have three kinds of knowledge
   A. He must be familiar with his product
   B. He must understand the demands and requirements of his customers
   C. He must know the principles of persuasion
II. A good teacher will have similar kinds of knowledge
   A. He will know his subject thoroughly
   B. He will understand the needs of his classes
   C. He will be skilled in the principles of effective communication
III. A good salesman and a good teacher have similar personality traits
   A. Enthusiasm
   B. Honesty
     [And so on]

6. Pattern of Cause and Effect

When you want to explain a topic in terms of what caused an event or when you want to explain the consequences of some event, you can use a cause-and-effect order. You would employ this pattern to explain either the *causes* for the stock-market crash of 1929 or the *effects* of radioactivity on the human body. In the following example, both cause and effect are combined in the same organizational pattern in order to clarify the subject more fully.

> STATEMENT OF PURPOSE: To inform the audience of the problem of smog in the Los Angeles Basin
>
> I. Effects of smog
>   A. Smog is harmful to the human body
>   B. Eleven billion dollars per year in property damage is incurred
>   C. Agricultural losses are sustained.
>   1. Plants and crops
>   2. Livestock
>   D. Visibility is limited
>   E. The area loses tourist trade
> II. Causes of smog
>   A. Chemical
>   1. Automobiles
>   2. Industrial plants.
>   B. Climatic
>   1. Temperature inversion
>   2. Weak winds

B. Using Multiple Patterns of Arrangement

In organizing an informative speech, you are not only trying to find *some method* of arrangement that will pull the points of the speech together, but you are also trying to find *the method* that best expresses and emphasizes the most natural sequence of ideas.

You need not confine your partitioning of an informative speech to a single method. It is quite possible that your ideas will become clearer if you combine two (or even more) of the methods mentioned. In some instances, the nature of the subject itself demands multiple levels of arrangement. When, for example, you explain the steps in building an automobile on an assembly line, you will necessarily combine chronological, spatial, and topical elements in the sequence of ideas. The following outline includes two methods of arrangement: topical and chronological.

> SPECIFIC PURPOSE: To inform the audience of the purpose of the three major honor societies open to speech and drama majors
> I. Phi Beta Kappa
> A. First on campus—1906
> B. Purpose—to recognize scholarship
> II. Delta Sigma Rho
> A. On campus—1916
> B. Purpose—to recognize forensic ability
> III. Alpha Theta Phi
> A. On campus—1934
> B. Purpose—to recognize dramatic ability

Here, the objective is to classify the purposes of the honor societies, but the chronological element in the arrangement of ideas is valuable in strengthening the unity of the material.

In contrast, notice the lack of order in the following outline:

> STATEMENT OF PURPOSE: To inform the audience of the essential nature of atheism
> I. Early Greeks
> A. Two meanings for atheism
> 1. Believing in foreign or strange gods
> 2. Believing that there are no gods
> B. The original Greek word was "atheos."
> II. Atheism and Communism
> A. Associated with international socialist movement
> B. Part of the state philosophy of the Soviet Union
> III. Atheists and agnostics differ in their beliefs
> A. Neither is convinced of the existence of God
> B. Negative evidence sufficient for atheists
> C. Proof one way or other needed for agnostics
> IV. Atheism today

Ignoring the lack of coherence in the organization of subheads, look at the basic partition of the main points. The first main point appears to promise a chronological development. The second point shifts ground, however, and introduces what must probably be identified as a topical heading of the central idea. The third point introduces yet another pattern in the form of comparison and contrast. The fourth point returns to the original chronological pattern. The result is a mishmash of tangled ideas. Even if each main point is made clear individually, the listeners will probably have only a confused notion of what atheism is.

It is clear, then, that imposing multiple patterns of organization on a speech is an advantage only as long as they are compatible and consistent throughout.

C. Number of Points in the Body of the Speech

No set rule can be given for determining how many points the body of a speech should have because the nature of the subject determines this figure. A reasonable number of main points would be from two to five. More than this number gives the audience too much to remember. Keep in mind at all times that you are trying to give your audience ideas they can carry away with them. The number of main points in the speech should be controlled to a large extent also by the time you have available for speaking. You should allow at least a minute to develop each of the major headings in the body. Thus, if your speech is to be 5 minutes long, considering the fact that you also need an introduction and a conclusion, four points in the body would be a maximum. Even in a 7-minute speech, three points are not too few. If you have more time, concentrate on extending the development of a few points rather than on increasing the number.

III. ADDING SUPPORTING DETAIL

After you have established the basic partition through which you will develop the central idea of a speech, you are ready to develop these points by adding supporting detail. The partitioning of a speech creates an orderly structure that helps the audience to follow the ideas and see the relationships among them; the supporting details are the sparks that strike fire to the cold logic of the outline. (See Chapter 6.)

When you choose supporting material for a speech, always keep in mind the fact that the key element in any speaking situation is the audience. Select material with the audience in mind. Use those materails which will best clarify your ideas and best sustain the interest of your audience.

Listeners usually grasp an idea more readily when it is associated with some object, person, or event which they already know or can easily comprehend. The more vividly your examples, statistics, definitions, and quotations revitalize experiences that listeners have had, the better are your chances of making your speech interesting and clear to them. For this reason it is a good beginning rule of thumb to use at least one supporting detail for every idea you bring into a speech.

Variety in supporting detail is a further help toward building interest. If you use statistics exclusively, or only hypothetical examples, or nothing but quotations, you may lose the attention of an audience because your materials lack variety. To be sure, having some supporting material, even if it does lack variety, is preferable to having no material at all, but get variety if you can.

IV. PREPARING THE CONCLUSION

When you have organized your ideas and materials into the body of the speech, you have a unified and coherent view of what you want your audience to understand. Then you prepare the conclusion of your speech. The function of the conclusion is to draw together all the diverse elements of the body of the speech, the main ideas and the supporting materials, in order that the audience may have an understanding of this subject that is as unified and coherent as yours. Whereas in developing your discussion it was necessary to partition the ideas, in concluding you try to give the audience an overview of the subject; you try to get them to see the topic as a whole. The conclusion should therefore contain, minimally, a restatement of the purpose and a recapitulation of the main ideas. In short, it should be a summary of the speech. This much is needed to assure clarity.

Clarity, however, is a minimal requirement. The conclusion can also lend a personal touch to the speech and bring it to a graceful close by adding a story, a joke, or a quotation that illustrates the total idea you mean to convey. The conclusion is your last chance to make sure that your audience has understood the central idea of the speech.

V. PREPARING THE INTRODUCTION

The last step in organizing a speech is developing the introduction. After the central idea has been logically partitioned; after the main points have been developed with clearly organized, interesting, and pertinent supporting materials; and after the conclusion has been planned—then you know to all intents and purposes what you are going to say. The major part of your preparation has been completed. The introduction of the speech is, in one sense, an added part. It is the part that prepares an audience to listen to the body of the speech. The introduction to an informative speech must accomplish two ends: It must gain the attention of the audience and it must disclose the subject of the speech. This much, then, must be included: material to *gain attention*, and a *subject sentence.*

Over and above these two essential elements, however, some introductions include a third kind of material. These are the additional items of information that may be needed to clarify the subject sentence or to orient the audience before you begin the development of the central idea. Such information is called *background material.*

A. Gaining Attention

It is often difficult to realize that an audience is not ready to listen as soon as you are ready to speak. You must *win* the attention of an audience before you can present your ideas. Talking serves no communicative end if the audience is not listening. Material must be provided in the introduction to catch the attention of the audience and direct its attention to the subject of the speech. Any of several means of gaining attention may be used. Here are a few: startling statistics, a story, an anecdote, a quotation, or a reminder to the audience of what it already knows about the subject of the speech. (See Chapter 5.)

Suppose you were planning to give a description of student government at your college. To show the importance of knowing what the student body officers do, you might begin by pointing out the amount of money collected by the student body each year, and by showing the way this money is spent. Or you might recall the last campus election, or quote an authoritative statement about the importance of student body government in college life. All of these ideas, and many others, may come to mind as a means of gaining attention.

359

Despite the value of such devices for winning the ear of a listener, the speaker must avoid misusing them. Nothing must be done to interfere with the primary object of a speech: to communicate an idea. The materials used to catch attention must lead the audience directly to the central idea of the speech. Avoid the practice of using any introductory device that gains attention but fails to focus this attention on the subject.

A speech student in a class of businessmen persistently used some startling means of getting attention, but consistently he failed to relate it to his subject. He would rise, for instance, go to the rostrum, and say, "Bob, I disagree completely with you on that matter. If I've told you once, I've told you a thousand times that you just don't know what you're talking about." A pause, and then, "Ladies and gentlemen, how much insurance does an unmarried man need? Here is a question I would like to speak to you about this evening." And so the speech would proceed. Needless to say his audience was bewildered. Bob would sit there waiting (with the rest of the audience) to find out what the speaker's opening remark had meant. They never did find out because it bore no relationship to the subject. It was nothing more than a gimmick to get attention.

B. The Subject Sentence

The opening you use to catch attention brings you directly to a specific statement of your subject. The statement of purpose that you formulate serves admirably to guide you in preparing your speech, but stylistically it leaves much to be desired. It will not be used in the speech in the form it originally takes. Instead, it will be replaced by a *subject sentence*. This, in effect, is the statement of purpose recast into a sentence of the sort you might use in conversation.

> STATEMENT OF PURPOSE: To inform the audience of the legislative, executive, and judicial branches of student government at Howard College.

would, in a speech, become a subject sentence somewhat as follows:

> SUBJECT SENTENCE: In order to understand how student government works at Howard College, let's look at the functions of the Student Council, Student Body President, and the Student Court.

C. Background Material

When an audience is not familiar with the subject at hand, it may be necessary to do more than state the subject sentence. When you choose a subject that is new to the listeners, you will often need to orient them to it. For example, when the attack on the citadel at Hue was in the news, there was no necessity for background material on a speech about it, but as the war in Vietnam fades in our memories, as every war ultimately does, it becomes more and more necessary to remind listeners of the earlier time. You would need to tell them, for instance, of the condition that existed in the war at the time. By doing this, you give your audience a clearer picture of the main ideas.

Such background material, however, should be limited to a few sentences and must not become an extended discussion. To spend 3 minutes of a 5-minute speech in giving background is a waste of valuable time. If this much background information is necessary for the audience's understanding, then revise your statement of purpose and make the background material the subject of your speech.

VI. PRACTICING THE DELIVERY

At all times it is well to remember that, until its delivery, a speech is a growing thing, representing your increasing awareness of the subject and the specific audience to which you speak. For this reason, your speech will continually change during the time you are working on it. You will be shifting points around, replacing one example with a better one, or considering new principles of partition.

Perhaps because so much of our training in school deals with written communication, we sometimes come to think that a speech is something that we write out and read. As a result of this attitude we are tempted to prepare a careful outline, and then when it is completed to stop revising it and begin to practice the oral delivery. But a speech is different from an essay. It will be judged by the impact its oral delivery has on the audience. Consequently, it should be tried out *orally*, in parts and in the whole, from the early stages of preparation. When the first rough approximation of your speech has been drawn up, begin to "talk it through." As you hear things in the speech you don't like, change them, and improve them. The outline should be developed in the atmosphere of *oral rhetoric*. With this kind of preparation, a speech will come to be part of you; more and more it will grow into a communication that reflects your ideas, your knowledge, and your individual personality.

SUMMARY

Of all the talking that goes in the world each day, a large part is occupied with the transmitting of information. Informative speaking is an important process; therefore, skill in this kind of communication is both necessary and desirable. To insure that the information you give will be interesting and clear, take six steps in preparing an informative speech:

1. *Select and narrow the subject, and formulate a statement of purpose.* The more conventional methods are to narrow the subject to a specific segment of time, or of space, or to a subproblem in a larger controversy, or to a single portion of a process. One or more of these methods of narrowing the subject may be used. A speech topic may also be narrowed by including in the discussion a series of treatments of selected aspects of the whole subject. Narrowing the whole gives a limited scope to the subject by developing in detail a very restricted view of the subject; narrowing the discussion to specific aspects of the subject gives a broader view without sacrificing concreteness and detail.

2. *Choose the basic method of partitioning the subject and determine the main points of the body of the speech.* One or more of several patterns of organization may be used to impose a clear and reasonable sequence on the ideas of the speech, both in the main points and in their subheadings: (a) chronological arrangement, (b) geographical arrangement, (c) topical arrangement, (d) arrangement by definition, (e) arrangement by comparison and contrast, and (f) arrangement by cause and effect. The total number of main points will usually be from two to five.

3. *Add the supporting details.* Use a variety of supporting materials to bring your ideas sharply into focus for your audience.

4. *Prepare the conclusion.* Summarize the main points of the speech, including a restatement of the subject sentence; bring the speech to a graceful close.

5. *Prepare the introduction.* Plan to open the speech in a way that will catch the attention of the audience and, at the same time, lead directly into the subject sentence. When necessary, include background material to orient the audience to the subject of the speech.

6. *Practice the delivery.* Familiarize yourself thoroughly with the ideas and materials of the speech by "talking it through" from the

early stages of preparation. With the contents thus firmly in mind, you will be able to deliver the speech with fluency, vigor, and conversational spontaneity.

QUESTIONS

1. List the six steps in preparing a speech.
2. How may a subject be limited?
3. How can you handle a broad subject with limited time?
4. Explain four of the six patterns of arranging the body of a speech.
5. Explain how to gain attention in the introduction of a speech.
6. Differentiate between a specific purpose and a subject sentence.
7. What care must be taken in using background material in the introduction?
8. Explain how to practice the delivery of a speech.

EXERCISES

1. Organize and deliver a 5- to 7-minute informative speech on a topic selected from the subject matter of a course you are now taking (other than Speech). Prepare the outline carefully and give your instructor a carbon copy of your speaking outline before you deliver the speech.

2. Select one item from the following list (or one supplied by your instructor) and prepare two statements of purpose for informative speeches on that subject. In the first instance, narrow the scope and limit the subject by using one of the methods explained in this chapter. In the second statement of purpose, do the same using another of the methods. Formulate a subject sentence for each statement of purpose.

The liberal arts	Southern hospitality
Biology	The national forests
The Civil War	College athletics
Summer jobs for students	Student government
Farming	Boating

3. Illustrate with a brief outline each of the six methods of partitioning the body of an informative speech.

4. Select an informative speech by one of your classmates and suggest how you might have tried to gain attention had you delivered the speech. Is your method better? Why?

5. With four of your classmates, select a subject for a symposium

(each speaker delivers a speech on one specific phase of the general subject). Divide the subject into five subtopics. Let each speaker deliver a 5- to 7-minute informative talk on a different one of the subtopics. The symposium topics might be:

    (a) The basic beliefs (nature of man, God, and the relationship between the two) of the five largest non-Christian religions of the world.

    (b) The main responsibilities of the five major executive officers of our state.

    (c) The extent of the five major types of crime in our city.

    (d) The main ideas about writing of five contemporary novelists.

    6. The following speech was delivered in a speech class by Charles F. Peters, a student majoring in mathematics. In a brief paper, analyze and evaluate the organization of the speech.

THE HOW AND WHY OF OLD FAITHFUL

When the American mountain men of the early eighteen hundreds, men like Jedediah Smith, Jim Bridger and Hugh Glass, came out of the West they brought with them incredible tales. "High in the Rockies," they said, "was a land where the earth boiled under your feet, where spouts of hot water as tall as a flagpole came roaring out of the trembling ground, and whole valleys steamed with sulphurous fumes as if the lid over Hell itself had been shot full of holes."*

These early descriptions astounded the folks on the eastern seaboard and taxed their credulity but they cause us no surprise today. What our forebears had watched in awe we know were the geysers of Yellowstone. All of us have read about these. Many of us have actually seen, at least in travel films or pictures if not in person, the most famous, "Old Faithful."

But for many of us the working of this geological phenomenon is just as mysterious as it was to Jim Bridger. It interested me enough to try to find out the how and why of geysers and you may be interested in what I learned about these natural fountains which intermittently erupt, hurling steam, boiling water, and sometimes mud to great heights above the surface. The particular theory I'm going to discuss is not the only explanation of how a geyser works but it's the oldest and most widely accepted. It was proposed in 1847, interestingly enough, by Robert Bunsen, the German chemist who invented the Bunsen burner.

Beneath the geyser's mouth is the geyser well, which is made up of a network of underground channels. These channels may be from ten to one hundred feet deep. The geyser well usually goes down a short distance as a single channel and then branches into many offshoots. These offshoots

* National Geographic Society, *America's Wonderlands* (Washington, D.C.: The National Geographic Society, 1959).

may be contorted and twist about each other. They may be jagged and narrow in some places, and broad enough to form large subterranean cavities in others. Most passages are between one and five feet in diameter.

Molten igneous rock material beneath the geyser well furnishes the heat that keeps the well and its water at a high temperature.

All levels of the well have a delicate balance between the temperature of and the pressure on the water. The water temperature on the surface is nearly 100 degrees centigrade, while on the bottom it is above 270 degrees. The hotter water near the bottom of the well does not boil or vaporize because of the pressure caused by the water above it. This variation of temperatures within the well is possible only because there is no *convection* to transfer the temperatures around evenly. That is, there can be no mass movement or currents because of the contorted and restricted nature of the passages that form the well. If there were convection, we would have a boiling spring, where all the water boils evenly, instead of a geyser, where the variable pressure situation causes an eruption. The eruption itself occurs when the temperature of the water near the bottom of the well becomes great enough to vaporize the water, and the resulting bubbles of steam become trapped in the crooked passages near the bottom. Under these conditions one cubic inch of water will vaporize into fifty cubic inches of steam. Thus, some water wells up and runs over at the mouth of the geyser. This loss of water eases the pressure throughout the entire column and permits water at all levels of the well to flash into steam. The enormous pressure caused by the new steam forces the boiling water out of the channel network and into the air, sometimes as high as two hundred feet.

After the eruption the well immediately begins to refill. Some of the erupted water drops back into the well. Subsurface water seeps into the well through permeable rocks and fissures, or water may run into the well from a nearby hot spring. When this new water flows into the well, it does not immediately boil: If it did we would have nothing but a steaming vent. Rather, the water goes back into the pressure relationships I have already described and the cycle begins again.

The interval between eruptions varies from ten minutes to several weeks. Its length depends upon such things as the rate at which the channel network refills, the proximity of the well to its source of heat, the amount of constriction in the well passages, the size of the entire channel network, and the amount of steam that escapes through the rocks that form the geyser well.

It would seem that the eruption of a geyser, then, is neither a mysterious nor an unexplainable occurrence as the early mountain men thought, but is rather an ordered process of nature where the balance between temperature and pressure in a geyser well and the peculiar configurations of the channels of that well determine how frequent, how high, and how faithful Old Faithful's eruptions will be.

I. The nature of persuasion
   A. Persuasion uses a variety of proofs
   B. The limitation of objectives
II. Organizing the speech to persuade
   A. Persuasive organization in general
      1. The introduction
      2. The body
      3. The conclusion
   B. Types of persuasive organization
      1. The proposition-to-proof pattern
      2. The problem-to-solution pattern
      3. The reflective pattern
   C. Determining the best persuasive order
   D. Determining the placement of arguments

Chapter $\mathbf{17}$

Speaking To Persuade

I. THE NATURE OF PERSUASION

To persuade is to cause someone to believe or act in a predetermined way. In persuasion, you present to your listeners impelling proofs that cause them to do or believe something. The effectiveness of persuasion depends upon your ability to satisfy your audience that the mode of conduct, the value judgment, or the factual condition you propose is expedient or good or true. In order to do this, you must offer proofs.

Proofs in persuasion may be considered successful when they help you to make an audience feel that it is "obligated" to do what you want. We use the word obligated here in a figurative sense. That is to say, you offer your audience some *motive* (expediency, profit, morality, or the like) which makes the audience feel a need to accept your proposition. You appear as one giving advice so sound, so reasonable that it *ought* to be accepted; it becomes almost a command. It is not necessarily you as the source of the argument who are seen as giving the command. The command comes from a source internalized within the listeners—"common sense," if you will. Given the audience's frame of mind, its beliefs, attitudes and values, its priorities and, given the impact on these factors by your arguments, it would seem unreasonable to the audience to reject your advice. When that happens, you have argued persuasively.

The proofs you offer an audience are not rigorous, however, because rhetorical argumentation does not either determine or demonstrate the truth of a matter. It only helps to determine what someone *believes* about it. For example, we might well ask whether propositions of fact should even be *argued*. Perhaps they should, instead, be *researched*. If they can be researched to the point that the truth is known and can be demonstrated, then no rhetorical argument (no persuasion, that is) is required. Most often, however, this level of certainty is unattainable and persuasion must be used.

Again, the proposition of a persuasive speech is *never* anything more than an expression of an opinion. You perceive, you make judgments, and you express these judgments in language. The expression is what we have called a proposition and it is your opinion, your judgment, of what you perceive. You have, in other words, no fund of absolute information on which you can draw and, in such cases, therefore, no certainty is available to you. Hence you cannot develop absolute proof. The tentative nature of rhetorical argumentation, known as the concept of probability in argument, is discussed in Chapter 8.

The examples you choose, the definitions you formulate, the comparisons and contrasts you draw must be within the scope of your listeners' comprehension. These and all the other supporting details you use are the raw materials from which arguments are built. The arguments themselves must be just as much audience-centered as the materials they are built of because an argument fired off blindly is not likely to knock down many pigeons. The thesis you advocate must likewise be advanced within the framework of the existing ideas, opinions, attitudes, beliefs, and values of your audience.

A. Persuasion Uses a Variety of Proofs

Speakers use a variety or combination of proofs to bring about persuasion. The rational and extrarational elements of proof combine to influence audience response. Indeed, they are so closely intermingled in any persuasive speech that only the critic who is consciously looking for them can isolate one aspect of the proof from another. In a single statement, the critic will often find evidence of each. As an example, when Winston Churchill became Prime Minister of England in the dark days of 1940, he assumed the fearful responsibilities of his office with a statement of policy that we know as the "Blood, Sweat and Tears," speech. The conclusion of this famous speech illustrates the intermingling of the different kinds of proof. Churchill says:

You ask, what is our policy? I say it is to wage war by land, sea and air. War with all our might and with all the strength God has given us, and to wage war against a monstrous tyranny never surpassed in the dark and lamentable catalogue of human crime.

That is our policy.

You ask, what is our aim? I can answer in one word. It is victory. Victory at all costs—victory in spite of all terrors—victory, however long and hard the road may be, for without victory there is no survival.

Let that be realized. No survival for the British Empire, no survival for all that the British Empire has stood for, no survival for the urge, the impulse of the ages, that mankind shall move forward toward his goal.

I take up my task in buoyancy and hope. I feel sure that our cause will not be suffered to fail among men.

I feel entitled at this juncture, at this time, to claim the aid of all and to say, "Come then, let us go forward together with our united strength."

Look at the individual sentences. Which parts are rational appeals, which are motive appeals, and which rely upon the audience's acceptance of the speaker? Each sentence is a mixture of each kind of proof.

B. The Limitation of Objectives

The extent to which you can hope to be persuasive must be kept in proper perspective. The dramatic picture of a speaker who meets a hostile audience and during the course of a half-hour address converts it into an audience of friendly partisans is not accurate. The concept of spellbinders who can mold audiences to their will on any subject is a myth. It is much more realistic to recognize the fact that under certain circumstances any attempt to persuade will be no more than a waste of time. Frequently, the differences in attitudes, beliefs, and values between you and a potential audience are irreconcilable. You would never in a million years win the support of the Roman Catholic Archbishop of Boston for legislation legalizing abortion. Other attitudes are held as firmly and unshakably by many people in many other areas of opinion such as politics, for example. To try to persuade them is a waste of time. In other instances, an audience *cannot* give a response you might seek. Would you look for financial support for some project from people who can't even pay their rent? In still other instances it would be wise to keep in mind the old Latin adage, "De gustibus non disputandum est." The notion here is that it's a foolish waste of time to argue a matter when the deciding factor is individual taste.

In cases such as these, it is easy to become frustrated. If you do, it might be useful to remember the prayer of Saint Francis of Assisi, who asked God to give him the courage to change what he could, the patience to live with what he could not, and the wisdom to know the difference. The wisdom to know the difference is the important point here, because it would be a mistake to confuse a difficult rhetorical situation with an impossible one. It is also a mistake to think that a speech to persuade may be counted successful only if it causes an audience to change its ways. The persuasive speakers most celebrated in history have frequently had to be satisfied with the knowledge that they moved the members of the audience only a little way. As a persuasive speaker, your objective is to move listeners in your direction, however short the journey may be, or to stop, if only for a short time, their movement in another direction. In many instances to expect more than this is to open the door to harsh disappointment.

II. ORGANIZING THE SPEECH TO PERSUADE

On September 11, 1941, President Franklin D. Roosevelt delivered from the White House a speech which has since been called "The Freedom of the Seas." In this speech, the president announced it to be the policy of the United States government to attack any German or Italian warship that entered what the United States had defined as her defensive waters. Previously, the policy of the United States had been to defend only her own ships from attack, but now she would protect all shipping in her defensive waters by sinking on sight any Axis submarine or surface raider. But notice the order in which the president presented his ideas.

He opened his speech with a detailed discussion of a number of unprovoked attacks on American vessels. He characterized these attacks as "international lawlessness" and as the manifestation of a design on the part of the Axis "to abolish the freedom of the seas and to acquire absolute control and domination of these seas for themselves." Next, he discussed the implications for America of the Axis plan. He pointed out that in time Germany would, through controlling the seas, be able to subjugate the United States. He said that something must be done: "When you see a rattlesnake poised to strike, you do not wait until he has struck before you crush him."

Only after he had elaborated this kind of background, building a strong case against the depredations of the Axis navies, did Roosevelt propose and defend the policy he had formulated. Why did he approach the subject in the way he did? Why did he withhold his statement of the proposition of his speech until so near the end? Why did he not state, bluntly and tersely, the policy of the American government? Because in September of 1941 a considerable segment of the American population felt that if the United States could stay neutral, and would attack Axis ships only when and if they attacked her own, she could avoid becoming entangled in the war and live in peace with whatever victor emerged.

Three months later, the United States was brought into the war by the Japanese attack on Pearl Harbor. After this time, a policy of attacking the ships of the Axis powers could be set forth bluntly. There would be less need to prepare the audience to give favorable hearing to such a policy. But in September, the president had to adopt a speech organization that took into account the desire of his audience to avoid conflict. The organization he chose helped his audience to dissociate from the then current policy of defense and to identify with his newly established policy.

This example not only shows the importance of organization in a speech to persuade, but it also indicates that the organization of a given speech will depend upon the temper of a given audience. Let's examine this latter concept in some detail.

A. Persuasive Organization in General

The general structure of the speech to persuade is the same as that for the speech to inform. Each has an introduction, a body, and a conclusion.

1. The Introduction

The introduction of a speech focuses attention on the subject and arouses the interest of the audience in it. In many instances, it will include a clear statement of the proposition the speaker wishes to prove. In other instances, the speaker may want to withhold for a time the specific thesis. (Franklin D. Roosevelt's speech on the freedom of the seas is an example). In such cases the speaker substitutes for a clear revelation of the proposition a more general statement to let the audience know what the speech will be about.

John F. Kennedy's introduction to his speech to the Greater Houston Ministerial Association during the 1960 Presidential campaign indicates clearly to his audience the subject of his speech.

> I am grateful for your generous invitation to state my views.
>
> While the so-called religious issue is necessarily and properly the chief topic here tonight, I want to emphasize from the outset that I believe that we have far more critical issues in the 1960 election: the spread of Communist influence, until it now festers only ninety miles off the coast of Florida—the humiliating treatment of our President and Vice President by those who no longer respect our power—the hungry children I saw in West Virginia, the families forced to give up their farms—an America with too many slums, with too few schools, and too late to the moon and outer space.
>
> These are the real issues which should decide this campaign. And they are not religious issues—for war and hunger and ignorance and despair know no religious barrier.
>
> But because I am a Catholic, and no Catholic has ever been elected President, the real issues in this campaign have been obscured—perhaps deliberately in some quarters less responsible than this. So it is apparently necessary for me to state once again—not what kind of church I believe in, for that should be important only to me, but what kind of America I believe in.

Both in Roosevelt's speech on the freedom of the seas and in Kennedy's speech on religion in government, the introduction is used to help the listener know what the speech is about, but only in Kennedy's introduction is the specific purpose revealed to the audience.

2. The Body

In the body of a persuasive speech, arguments are stated and supported. The arguments and their supporting material are selected with an eye to influencing the audience to believe or act in a specified manner.

3. The Conclusion

The conclusion of a speech to persuade will rarely be like the conclusion of an informative speech—a summary of the ideas in the body.

It will usually be a climax which summarizes only in the sense that it is the final outcome of all that has come before. The Reverend Martin Luther King, Jr., founder and President of the Southern Christian Leadership Conference, delivered his speech, "I Have a Dream," at the Lincoln Memorial on August 28, 1963, at the climax of the Civil Rights March on Washington. He told of the failure of the nation to make good on its "promissory note." He called for the nation to continue to advance civil rights, for black people to continue to press for their rights. Then he gave a series of nine statements beginning "I have a dream," followed by five statements containing the phrase "Let freedom ring," and ended:

When we let freedom ring, when we let it ring from every village and every hamlet, from every state and every city, we will be able to speed up that day when all of God's children, black men and white men, Jews and Gentiles, Protestants and Catholics, will be able to join hands and sing in the words of the old Negro spiritual, "Free at last! free at last! thank God almighty, we are free at last!"

Such a steady building makes it almost impossible to say where the conclusion begins. It could begin with the first "I have a dream" or with the first "Let freedom ring." The whole section is climactic. The last phrase is a summary, not of content but of attitude—"we are free at last!"

The conclusion to William Jennings Bryan's speech at the Democratic National Convention in 1896 was a metaphorical statement which, in a sense, summarized his whole argument in favor of the free silver plan, in the platform:

. . . [We] will answer their demands for a gold standard by saying to them: You shall not press down upon the brow of labor this crown of thorns, you shall not crucify mankind upon a cross of gold.

James B. Conant, former president of Harvard University, speaking in Washington, D.C., on May 24, 1961, to a national conference on the unemployed, out-of-school youth, concluded his more analytical speech with more of a content summary:

In conclusion, let me repeat my sense of shock as I contemplate conditions in our big cities with respect to youth in slum neighborhoods. The problems are the result of a social situation the roots of which run back to the days of slavery and the result of an economic problem which is in part a reflection of the total unemployment situation and in part a result of racial discrimination among labor unions and employers. To improve the work of the schools requires an improvement in the lives of the families who inhabit these slums, but without a drastic change in the employment prospects for urban Negro youth, relatively little can be accomplished. I close by urging that our large-city problems be analysed in far more detail than in the past and with a far greater degree of frankness. Neighborhood by neighborhood we need to know the facts, and when these facts indicate a dangerous social situation the American people should be prepared to take drastic measures before it is too late.

In these three examples one can see how differences of occasion and audience call out different kinds of conclusions. Dr. Conant speaks to a conference of experts who are aware of the problem. His speech (and its conclusion) has a more informative tone. Mr. Bryan concludes his speech as a part of a debate on the resolution. He is more conscious of the need to reinforce argument. The Reverend Mr. King is building an attitude; he wants, not an acceptance of a specific proposal, but an identification with a way of life.

B. Types of Persuasive Organization

Any persuasive speech in support of any proposition may be organized in any one of three patterns. Choose the one that you think will make arguments most effective with a specific proposition. The question of which format to use requires some discussion, and the discussion requires that you understand more fully what the three patterns are.

The patterns of arrangement discussed in Chapter 16 ("Speaking To Inform") are usually unsatisfactory for a persuasive speech because they emphasize understanding and clarification. In persuasion, the emphasis is on influencing the way an audience will think or act in addition to understanding. For this purpose, there are other ways of organizing a speech. Three of these methods are widely enough applicable and of sufficiently general character to warrant specific mention. In using the first of these, you would identify your proposition *early* in the speech and then present supporting arguments. We may call this the *proposition-to-proof* pattern. It is frequently referred to as a deductive pattern or organization. The term *deductive* is probably unfortunate because it invites confusion with the kind of reasoning that bears the same name. In the other two patterns you identify your proposition *later* in the speech. In varying degrees, these two patterns use what may be called a proof-to-proposition order. They are frequently called *inductive* organization, although the use of inductive has the same disadvantages inherent in the practice of calling proposition-to-proof order deductive. When these patterns are used, at least a portion of your supporting proof is presented before your proposition is identified. These patterns are named, respectively, the *problem-to-solution* pattern and the *reflective* pattern.

1. The Proposition-to-Proof Pattern

A proposition-to-proof pattern of organization is one in which you state the proposition in the introduction of the speech and then develop a series of supporting arguments in the body. The main idea is revealed from the very beginning, and the proofs are developed and heightened by building up subpoints. The speech concludes with an appeal for acceptance of the proposition.

Suppose you were to speak in favor of a compulsory student body fee to support extracurricular activities at your college. You look over your arguments and you find several good reasons for adopting the fee.

1. It will provide more opportunity for participation by all of the students.
2. It will provide a program of higher quality.
3. It will provide finances for some smaller activities that would not exist at all without funds from such a source.
4. It will mean better public relations for the college.

You also note that the one strong argument against this proposal is its unfairness to those who would not participate in student activities.

1. Students who aren't interested in student activities will have to pay for something they don't intend to use.

You recognize your reply to this objection:

1. Even those who do not use the student body card benefit indirectly through the improved public relations of the school. (Note the relationship of this to Point 4 above.)
2. It is the democratic principle that everyone must share in the expense of maintaining the group when the membership of the group are agreed by majority vote.

Here you have four arguments in favor of the fee and one against, with the answer to the opposition argument contained within one of the original arguments in favor, and the opposition argument further countered by an appeal to democratic principle. How might these be presented in the proposition-to-proof pattern of organization? The following example is given to show the main points. (Obviously, if you were to give the speech, you would need evidence and supporting detail that are not shown here.)

INTRODUCTION

I. The current student body election has aroused the interest of us all.

II. I would like to enlist your support in favor of the compulsory student body fee to support extracurricular activities.

BODY

I. It will provide more opportunity than now exists for everyone to participate.

II. It will provide financing for the smaller activities.

III. It will provide a program of higher quality than the present one.

IV. It will mean better public relations for the college, and thus eventually benefit even the students who do not participate in extracurricular activity.

V. The only democratic way to gain these advantages is with a compulsory student body fee.

CONCLUSION

I. Because of the opportunity it will provide for everyone, the aid it will bring to the smaller activities, and better public relations it will bring to the college, all of us should agree to the imposition of this compulsory fee.

II. The way to achieve these advantages is for all of us to vote for the fee at the election so that we can all benefit from it.

2. The Problem-to-Solution Pattern

In using the problem-to-solution order, first get the attention of the audience and present a problem that needs to be solved. Then recommend a course of action and show how it will solve the problem. Conclude with an appeal to act on the suggestion. The solution which you wish to propose is withheld from the audience at the beginning of the speech, at least until the problem has been presented. How long it will be withheld is determined by the situation. Here's how the argument in support of a compulsory student body fee would look in a problem-to-solution pattern:

INTRODUCTION

I. The current student body election has aroused the interest of us all.

BODY

I. One of the problems of this college is the lack of financial support for student activities.
   A. Currently the activities program is so limited that few students can participate.
   B. Activity is limited to events like proms and intercollegiate athletics.
   C. Little publicity is given to our school in the local newspapers because we lack a program which will draw the attention of people outside the college.
II. The solution to this problem is in a "yes" vote for a compulsory student body fee.
   A. It will solve the problems I have already discussed.
   B. It will help to put our activities program on a democratic basis with everyone sharing the load equally.

CONCLUSION

I. So support the solution to these problems—vote "yes" next Tuesday.

3. The Reflective Pattern

A third type of persuasive organization, the reflective pattern, also withholds the presentation of the solution until later in the speech. In using the reflective pattern, describe a problem situation and suggest several possibilities for solution. Next, evaluate each of these. Finally, propose the one which you present to the audience as the best. This form looks like a thoroughly objective approach to the subject. Your purpose, however, is quite argumentative. Far from being purely analytical, you know before you begin to speak exactly what course of action you will advocate. Everything you say is intended to move the audience toward accepting it.

377

Organized in the reflective pattern, the outline of a speech supporting a compulsory student body fee would look like this:

INTRODUCTION

I. The current student body election has aroused the
interest of all of us.

BODY

I. One of the problems of this college is the lack of
financial support for extracurricular activities.
   A. Currently, the activities program is so limited
   that few students can participate.
   B. Activity is limited to events like proms and intercollegiate athletics.
   C. Little publicity is given to our schol in the local
   papers because we lack a program that will draw
   the attention of the people outside the college.

II. The causes for this unsatisfactory condition are two:
   A. Receipts from year to year under the voluntary
   student activity fee have been uneven.
   B. The percentage of students who pay the voluntary fee is small.

III. We need some system that will satisfy two require-
ments.
   A. It should furnish enough money.
   B. It should furnish a consistent amount of money.

IV. The choice is between our present system and the
proposed compulsory fee system which will be on
the ballot at the next election.

V. The new compulsory fee system will best meet our
needs and in the most democratic fashion.

CONCLUSION

I. When you go to the polls Tuesday, vote for the
compulsory fee.

With this brief explanation as background, let's see how you make
your decision about which type of persuasive organization to use.

C. Determining the Best Persuasive Order

The choice of persuasive order is based on many factors, among
them: the complexity of the proposition, the attitudes of the listeners,

your credibility with the audience, and the presence or absence of opposition speakers. The proposition-to-proof order is easier to develop with clarity because the proposition is constantly before the listener and the relationship between your purpose and your individual arguments can be continually reinforced. Both the problem-to-solution and the reflective pattern, on the other hand, have the advantage of presenting an idea gradually and thus permit you to support your position before the audience can form a clear notion of rejecting it. Although research into this aspect of persuasion is still tentative, here are some general principles that you can keep in mind when you select your organizational pattern.

1. *Listeners do not like to be undecided.* Consequently, there is a point in every persuasive speech at which the audience decides for or against the speaker. During the course of a speech several such points may occur as the listeners change their minds or shift along a continuum between credence and disbelief. The listener's initial decision may be made before the speech even begins. An audience whose opinions are contrary to yours will tend to reject your ideas once your position is made known. Therefore, when an audience is opposed to your position and knows the argument in support of its own view, it will be to your advantage to delay associating yourself with the position your listeners oppose. Obviously, however, such a practice is unprofitable if the audience knows your position in advance. In such a case, using the proposition-to-proof order would be a sign of candor, thereby strengthening your *ethos* and tending to lessen somewhat the listeners' objections.

2. *When listeners already agree with you, you can do little wrong.* Virtually all you say will reinforce the listener's beliefs. The proposition-to-proof order would seem best to give such an audience immediate and continued reinforcement of its views.

3. *Variations in the intelligence, education, and sophistication of audiences influence their response to persuasive order.* Some listeners, regardless of what position they hold, are influenced by an orderly, logical approach. These hearers might be more easily influenced by a proposition-to-proof order. Other listeners respond more readily to the identification you make with their needs. In the latter case, a problem-to-solution order may be best because it groups together the needs of the listener and emphasizes them at one point in the speech for maximum immediate effect.

4. *The reflective pattern is designed for the situation wherein the audience has little knowledge of the subject.* It creates understanding first and gets to the issues later. Using this order, you can approach

the subject in such a way that the audience understands more clearly what kinds of decisions it must make before it makes them. The reflective pattern has another and perhaps more important advantage. In using it, you impose your analysis of the topic on the audience. Because the audience is thereby conditioned to your analysis, later speakers will find it more difficult to undo your persuasive effect; to do so, they must contradict not only your conclusions but your analysis as well.

D. Determining the Placement of Arguments

Once the problem of general arrangement has been resolved, a more specific question arises: "In what order should individual arguments be put?" Some will say that you should save your strongest argument to give the speech a greater impact at the end. Another will claim the contrary, that putting the best argument first gives the speech a strong start. Experimental investigations of the question have produced mixed results. The decision, as in all other questions in rhetoric, depends upon the state of the audience. However, some general, though tenative, principles are worth considering.

1. While disagreement exists over the relative importance of the first and last positions, arguments presented early and late are clearly better remembered than those presented in the middle of the speech.

2. When one argument depends on another for its meaning, the dependent argument must obviously follow the one on which it depends. It is useless, for instance, to argue that some federal medical plan will alleviate the shortage of physicians in rural areas before your audience believes that such a shortage exists.

3. If the ideas in a speech are sufficiently unrelated, the speech will appear to lack a unifying theme. It becomes something like a grocery list. The advantage of primacy (putting the strongest argument first) has been observed to be considerably weakened on these occasions. When, for example, a political candidate speaks on a number of relatively unrelated points, the audience will give greatest attention to items that it considers most important, regardless of the order in which they are presented.

4. When you have high status in the eyes of the audience, it will tend to see greater strength in arguments presented early in the speech. Listeners have greater expectations of high-credibility sources, and it is only after you have failed to reinforce their expectations that they will be less attentive.

5. Generally, arguments against your position, even when you refute

them, should not be presented first because they tend to build opposition in the listener's mind. Then you must overcome not only the opposition, but also whatever mechanisms the audience establishes to permit it to ignore or avoid your arguments. There is an additional danger. Once an audience makes a decision in the course of the speech, it tends to pay less attention to what follows. Thus, even if the opposition arguments are refuted, the listener will be less likely to "hear" your argumnets in your behalf.

There is an exception to this principle. When an audience has firmly held arguments opposing your position, it is probably best to refute those arguments early or the listener may rehearse them throughout the speech and ignore the arguments you use to support your position.

SUMMARY

In persuasion, select arguments and motivations that will cause a listener to identify your proposal with what the listener already knows and believes. Proof in a persuasive speech has both rational and extra-rational elements. These elements are so thoroughly blended that one can hardly be distinguished from another. Success in persuasion is not always likely to be dramatic. With some audiences, even the most persuasive speaker can win no more than a slight shift of position.

Three different types of organization are useful in persuasion: the proposition-to-proof, the problem-to-solution, and the reflective patterns. Determine which of these to use for the over-all structure of a speech on the basis of audience attitude. The complexity of the proposition, the attitudes of the listeners, source credibility, and the presence or absence of opposition speakers all help to determine the choice of persuasive order. The placement of arguments in a speech influences the ease with which they will be remembered and the degree to which they will reinforce agreement and diminish opposition.

QUESTIONS

1. What is persuasion?
2. Was the Reverend Martin Luther King, Jr., an emotional or a logical speaker?
3. Must a specific statement of what you want to prove be made in the introduction to every persuasive speech?

4. What is the nature of a persuasive conclusion?

5. How is the deductive pattern basically different from the problem-to-solution and the reflective patterns?

EXERCISES

1. Organize and deliver a 5- to 7-minute persuasive speech. Turn in to your instructor a copy of your outline, a brief analysis of your audience, a brief statement of what motivation you will use and why you will use it, and a brief statement of what organization you will use and why you will use it.

2. Listen to some persuasive speeches in class. What persuasive order did the speakers use? Could you improve the speeches by changing the order?

3. Write a brief analysis of one of your classmates' speeches evaluating the method of organization and the use of motive appeal in relation to the classroom audience to which the speech is delivered.

4. Formulate a proposition of policy from one of the general topics listed at the end of Chapter 2. Sketch the outline of a persuasive speech on this proposition, showing each of the three methods of persuasive organization.

5. Examine one of the three speeches at the end of this chapter and write a paper evaluating its persuasive techniques.

6. Examine the following three speeches and compare and contrast the rhetorical techniques used.

TOMORROW IS NOW!

Wilma Scott Heide°

Eleanor Roosevelt, who I'd like to think would be with us in spirit, once wrote: "We face the future fortified only with the lessons we have learned from the past. It is today that we must create the world of the future . . . In a very real sense. Tomorrow is NOW."

We return to the birthplace of NOW in our nation's capital to declare that feminism is a bona fide occupational qualification (b.f.o.q.) for every

° Wilma Scott Heide, then president of NOW, National Organization for Women, Inc., delivered her speech at the Sixth National Conference of NOW, Washington, D.C., February 17–19, 1973. Reprinted by permission from *Vital Speeches of the Day*, May 1, 1973, pp. 424–28.

human endeavor. Every social issue, every public policy, every institution of our society needs feminist analyses and leadership and we will provide it as a basic requirement for a humanist world. What we are about is a profound universal behavioral Revolution: Tomorrow is NOW!

It is for any remaining status quoters, via institutions or persons, who would deny us by behavior or priorities to justify (if they can) any humaneness, legality or justice of their recalcitrance. For the news media, we insist that you communicate to the world that our lively discussions of issues, our diversity of views and styles, our disagreements are transcended by our togetherness that sexism is a societal disease and feminism is caring enough to cure it. What feminists in NOW have lovingly and vibrantly put together, no news media *or* other forces can put asunder. The no longer silent majority *will be* heard with our own voices as we choose to articulate our values and intentions.

Our diversity is our richness; NOW members' creativity and commitment are our greatest resources and a source of daily inspiration to me. Such seeking of funds as we do to support our revolution and the revolutionaries accommodates our fund-raising to our politics, never vice versa. It's a matter of individual and organizational integrity.

As a further matter of integrity, feminism includes the freedom and power to love ourselves *and* each other as women, as men and as women and men loving each other as persons and embracing such children as we choose to have or have had in that love. No particular sexuality preference, if any, is either a requirement of or a barrier to feminism in NOW. That orientation, in my view, is the sine qua non for getting on with the business of educating and being educated by our children vis à vis the full potential of human sexuality. We do not equate normal with natural and in neither do we see bases for praise or censure. Our sexuality is; that is its own validity and though often vital is not the totality of our identity. I would propose that philosophy as a societal imperative to help hang up our sex hang-ups. Though we've resolved this in NOW, we have yet to exhibit the courage of our convictions. This Conference must move beyond resolution to action programs for NOW and society.

What we are about is love in its deepest, most abiding sense. If we did not care, NOW would not be.

It is about daring to care that I want to share some thoughts. In the process, I trust you will note a fundamental belief that every person, at some time, if not always, wants to be humane and courageous in our human interrelationships. It has been said that where there's the will, there's the way; at least equally true must be the maxim that where there is the way, there is the will. Our institutions of religion, family, law, education, health, economics, politics and child rearing have not provided the way, thus superhuman transcending will has been necessary to be courageous and humane. Most of us are not superhuman. Thus, we must create human institutions responsive to our needs; we are less daughters, and sons, of the American revolution than we are designers of the American revolution of feminism which is spreading throughout the world.

In daring to care, we must care *enough* to dare to know poverty in gut-level, existential terms and/or feelings else we will never reach or be reached by our poor sisters or brothers and *all* women are somehow poor in a male-dominated society as is society itself. We must dare to know that economic poverty means *if* to eat as much as what to eat, it means *if* anything to wear as much as what to wear; it means *if* adequate housing and schooling not the luxury of where to live or attend school. It means knowing the ghetto of one's home *and* the ghettos of our minds. It means also knowing the damning luxury of ennui of some affluent women who dilettante at still acceptable band aid volunteerism instead of radical feminism, e.g. to change the conditions their auxiliary status perpetuates.

Recommending the professionalization of volunteerism in Nixon's centers for voluntary action and most other establishment volunteerism without a contract to pay the ostensible "beneficiaries," potentially those most able to lead and needy of change, makes healthy redirection of effort more apparent than real. Co-optation by the existing system comes in many guises. We would do well to study and be wary of some of the current fashions in volunteerism that acknowledge the symptoms of subservience (since NOW adopted its position on change-directed volunteerism in preference to status quo efforts) but some of these current fashions still assure that the unhealthy donor-donee power relationships will be solidified.

Just as the poor, the majority of whom are women of all races and ages and our dependent children, must have whatever is necessary to survive and thrive as a basic right so must these poor know that even, if not especially, our affluent sisters and brothers must become psychologically if not economically liberated from materialism for humanism to begin. We all have so much to learn from each other.

First, we must all survive and to do that, we must get the affluent off public welfare by virtue of vested lobbying and unequal access to public funds and private profits often in obscene amounts. The real empowerment of women augurs more for the elimination of poverty than any so-called welfare reform advanced so far by any political system in any country. All we are saying is: give feminism a chance.

Johnnie Tillmon of the National Welfare Rights Organization is correct; every woman not economically independent or confident of and prepared for her capacity to be so may be just one man away from "welfare." Which brings me to the "housewife" syndrome though I do accept that *anyone* can marry a house. Ponder the term "househusband." No wonder so many women are so alienated and dropped out from society and say in shy self-deprecation: "I'm *just* a housewife" though their and much of our labor and love have powered and emotionally supported men and children and such economic—political—social—educational—religious institutions of society as we have. There is the homemaker role for men or women and its devaluation is not created by feminists but by such phenomena as the U.S. Labor Department's Dictionary of Occupational Titles that still gives the homemaker the lowest classification of 23,000 + titles and insensitively describes it as of "no significant function except the serving function." I am delighted that NOW feminists from Wisconsin are addressing that significant and related problems.

We must reach out more to our sisters who currently accept the term "housewife" and offer alternatives of personhood to things like: HOW (The Happiness of Womanhood), MOM (Men Our Masters), Pussycats (a pet is not a person), and Fascinating Womanhood to make being a person who is a woman truly dynamic. The less respect one receives as a person, the more one values the superficial "respect" accorded as a woman. Dana Densmore has correctly called chivalry "The Iron Fist in the Velvet Glove."

If the life career of support of a fragile male ego is innate and healthy, why train so assiduously for what is natural and why do women of many traditional marriages have such a disproportionate rate of mental illness especially depression? Wait'll Barbie Doll, their plastic model, becomes a feminist! These, our potential allies and surely our sisters already affected enough by feminism to speak out publicly and assertively (so unfeminine) about *something* for the first time in their lives, will eventually experience raised consciousness and you know what that means. Scratch the surface of any woman—and somewhere there's a feminist.

What of the men in NOW or who could be? I'm tempted to say: "Bless their ever-loving hearts!" But that would be matronizing and I no way exclude men from the need and potential of human liberation from sexism. Feminism is more difficult for most men to live, if not to think about. Shall we have commissions on the status and roles of men or commissions on sex role policy as has been suggested? Shall we examine if men qua men are fit for leadership, at least those men victims of the masculine mystique (mistake)? Can those people conditioned to violence as the final assertion of "manhood" (currently synonymous with nationhood) be permitted to exercise power?

Is aggressiveness against people a consequence of incompatibility of one's transcending human mystique with the constraints of the stereotyped "masculine" and the consequent accommodating "feminine?" I think so. Shall we give academy awards for performances of women and men living lives of private and/or public desperation to adjust to expectations often foreign to their individuality and then retire them from their acts and habilitate them for personhood?

Most men have not had the potentially humanizing experience of child care, the gut-level issue of feminism and of society, in my view. Why not see that *every* boy who wants one has a doll (not G.I. Joe) and be supported as he plays with it in anticipatory socialization for his parent role, *if* he *and* a woman so choose. We *can* care enough about children to assure them the right to be wanted, the right to paternal and/or maternal care and the right to supplemental child care to broaden theirs and their parents' horizons and to provide our children adult models of caring, daring, competent, sensitive adults cured of masculinity and feminity and committed to humanity. That might really strengthen such families as we choose.

On the subject of the family, is the white patriarchal model of family itself or nation state viable? Should it be? The black family has inaccurately been called matriarchal. Matriarchy denotes power but women and power have been virtually mutually exclusive. Minority women who finesse/transcend racism and sexism are superb individual role models for us all. However, their institutionalized exclusion from power is no less than white women's. For Moynahan in his infamous study "The Negro Family: the Case for National Action" to consider matriarchy pathological is the epitomy of misogyny. It is the white patriarchy of the Moynahans and their boss that is the manifest pathology of our time and all time as I suspect Indira Ghandi will have the 'guts' to inform "our" Ambassador of racism and sexism when and if he indeed goes to India.

We've had affirmative action programs for white men for centuries; we just haven't called them that. It's time we get together as women of all races and minority men and educate ourselves and each other on the interrelationships of racism and sexism and then educate the rest of society: white men that *they* are the minority. Some minority women may be understandably attracted to the physical comforts of the "kept woman" but my black and brown sisters and brothers can no more afford the "feminine mystique" life style than can I. We all need less of the feminine mystique and more of a joint feminist-humanist manifesto (or should we call it womanifesto—that includes man)?

We will come together as we of NOW have in creating and giving leadership and womanpower to the National Women's Political Caucus and its counterparts all over the U.S. to acknowledge that a white male club is not a democracy. We are coming together as women of all races and minority men to rank down General Mills for its sexism and racism. NOW and other human rights groups, by direct action and pressure on the Equal Employment Opportunity Commission (EEOC) and the Office of Federal Contract Compliance (OFCC), created the conditions and compliance of A.T.&T., that's "Pa" Bell (not "Ma" Bell), with (civil rights) law and (executive) order. Even as "Pa" Bell still owes women employees of all races at A.T.&T. a remaining $3,962,000,000 for illegal economic disadvantages, still the $38,000,000 settlement is a landmark for other industries to beware. Already "Pa" Bell is bragging about some behavioral changes that they were forced to institute. Who says we can't legislate morality; we've been doing it for centuries *when* we have the laws *and* the enforcement.

We have begun, often in coalitions with other civil rightists, to rid the airwaves of the unhealthy pollution of sexism and racism, both anti-human. We aren't sure yet if the Federal Communications Commission, F.C.C., is part of the solution or part of the problem, but we are assuming that they are educable at least more than their bosses who are introducing legislation that would make broadcasters even less accountable to the public and make access to the public forum more difficult for the excluded peoples, most of whom are women.

We must gain access to the public forum (preferably without interruption for thousands of years) for many of the significant questions have yet to be asked and the dramatic actions have yet to be taken to create the institutional, behavioral changes to which we are committed. Following are only a few of the questions:

Are men smart and humane enough to manage a home and loving child care or can they too be educated for these important roles.

Are people unbalanced with the masculine mystique qualified for responsible leadership?

If medicine were sanctioned for administration to people who are aggressive (not just to achieve goals) but against people as has been suggested, who would be the candidates? Without sanctioning such, even *that* would be more humane than psychosurgery that uses women and others powerless as subjects and considers women's adjustment to the "feminine mystique" as success.

If women are "natural" Secretaries (and typing is not a secondary sex characteristic of all females), why not Secretary of Labor, of Defense, of Health, Education and Welfare, Transportation, Commerce, Housing and Urban Development, Interior and Agriculture?

If the best communication is indeed "telewoman," why not a woman for Postmaster or Postperson or Postone General?

If women "intuitively" sense and value the good of the whole—family or community and the justice of this, then are not women the "naturals" for Attorney Generals and Supreme Court Justices? While the recent U.S. Supreme Court decisions vis à vis abortion may represent *something* of our "emancipation proclamation," can we continue to depend on the suffrance and largesse of men only for this and related overdue decisions?

If black defendants have a right to determine if jurors and/or judges are racists (and I support this approach) must not women of all races demand non-sexist judges and juries and police of both sexes?

If power corrupts and absolute power corrupts absolutely, is not the corollary true i.e. that weakness tends to corrupt and impotence corrupts absolutely?

If any religion is to be fully human and thus more humane, should we not send sympathy letters (as I have) to the Pope and his counterparts for their myopia in failing to yet realize that the rebirth of feminism means *"She Is Risen?"*

If education is to fully educate the full human family, must we not insist that feminism be a bonafide occupational qualification for educators whether in our schools, our homes, our art or our literature?

If, and it's a big if, contests for models in America are healthy, how about a *Ms.* America program with feminist criteria for the ideal; if it's what's up front that counts, why not advance whole women not just our breasts? Can we not recognize that ageism as it currently dehumanizes especially women denies us all of wise, brave, mature models of courage and caring? Is it too immodest of me to observe the relevant facts and the current president of NOW is over 40, "overweight" (actually a liberated body), but not "over the hill?"

If veteran's preference is fair to aid those endangered or disadvantaged by national demands, are not women also disadvantaged by institutional sexism, minorities by racism, the poor by classism and all women endangered by childbirth and rape? Do we not need additional concepts of the veteran and benefits accordingly?

Can we wage war like physical atomic giants and consider peace like intellectual midgets equating a partial cease-fire with peace when a fundamental cause of war is the ultimate expression of violence from the masculine mystique and the adoring feminine mystique that sustains it? Must we not develop the transcending human mystique not as the nirvana but as a search for wholeness of persons and society?

Must not we expect the "think tankers" like at the Center for the Study of Democratic Institutions to see that undemographic institutions are undemocratic and futurists iike of The World Future Society to begin to transcend current cultural biases to project a feminist-humanist world? Some of us from NOW are working in a Women's Coalition for the Third Century to do just that.

Should we, as women, continue to obey laws made mostly, if not entirely, by men, enforced by men, judged by men? Is this or should is not be unconstitutional? Is there not taxation without representation involved here and is that not tyranny? Should we not test this in the courts and in our lives? Our founding fathers in The Declaration of Independence (where *were* the mothers?) wrote that when government does not represent people, those people have not only the right, but the *duty*, to throw off such government. This government has never, nor does it yet, represent women as people let alone include us beyond tokenism. Shall we in NOW gather our forces and obey that dictum in the Declaration of Independence?

If a President impounds funds appropriated by Congress, gives public support to church teaching and promises public aid to sectarian schools does he not violate the separation of powers and separation of church and state he is sworn to uphold? When he vetoes health, education, child care and/or welfare legislation and/or funds as politically unsuitable or inflationary (while defense money is not called inflationary) is this not a corrupt use of veto power?

Can the foreign policy of this or any other nation continue to be a foreign affair to most women as is what it means to live life as a woman a foreign affair to most policy makers and yet expect to develop fully human

388

let alone humane policy from roughly (literally) one half the population? Can population policy alone address itself to population choice and quality (while we still have the chance) with the women majority of the population only tokenly represented, if that?

Dear God, Heavenly Mother, Parent or Spirit, what *do* some men want? To possess women is not to incorporate the so-called "feminine" part of their nature they may need and covet (often covertly and deviously). Or is god an *idea* of the divine we can become ourselves by transcending the feminine only or masculine only to incorporate the best of each traits in ourselves to develop humane and courageous personhood and society?

To ask these and more questions and to create the behavioral actions they imply, let's remember the words of our foremother Susan B. Anthony, whose birth and courage we honor with the date and theme of our Conference: "Cautious, careful people always casting about to preserve their reputation or social standards never can bring about a reform (let alone a revolution—W.S.H.). Those who are really in earnest must be willing to be anything or nothing in the world's estimation and publicly and privately, in season and out, avow their sympathies with despised ideas and their advocates and bear the consequences."

The Equal Rights Amendment Blood Money program is one sample of dramatic action to behaviorally communicate that we will not only figuratively but literally give our blood to assure that women are included in the basic legal domument of this alleged democracy.

If broadcasters and the Federal Communications Commission do not develop adequate feminist consciousness and effective affirmative action (as they have not yet) by the important license challenge and denial method, then perhaps we must educate by station and network takeover actions to assure them we are in earnest.

Heaven and feminists know the corporate world needs the authentic voice and talents of women beyond tokenism not only for fair employment but to challenge some products and services they produce, the dehumanization of much work/job design, and sexploitative advertising with which they still bombard us. If our writing, speeches, protest by selective buying/non-buying continue to be substantively non-persuasive, some continuous sit-ins, teach-ins, consult-ins are obviously necessary.

Creative, dramatic actions, it appears, may continue to be necessary vis à vis toys, films, male-only athletic programs with public funds, otherwise uneducable school boards and departments of education, public education textbook publishers, guidance counselors, airlines, unions, national and local committees of political parties, federal cabinet level practices, and sexist social agencies. Women tithing for women and women leading an exodus from misogynous churches are great educators as is refusing to donate for United Funds united only in giving an average of twice as much to male programs (like Scouts and the Y) as to female programs.

When did Congress begin to take us seriously on the Equal Rights

Amendment? When about 20 of us from Pennsylvania NOW interrupted a Senate Subcommittee on constitutional amendments February 17, 1970! When did the Office of Federal Contract Compliance of the U.S. Labor Department begin to implement Executive Order 11375 and issue Order #4 with goals and timetables to be applied to women? When we repeatedly visited, sat in the Labor Secretary's office and got on or took over their closed circuit television program in 14 cities in July, 1970! When did *New York Times* and others desegregate want ads? When NOW picketed! When did Southern Bell obey a court order to give sister Lorena Weeks her job? When NOW demonstrated all over the country! We could share thousands of other examples that when polite letters, proffered meetings, documented evidence, detailed offensiveness to our personhood do not penetrate and/or produce significant behavioral change, then it is irresponsible of us not to change our behavior and tactics.

For a manual for wave-makers, I recommend to your attention, the warmly humane and full of good humor book by NOW Board member Tish Sommers: "The Not-So-Helpless Female." Here is a practical how-to that recognizes that the processes of change are central to the quality of change itself.

In urging the courage of our convictions, I truly regret the necessity. It seems part of my personal preference to quietly persuade, softly negotiate change, cite the justice of our case. Yet, we haven't always the "luxury" of relative passivity or even limited activity. Our militancy and programs to get out into what has been "man's world" must be seen as a rejection of nearly total passivity through self-denial and vicarious half-lives. The so-called "man's world" is our world and it's in trouble. We're hell-bent or heaven-bent (depending on one's view) to join it, determine the the action and redirect it, share it, lead it—differently we hope but participate we *will*.

Even as we confront institutions, practices, and people, we must develop methods of non-adversarial human interrelationships. Even as we discuss NOW and its structure, leadership and its potential and limitations, *whatever* the structure is only justified if it facilitates the function of achieving our common goals. We must continue to experiment with new values and styles of leadership only now in embryonic stages of creation. We have yet to adequately facilitate the local and national participation and leadership in NOW independent of personal economic resource. Leaderlessness, absence of structure, and impoverishment from inadequate dues imposes a tyranny that is even less healthy. Our challenge is to develop the values, resources, and caring, sharing participation and leadership opportunities that promotes corporate responsibility and reparations from institutions that "rip us off" in grievous sex-ploitation to positively fund our healthy activities.

The Now finance committee and NOW's tax-deductible (for donors)

390

Legal Defense and Education Fund as well as our public advertising ad campaign have begun that vital process. We are learning and teaching each other and society how to share the wealth (women never have and we don't want to control it exclusively) and educate society to the *wealth* of value in what NOW feminism is *really* all about and can mean for women, men and all of our children.

To challenge and change sexist institutions to become feminist-humanist institutions, it is unrealistic to think that vital local action alone and/or *only* "doing our own thing" negates the imperative for strong national organization. The resistance to change is not only organized, it is universally institutionalized. Healthy local, state and national organization is, of course, not mutually exclusive, it is mutually supportive and vital. And the world is our stage as evidenced by our June International Feminist Planning Conference. We have or could have the whole world in our hands and our heads and our hearts.

No other movement however just, overdue, needful of national commitment examines as does feminism the most basic of human power interrelationships, that between woman and man. Only those women and men free enough from stereotyped notions of "feminity" and "masculinity" to be secure about our common humanity are as yet liberated enough to move with the level of self-confidence to create a gynandrous society and world. For that, the power of love must exceed the love of power. Love is the only "game" in which two or more can play and everyone wins.

For feminism to be viable (and it is), then we must empower girls themselves and as women; we must prepare boys to find it livable as men and succeeding generations of children to thrive in its warmth, choices, and vitality. Even with the end of feigned or real innocence for women is the end of the age of guilty privilege of male "birthrights" denied to women and girls. The masks are off: this drama is for *real*.

As your president these past 18 months, I am one of thousands of us privileged to experience the joy, the risks, the gratifications, bone weariness, tragedies and triumphs of activist feminism. There are women and men and children in our lives and whose lives we touch who may never know how profoundly we care about ourselves and them and the quality of the world we must share and make livable for all. We are self-helpers with the courage of our commitment.

Let us, of course, commit ourselves to the ratification of the Equal Rights Amendment by August 26 of this year (if humanly possible). On that date let us celebrate not only the vote won by our brave foremothers and still living sisters but a truly democratic constitution. Further, if we all believe, as I do, that feminism is a bona fide occupational qualification for every human endeavor, then I ask that by August 26, 1973 we develop a feminist womanifesto applicable to every organization, institution, agency, social unit, individual of our society. On that date, whatever else we demonstrate, let us not fear to demonstrate by our presentation of womanifestos everywhere that feminism has universal potential and imperatives.

To date, we have taught men to be brave and women to care. NOW, men must become brave enough to care about the equality and thus the quality of our common life. NOW, women must care enough to bravely assert our talents and intentions not only to rock the cradle but rock the boats and share equally in guiding the ship of state of all our institutions.

Edwin Markham once wrote: "You drew a circle that shut me out; Rebel, heretic, a thing to flout. But love and I had the wit to win. We drew a circle that took you in." Just as the Reverend Dr. Martin Luther King, Jr. insisted that whites must be included in our other related behavioral revolution, so will we include men, even Richard Nixon, whom I (for the third time in a January 17 letter) offered the opportunity to meet with us. We do not want partnership in the world that is but offer the Nixons of the world partnership in what we are creating.

The (other) President has rejected our offer (at least for the suggested dates). In reality, Nixon and his other more or less powerful counterparts are hereby publicly challenged: 'Ask not what you can do for feminism (that's obvious: raise your consciousness and commitment of resources) but ask what feminism can do for you and for this heretofore "man's" world! Men are demonstrably unable, without the equal partnership of women at every level of public life, to fully conceptualize let alone solve our deepest problems that have their roots in sexism, racism, poverty and organized violence. Indeed, the very absence of women may *be the problem* itself. Even more than the brotherhood of all men may we need the sisterhood of all women and together to create the integrated humane family.

That would indeed be a behavioral Revolution: Tomorrow *is* NOW. Let's get on with it today. *And* in the process, please know you have my hands, my head, my heart, and my love.

I HAVE A DREAM

Reverend Martin Luther King, Jr.*

Five score years ago, a great American, in whose symbolic shadow we stand, signed the Emancipation Proclamation. This momentous decree came as a great beacon light of hope to millions of Negro slaves who had

* Address at the Lincoln Monument, Washington, D.C., August 28, 1963. From *Representative American Speeches 1963–1964*, Lester Thonssen, ed. (H. H. Wilson Company: New York, 1964), pp. 44–48. Reprinted by permission of Joan Daves. Copyright © 1963 by Martin Luther King, Jr.

been seared in the flames of withering injustice. It came as joyous daybreak to end the long night of captivity.

But one hundred years later, we must face the tragic fact that the Negro is still not free. One hundred years later, the life of the Negro is still sadly crippled by the manacles of segregation and the chains of discrimination. One hundred years later, the Negro lives on a lonely island of poverty in the midst of a vast ocean of material prosperity. One hundred years later, the Negro is still languished in the corners of American society and finds himself an exile in his own land. So we have come here today to dramatize an appalling condition.

In a sense we have come to our nation's Capital to cash a check. When the architects of our republic wrote the magnificent words of the Constitution and the Declaration of Independence, they were signing a promissory note to which every American was to fall heir. This note was a promise that all men would be guaranteed the unalienable rights of life, liberty, and the pursuit of happiness.

It is obvious today that America has defaulted on this promissory note insofar as her citizens of color are concerned. Instead of honoring this sacred obligation, America has given the Negro people a bad check; a check which has come back marked "insufficient funds." But we refuse to believe that the bank of justice is bankrupt. We refuse to believe that there are insufficient funds in the great vaults of opportunity of this nation. So we have come to cash this check—a check that will give us upon demand the riches of freedom and the security of justice. We have also come to this hallowed spot to remind America of the fierce urgency of *now*. This is no time to engage in the luxury of cooling off or to take the tranquilizing drug of gradualism. *Now* is the time to make real the promises of Democracy. *Now* is the time to rise from the dark and desolate valley of segregation to the sunlit path of racial justice. *Now* is the time to open the doors of opportunity to all of God's children. *Now* is the time to lift our nation from the quicksands of racial injustice to the solid rock of brotherhood.

It would be fatal for the nation to overlook the urgency of the moment and to underestimate the determination of the Negro. This sweltering summer of the Negro's legitimate discontent will not pass until there is an invigorating autumn of freedom and equality. 1963 is not an end, but a beginning. Those who hope that the Negro needed to blow off steam and will now be content will have a rude awakening if the nation returns to business as usual. There will be neither rest nor tranquility in America until the Negro is granted his citizenship rights. The whirlwinds of revolt will continue to shake the foundations of our nation until the bright day of justice emerges.

But there is something that I must say to my people who stand on the warm threshold which leads into the palace of justice. In the processes of gaining our rightful place we must not be guilty of wrongful deeds. Let us not seek to satisfy our thirst for freedom by drinking from the cup of bitterness and hatred. We must forever conduct our struggle on the high plane of dignity and discipline. We must not allow our creative protest to degenerate into physical violence. Again and again we must rise to the majestic heights of meeting physical force with soul force. The marvelous new militancy which has engulfed the Negro community must not lead us to a distrust of all white people, for many of our white brothers, as evidenced by their presence here today, have come to realize that their destiny is tied up with our destiny and their freedom is inextricably bound to our freedom. We cannot walk alone.

And as we walk, we must make the pledge that we shall march ahead. We cannot turn back. There are those who are asking the devotees of civil rights, "When will you be satisfied?" We can never be satisfied as long as the Negro is the victim of the unspeakable horrors of police brutality. We can never be satisfied as long as our bodies, heavy with the fatigue of travel, cannot gain lodging in the motels of the highways and the hotels of the cities. We cannot be satisfied as long as the Negro's basic mobility is from a smaller ghetto to a larger one. We can never be satisfied as long as a Negro in Mississippi cannot vote and a Negro in New York believes he has nothing for which to vote. No, no, we are not satisfied, and we will not be satisfied until justice rolls down like waters and righteousness like a mighty stream.

I am not unmindful that some of you have come here out of great trials and tribulations. Some of you have come fresh from narrow jail cells. Some of you have come from areas where your quest for freedom left you battered by the storms of persecution and staggered by the winds of police brutality. You have been the veterans of creative suffering. Continue to work with the faith that unearned suffering is redemptive.

Go back to Mississippi, go back to Alabama, go back to South Carolina, go back to Georgia, go back to Louisiana, go back to the slums and ghettos of our nothern cities, knowing that somehow this situation can and will be changed. Let us not wallow in the valley of despair.

I say to you today, my friends, that in spite of the difficulties and frsutrations of the moment I still have a dream. It is a dream deeply rooted in the American dream.

I have a dream that one day this nation will rise up and live out the true meaning of its creed: "We hold these truths to be self-evident; that all men are created equal."

I have a dream that one day on the red hills of Georgia the sons of former slaves and the sons of former slaveowners will be able to sit down together at the table of brotherhood.

I have a dream that one day even the state of Mississippi, a desert state sweltering with the heat of injustice and oppression, will be transformed into an oasis of freedom and justice.

I have a dream that my four little children will one day live in a nation where they will not be judged by the color of their skin but by the content of their character.

I have a dream today.

I have a dream that one day the state of Alabama, whose governor's lips are presently dripping with the words of interposition and nullification, will be transformed into a siutation where little blacks boys aand black girls will be able to join hands with little white boys and white girls and walk together as sisters and brothers.

I have a dream today.

I have a dream that one day every valley shall be exalted, every hill and mountain shall be made low, the rough places will be made plains, and the crooked places will be made straight, and the glory of the Lord shall be revealed, and all flesh shall see it together.

This is our hope. This is the faith with which I return to the South. With this faith we will be able to hew out of the mountain of despair a stone of hope. With this faith we will be able to transform the jangling discords of our nation into a beautiful symphony of brotherhood. With this faith we will be able to work together, to pray together, to struggle together, to go to jail together, to stand up for freedom together, knowing that we will be free one day.

This will be the day when all of God's children will be able to sing with new meaning

> My country, 'tis of thee,
> Sweet land of liberty,
>   Of thee I sing:
> Land where my fathers died,
> Land of the pilgrims' pride,
> From every mountain-side
>   Let freedom ring.

And if America is to be a great nation this must become true. So let freedom ring from the prodigious hilltops of New Hampshire. Let freedom ring from the mighty mountains of New York. Let freedom ring from the heightening Alleghenies of Pennsylvania!

Let freedom ring from the snowcapped Rockies of Colorado!

Let freedom ring from the curvacious peaks of California!

But not only that; let freedom ring from Stone Mountain of Georgia!

Let freedom ring from Lookout Mountain of Tennessee!

Let freedom ring from every hill and molehill of Mississippi. From every mountainside, let freedom ring.

When we let freedom ring, when we let it ring from every village and every hamlet, from every state and every city, we will be able to speed up that day when all of God's children, black men and white men, Jews and Gentiles, Protestants and Catholics, will be able to join hands and sing in the words of the old Negro spiritual, "Free at last! free at last! thank God almighty, we are free at last!"

MESSAGE TO CONGRESS

President Gerald R. Ford*

Mr. Speaker, Mr. President, distinguished guests and my very dear friends:

My fellow Americans, we have a lot of work to do.

My former colleagues, you and I have a lot of work to do.

Let's get on with it.

Needless to say, I am deeply grateful for the wonderfully warm welcome. I can never express my gratitude adequately.

I am not here to make an inaugural address. The Nation needs action, not words.

Nor will this be a formal report on the State of the Union. God willing, I will have a least three more chances to do that.

It's good to be back in the People's House.

But this cannot be a real homecoming. Under the Constitution, I now belong to the Executive branch. The Supreme Court has even ruled that I am the Executive branch, head, heart, and hand.

With due respect to the learned Justices—and I greatly respect the Judiciary—part of my heart will always be here on Capitol Hill. I know well the co-equal role of the Congress in our Constitutional process. I love the House of Representatives. I revere the traditions of the Senate despite my too-short internship in that great body. As President, within the limits of basic principles, my motto toward the Congress is communication, conciliation, compromise and cooperation.

This Congress, unless it has changed, I am confident, will be my working partner as well as my most constructive critic. I am not asking for conformity. I am dedicated to the two-party system, and you know which party I belong to.

I do not want a honeymoon with you. I want a good marriage.

I want progress and I want problem solving which requires my best efforts, and also your best efforts.

I have no need to learn how Congress speaks for the people.

As President, I intend to listen; but I also intend to listen to the people themselves—all the people—as I promised last Friday. I want to be sure that we are all tuned into the real voice of America.

* Address to a joint session of the Senate and the House. Delivered in the House chamber three days after President Ford's inauguration. *Congressional Record*, Aug. 12, 1974, pp. H8160-8162.

My Administration starts off by seeking unity in diversity. My office door has always been open, and that is how it is going to be at the White House. Yes, Congressmen will be welcomed—if you don't overdo it.

The first seven words of the Constitution and the most important are these: "We the People of the United States." We, the people, ordained and established the Constitution and reserved to themselves all powers not granted to Federal and State governments. I respect and will always be conscious of that fundamental rule of freedom.

Only eight months ago, when I last stood here, I told you I was a Ford, not a Lincoln. Tonight I say I am still a Ford, but I am not a Model T.

I do have some old-fashioned ideas, however. I believe in the very basic decency and fairness of America. I believe in the integrity and patriotism of the Congress. And while I am aware of the House rule that no one ever speaks to the galleries, I believe in the First Amendment and the absolute necessity of a free press.

But I also believe that over two centuries since the First Continental Congress was convened, the direction of our nation's movement has been forward. I am here to confess that in my first campaign for President— of my senior class in South High School in Grand Rapids, Michigan—I headed the Progressive Party ticket, and lost. Maybe that is why I became a Republican.

Now I ask you to join with me in getting this country revved up and moving.

My instinctive judgment is that the State of the Union is excellent. But the state of our economy is not so good.

Everywhere I have been as Vice President, some 118,000 miles in 40 States and some 55 press conferences, the unanimous concern for Americans is inflation. For once all the polls seem to agree. They also suggest that the people blame government far more than either management or labor for the high cost of everything they have to buy.

You who come from 50 States, three territories and the District of Columbia know this better than I do. That is why you have created, since I left here, your new Budget Reform Committee. I welcome it and I will work with its Members to bring the Federal budget into balance in fiscal year 1976.

The fact is that for the past 25 years that I had the honor of serving with this body the Federal budget has been balanced in only six.

Mr. Speaker, I am a little late getting around to it, but confession is good for the soul. I have sometimes voted to spend more taxpayer's money for worthy projects in Grand Rapids, Michigan, while I vigorously opposed wasteful spending boondoggles in Oklahoma.

Be that as it may, Mr. Speaker, you and I have always stood together against unwarranted cuts in national defense. This is no time to change that nonpartisan policy.

Just as escalating Federal spending has been a prime cause of higher prices over many years, it may take some time to stop inflation, but we must begin right now. For a start, before your Labor Day recess Congress should reactivate the Cost of Living Council through passage of a clean bill, without reimposing controls, that will let us monitor wages and prices to expose abuses. Whether we like it or not, the American wage-earner and the American housewife are a lot better economists than most economists care to admit. They know that a government big enough to give you everything you want is a government big enough to take from you everything you have.

If we want to restore confidence in ourselves as working politicians, the first thing we all have to do is to learn to say no.

The first specific request of the Ford administration is not to Congress, but to the voters in the upcoming November elections. It is this, very simply: Support your candidates, Congressmen and Senators, Democrats or Republicans, conservatives or liberals, who consistently vote for tough decisions to cut the cost of government, restrain Federal spending and bring inflation under control.

I applaud the initiative Congress has already taken. The only fault I find with the Joint Economic Committee study on inflation authorized last week is that we need its expert findings in six weeks instead of six months.

A month ago the distinguished Majority Leader of the United States Senate asked the White House to convene an economic conference of Members of Congress, the President's economic consultants and some of the best economic brains from labor, industry and agriculture.

Later this was perfected by resolution to assemble a domestic summit meeting to devise a bipartisan action for stability and growth in the American economy.

Neither I nor my staff have much time right now for letter writing, so I will respond: I accept the suggestion and I will personally preside.

Furthermore, I propose that this summit meeting be held at an early date in full view of the American public. They are as anxious as we are to get the right answers. My first priority is to work with you to bring inflation under control. Inflation is domestic enemy No. 1. To restore economic confidence , the Government in Washington must provide some leadership. It does no good to blame the public for spending too much when the Government is spending too much.

I began to put my Administration's own economic house in order, starting last Friday.

I instructed my Cabinet officers and counselors and my White House staff to make fiscal restraint their first order of business and to save every dollar that the safety and genuine welfare of our great nation will permit.

Some economic activities will be effected more by monetary and fiscal restraints than other activities. Good government clearly requires that we tend to the economic problems facing our country in a spirit of equity to all of our citizens in all segments of our society.

Tonight, obviously, is no time to threaten you with vetoes. But I do have the last recourse. And I am a veteran of many a veto fight right here in this great chamber.

Can't we do a better job by reasonable compromise? I hope we can.

Minutes after I took the Presidential oath, the joint leadership of Congress told me at the White House they would go more than half way to meet me. This was confirmed in your unanimous concurrent resolution of cooperation, for which I go more than half way to meet the Congress, maybe we can find a much larger area of national agreement.

I bring no legislative shopping list here this evening. I will deal with specifics in future messages and talks with you. But here are a few examples of how seriously I feel about what we must do together

Last week the Congress passed the Elementary and Secondary Education bill, and I found it on my desk. Any reservation I might have about some of its provisions—and I do have—fade in comparison to the urgent needs of America for quality education. I will sign it in a few days.

I must be frank. In implementing its provisions, I will oppose excessive funding during this inflationary crisis. As Vice President, I studied various proposals for better health care financing.

I saw them coming closer together, and urged my friends in the Congress and in the Administration to sit down and sweat out a sound compromise. The Comprehensive Health Insurance Plan goes a long way towards providing early relief to people who are sick. Why don't we write—and I ask this with the greatest spirit of cooperation—why don't we write a good health bill on the statute books in 1974 before this Congress adjourns?

The economy of our country is critically dependent on how we interact with the economies of other countries. It is little comfort that our inflation is only a part of a world-wide problem, or that American families need less of their pay checks for groceries than most of our foreign friends.

As one of the building blocks of peace we have taken the lead in working toward a more open and a more equitable world economic system. A new round of international trade negotiations started last September among 105 nations in Tokyo. The others are waiting for the United States Congress to grant the necessary authority to the Executive Branch to proceed. With modiflcations, the Trade Reform bill passed by the House last year would do a good job.

I understand good progress has been made in the Senate Committee on Finance. But I am optimistic, as always, that the Senate will pass an acceptable bill quickly as a key part of our joint prosperity campaign.

I am determined to expedite other international economic plans. We will be working together with other nations to find better ways to prevent shortages of food and fuel. We must not let last winter's energy crisis happen again. I will push Project Independence for our own good and the good of others. In that too I will need your help.

Successful foreign policy is an extension of the hopes of the whole American people for a world of peace and orderly reform, and orderly freedom. So I would say a few words to our distinguished guests from the governments of other nations where, as at home, it is my determination to deal openly with allies and adversaries.

Over the past 5½ years in Congress and as Vice President, I have fully supported the outstanding foreign policy of President Nixon. This policy I intend to continue.

Throughout my public service starting with wartime naval duty under the command of President Franklin D. Roosevelt, I have upheld all our Presidents when they spoke for my country to the world. I believe the Constitution commands this.

I know that in this crucial area of international policy I can count on your firm support.

Now let there be no doubt, or any misunderstanding anywhere, and I emphasize anywhere, there are no opportunities to exploit, should anyone so desire. There will be no change of course, no relaxation of vigilance, no abandonment of the helm of our ship of state as the watch changes.

We stand by our commitments and we will live up to our responsibilities, in our formal alliances, in our friendships, and in our improving relations with potential adversaries. On this Americans are united and strong. Under my term of leadership I hope we will become more united. I am certain America will remain strong.

A strong defense is the surest way to peace. Strength makes detente attainable, weakness invites war as my generation, my generation knows from our very bitter experiences. Just as America's will for peace is second to none, so will America's strength be second to none.

We cannot rely on the forbearance of others to protect this Nation. The power and diversity of the armed forces, active guard and reserve, the resolve of our fellow citizens, the flexibility in our command to navigate international waters that remain troubled are all essential to our security.

I shall continue to insist on civilian control of our superb military establishment. The Constitution plainly requires the President to be Commander in Chief and I will be.

Our job will not be easy. In promising continuity I cannot promise simplicity. The problems and challenges of the world remain complex and difficult. But we have set out on a path of reason, or fairness, and we will continue on it. As guide-posts on that path, I offer the following: To our allies of a generation in the Atlantic community and Japan, I pledge continuity in the loyal collaboration of our many mutual endeavors.

To our friends and allies in this hemisphere I pledge continuity in the deepening dialogue to define renewed relationships of equality and justice.

To our allies and friends in Asia I pledge a continuity in our support for their security, independence and economic development. In Indo-China we are determined to see the observance of the Paris agreement on Vietnam, and of cease-fire and negotiated settlement in Laos. We hope to see an early compromise settlement in Cambodia.

To the Soviet Union I pledge continuity in our commitment to the course of the past three years, to our two peoples, and to all mankind we owe a continued effort to live, where possible, to work together in peace, for in a thermonuclear age there can be no alternative to a positive and peaceful relationship between our nations.

To the People's Republic of China, whose legendary hospitality I enjoyed, I pledge continuity in our commitment to the principles of the Shanghai communique. The new relationship built on those principles has demonstrated that it serves serious and objective mutual interests, and has become an enduring feature of the world scene.

To the nations in the Middle East I pledge continuity in our vigorous efforts to advance the progress which has brought hopes of peace to that region after 25 years as a hotbed of war. We shall carry out our promise to promote continuing negotiations among all parties for a complete, just, and lasting settlement.

To all nations I pledge continuity in seeking a common global goal, a stable international structure of trade and finance which reflects the interdependence of all people.

To the entire international community, to the United Nations, to the world's non-aligned nations, and to all others, I pledge continuity in our dedication to the humane goals which throughout our history have been so much of America's contribution to mankind.

So long as the peoples of the world have confidence in our purposes and faith in our work the age-old vision of peace on earth will grow brighter.

I pledge myself unreservedly to that goal. I say to you in words that cannot be improved upon, let us never negotiate out of fear, but let us never fear to negotiate.

As Vice President, at the request of the President, I addressed myself to the individual rights of Americans in the area of privacy. There will be no illegal tappings, eavesdroppings, buggings or break-ins by my administration. There will be hot pursuit of tough laws to prevent illegal invasion of privacy in both government and private activities.

On the higher plane of public morality there is no need for me to preach tonight. We have thousands of far better preachers and millions of sacred scriptures to guide us on the path of personal right living and exemplary official conduct. If we can make effective and earlier use of moral and ethical wisdom of the centuries in today's complex society we will prevent more crime and more corruption than all the policemen and prosecutors and governments can ever deter. If I might say so, this is a job that must begin at home, not in Washington.

I once told you that I'm not a saint, and I hope never to see the day that I cannot admit having made a mistake.

So I will close with another confession. Frequently along the tortuous road of recent months from this Chamber to the President's House I have protested that I was my own man. Now I realize that I was wrong. I am your man, for it was your carefully weighed confirmation that changed my occupation. The truth is I am the people's man for you acted in their name, and I accepted and began my new and solemn trust with a promise to serve all the people and do the best that I can for America. When I say all the people I mean exactly that—to the limits of my strength and ability I will be the President of black, brown, red and white Americans, of old and young, of women's liberationists and male chauvinists, and all the rest of us in between, of poor and the rich, of native sons and new refugees, of those who work at lathes or at desks or in mines, or in the fields or of Christians, Jews, Moslems, Buddhists, and atheists if there really are any atheists after what we have all been through.

Fellow Americans, one final word. I want to be a good President. I need your help. We all need God's sure guidance. With it, nothing can stop the United States of America.

Thank you very much.

I. Topics
II. Organization
III. Humor
    A. Sources of humor
    B. Forms of humor
       1. Overstatement
       2. Understatement
       3. Irony
       4. Unexpected turns
       5. Play on words
       6. Burlesque
    C. Making humor effective
       1. Be objective.
       2. Show kindliness.
       3. Use good taste.
       4. Learn to laugh at yourself.
       5. Let the humor label itself.
       6. Stop when you're ahead.
IV. Heightening the interest
    A. Suspense
    B. Conflict
    C. Vividness
    D. Novelty and familiarity

Chapter 18

Speaking To Entertain

On occasion, your purpose might be to interest, divert, or amuse your audience. A fairly obvious example of such an occasion is the after-dinner speech. Someone once introduced an after-dinner speaker by asking the audience to divert its attention from a turkey stuffed with sage in order to hear a sage stuffed with turkey. It would be a brave man who dared approach that audience hoping for their serious consideration of a weighty topic. But what kind of topics are suitable for you when you want to entertain?

I. TOPICS

Look primarily to personal experience for the subject of a speech to entertain. Nearly everyone has had adventures, exciting experiences or just experiences that will make good speech subjects. You may have made trips to interesting parts of the country or to foreign countries. You may have had interesting jobs, met unusual people, developed unique hobbies, or done exciting things. Any of these activities is a potential subject for an interesting and entertaining speech.

To be entertaining, a speech need not be devoid of meaningful ideas. It can have a very real and useful point to it. For example, if you were to talk about the glories of growing up and described the dubious advantages of maturity—with its responsibilities, debts, taxes, and the like—you would surely make something of a point. Nonetheless, you could amuse and divert your audience by approaching the subject from a deliberately offbeat, eccentric point of view. What distinguishes a speech to entertain from one to inform or to persuade is the light touch with which you take up the subject.

Even if we were to suppose that you had never had any exciting or interesting experiences, you would still not lack an abundance of suitable topics. Being able to entertain others lies not so much in the excitement or amusement inherent in what you have to say as in the exciting or amusing way you look at things and make others see them. If you have never traveled, here or abroad, or fought a war, or had a hobby, you can still find entertaining subjects, provided that you have a sense of humor. Of course, if you have done nothing, seen nothing, felt nothing, never have been amused or excited, and have no sense of humor, we must admit you face something of a problem. But certainly you don't consider yourself an amoeba. As long as you are alive, you are in a world filled with situations and people—and these are the basis of entertainment. They are the subjects of speeches to entertain.

II. ORGANIZATION

A speech to entertain is not merely a collection of funny stories. It is a speech and, as such, must have at least a semblance of order. You devise a central idea and then proceed to "develop" it. Some of the audience's pleasure may come from the zany way the idea is developed, but you must give the appearance of starting from a logical base. Digressions need only seem to be appropriate in order to be perfectly acceptable. But be aware of your diversions. Then you can use them consciously as a source of humor.

A lawyer gave a speech that offers a good example of this point. He talked about the problems of forming the then-new American Football League. His starting point was that the initials of the group, AFL, had led to all kinds of confusions—including labor problems. He moved next to the fact that forming the League required the work of many lawyers. Having thus mentioned lawyers, he digressed purposely into a discussion of the evils of having too many lawyers around. His audience, knowing that he was a lawyer, laughed with him as he moved into the conclusion of his speech.

Good transitions are a useful device for imposing a sense of order on a speech to entertain. The temptation to say, "That reminds me of a story," is a strong one. Resist it. Look instead for transitions that move the speech from point to point, not from joke to joke. The stories and quips then fall into place with the force of properly used supporting material. If your transitions emphasize the gist and not the jests, the audience will see in your speech a plausible (though perhaps zany) coherence.

III. HUMOR

There has been strong implication in what we have said so far that much of the success in an entertaining speech springs from the ability to use humor well. It does, indeed. Therefore, we must say something about the use of humor.

Humor is as universal as language. It is found in the gentle teasing of a friend, in subtle quips understandable only to a few, in bitter satire that strikes at folly and vice. The things that cause amusement range widely from the most highly intellectual delicacies of wit to the broadest sort of slapstick, custard-pie comedy. In life's most serious moments, laughter intrudes to break tension. The grim jests of war are clear proof that individuals need release and frequently seek it in humor.

Just what it is that makes humor has often occupied the thoughts of psychologists, rhetoricians, philosophers, and philosophical comedians. Quintilian, who taught speech at Rome in the first century of the Christian era, said,*

I do not think that anybody can give an adequate explanation, though many have attempted to do so, of the cause of laughter, which is excited not merely by words or deeds, but sometimes by touch. . . . There are no specific exercises for humor nor professors to teach it.

* *Institutio Oratoriae*, VI, 3. Translated by H. Rackham. Loeb Classical Library.

A. Sources of Humor

Whatever other points may be at issue about the nature of humor, one must agree that it is exclusively a human characteristic. Only human beings among all living creatures laugh. They have even been defined as "animals that laugh." Upon no more than casual examination, it becomes evident that what seems to be laughter in animals is only a caricature of human amusement. Probably the simplest explanation for humanity's sole proprietorship over laughter lies in the fact that it requires intelligence somewhat above that of a chimpanzee, a horse, or a dog to understand the things that cause amusement.

It has also been said that the comical does not exist outside of what is strictly human.* To borrow examples from Bergson, landscapes may be dull, or beautiful; they are never laughable. Human beings laugh at animals only when the latter exhibit some human characteristic, attitude, or expression. A hat is "funny" not of itself but because of the human whimsy that gave it a shape out of the ordinary.

Bergson's observations lead him to two other conclusions that are of interest here. First, emotions tend to silence laughter. Disinterestedness, emotional detachment, seems to be a necessary condition for amusement. The comical appeals only to intelligence. Bergson points out, secondly, that laughter needs an echo. It is social; it occurs in a *group*. Regardless of how large it may grow, the circle of those who laugh is a closed one. Those not privy to a joke feel no desire to laugh.

There seem to be many different kinds of laughter, only one of which is the sort that arises out of amusement. J. C. Gregory has attempted to show that laughter of all kinds springs from one form or another of relief.† Among these is the laughter caused by tickling, said to be relief springing from the recognition that an attack on the sensitive areas of throat or ribs is not made by fangs but by friendly fingers. Again, there is the laugh of greeting, which arises from relief felt when a potential enemy is seen to be a friend. Laughs of contempt, superiority, and self-congratulation may arise out of the relief one feels at victory and an end to danger, or at escaping the misfortunes that befall another. Gregory rather pointedly denies Bergson's contention that emotion is absent from the reaction to what is comical. It need not be of great concern which of the two theories is correct. If emotion accom-

---

* For a more thorough discussion of ideas merely sketched in this paragraph and the next, see Henri Bergson, *Laughter* (New York: Macmillan Publishing Co., 1911).

† J. C. Gregory, *The Nature of Laughter* (New York: Harcourt, Brace, Jovanovich, 1924).

panies laughter, it is human emotion and it is clear that intelligence is needed to appreciate humor.

Despite the modesty with which students of humor approach an attempt to isolate the sources of humor and its constituents, there is some agreement as to what these are. Whether other elements may be present in comic situations, in amusing language, or in droll characters, *incongruity* and *surprise* seem to be sufficient to cause laughter. The humor springs from recognition of the incongruity or from the failure of an expected outcome to be realized.

It is not always possible to judge what will cause amusement in an individual. The great German philosopher Schopenhauer is said to have chuckled when he saw a tangent to a circle. The straight line of the tangent led him to expect it to meet another straight line at an angle but the curving circumference of the circle failed to follow through. To Schopenhauer, this unexpected geometry seemed ludicrous. Who could anticipate this reaction?

A speaker faces a somewhat analogous situation. The specific instances of circumstance or language that will amuse an audience are not always anticipated by the speaker. A young woman launching a vigorous attack on the foreign-aid policy of the United States offered evidence of its wastefulness by citing the amount of money spent in India to build grain elevators that are "better than our own." "But," she said, "they are empty." When her audience laughed, a look of surprise crossed her face. She seemed a little vexed to find such levity in the audience. She was talking about *quite* serious matters. Recovering her poise, she went on to show that money had also been spent "to build elaborate cotton mills in Korea. But cotton doesn't grow there." When the audience laughed again, she was quite disconcerted. She looked out over the group with a puzzled frown, and then as she realized the incongruity in the conditions she described, her expression gave her listeners still another moment of unintended delight. Had she seen the incongruity in the situation sooner, she could have used it to advantage.

B. Forms of Humor

The list of things that bring laughter is long and varied. We will mention here six types of humor that seem especially useful in speaking to entertain.

Late last year, a speaker addressing the French Chamber of Commerce in the United States wanted to dramatize the effect a recent devaluation of the American dollar was having on its purchasing power throughout the world. To make the point, he reminded the audience of Arthur Frommer's "Europe on $5 a Day," a book very popular a few years ago among American travelers looking for economical meals and accommodations in Europe. Then he told them a story of an American business man who had managed to get by on $500 a day on a trip to Europe. Asked how, he replied, "Easy. I skipped lunches."

1. Overstatement

It is well to understand that humor is not always pleasant or funny. Recognizing incongruity or being surprised by an unexpected outcome can cause laughter under grim conditions as the following example of overstatement shows.

A young man driving a car around Rim of the World Highway near Crestline, California, drove off the road and down the side of the mountain. When the accident was discovered, a police car and an ambulance were dispatched to the area. While the ambulance attendants were giving what comfort they could to the battered young man, a zealous policeman badgered the poor fellow with questions. The officer seemed to be particularly concerned about speed and kept forcing the question, "How fast were you driving when you went over the cliff?" Finally the injured man looked up at the policeman and said, "Three hundred and seventy-five miles an hour."

2. Understatement

If one may believe them, the stories that are told about President Calvin Coolidge make him the champion understater of all time. "Silent Cal" wasn't much of a talker anyway and what little he had to say didn't tend toward elaboration.

Mr. Coolidge returned home from church one Sunday morning and was asked by Mrs. Coolidge what the minister had talked about.
"Sin."
"Well, what did he have to say?"
"He's against it."

3. Irony

Intending a meaning which is the opposite of the literal sense of the words. According to Abraham Lincoln:

A politician of less than ideal quality so aroused the citizenry of a small midwestern town that they decided to tar and feather him and ride him out of town on a rail. As they put him on the rail, he remarked, "If it weren't for the honor of the thing, I would just as soon walk."

4. Unexpected Turns

A Texan and an Ohioan were riding through the Middle West on a train. The Texan spent considerable time telling his fellow passenger about the vastness of the state of Texas, "Why" he said, "do you know that in Texas you can ride all day and all night and all the next day and never leave the state of Texas?"

"I know what you mean," said the Ohioan, "the trains are terribly slow in Ohio, too."

5. Play on Words

One evening during a terrible storm on the English countryside, a knight rode up to an inn on a greyhound dog. He inquired of the inn-keeper whether he could find a place to sleep. The innkeeper at first told him that there was no more space. It looked as if the knight would have to go back out into the storm. But then the innkeeper noticed that the greyhound was sorely fatigued and in general quite the worse for wear. So he changed his mind, saying, "I wouldn't send a knight out on a dog like this."

"Oh Mr. Gilbert," said a wealthy lady to William Gilbert at a dinner party, "your friend Mr. Sullivan's music is really too delightful. It reminds me so much of dear Baytch [Bach]. Do tell me: What is Baytch doing just now? Is he still composing?"

"Well, no madam," Gilbert returned, "just now, as a matter of fact, dear Baytch is by way of decomposing.*

6. Burlesque

Ludicrous treatment of the sensible and sensible treatment of the ludicrous. Ambrose Bierce† had this way of dealing with Ben Franklin's sayings from *Poor Richard's Almanac.*

A penny saved is a penny to squander.
A man is known by the company he organizes.
A bad workman quarrels with the man who calls him that.

* Hesketh Pearson, *Gilbert and Sullivan* (Baltimore: Penguin Books, 1950), p. 93.
† As quoted in R. P. Falk, *The Antic Muse* (New York: Grove Press, 1955), p. 27. This book is worth consulting.

What is worth doing is worth the trouble of asking somebody to do it. Think twice before you speak to a friend in need.

C. Making Humor Effective

The following suggestions will help to get the best results from your use of humor in speaking.

1. Be Objective

Overriding all use of humor should be a sense of objectivity toward the situations and people you poke fun at. Listeners must feel that the weaknesses you see in them and others are the normal weaknesses of human beings. Outlandish techniques may be used to point up these foibles, but listeners can laugh more freely if they are confronted with what is at base a true picture (though drawn in caricature), presented impartially and without prejudice.

2. Show Kindliness

Speakers are constantly tempted in using humor to be sarcastic, to ridicule some person, group, or idea. Sarcasm and ridicule are properly classed as forms of humor and they are effective weapons in the arsenal of a persuasive speaker. But in a speech meant to entertain, they strike a sour note. Barbed attacks may seem to find favor with an audience, but the truth is that although they may please, they do so by inviting the audience toward smugness and the speaker toward insolence. Speakers also run the danger of offending their listeners or of having them realize that they have been cheapened by their part in the act. Pointing out incongruities is not in itself an act of unkindness. But to do so with bitterness is out of place in a speech to entertain. Raillery and banter lack the bitterness of sarcasm and ridicule. These may be used in a spirit of good will.

3. Use Good Taste

Good taste is difficult to define and audiences differ in what they consider to be acceptable. Therefore, arbitrary prescriptions to avoid jokes about nationality, race, religion, and sex do not always hold true. A good rule to follow is that if any bit of humor is at all likely to offend, avoid it. On the public platform, therefore, avoid any humor that even hints at vulgarity or obscenity. The stock in trade of the burlesque stage comedian has no place in the kind of speaking that is of interest

412

to us here. The world is full of fine humor that can be drawn upon without invading areas which may give offense. The cost of a laugh is too high if the price you pay for it is making yourself look tawdry.

4. Learn to Laugh at Yourself

One way you reveal both objectivity and kindliness in humor is to laugh at yourself. Before you can find effective humor in the weaknesses of others, you must first sense the foibles in yourself.

5. Let the Humor Label Itself

There is no joke that has to work so hard for a laugh as the one that is introduced with the suggestion that it is intended to be funny. If you let it appear that you are working at being witty, you will never make it. The humor that is worth using needs no identification. Then, too, some audiences are strangely perverse in that if you tell them an amusing incident to recount, they either expect too much or set themselves (unconsciously or not) to resist. The most effective humor slides into the mind without announcement or fanfare.

6. Stop When You're Ahead

There are few things for which people develop a taste more easily than applause. And the taste for applause is virtually insatiable. It is difficult to stop when you know you are doing a good job, when an audience is responsive, and you feel that you could hold it indefinitely. There is always a tendency to exploit the favorable reaction of the audience just a little more. But just those few extra stories or jokes may be all it takes to push the speech past its peak of effectiveness. From then on, it goes downhill. It is much better to quit while you're winning. Paradoxically, your listeners will be better satisfied if you leave them feeling that they still want more.

IV. HEIGHTENING THE INTEREST

Humor is only one of the sources from which entertainment is derived. Any device you use to heighten the interest of your audience in what you say can contribute to the success of a speech to entertain. Some of these devices demand brief mention now. Several of them have already been noted either in Chapter 5 ("Attention and Response") or in Chapter 12 ("Language and Oral Style"). It is proper that they should have been, for there is no way of separating these methods of heightening the effect of a speech from the principles of attention and interest or from the element of language.

A. Suspense

Curiosity, the desire for information, is not the exclusive property of monkeys, cats, and children. Every normally alert person has some degree of inquisitiveness. In human beings, curiosity evidences an eagerness to learn. You can use this to catch and hold the attention of an audience and to heighten its interest in what you have to say. If listeners want information, they will be interested in the source from which it may come to them: you and your speech. The "information" they want can be about the outcome of some point at issue, the identity of the murderer in a crime story, or the punch line of a joke.

Suspense is created when you withhold from the audience for a time the information required to forecast the final outcome of what you are talking about. As long as you can keep your listeners guessing, you can keep them interested. Suspense is thus a means of heightening their interest.

B. Conflict

An interest in conflict seems to be natural. The enormous popularity of westerns on television is a case in point. All sports involve competition in one form or another and the essence of competition is conflict, hence the popularity of sports. The more obvious competition is, the greater the interest becomes. Anything that suggests a fight draws interest, whether it is a schoolyard brawl, a chess game, professional boxing, or athletic teams in competition. The interest of plays and stories is almost always in some kind of conflict. You can create a similar interest when the materials you use suggest conflict or struggle. A conflict has an outcome; listeners want to know the outcome of stories and situations you use. Thus conflict heightens the audience interest in a speech. Moreover, by timing the revelation of the outcome to create suspense, you can heighten the interest still further.

C. Vividness

The more vividly a scene or incident can be visualized, the more colorful it becomes. Adding concrete details to the telling of a story heightens interest by making the ideas immediately clear and easy to grasp. Language that is vague, general, and abstract makes the audiences struggle for the ideas it is supposed to communicate; and they quickly cease to struggle. Specific language, on the other hand, builds images that make the ideas sharp and clear.

Dialogue and dialect also lend vividness to the telling of a story. If, instead of translating what is said, you let the characters talk in their own words, they come alive in a way they otherwise would not. If the characters speak in a regional or other dialect, you can use it to add another dimension of reality and vividness to the telling—*provided that* your rendition of the dialect is accurate enough to be believable. Using dialects well is not a skill that comes naturally; it must be developed through practice. Moreover, it requires a good ear for the sounds of language and for the tone and the tempo patterns of speech. Lacking this, you will do better to ignore a dialect rather than imitate it poorly.

D. Novelty and Familiarity

New ideas lose their strangeness and become welcome when they are associated with ideas that are familiar. Something you have never seen or even heard of makes no sense to you until you can join it to something familiar. A distributor for one of the major oil companies, an engineer and a graduate of Princeton University, said that when he first went to a small town in southwest Texas to represent his company, he found it difficult to overcome barriers between himself and the dealers who retail his company's petroleum products. As soon as he learned to talk their kind of language, however, his problem dissipated. At first he had been something wholly novel to their experience; now his language had become a linking familiarity.

Interest in new ideas comes from finding something known in what is unknown. Novelty is effective for heightening interest only when there is a familiar peg to hang it on. Illustrative analogies and apt examples can be used to help listeners see the familiar in novel ideas and situations.

Speakers often have the reverse opportunity: to heighten interest in familiar ideas by giving them a novel treatment. No matter how stale a subject is, a clever treatment and fresh materials can give it a slant that will delight an audience. Here again, as we said earlier, the way a subject is handled is what determines its ability to entertain.

SUMMARY

Virtually any topic that would be suitable and in good taste in a friendly conversation can be converted into an entertaining speech. The central idea may be organized in either a conventional or unconventional way, but the development of the speech should emphasize the central idea rather than lose it among jokes or stories.

The major emphasis in speeches to entertain is ordinarily put on humor. This is found in the recognition of incongruity or in the surprise that springs from an unexpected outcome. Humor takes several forms, among them, overstatement, understatement, irony (saying one thing but meaning the opposite), unexpected turns, plays on words, and burlesque (giving ludicrous treatment to sensible subjects and sensible treatment to ludicrous subjects).

For greatest effectiveness, humor should be objective, without malice, and in good taste. If you learn to laugh at yourself and your own shortcomings, you will be better able to enjoy and help audiences enjoy the foibles of others. Humor that is labeled as such will tend to have less effect. The best humor will identify itself without being labeled. Plan the speech to entertain so that it reaches its peak of reaction in the audience very near the end. Letting a humorous speech drag on after this peak has been reached may destroy the whole effect.

Other than humor, there are several devices that you can use to heighten the effectiveness of your speaking. These devices stimulate the interest of an audience: suspense, conflict, concreteness, novelty, and familiarity.

QUESTIONS

1. What is the purpose of an after-dinner speech?

2. What is the primary source for topics for the speech to entertain?

3. Comment on the notion that the speech to entertain should avoid the discussion of meaningful ideas.

4. What is the function of the transition in a good speech to entertain?

5. Comment on the idea that "the comical does not exist outside of what is strictly human."

6. Do you believe that humor is an intellectual and not an emotional experience?

7. What are the two basic constituents of humor?

8. Define the six forms of humor discussed in the text.

9. Why should sarcasm be avoided?

10. Should you let an audience know you intend to be humorous? Explain your answer.

11. Comment on the idea that a speaker should exhaust the humor in a situation before closing the speech.

12. Explain three of the four methods discussed in the text for heightening interest.

EXERCISES

1. The following speech by renowned humorist Mark Twain was delivered in Hartford, Connecticut, at a dinner honoring an Englishman named Cornelius Walford. Read the speech, and then write a brief paper discussing the following points:

   (a) What seems to be the specific nature of the occasion?
   (b) Who would seem to make up the audience?
   (c) What is the structure of the speech?
   (d) What are some of the forms of humor Twain uses?
   (e) Can you see any serious purpose underlying his use of humor?

ACCIDENT INSURANCE—ETC.*

Mark Twain

Gentlemen,—I am glad, indeed, to assist in welcoming the distinguished guest of this occasion to a city whose fame as an insurance centre has extended to all lands, and given us the name of being a quadruple band of brothers working sweetly hand in hand—the Colt's arms company making the destruction of our race easy and convenient, our life-insurance citizens paying for the victims when they pass away, Mr. Batterson perpetuating their memory with his stately monuments, and our fire-insurance comrades taking care of their hereafter. I am glad to assist in welcoming our guest— first, because he is an Englishman, and I owe a heavy debt of hospitality to certain of his fellow-countrymen; and secondly, because he is in

* From *Mark Twain's Speeches*, with an introduction by William Dean Howells (Harper Brothers Publishers: New York, 1951), pp. 249–251. Copyright 1923, 1951 by The Mark Twain Company. Reprinted by permission of Harper & Row, Publishers.

sympathy with insurance, and has been the means of making many other men cast their sympathies in the same direction.

Certainly there is no nobler field for human effort than the insurance line of business—especially accident insurance. Ever since I have been a director in an accident-insurance company I have felt that I am a better man. Life has seemed more precious. Accidents have assumed a kindlier aspect. Distressing special providences have lost half their horror. I look upon a cripple now with affectionate interest—as an advertisement. I do not seem to care for poetry any more. I do not care for politics—even agriculture does not excite me. But to me now, there is a charm about a railway collision that is unspeakable.

There is nothing more beneficial than accident insurance. I have seen an entire family lifted out of poverty and into affluence by the simple boon of a broken leg. I have had people come to me on crutches, with tears in their eyes, to bless this beneficent institution. In all my experience of life, I have seen nothing so seraphic as the look that comes into a freshly mutilated man's face when he feels in his vest pocket with his remaining hand and finds his accident ticket all right. And I have seen nothing so sad as the look that came into another splintered customer's face when he found he couldn't collect on a wooden leg.

I will remark here, by way of advertisement, that that noble charity which we have named the Hartford Accident Insurance Company is an institution which is peculiarly to be depended upon. A man is bound to prosper who gives it his custom. No man can take out a policy in it and not get crippled before the year is out. Now there was one indigent man who had been disappointed so often with other companies that he had grown disheartened, his appetite left him, he ceased to smile—and life was but a weariness. Three weeks ago I got him to insure with us, and now he is the brightest, happiest spirit in this land—has a good steady income and a stylish suit of new bandages every day, and travels around on a shutter.

I will say, in conclusion, that my share of the welcome to our guest is none the less hearty because I talk so much nonsense, and I know that I can say the same for the rest of the speakers.

I. Why speeches are criticized
II. The steps in rhetorical criticism
    A. Analysis
        1. Argument
        2. Motivation
        3. Credibility
        4. Structure
        5. Language and style
            a. Clarity
            b. Interest
        6. Delivery
    B. Synthesis
    C. Evaluation
III. Preparing the criticism
    A. Begin the criticism with evaluation.
    B. Point up the relationship of evaluation to synthesis.
    C. Use the analysis to support both synthesis and evaluation.

Chapter 19

Criticizing Speeches

The primary concern of this book has been to outline the principles that you apply to make messages more effective with audiences. An understanding of such principles is important not only for speakers, but for listeners as well. Everyone spends more time as a receiver of communication than as a sender. Consequently, everyone must lend a critical ear to the communication of others. In your speech class you are called upon to evaluate your colleagues' speeches. The lectures of your professors are continuing objects of critical evaluation by students. Community leaders and public officials are subjects of continued evaluation as they try to affect others in situations ranging from small group meetings to nationwide television broadcasts. This evaluation is called rhetorical criticism.

The principles of rhetorical criticism are applicable to *all* verbal communication: essays, novels, plays, motion pictures, and television, among others; but because our major concern is with oral communication, we shall emphasize the criticism of speeches. As an object of rhetorical criticism, a speech may be presented to a critic through many different media and in a variety of places. Sometimes the only source of speeches is a printed text. This is particularly true of speeches delivered before recording and motion pictures were available. Although there are important additional factors that specialized media, such as television, bring to bear on the situation, because of lack of space, we shall look only at those factors which are operative in all speech communication situations.

Regardless of how the speech comes to you as a rhetorical critic, the primary dimension of your evalutaion will be an examination of that speech in light of the interaction between the speech and its audience. In examining a speech of Daniel Webster, Thomas Jefferson, or Abraham Lincoln, you would make a judgment of the extent to which the speaker, in the words of Aristotle, discovered "the available means of persuasion" to influence the beliefs and actions of his audience.

I. WHY SPEECHES ARE CRITICIZED

The criticism of speeches is useful for several reasons. Perhaps the most obvious is the improvement of your own speaking. By examining the techniques used effectively by other speakers, you can better see what techniques to use. The criticism you do in class lets you see in action the methods discussed in this book. What may be effective at one time with one audience will not necessarily be effective in other circumstances; nonetheless, by seeing how an audience responds to techniques you gain insights into the kinds of situations wherein certain techniques are most useful.

Criticizing speeches will also improve your listening skills. Frequently, you hear a speech and judge it to be good or poor without testing your conclusion by asking what, specifically, makes it good or poor. By asking this question, a listener sees the specifics of what the speaker says and thus gets more out of the experience.

The criticism of a speech also gives insight into the total significance of the speaking situation. It helps you to see the interrelation of speaker, speech, and audience. When Franklin D. Roosevelt said in his first inaugural address, "We have nothing to fear but fear itself," his statement had great significance for the depression-ridden people of the 1930s. To read that speech and analyze it against the background of the times will bring more sharply into focus the problems of the era and the attitudes of the people who lived in America at that time.

The criticism of speeches not only offers an understanding of some particular point in history but, more broadly, it gives insights into the nature of mankind in general. When you study speeches from a number of eras you soon become aware that, although issues change and techniques change, many attitudes and feelings remain constant. The arguments advanced during the late 1960s and early 1970s by opponents of the war in Vietnam are essentially the same as those advanced in the 1840s by opponents of the Mexican War, such as Senator Tom Corwin. Effective public speakers, whether purposely or not, reflect the prevailing ideas of the times; they reflect, in addition, their own insights into all mankind. The rhetorical greatness of William Shakespeare is that he so thoroughly understood the Elizabethan audience that he provided insight into all people of every age.

II. THE STEPS IN RHETORICAL CRITICISM

A volume could be written on each of the three major steps of rhetorical criticism. This chapter will provide only a broad outline of these three steps: analysis, synthesis, and evaluation. A speech is first *analyzed*; that is, it is taken apart so that its various elements can be seen individually: argument (including supporting material) motivation, credibility, structure, language, and delivery: This analysis is then *synthesized* around the most important critical points and the less important points are viewed in relation to them. Finally, there must be *evaluation*, not merely a statement that a speech is "good" or "bad," but an indication of strengths and weaknesses, and of reasons why the speech is worth study or emulation. If evaluations are made on the basis of judicious analysis and synthesis, they will be worth the attention of others. No one expects that in a beginning speech class you will be an accomplished rhetorical critic, but you should begin early to develop critical ability.

A. Analysis

The analysis of a speech begins with the speaker's ideas and support. From classical times rhetorical criticism has recognized three elements in proof. The argument (frequently called "logical" proof), motivation, and credibility. Although all three are viewed as equally important and involve the interrelation of audience, speaker, and speech, the argumentative function is more directly related than the others are to the message, motivation bears most upon the audience, and credibility seems to reside in the speaker.

1. Argument

The analysis of the message itself emphasizes the speaker's ideas and support for them. Reference to Chapter 3 will help you to identify the issues in the controversy and to discover what are (or might conceivably be) the most effective arguments in support of a particular proposition. Here are some questions to consider in analyzing the argumentative dimension of the speech:

1. Is the speaker aware of the issues that divide opinion?
2. What ways of looking at the issues does the speaker propose?
3. Does the speaker meet opposition arguments?
4. What reasoning does the speaker use in developing the arguments?
5. What supporting materials does the speaker provide?

2. Motivation

The motivational appeals a speaker makes to the audience must be identified. Your analysis must examine the specific value system revealed and the motivation developed from that value system.

Identifying value systems is not easy. But you can begin by looking carefully at those words which carry value judgments. Your analysis should identify the positive and negative terms in the language of the speech. You then determine from your examination of these terms what the speaker's value system appears to be.

In his first Inaugural Address, President Woodrow Wilson called for reform of the nation's economy in the interest of a "New Freedom." In the following passage from that speech, terms labeling notions Wilson considers *good* are printed in italics and those he considers **bad** are printed in boldface.

But the **evil** has come with the *good*, and much *fine gold* has been **corroded.** With *riches* has come **inexcusable waste.** We have **squandered** a great part of what we might have *used*, and have not stopped to *conserve* the exceeding *bounty* of *nature*, without which our *genius for enterprise* would have been **worthless** and **impotent, scorning** to be careful, **shamefully prodigal** as well as *admirably efficient.* We have been *proud* of our industrial *achievement*, but we have not hitherto stopped *thoughtfully*, enough to count **human cost**, the **cost** of *lives* **snuffed out,** of *energies* **over-taxed** and **broken,** the **fearful** *physical* and *spiritual* **cost** to the men and women and and children upon whom the **dead weight** and **burden** of it all has fallen **pitilessly** the years through.

From an examination of the value words that carry Wilson's argument, you can see the value system underlying what he says. To paraphrase him, we must with candid and fearless eyes conserve our riches (the bounty of nature) through careful, efficient use of our genius for enterprise with due pride in our industrial achievements. We must reject the corrosion of fine gold through waste, squandering, overtaxing, the snuffing out of lives, and the great spiritual and physical costs. Further, we must discontinue our attention to worthless things. We must stop being impotent, prodigal, and selfish.

Wilson appeals to the Puritan values so basic to American society: a respect for nature and enterprise; a rejection of selfishness, waste, and false pride. These values form a base for him to tap the self-esteem motivation of his audience. Further examination will show that the emphasis of this passage is negative; that is, President Wilson uses the words of his value system to reject what he considers bad more strongly than to identify what he supports.

This illustration identifies the basis for some of the analytical questions you will ask:

1. To what value systems does the speaker appeal?
2. What motivation does the speaker emphasize at the most critical points in the speech?
3. Is the motivation justified by the subject?
4. Does the motivation remain consistent throughout the speech?

Other questions will be brought to mind by the discussion of motivation in Chapter 9.

3. Credibility

Credibility is established when an audience perceives a speaker to be worthy and competent. Speakers can establish credibility by projecting "good" images of themselves and "bad" images of their opponents. When you analyze credibility, ask yourself what qualities the speaker seems to claim and what qualities he assigns to the opposition.

In the election of 1952 the Republicans pictured their candidate (General Eisenhower) as tough and hard-thinking, a man of action with the experience needed to solve the problems of the Korean war. They characterized their opponent (Adlai Stevenson) as a dreamer, an idealist who had been taken in by the "Truman gang."

The speech to be criticized may not have an opponent in the form of a specific person. The antagonist may be an idea, a party, a way of life. The speech of Martin Luther King, Jr., "I Have a Dream," has an opponent in certain existing ideas in the society. True, there are people who hold these views, but the speaker does not identify them directly. Who could deny that there is an opponent with whom Dr. King had to deal? When, for instance, the audience agrees with the speaker but is apathetic, one could say that apathy is the opponent. Much patriotic ceremonial oratory is of this nature, as is a reasonable proportion of all preaching.

Credibility is further classified as either direct or indirect. In direct credibility the speaker's attributes and accomplishments, as well as the defects of the opponent are referred to directly. Indirect credibility is developed more subtly. Two examples will show the difference.

On September 23, 1952, Richard Nixon, then a Senator and a candidate for the Vice-presidency, appeared on television to defend a fund that had been raised for him by wealthy Californians. In that speech, Mr. Nixon made heavy use of direct credibility.

I worked my way through college and, to a great extent, through law school. And then in 1940, probably the best thing that ever happened to me happened; I married Pat—sitting over here. We had a rather difficult time after we were married, like so many of the young couples who may be listneing to us. I practiced law; she continued to teach school. I went into the service.

Let me say that my service record was not a particularly unusual one. I went to the South Pacific. I guess I'm entitled to a couple of battle stars. I got a couple of letters of commendation but I was just there when the bombs were falling and then I returned. I returned to the United States and in 1946 I ran for Congress.*

When as president he delivered the Commencement Address at the University of Rochester on June 5, 1966, Mr. Nixon built his credibility in a very different, very indirect way by identifying himself with ideas that would bring him respect. Although he never mentions himself, this passage reveals something of the image of himself he wants the audience to share.

A generation ago, "Four Freedoms" became a rally cry for the forces of democracy: Freedom of speech and of worship, freedom from fear and from want. Today let us discuss the *Four Academic Freedoms.*

There is the academic freedom of the student to investigate any theory, to challenge any premise, to refuse to accept old shibboleths and myths.

There is a second academic freedom of the student to espouse any cause,

* Richard M. Nixon, "Apologia," *Representative American Speeches, 1952–1953,* A. Craig Baird, ed. (New York: H. W. Wilson Co., 953), p. 78.

to engage in the cut and thrust of partisan political or social debate, both on and off campus, without jeopardy to his academic career.

The third academic freedom is for the teacher—freedom from fear of reprisal while speaking or publishing the truth as he sees it, governed by the dictates of his own intellect and of the disciplines of scholarship.

Finally, there is a fourth academic freedom—this one within the academic community—that is the freedom of the student from tyranny of the faculty, and conversely, freedom of the faculty from student tyranny.*

4. Structure

The structure of the speech helps you to see how well the speaker gives the message *unity*, *order*, and *coherence*.

The primary constituent of unity is singleness of theme. You must ask whether all the ideas, arguments, and motivations of the speech are relevant to one main theme. Suppose there seem to be several themes. Are they related to one another and developed in such a way as to give a sense of unity?

Similarly, *scope* is a function of unity, for the impression of unity is created not solely by the singleness of the speaker's theme but is influenced by the listener's perception as well. Is the speech limited to what the audience can attend to and yet broad enough to continually engage listener interests?

Order is the sequence of ideas in a speech. It is found in what can be called *thematic emergence*, the manner in which the main idea (the theme) of the speech emerges. Is the cat let out of the bag one whisker at a time? Does this main theme become clear somewhere around the middle of the speech? Does the theme emerge at the beginning, full blown and stated unequivocally to the audience? In addition, ask how the speech is organized: chronologically? geographically? to judge whether the order of the speech is the one best calculated to achieve the speaker's purpose.

Coherence is directly related to both unity and order. It can be thought of in terms of the transitions a speaker uses to link one thought with another and to what extent these transitions will help a listener develop a clear and correct understanding of what the speaker says. Thus the critic analyzes a speech to discover how its theme emerges, what order is used to organize the material, and what means are used to link one idea with another.

* Richard M. Nixon, "Academic Freedom," *Vital Speeches of the Day*, 32 (July 1, 1966), p. 550.

5. Language and Style

Language is the fundamental "hardware" of a speech; it is the vehicle that carries the other objects of critical study (idea and support, motivation, credibility, and structure). In a very real sense, therefore, whatever you learn about these when you criticized a speech must come through analysis of the speaker's language. But in addition to making this kind of analysis, your rhetorical criticism examines the language of a speech in order to evaluate how well the speaker's language exemplifies the primary constituents of style: clarity and interest.

a. Clarity. In judging whether a speaker's language will be clearly understood by a listener, you ask questions about the levels of language used. No speaker wants to use a vocabulary that is insulting because of its simplicity or confusing because of its complexity. Imagine addressing an adult audience in the language of the first-level reader. "See Puff. See Puff run. Run, Puff, run. Run, run, run." Or imagine the response of an audience addressed in the complex jargon of a field that it does not understand. Your criticism must, therefore, determine something about the level of vocabulary within the audience's understanding.

Syntax is potentially as serious a problem as vocabulary. Given words it understands, an audience can often do a reasonably good job of straightening out unclear sentences but, to the extent that syntax is awkward and unsure, the communication of both denotative and connotative meaning will be impaired. The problems syntax may generate, however, do not necessarily mean that simple sentences are to be preferred. A well-developed complex sentence may be just as clear as a series of short ones, perhaps even more so. Indeed, subtle ideas or shades of meaning may be lost in simple sentences.

As a critic of the printed speech text you must learn to listen with your eyes. From what you have heard about the speaker's delivery, you must imagine pauses and other factors of delivery that help to clarify meaning.

b. Interest. In judging the interest values of language your analysis must give attention to embellishment, the stylistic devices that the speaker uses. First, you must consider the *level* of embellishment used. To a degree, you can determine how embellished the style of a speech is by comparing the language with that of other speakers in similar situations. Your analysis will consider next what *kinds* of figures this speaker tends to use. The late President John F. Kennedy became well known for his use of antithesis. Some speakers make extensive use of metaphor, others do not. These stylistic characteristics should be noted.

Having considered such factors as vocabulary, syntax, and embellishment, you should be able to characterize the language of the speech. Is it plain, given to short direct sentences, simple vocabulary, and few figures of speech? Or is it highly embellished with complex sentence structure, vocabulary, and many figures of speech? Perhaps the language is somewhere between these two extremes, characterized, for example, by a simple vocabulary but an extensive use of figures of speech. From your examination of these factors, you make your judgment about the merits of the speaker's style.

6. Delivery

The facial expressions, gestures, vocal quality, and vocal emphasis of a speaker are all agents of speech that tell the listener what the speaker wants to say. The policeman holds up his hand to say "Stop." When the Indian of the Western movie holds up his hand, he means "Peace." Whether a speaker smiles or frowns, speaks loudly or softly, emphasizes one word or another, it says something to the audience.

In analyzing a speaker's delivery, you will ask such questions as these: Do the gestures, vocal quality, and other elements of delivery help to communicate the speaker's meaning? Do they draw attention to themselves? In short, is the delivery an aid or a hindrance in eliciting the meaning the speaker wants the listener to have? You must judge whether gesture, facial expression, vocal quality, and loudness are coordinated with the ideas of the speech; whether they add emphasis or merely exhibition.

The first step in rhetorical criticism, then, is analysis, that is, the examination of argument, motivation, credibility, structure, language, and delivery to discover what a speaker does in a speech. In this examination and the conclusions you as a critic draw about the interrelationship of speaker technique and audience response, you find the basis for a synthesis of these independent points of analysis.

B. Synthesis

The purpose of synthesis is to reconstruct the speaking situation in order to emphasize the important factors of your analysis. That is to say, you ask, "Given this audience with its attitudes, beliefs, and values, what strategy did this speaker use?" An adequate answer to this question is not a catalog of appeals but a specification of the emphasis the speaker has given them.

For one speaker, an argumentative development may be central: the basic appeal is to reason; credibility is generated by building the image of a "reasonable" person. Another strategy will emphasize the trustworthiness of the speaker. In such a case other rhetorical elements will be subservient to credibility. Still another speaker may create a rhetorical strategy centered in the deeply felt needs of the audience. This strategy reveals itself through the emphasis given to a particular appeal throughout the speech and especially at critical junctures.

Although the term *strategy*, used here to characterize the emphasis of a speech, usually implies design, you will not necessarily know the speaker's design. It is useful to know what the speaker intended to do, but it is not essential to an understanding of what happened on a particular occasion. It is more important to discover what actually happened between speaker and listener, irrespective of the speaker's intent.

The presidential election campaign of 1952 has ben synthesized in the following way: The major attack of the Republican campaign was calculated to dramatize the nation's obvious problems: the seemingly endless stalemate in Korea, corruption in government, the problem of inflation, and the inability of America to do more than contain communism. The Republican candidate, General Dwight D. Eisenhower, attacked an administration that seemed unable to handle these problems. Eisenhower, therefore, shifted the emphasis from issues to frustrations. His battle cry was "Leadership" and it was consonant with the voter's dilemma of favoring a policy and objecting to its results. In short, Eisenhower asked no one to give up a single view on policy but only to trust him. This approach was most evident in the dramatic statement, "I shall go to Korea" in his October 24 speech at Detroit. But, more than dramatic, this statement was symbolic of the campaign. Eisenhower submitted himself on every issue. His only real promise was that he would be "fair" to the American people and would, through his fairness, bring an end to national and international conflicts, frustrations, and fears. The problem was frustration, and the solution was an esteemed national leader.

Democratic candidate, Adlai Stevenson, on the other hand, was a speaker in the tradition of classical rhetoric. Perhaps this is part of the reason for the impression he made on the intellectuals in 1952. He addressed himself to issues that political thinkers have examined throughout the history of the western world. Such concepts as the nature of man, of the state, and of society, and the methodology of political action were of far greater concern to Stevenson than to Eisenhower. In all probability these problems were of greater concern to

Stevenson than to any major American politician since Woodrow Wilson.

His argument was more thorough than that of most contemporary political speakers. His motive appeals were restrained and linked to the ideas that he wished to develop. Stevenson called on the American people to rise to the tremendous problems facing them. He emphasized the ego-expansion of the people through their capacities of patience, struggle, and intelligence. He did not, as Eisenhower did, relieve the people of responsibility. Stevenson's ethical proof, while bold, was not flaunted. He spoke of his wide variety of administrative experience. He linked his cause with names of intellectual and political stature from Aristotle to Roosevelt. Always he was careful to point out that he was human and therefore fallible. An examination of post-election studies supports the contention that those who voted for Stevenson were not particularly impressed with his personality, but were solidified on issues and favored him because of his position on the issues.

C. Evaluation

Writers on rhetorical criticism generally identify four forms it may take. Some theorists maintain that a critic should make only pragmatic judgments about the immediate and long-range *effects* of a speech on a listener and on society. Only the naïvest evaluation of effects considers the merit of speech to depend solely upon whether the speaker succeeded in getting the audience to do what the speaker wanted it to do. One speech, standing alone, may have little discernible effect, but the results of a series of speeches may be cumulative. A speaker, moreover, may produce results not even intended but which, nonetheless, introduce noticeable changes into society. It may very well be that in a particular case no adequate means of persuasion are available to *any* speaker. Nor does counting votes after an election determine the more effective speaker of a pair of candidates. Others say that the critic must consider the *artistic merit* of the speech. This variety of criticism aims at evaluating the techniques to determine the literary beauty and grace of the product. Some critics look for the *historical truth* of the ideas. They ask whether or not history bears out the truth of what the speaker said. They evaluate the extent to which the speaker reflects, leads, or trails behind the society in what he believes and says. Judgments are made by some critics as to the *ethical worth* of what the speaker says. An evaluation of this kind determines the merits of a speech by weighing the speaker's ideas in the balance of the critic's ethical norms.

Regardless of whether your critical method emphasizes one or all of these standards of evaluation you must, nevertheless, make your judgments in terms of the audience and the times in which the speaker lived. Certainly, most would agree that it is generally unethical to be untruthful, but for the rhetorical critic it is more important to know why an untruthful speaker is successful than it is to know that the speaker is untruthful. To evaluate the historical truth of a speech without being aware of the knowledge that was available to the speaker and the audience of the time is foolish. John C. Calhoun argued that slavery was a positive good, yet he is regarded as a genius and one of America's great orators. The same arguments today are deemed nonsense. We judge Calhoun by his times and the contemporary racist by ours. The long periodic sentence, the parallel structure, the classical and Biblical allusions, and the involved metaphor so prized in the style of earlier oratory seem overdone today, but yesterday is not judged by today.

Your criticism, therefore, renders an evaluation of the speech based not upon how the world ought to be, or ought to have been, but upon how well the speaker discovered and used the available means of persuasion. While Dwight D. Eisenhower might capitalize on his credibility as a military hero by saying "I shall go to Korea," it would have been ludicrous for Adlai E. Stevenson, his political opponent, a man without a military reputation, to have used the same phrase in 1952. That was simply not a means of persuasion available to Stevenson. "Don't change horses in midstream" represents an argument that only an incumbent officeholder can use. The attitudes, beliefs, and values of the audience about the speaker, about the issues, and about the times constitute the bases for criticizing the speaker's efforts.

III. PREPARING THE CRITICISM

Obviously, the form and depth of critical analysis will differ as situations differ. When you criticize a classmate's speech, you will have far less time to consider, study, and prepare than when you have several weeks in which to pore over a text, check items in the library, and write a paper with care. However, the basic approach and attitude will be the same.

Variety in critical approach is unlimited but a few general principles will be helpful as you begin to express your evaluative judgments.

A. Begin the Criticism with Evaluation

Evaluations are what your listeners or readers are most interested in. Avoid at all cost the "laundry-list" analysis ("He said this, . . . then this, . . . then this . . ."). Center on the two or three important evaluative statements about what you regard as good or poor in the speech.

B. Point up the Relationship of Evaluation to Synthesis

Reveal in your evaluation that you see the strategy of the speech. Reconstruct, if necessary, the situation that led you to your evaluation. Show how individual judgments join to provide an over-all impression of the speech.

C. Use the Analysis to Support Both Synthesis and Evaluation

To say merely that something was good or bad, or that it was central to the persuasive effort, is not enough. The critic must show how arguments, motivation, credibility, style, delivery, or structure illustrate the strategy of the speech and the evaluation. Of course, not everything discovered through analysis will be used but only what is necessary to support your evaluations.

Analysis, synthesis, and evaluation—the three elements of criticism —are closely comparable to the elements of communication discussed in earlier chapters. Your critical judgments are like the specific purpose of a speech. They identify what you want the audience to know or to believe. Synthesis provides a basis for identifying major critical points and for giving order to the criticism. Your analysis provides the specific supporting materials necessary for understanding your final evaluation. It is equally incumbent on speaker and critic to have something to say and to say it well. These are the objects of criticism and the end of speech: content and communication.

QUESTIONS

1. In what sense can rhetorical criticism be said to apply to all forms of communication?
2. Why are speeches criticized?
3. Name and explain the major steps in rhetorical criticism.

4. What effect would it have on the criticism to omit any one of the three major steps?

5. Can you adequately criticize a speech you have only read?

6. What kind of questions does a critic ask about rational proof in a speech? About motivation?

7. What is the difference between direct and indirect credibility?

8. How are unity, order, and coherence related?

9. What kind of judgments does a critic make about a speaker's style?

10. What are the varieties of criticism?

11. Compare the method of preparing a criticism with that of preparing a speech.

EXERCISES

1. Act as a critic for your classmates' speeches. In your oral criticism explain what you believe to be the two greatest strengths and the two greatest weaknesses of the speech. Give specific examples to support your judgment.

2. Hear a speech by some local person (your minister, for instance) and write an evaluation of the speech.

3. With a group of classmates prepare and hold a group discussion evaluating a speech by some nationally known person delivered on television.

4. Write an evaluation of a speech of historical importance such as Abraham Lincoln's "Second Inaugural Address," Booker T. Washington's "Atlanta Exposition Address," or Woodrow Wilson's "Speech at Des Moines on the League of Nations." Emphasize the ways in which the same speech delivered today might be differently received.

5. Hear a speech by a person appearing on campus and write a paper on some phase of analysis assigned by your instructor.

Index